D1200932

The
NORTHSIDE

The

NORTHSIDE

African Americans and the Creation of Atlantic City

Nelson Johnson

Plexus Publishing, Inc.
Medford, New Jersey

Second Printing, February 2011

The Northside: African Americans and the Creation of Atlantic City

Copyright © 2010 by Nelson Johnson

Published by:
Plexus Publishing Inc.
143 Old Marlton Pike
Medford, NJ 08055

Library of Congress Cataloging-in-Publication Data

Johnson, Nelson., 1948-
  The Northside : African Americans and the creation of Atlantic City / Nelson Johson.
    p. cm.
Includes bibliographical references and index.
  ISBN 978-0-937548-73-8
  1. African Americans--New Jersey--Atlantic City--History. 2. Atlantic City (N.J.)--History. 3. Atlantic City (N.J.)--Race relations. 4. Seaside resorts--New Jersey--Atlantic City--History. I. Title.
  F144.A8J66 2010
  305.896'073074985--dc22

                                                                    2010038235

ISBN 978-0-937548-73-8

Printed and bound in the United States of America.

President and CEO: Thomas H. Hogan, Sr.
Editor-in-Chief and Publisher: John B. Bryans
Managing Editor: Amy M. Reeve
VP Graphics and Production: M. Heide Dengler
Book Designer: Kara M. Jalkowski
Cover Designer: Denise M. Erickson
Marketing Coordinator: Rob Colding

Original cover art by Tyrone L. Hart
Photo of Nelson Johnson on dustjacket courtesy of ANTONIMAGES.COM

www.plexuspublishing.com

In memory of:

Horace J. Bryant Jr., a mentor
whose wit and wisdom is sorely missed,
and
Pierre Hollingsworth, a friend and ally
who launched me on my adventure
with Atlantic City.

Both were tireless warriors for freedom.

And, alas,
Redenia Gilliam-Mosee,
who left us too soon.

We had our own special place in time.
Family, friends, work, and play—it was all right here.
Was nothin' like it. Never will be again.
Damn shame it's gone.

—Sid Trusty,
Renaissance man

On the Cover

The illustrations by Tyrone L. Hart appearing on the front cover of *The Northside* were commissioned specially for this book. A lifelong resident of Atlantic City whose work is exhibited throughout the region, Mr. Hart specializes in contemporary and historic scenes of people and places on the Northside.

The artist recalls how reading an early draft of *The Northside* brought to mind his late grandmother, Katie Bell Gardner, who arrived in Atlantic City in 1921 at the age of 21. Mr. Hart dedicates the work seen here to this inspiring woman who, more than anyone he has known, lived the story told in these pages.

Tyrone L. Hart can be reached at bctartworks@comcast.net.

Contents

Acknowledgments

"You've written a serious book," the publisher began, letting me down gently. She continued, "We publish serious books for scholarly audiences and nonserious books for general audiences. But we don't publish serious books for the general audience. It's a fine piece of history, but I don't know what to do with it."

Fortunately, after many rejections, another publisher knew what to do with "it"—*Boardwalk Empire*—and so began my relationship with John B. Bryans and Plexus Publishing, Inc. To say that either John or I knew that *Boardwalk Empire* would lead to an HBO series would be twaddle. I was trying to "make sense of" Atlantic City's history, and John was abiding by his commitment to treating both authors and readers with respect.

Why not a serious book for a general audience? Happily, John was quite comfortable with the idea, and he thought *Boardwalk Empire* would "find its audience." Although we sometimes disagree on language, his support for the message is constant. I am grateful for John's confidence and the time he's spent cultivating my avocation as a historian.

So many people were helpful in making both *Boardwalk Empire* and *The Northside* possible that I know I will fail to mention someone—my apologies here and now. My Source Notes for *Boardwalk Empire* and those at the end of this work recite individuals to whom I owe a debt of gratitude. Nevertheless, some contributors warrant special recognition.

The late Sid Trusty was an inspiration. When we first met, he said to me, "I want to shake the hand of the man who wrote *Boardwalk Empire—especially* Chapter 3. I think I've read it nine times. God bless you." Sid was invaluable in getting me grounded. It's a heartache that he's not here to revel in this moment.

After Sid, there are many people who graciously took me into their homes, met with me over lunch and dinner, or allowed me to pester them with follow-up calls and email. The following people supported my research and writing in important ways.

The professionals at the Atlantic City Free Public Library (ACFPL) are a treasure. Maureen Frank, Heather Halpin Perez, Pat

Rothenberg, Julie Senack, and others were always helpful in finding archival materials. One of the real finds at the ACFPL was a series of interviews conducted many years ago by Cynthia Ringe. Those interviews helped fill gaps in my narrative with excellent first-person accounts from people no longer with us.

Historian Dr. Richlyn F. Goddard of the Richard Stockton College of New Jersey is an indefatigable researcher, and I excavated her doctoral dissertation, "Three Months to Hurry and Nine Months to Worry: Resort Life for African Americans in Atlantic City, NJ (1850–1940)." The curatorship skills of Ralph Hunter and Dennis Burroughs were crucial to my work on the life of C. Morris Cain, as is true for Madame Sara Spencer Washington. I am also grateful for the insights and photographs provided by Madame Washington's grandson, Royston Scott. Michael Everett was most generous in sharing his wealth of knowledge on Pop Lloyd's career and in the many hours he granted me.

Both Lillian Bryant and Joe Bair mined their memories to share anecdotes of their fathers and precious tidbits from their family life I could find nowhere else. The same is true of my friend Joe Jacobs, who many times was my "go-to guy" when I was stumped for a name or reliable source on a particular issue.

Fellow historian Vicki Gold Levi was an early sounding board and steered me to Giles R. Wright, the former director of the New Jersey Afro-American History Program who reviewed several chapters prior to his untimely demise. The late Dr. Charles Wilson permitted me to probe his memory, as did retired Police Captain Hank Tyner. I have leaned on Karlos and Joanna LaSane many times and never came up wanting on questions critical to my research.

Alma Dobson, wife of the late Ted Dobson, graciously permitted me to utilize her husband's historical collection. Mary Ward shared experiences from her years of working in her family's business. My friend and co-worker Alma Johnson recruited her reading club to review early drafts, and their candid assessments provided guidance in my research and writing. My friend Professor Wendell White of Stockton College reviewed early drafts and lent his photographic talents to the book. My friend Tyrone Hart, a gifted artist, gave me valuable feedback on early drafts and created an original piece of art to grace the book's cover. At Plexus, Amy Reeve, Heide Dengler, Kara

Jalkowski, and Denise Erickson brought expertise and enthusiasm to the publishing process.

Two persons who were priceless to my work in pulling things together are Ada McClinton and Elwood Davis. Along with Sid Trusty, they are my "conscience" in the writing of *The Northside*. Both are veterans of the "Summer of Freedom" and are steeped in the Northside's history. They know where the bones are buried. I am grateful for their advice and consider it a privilege and an honor that they befriended me.

Finally, two people who were with me in the writing of both *Boardwalk Empire* and *The Northside* and worked on more drafts than I had a right to thrust upon them are my former colleague, the Honorable Steven P. Perskie (Ret.) and my aide-de-camp of many years, Sheryl McGrotty. Steve is an astute editor and a constructive critic. He has a keen sense of history. Sheryl is an exceptional assistant and a tireless proofreader. She has my back. I *probably* could have written both books without them, but it would have been a lot more difficult and not nearly as much fun.

Foreword

We often imagine the modern African-American experience within a bi-furcated framework. That framework places sentimentalized notions of black people, a veritably monumentalized people, in triumph over extraordinary odds alongside a stark reality that well over a century after the Great Emancipation, many black Americans exist on the far margins of our society, not really making it into the future. This book, a fascinating study of Atlantic City's African-American community experience, suggests that both perspectives are off the mark, if not irrelevant.

Nelson Johnson's sweeping study of African-American life and history in Atlantic City, *The Northside: African Americans and the Creation of Atlantic City,* places the city's history at the center of what the black experience and race have come to mean in American life, especially that part of the nation's life that has been shaped by the culture of leisure, by white middle class and working class fantasies and aspirations, and by attempts by blacks to carve out honorable spaces for themselves.

Late 19th-century Atlantic City's emergence as the nation's first urban space devoted primarily to the conceits of leisure coincided with deepening racial stratification in the nation, the legalization of Jim Crow, and attempts by blacks to make freedom from slavery matter in their lives. It was, in fact, a terrible period for blacks, which the historian Rayford Logan years ago called the nadir of American race relations. For over a generation, other scholars have drawn our attention to the starker episodes of the period—lynching and other forms of violence against blacks—which were, to be sure, tragically important. Also important was the diminishing voting rights of black men in the Southern states and the reconciliation of Southern and Northern whites with memories of the Civil War, reconciliation at the expense of the nation's aspiring black citizens. Atlantic City took shape, and found its purpose, within this historical context.

In its early days, Atlantic City was unlike any other place in the Republic. It was created out of surf and sand, or better put, out of the imagination of what the seaside might mean to white and black Americans seeking to exploit each other's place in a modernizing nation. For whites, Atlantic City was an opportunity to experience their small measure of success—a vacation by the sea—in real time, in a new place. Atlantic City helped create an important part of white identity—the ability to take it easy, to escape the city, and to be doted upon by blacks who served them, washed their clothes and linen, and appeared, at least on the surface, to accept their superiority through rituals of subservience and silence. For rising numbers of blacks, Atlantic City was a place where a recreational and leisure industry created black employment opportunities and, equally important, a black community. The city became an extraordinarily complex environment in which blacks performed subservience, created community, enjoyed their safety in numbers, and prepared themselves for opportunities that would come in the future. Black Atlantic City, the Northside, was an incubator for black social and cultural ingenuity.

As a place carved out to serve modern leisure conceits, Atlantic City might be far more important than better known communities that race and racism forged. Consider this: When slavery ended as the longest experience involving the engagement of blacks and whites in America, the future of race relations, especially for whites and those seeking to become white, was uncertain. In a sense, Atlantic City was an experiment, a bold one to be sure, that prepared a post-Emancipation America for freedom with the white over black social equation still very much intact. White leisure was a corollary to black freedom and black second class status.

Nelson Johnson is a conscientious and imaginative historian. His contributions to African-American history, New Jersey history, and ethnic studies are underscored by *The Northside*'s richly textured narrative on local politics, race relations, the intersection of transportation technology and greed, and black agency under enduringly difficult circumstances. Marshalling a constellation of primary sources, many of them new to historians, and building upon the existing historiographical literature, Johnson weaves a complicated and persuasive narrative that contributes to our understanding of Atlantic City's prominence in the aspirations of the black urban experience. Prior to the rise of Harlem as the titular capital of Negro America, the Northside of Atlantic City was, in fact, among the most interesting, and important, black communities in the United States. As Johnson shows, it was created out of white racial fantasies of black inferiority and subservience to the needs of white vacationers. As such, the community was imagined into existence. But Johnson also sheds a brilliant light on how the Northside, despite or perhaps because of its image by an expanding class of leisure-loving whites, developed itself as a city within a city. That inner city enabled thousands of black people over the course of the late 19th century and well into the next to prevail over the most debilitating aspects of racial injustice. That inner city also contributed broadly to American society by nurturing African-American traditions that by the mid-20th century found their way into the nation's mainstream culture.

The Northside was a richly textured black community that revealed how African Americans took advantage of the freedom of racial assembly. Through religious and secular organizations, and rituals unique to the segregation era, through the efforts of an entrepreneurial class of blacks, and the rise of leisure as a part of black life in the 20th century, the community actually thrived despite its challenges. Within its confines, a lineage of remarkable black residents contributed to the Northside's energy and to its self-referential identity. And because the Northside, not unlike the Atlantic City Boardwalk, was a destination for two generations of vacationing black Americans, it became over time a veritable arena of memories. In short, black Americans who came to Atlantic City over the course of the last century remembered their time spent there as yet another measure of what freedom and blackness meant.

Some years ago, in 2001, the Civil Rights Garden opened in Atlantic City. It is the largest monument to the Civil Rights Movement in a northern state, located in Atlantic City as an acknowledgement of a historically important turning point, in 1964, when the Democratic Party Convention met there. The convention, especially the controversy over the seating of the Mississippi Freedom Democratic Party delegation, brought into high relief the urgency of the black freedom struggle in the South. The garden's location will now also remind us, all the more because of Nelson Johnson's extraordinary narrative history, that the life and times of Atlantic City's Northside was at the center of a long quest for freedom, dignity, and an honorable place for African Americans.

Clement Alexander Price
Board of Governors Distinguished Service Professor of History
Rutgers University
Newark, New Jersey

Prologue

We have a wonderful history behind us ... It reads like the history of a people in a heroic age ... We are going back to that beautiful history, and it is going to inspire us to greater achievements.

—Carter G. Woodson, historian

Waiting wasn't something he did well. Ever eager to move on to the next thing, Morris Cain had a fire in his belly. Orphaned, uprooted, put on a train, and sent north while still in his teens, Atlantic City was now home. A divinity student, Cain aspired to lead a church without walls. His congregation would be the people of his adopted hometown. But he wasn't home. He was sitting in a railroad station. The train from Lincoln University in southeastern Pennsylvania to Philadelphia had arrived late, and he'd missed his connection to Atlantic City. Despite his impatience, he knew the next train would be along soon. Even in November, in the early 1900s, trains left for the resort hourly.

Partly partying, partly spending time with family, and mostly working, Cain knew Thanksgiving weekend would fly by. His uncle was head bellman at a large Boardwalk hotel that hosted a bountiful holiday spread. Extra help was needed for the weekend. From his several years of working at the hotel to save money for college, Cain had earned a reputation as a reliable worker. His uncle had no difficulty getting him a slot to work at the busiest times during the holiday weekend. Thursday would be a long day of carrying bags, serving meals, and busing tables, but the tips would go a long way at school. As was true for many black households in Atlantic City, the Thanksgiving holiday wouldn't begin for Cain and his uncle until the hotel's white guests had been pampered and their bellies filled with all the fixings.

Black hotel workers catering to the needs of white vacationers is a critical part of Atlantic City's history. Their labor was vital to the town's existence. Yesterday's Atlantic City, the resort that rose to national prominence in the final years of the 19th century and the early decades of the 20th, relied heavily upon the labor of African Americans for its success. The black experience in Atlantic City wasn't just part of the show. It was the main event. It's time to tell the tale of this fabled American resort in all its fullness.

Four cornerstones anchored Atlantic City's growth from a wilderness island visited by thousands of day-trippers into a bustling city hosting millions of vacationers staying in hotels. Each was critical to the success of the nation's first experiment in creating an urban center based solely on tourism. In ascending order of importance, the cornerstones were *first,* the railroad—without a train linking the booming industrial center of Philadelphia to what was at the time a desolate patch of sand, Absecon Island would have remained sand dunes and salt marshes for generations; *second,* money and know-how required to develop a major hotel-recreation economy brought to the island by buccaneer-like businessmen who had migrated to town from Philadelphia and New York; *third,* a community mind-set that not only welcomed visitors but embraced violations of the law needed to make them happy and keep them returning; and *fourth,* a hotel workforce comprised almost entirely of African Americans, essential to building a resort and servicing vacationers.

Black people built Atlantic City. In the early days, 1854 to 1890, starting with construction of the railroad (many working as freedmen, while some, possibly, as slaves), black people provided the muscle and sweat for everything from wrestling timbers for laying railroad tracks to shoveling sand for carving out streets. As Atlantic City grew from a sleepy beach village to a major resort, freed slaves and the children of slaves were recruited from the upper South by the resort's hotel industry. The men worked at everything from carpentry and painting to waiting on tables and carrying bags. Women's work included cooking and cleaning, laundering clothes, and caring for children, black and white alike.

Between 1880 and 1930, approximately 95 percent of the hotel workforce was African American. Black workers were the mortar that held the hotel economy together, making it possible to build America's first national resort. Servants are the lynchpin of a resort economy. Erase them from Atlantic City's history and the town we know today never comes to be.

Servants don't have names and black people all look alike, or so segments of white society have often believed. Despite being the primary source of labor for the resort's economy, black people were taken for granted. They were anonymous. This nearsightedness relegated an entire portion of the population to a brutally inferior status. Racism, segregation, and poverty threatened to eat away at the black community's self-esteem and pride. But Atlantic City's blacks had plans of their own. They rejected the anonymity thrust upon them by racism and refused to live a second-rate existence. When blacks encountered the racial prejudice of their employers and the town's white population, they reached inward to construct a community structure and social life that expressed their experiences. As we shall see, many talented and educated African Americans were attracted to the resort. They led the way in building a society all their own, a virtual city within a city that came to be known as "the Northside."

White racism may have forced the creation of a physical ghetto, but it was civic-minded upper- and middle-class blacks who led their community to create an institutional ghetto in order to provide services the white power structure had denied African Americans. It was no small task. Nevertheless, a tree is best judged by the quality of the fruit it bears, and, at full bloom, the Northside yielded a remarkable crop of talented individuals. A self-contained metropolis in miniature form, it offered its residents a wide range of business, social, entertainment, recreational, and religious opportunities. It was a micro-colony within a city indifferent to its black population as anything more than a hotel workforce. On the Northside, black people could live with dignity.

Perhaps most importantly, the Northside was an incubator of local talent. That it succeeded in encouraging the development of individuals who went on to become leaders in their fields is a lasting hallmark of the community and a tribute to those who created and maintained it. A brief catalog of key figures who weathered adversity to excel in their professions is in order. The lives and contributions of these individuals (each of whom has a substantial presence in this work) are major components of the Northside's history.

Education was a polestar during the several generations following the American Civil War, and educated blacks were revered by their communities. Claiborn Morris Cain was such a person. He was a giant of his generation, and the tale of his life needs revival. A graduate of Lincoln University, a historically black college and university, and longtime director of the "Northside Y" (the segregated

YMCA), Cain was responsible for molding the lives of hundreds of successful young men in Atlantic City. History can play mean tricks, and one of the meanest in this story is how what may be Cain's proudest accomplishment—the development of housing at Stanley S. Holmes Village—became a canker sore on the community long after his demise. Morris Cain's career personifies the spirit that made the Northside one of the leading African-American communities in the Northeast.

Business ownership was aspired to by many but few black people succeeded the way Sara Spencer Washington did. She was an entrepreneur who demanded and earned respect from everyone she encountered. Shortly after arriving in town in 1913, "Madame" Washington promptly started her own hairdressing business. Quickly developing a reputation as a trendsetter, Madame Washington set the goal that her customers were to leave her shop feeling better about themselves. With Atlantic City as her base, she created an international empire of franchised salons, fostering opportunities for thousands of black businesspeople. Sara Washington's story is one of creativity, determination, and shrewd business instincts.

Government presented one color barrier after another, and Horace J. Bryant Jr. smashed them all. Bryant was the first African American to serve as a member of a New Jersey governor's cabinet and a bold leader on social issues. Whether serving in Trenton and mastering the intricacies of finance and insurance, agitating as a civil rights activist years before Rosa Parks refused to sit in the back of the bus, or running for office in Atlantic City, and then running again and again when a black man was supposed to know better, Horace Bryant was a born leader. Few people can match his pluck and wisdom.

Athletics had barriers of its own, and they were broken before many others, but not without the talent and persistence of earlier sportsmen who cleared a path for those who followed. One of those was Atlantic City's John Henry "Pop" Lloyd. Pop Lloyd was arguably the best all-around baseball player of his generation (circa, 1910–1940) and beyond question one of the greatest of all time, despite being confined to the "Negro League." Thanks to his long and brilliant career as a player and coach, he earned induction (posthumously, in 1977) into the Baseball Hall of Fame in Cooperstown, New York. Pop was also a patient teacher of the game and an excellent role model as a gentleman. His life is an inspiration and a lesson in humility.

Entertainment was segregated, too, but that didn't stop black talent from emerging in Atlantic City. The Northside provided opportunities for hundreds of musicians, dancers, and singers who went on to successful careers across the nation. One local legend was drummer Chris Columbo. His career reveals how the Northside's entertainment district became a critical part of the resort's economy. Thousands of music fans (white and black alike) were drawn to Atlantic City to see black entertainers. These fans returned each summer and were a vital source of income to the entire town. The center of black entertainment in the resort was Kentucky Avenue, home to nightclubs, restaurants, and dance halls that featured live entertainment equal to anything performed in New York's Harlem, including the Paradise Club, the Wonder Gardens, the Little Belmont, and the nationally renowned Club Harlem.

Distressfully, Club Harlem was where the music died. It was there, on Easter Sunday 1972, that gangsters' bullets ripped though the hearts of the Northside, sounding the death knell for Atlantic City. Among the performers who either got their start on Kentucky Avenue or rose to prominence after appearing in its venues were Cab Calloway, Count Basie, Pearl Bailey, Billy Daniels, Sarah Vaughan, "Moms" Mabley, Sammy Davis Jr., Sam Cooke, and Tina Turner. Not surprising, many of these show people were nurtured in their church choirs.

Success in every field has its own formula but one constant ingredient in the Northside's achievements was the church. It is difficult to overstate the importance of the church to black America, especially in Atlantic City. For the better part of the first one hundred years of the resort's history, the network of traditional black churches played a vital role in developing the talents of its members. In addition to reaching out to their congregants' spiritual needs, Atlantic City's black churches were actively about the business of cultivating community leaders. They built a solid social base that generated mature, responsible citizens able to play meaningful roles in their society, seven days a week. The church was the thread that tied the community together, creating a dazzling fabric of active and engaged citizens.

The Northside was so vibrant it was known and respected by black people throughout the Northeast region. Other than for work, black residents had no need to leave their part of town. But the resort's decline and the changes in American society brought about during the 1950s to 1970s prompted an exodus of local leaders and a dramatic deterioration of the Northside's social fabric, which no one could have foreseen when the resort was in its prime. No enlightened person wants to turn back the clock and undo the progress of the American Civil Rights Movement, but the societal changes it fostered had implications for black people in Atlantic City that few people appreciated at the time.

Particularly ironic with regard to the history of race relations in America is the "Summer of Freedom," the summer of 1964, when the Democratic National Convention was held in Atlantic City. Events that summer had a profound impact on Atlantic City and America. For the resort, the Democratic Convention fractured its image beyond repair. It was a seismic event for the nation in both race relations and the American two-party political system.

More central to our story was the impact of the Civil Rights Movement on Atlantic City. It was a noble quest for justice and undid decades of institutionalized racism in America. The movement also disrupted the status quo in ways that tore at the fabric of many stable and prosperous African-American neighborhoods across America. The results were tragic and heartbreaking for Atlantic City residents, nowhere more so than on the Northside. The wheels of time never turn backward and that's probably for the best. Nevertheless, in our march through history, the struggle by which an evil is vanquished can also destroy an asset for which that evil was the catalyst. With the perspective afforded by more than 40 years, it's clear that the Northside was a casualty of the law of unintended consequences. The result is a community struggling to find its way in the new city being created by the presence of casino gaming.

Understanding the past is more than an intellectual exercise. It can be a path to comprehending the present and creating the future. Nevertheless, telling a portion of the story of the Northside through the lives of several significant people, three of whom were contemporaries—Morris Cain, Sara Spencer Washington, and Pop Lloyd—poses challenges. Of necessity, the story line advances, and at times digresses, to cover important issues as they relate to the biographical sketches. What is revealed is an important chapter in the annals of America. The role of black people in the creation of Atlantic City has been overlooked far too long, and the town is not the better for it. The goal of this work is to preserve the life stories of some extraordinary people and of a special place in time in danger of being forgotten.

Morris Cain and the many Northside leaders portrayed in this book were pivotal players in Atlantic City's history. Their legacy remains relevant. Cain believed that life has no purpose if we aren't about the business of helping one another. His message is a challenge to us all. The perseverance, courage, and creativity revealed through the lives of Cain and others are an inspiration, but they need to be revived and understood in the context of their era. The labor of black people was indispensable to the creation of America's first resort, but African Americans created something more enduring—an inspiring heritage. Making sense of how the Northside arrived at where it is today, and why the resort's success is tied to the health of that community, requires a look back to the era in which Atlantic City emerged.

1

Indispensable

The story of America is incomplete without history from the bottom up.

—Donald DeVore, historian

Cobwebs were at the top of her list. They were a nuisance. She wasn't launching her attack without a hairnet. Fall had been warm and winter mild for Atlantic City—perfect conditions for spiders. Although few of the long-legged creatures could have survived, their remnants would be everywhere. It reminded her of spring cleaning several years earlier when she was interrupted by the delivery of her neighbor's baby boy. The child's father had come running to fetch her away from work. What a joy that was! Her mother, and *her* mother, and *her* mother, as far back as anyone knew, had all been midwives. The privilege of ushering a life into the world was a special gift, even if it sometimes meant being present for the heartache of losing a child. But this was no time for daydreaming. She had a war to wage.

Cotton mops and a long-handled cornstalk broom were her weapons of choice. She leaned on the door and set her metal pail and bag on the porch. Before putting the key in the lock, she pulled her hairnet from her crisply starched apron together with one of her husband's worn handkerchiefs and fixed them in place. Steeling herself for the toil ahead, she opened the door and chuckled as she might at a bad joke she'd heard before. Her brief cheerfulness came from the satisfaction of finding what she had expected and finally getting back to work. Any rejoicing was gone in a heartbeat. She looked around and knew there was much to be done.

Arms outstretched, swinging her broom much like a machete, she began making her way through the boardinghouse, room by room.

The staircase, hallways, and every lighting fixture were decorated with delicate gray strands. Some of them clung to her head, contrasting with her brown skin and black hair. They were pesky, forcing her to stop and swipe them away. Bit by bit, constantly scraping the broom with her hand and flicking clumps of what-all she'd rather not think about to the floor, she swept small bundles into piles. Then she picked up several throw rugs, mats, and runners and shook them out on the porch, draping them over the railing to air in the sun. Once the cobwebs were conquered, she switched to her wet mop and washcloths. Retracing her steps, every floor, baseboard, and door was wiped clean with a solution of Lysol and water. She liked the clean smell it left behind and knew the owner did, too. But a better smell was her lunch.

Placed snugly to one side of her burlap bag, wrapped in a dishtowel, was a large sandwich. It was a favorite: cooked cabbage between two thick slices of hard-crusted, homemade bread, slathered with coarse brown mustard. Her sandwich had a familiar aroma all its own. Sitting at the head of a long table where, during "the season," guests gathered for breakfast, she was accompanied by a dozen ghost-like figures created by tall-back chairs covered with sheets. Munching slowly, she smiled to think that in a few weeks she'd be at her regular job as head laundress and seamstress at the Chalfonte Hotel. Someone else would be serving meals to the vacationers from Philadelphia seated at the table. Let *them* try to make the guests happy. She had waited tables in a boardinghouse as a teenager. It wasn't fun. She had jumped at the chance to use her sewing skills and wasn't looking back.

She enjoyed every morsel of her sandwich, washing it down with sweet tea from a milk bottle stopped with a cork. When she was done, she wrapped the bottle in the towel and placed it in her bag. In a moment, she was back on her feet.

Next, she washed the windows—inside and out—scrubbing them with water and vinegar, leaving them open to let out the staleness. After each room was free of cobwebs and dust, and the windows were sparkling, she attacked the bathrooms, scouring the sinks and toilets with Bon Ami. Winding down, she brought the rugs back in from the porch and went room to room closing the windows. Her final step was wiping down every chair, table, chest of drawers, handrail, and doorknob with a mild solution of Fels Naptha.

She breathed a sigh of relief and exhaustion, knowing what pleased her most was getting everything done in one day. Had her work spilled over to a second day, there would have been no extra pay from the owner. Worse still, her schedule would have been side-tracked. She had another boardinghouse waiting for her tomorrow and each day after that, nonstop 'til Good Friday. And she wasn't alone. The same routine was being played out all over town. As Atlantic City of yesteryear readied itself for the annual onslaught of visitors, black people were there to make it all happen.

Throughout most of Atlantic City's history, if the job was dirty, difficult, or dangerous—the "three Ds"—black people were there to perform the task. Remove the black experience from Atlantic City's history and it becomes nothing more than a beach village.

Understanding what a wondrous thing it was that blacks came to play an essential role in Atlantic City's rise to prominence requires historical context. Some facts: First, in 1804, New Jersey became the last northern state to abolish slavery, and later laws weren't friendly to runaway slaves. Second, in the presidential election of 1860, New Jersey was the only northern state that refused to support Abraham Lincoln (the same was true in 1864). Third, during the Civil War, the New Jersey Legislature adopted several "Peace Resolutions" supporting the Confederacy and denouncing the Emancipation Proclamation. Fourth, New Jersey initially rejected the 13th Amendment to the U.S. Constitution, which abolished slavery; it wasn't until 1866, after 31 other states (including most of the Confederacy) had acted favorably that New Jersey ratified the 13th Amendment. Finally, following adoption of the 15th Amendment in 1870, guaranteeing blacks the right to vote, New Jersey's Legislature waited five years to permit freedmen to vote.

Throughout the 19th century, on the issue of race New Jersey was the least progressive state in the Northeast. That the southern part of the state would become a destination for freed slaves and their children venturing north in hope of a better life, less than a generation after the Civil War, is one of the marvels of American history. The story begins with a country doctor.

Jonathan Pitney was an unlikely real estate developer. A physician whose medical practice took him to the small towns along South Jersey's coast, Pitney was frustrated by his struggle to make ends meet. After 30 years of serving his patients, he was broke—some say dependent on his mother-in-law. Living in the mainland community of Absecon, Pitney could see "Further Island" from his office. Created by the tides and storms, this barrier island was a wild place, dominated by sand dunes, marshes, and waterfowl. Before the American colonists arrived, the island was used as a summer campground by the Native American Lenni Lenape of South Jersey, who called it "Absegami," or "Little Sea Water." Few people in the state even knew where it was.

Further Island was a pristine but desolate place when Pitney first ventured there in the 1830s. The only people living on the island were descendents of a Revolutionary War veteran, Jeremiah Leeds. Before Pitney even began thinking aloud about his fantasy, the Leeds families owned nearly the entire island. Returning often, Pitney was charmed by the serenity and natural beauty of "Absecum Beach," as it was referred to on state maps at the time. Pitney believed that this wild, sandy island (which would eventually be named "Absecon Island") had potential as a health resort, a place where doctors could send their well-to-do patients to convalesce. The problem was getting people there. Roads of the day connecting the many villages of South Jersey were often little more than footpaths. Pitney knew that travel by stagecoach wouldn't do. A railroad from the Delaware River in Camden to the Atlantic Ocean at Further Island was the answer.

Pitney dreamed big but floundered about for several years until he won the support of Samuel Richards. "Richards" was a name known and respected throughout New Jersey. The family was the most powerful south of Trenton and among the largest landholders in the eastern United States. At its peak, the family's holdings collectively totaled more than one-quarter of a million acres. Samuel Richards understood the importance of a rail line between Philadelphia and Absecon Island. A rail line linking his landholdings to Philadelphia would increase their value, making it possible for him to turn some of his vast acreage into cash. Richards latched on to Pitney's idea and all but made it his own. Lobbying state legislators, he secured a charter for the Camden-Atlantic Railroad in 1852.

With the granting of a railroad charter, Richards recruited investors, primarily other large landowners hoping that a railroad would increase the value of their holdings. Construction began in earnest in August 1853. Starting at the Delaware River, the right-of-way slashed through a vast pine forest known as the Jersey Pine Barrens. Trees were cut, hills leveled, and swamps filled as the new railroad made its way east. A straight line was surveyed from Cooper's Ferry in Camden directly to Absecon Island. The train tracks went around nothing. This new railroad was built by the quickest and cheapest means possible: that meant African-American workers who had escaped slavery and Irish laborers who had fled famine in their homeland.

Clearing the right-of-way involved the backbreaking work of pulling stumps, hauling gravel and stones for the railroad bed, wrestling with timbers, and lugging rails. Cutting a path through South Jersey's vast, mosquito-infested Pine Barrens was tough going, but things got worse as the right-of-way left firm ground and approached the meadows. The mosquitoes were replaced with swarms of greenhead flies, and the chores involved in draining the meadows and marshlands in order to create the railroad bed were dreaded tasks. Standing knee-deep in salty, murky waters, wearing flimsy, homemade clothes and usually barefoot to keep their shoes from being destroyed, black workers wielded axes or pushed and pulled the end of a two-person saw to fell trees and large bushes. Often stumps had to be removed. Then the workers had to handle rope and chains without gloves while trying to steady a team of horses no happier than they were to be standing on the slimy bottom as the stumps were pulled. Finally, these African-American and Irish laborers lugged shovels filled with muck and mire to create channels directing the flow of water away from the railroad bed.

Although there are no hard numbers on the makeup of the workforce that built the Camden-Atlantic Railroad, we know that black hands were involved from the beginning. If the work to be done entailed the three Ds, it's a safe bet black workers were the first assigned.

"The First Colored Man" as described in an early volume of Atlantic City firsts was "Billy" Bright. Mr. Bright, along with his wife, Mary, and son, Daniel, lived in a shanty on Rhode Island Avenue in 1859. The 1860 U. S. Census reveals that the Bright family had taken in a boarder, a practice that would later become the norm for many black families in Atlantic City. The boarder was one Daniel Thompson, a 75-year-old native of Delaware whose occupation was described as "gunning." Before moving to Absecon Island after likely working as a laborer on the construction of the railroad, Billy Bright and his family lived in a small village comprised of seven black households in Hamilton Township, a heavily forested community 15 miles west of Absecon Island. This tiny village of farmers, craftsmen, and laborers dated back to the 1840s and was comprised of freed people hailing from Northeastern states, primarily New Jersey, Pennsylvania, and New York.

South Jersey was home to African Americans long before Atlantic City came to be. According to the 1850 U.S. Census, "Freed Colored" families lived in neighboring Egg Harbor Township, Galloway, Hammonton, Mullica, and Weymouth. Runaway slaves from the Upper South were attracted by the solitude and, more importantly, the isolation of the Pine Barrens. For modest sums, they could acquire or rent a small plot of woodlands, carve out a farm, and make a place for their families. These people did their best to live in anonymity knowing that New Jersey's laws granted them no protection from being reclaimed by slave masters. The men of these communities—where many lived by their wits as farmers and craftsmen relying on bartering—would have jumped at the opportunity to earn real money. There's every reason to believe they played a major role in building the railroad to Atlantic City. What's not known is whether everyone who labored on construction of the railroad was a *paid* worker.

Historians speculate that not all the African-American workers were freed persons at the time Atlantic City was being developed. Even after the elimination of slavery by the legislature, given New Jersey's mind-set, which respected the "right" of visitors to bring slaves with them, the transporting of slaves to work on the railroad may have occurred. According to historian Richlyn Goddard:

> The Atlantic City population was recorded as part of the county census prior to receiving its municipal charter in 1854; therefore, the first census for the city was reflected in 1860. When comparing the manuscript census from 1850 to 1860, the differences were striking because only two free-black households, the Brights and the Jeffries, a shoemaker, were recorded on June 5, 1860 by the census enumerator, F. R. DeVinney as "Free Inhabitants in Egg Harbor Township, Atlantic City Post

Office." Live-in servants at three hotels were also
recorded, thus a total of 19 blacks were documented that
year. In light of the fact that the census schedules reported
a total of 164 black persons residing in Atlantic City in
1860 ... it is feasible to deduce from the evidence that the
145 undocumented blacks in that census were enslaved
laborers.

New Jersey's attitude toward slavery being what it was, Goddard's
analysis is persuasive.

That slave labor was used to some extent in constructing the railroad and the early buildings on Absecon Island is more likely than
not. As for freed black workers, there's no need to speculate as to
whether they provided the bulk of the labor given how affordable
they were relative to their white counterparts. With the cheap labor
of African-American workers, the new rail line was ready for use in
less than a year.

Cooper's Ferry Terminal in Camden was the site at which guests
gathered for the inaugural trip of the Camden-Atlantic Railroad on
July 1, 1854. The first train, an "official special," consisted of nine
passenger cars, all filled. Ferryboats from Philadelphia brought a
stream of guests, each with a printed invitation, and hundreds of the
curious who came to see the first iron horse leave for the seashore.
More than 600 passengers—newspapermen, politicians, and nota-
bles of the day—were invited to help promote the resort. There were
several black persons on board as well: They were the porters who
handled the passengers' baggage and the wood tenders who split the
oak logs and fed them into the locomotive's furnace.

Huge clouds of smoke signaled the train's arrival as it reached the
end of the rail line in Absecon at water's edge, shortly before noon.
The guests were given life preservers and then herded onto large row-
boats for the trip across the bay, the rowing likely done by African
Americans and/or Irish immigrants, as this was the type of work only
they performed in that era. A second train chugged through the sand
dunes delivering the visitors to the door of the resort's first public
lodging, the United States Hotel, where black servants awaited them,
handling their bags and escorting them to their rooms.

After a sumptuous meal, prepared and served by black hands, the
guests strolled along the ocean's edge, taking in the remains of six

shipwrecks visible from the shore. A sprawling four-story structure built to house 2,000 guests, the United States Hotel was owned and operated by the railroad. By year's end, when fully constructed, it was not only the first hotel in Atlantic City, but—at 600 rooms—the largest in the nation. Once the private debut was over, the public was invited. The remainder of the summer was a success, with nearly every train leaving Camden filled to capacity. The first season earned rave reviews from visitors. Philadelphia area patrons were charmed by the novelty of the entire idea—a train ride through the forest, ending at the seashore. Although it was a proud time for Jonathan Pitney, his beach village was a long way from a full-fledged resort. It was *rustic*, to put it mildly.

True to its beginnings as a farm island, the cattle of local farmers were allowed to run free. Atlantic City's main thoroughfare, Atlantic Avenue, was originally a cow path. Cattle were driven by farmers in the inlet area to the lower end of the island to graze in pastures that later became the cities of Ventnor and Margate. As late as the 1880s, one could see dozens of cows being herded by black farmhands from one end of town to the other and then returned at night through the center of the village on Atlantic Avenue. Faithful to their heritage, black farmhands supplemented their families' diets by trapping muskrats, rabbits, fox, and turtles, which they harvested on their treks to graze cattle. By the 1880 U.S. Census, nearly 1,000 black persons called Atlantic City home. They worked at everything from washing clothes and cooking meals to tending cattle and building hotels. But the town grew slowly.

Finding the money for the improvements needed to establish a permanent community on Absecon Island was much more difficult than securing investors for the railroad. Richards and his friends had what they wanted. Their land along the railroad right-of-way was selling to small businessmen and farmers. Plans for cutting through streets, leveling the dunes, filling ditches, and constructing the infrastructure needed to establish a permanent presence simply had to wait. For the next 20 years, Atlantic City limped along, remaining a wilderness island.

Predictions by early critics proved true. Pitney's plans for a health spa didn't materialize. The wealthy visited the resort occasionally, but few returned. As for the growing numbers of new people in Philadelphia, the cost of vacationing remained beyond their reach.

But that was about to change. As he had a generation earlier, Samuel Richards decided it was time to build a railroad. What he lacked in youth, he made up for in savvy and enthusiasm.

Richards understood what was happening in Philadelphia. Its population had exploded from 120,000 in 1850 to 850,000 by 1880. Thousands of immigrants arrived daily to work in the city's factories. Home to a staggering number of manufacturers in the iron and steel industry, Philadelphia's foundries produced one-third of the country's manufactured iron. They turned out everything from nuts, bolts, horseshoes, and machine tools to cast iron building fronts, ship plates, sewing machines, and—important to Atlantic City—amusement rides. Additionally, by 1857, Philadelphia had more textile factories than any other city in the world—more than 260, manufacturing cotton and woolen clothes, making fashionable attire affordable to the masses. At the time, Philadelphia had the most diversified industrial economy of any American city.

Factory workers were beginning to have expendable income for leisure-time activities, and Richards believed that if Atlantic City could tap Philadelphia's working class, it would spur growth. He knew it could only happen if working men were able to afford a train ticket. For several years, Richards tried to sell his idea to the railroad's shareholders, but the directors of the Camden-Atlantic Railroad repeatedly rejected his idea for making travel to the resort more affordable. By 1875, Richards lost patience with his fellow directors and decided to build a new railroad of his own, the Philadelphia and Atlantic City Railway Company.

Prospects of a second railroad coming to Atlantic City divided the town. Jonathan Pitney had died six years earlier, but his dream of a sedate resort for the wealthy persisted. Most year-round residents were content with their island remaining a sleepy beach village where things perked up during summer but always at a genteel pace. But their opinions counted for little. As he had done 24 years earlier, Richards went to the Legislature and obtained another railroad charter. With his money and a second charter in hand, Richards set about constructing his new railroad. Nothing would stand in his way.

Construction proceeded at a fever pitch, with crews of black laborers working double shifts seven days a week. To cut down on construction costs, Richards decided to construct a "narrow gauge" railroad, so named because it was 14 inches narrower than conventional railroads. Fifty-four miles of railroad track were laid in just 90 days. The first train arrived on July 7, 1877. The world had never seen anything like it. With the exception of rail lines built during wartime, no railroad had ever been constructed at such speed.

Matching the swiftness of the construction was the number of Philadelphians who lined up to board the new train. Tickets were priced for a class of customers who cared little that the cars they rode in were the dregs of the train yards. The price of a round-trip ticket was slashed in half, from the $3 charged by the Camden-Atlantic Railroad to $1.50. There were even "excursion" rates of $1 for a round-trip ticket. To a majority of Richards's customers, the price was all that mattered. The less visitors spent on train fare, the more they had to spend while visiting Atlantic City. Because there were no mass-oriented facilities at the time the second railroad began service, the Philadelphia and Atlantic City Railway Company developed "excursion houses" that provided a reception point, locker facilities, a dining hall, and an entertainment pavilion where musicians, singers, and jugglers performed for coins from the customers. Patrons could purchase a meal, see live entertainment, shoot pool, bowl, rent a bathing suit and locker for 25 cents, and take a shower before returning home on the last train to Philadelphia.

Increased train ridership and the development of larger excursion houses created job opportunities for black workers. There were no washers, dryers, vacuums, vending machines, paper plates, or microwave ovens. Towels, blankets, and bathing suits had to be hand washed. Meals had to be prepared, and cooking and eating utensils cleaned for re-use. The day-trippers from Philadelphia left behind a lot of work, and newly freed persons from the Upper South performed the necessary chores. But not all African Americans who arrived in town came to work.

After the development of the second railroad, blacks living in Washington, D.C., Baltimore, Philadelphia, and Camden, working primarily as domestic servants or janitors, found that a trip to Atlantic City was also within their reach. To accommodate the "colored trade," most excursion houses scheduled what were known as "Colored Excursion Days" as early as the 1880s. They quickly became an annual event. At the end of each season, generally in September, the railroads offered their lowest priced outings. Many black people in the Northeast had relatives, friends, or fellow church members who worked in Atlantic City. Some of these local black workers lived in the resort year-round, others left in the fall. With the encouragement of the railroads, these black hotel employees invited their friends to the shore.

Regardless of the railroad's business interests, the local establishment couldn't hide its feelings about black vacationers. "Dagos" and "kikes"—that is, first-generation immigrant Italians and Eastern European Jews—were one thing, but "coons" were quite another. African Americans were acceptable as workers, but seeing them as vacationers was disturbing for many of the town's white residents.

Speaking for many in the resort regarding Colored Excursion Days, a local newspaper, the *Atlantic City Daily Union*—never one to hide its feelings about "colored folk"—noted in 1892, "There's more than one new coon in town today; fully 8,000 of 'em." In 1898, the same newspaper reported:

> They are patronizing the street cars and the busmen are doing a good trade. The lunch counters and the buffets are gathering in plenty of nickels and dimes, for the colored folk are generous and, like Pittsburghers, spend every dime they bring with them and have only the return coupons of their tickets left when the day is done … Tomorrow they will be gone, and it is estimated that they will leave behind no less than $20,000 in hard-earned cash.

Two years later, the *Atlantic City Daily Press* commented on the excursion of 1900:

> Yesterday was a great day for the colored population. Over eleven thousand were brought in by the two railroads on the excursion train … A great long line of Sambos and Liza Janes was seen like a huge cineograph moving picture along the ocean front … The loud laugh of the happy Negro and the "yaller girl" made the Boardwalk ring … Considering the event and the low price of razors, it is wonderful that so few disturbances occurred during the day.

Through cheap train fare and excursion houses, Atlantic City was making vacations affordable for blacks and whites alike. The excursion houses proved that something besides hotels for the wealthy could succeed in the resort. As Atlantic City marched into the future, it wasn't possible for it to exist without the railroads, and the railroads could not have existed without Philadelphia's masses. Nevertheless, each year the precariousness of the town's existence became clearer. Repeat business was crucial. Visitors had to leave happy or they might not return. Year-round residents understood that the prosperity of both Atlantic City and the railroads hinged on success of "the season"—the 12 to 14 weeks from June through August. Whatever their tastes, guests had to have a good time.

Richards's new railroad prospered but had a short life. It was acquired by the Philadelphia and Reading system in 1883, which was part of the Pennsylvania Railroad. This was no small occurrence in the resort's history. Headquartered in Philadelphia, the "Pennsy," as it was called, was gargantuan. By traffic and revenue, it was the mightiest railroad in the nation. At its peak, it controlled nearly 10,000 miles of rail line. Atlantic City was now tied into that extensive network. As historian Harold F. Wilson has noted, "Immediately the name of Atlantic City became familiar in every ticket office in the land in control of that great and powerful corporation [the Pennsylvania Railroad]. The reputation of the place became national, and people from all parts of the country began to appreciate its health imparting properties."

After the advent of Samuel Richards's second railroad, there was no turning back. New buildings sprouted in Atlantic City like daffodils. Where once there had been a sand dune or a pond, there now was a boardinghouse or a hotel. The air was filled with the sounds of shovels, hammers, saws, and masonry tools. The people performing the work were an ethnic stew of Italians, Irish, Germans, and Jews. Generally, the masons were Italian, the carpenters were German, and the roofers and general construction workers were Irish. The merchants who sold tools, supplies, and work clothes were often Jewish. Women and young children, many of them Italian or Jewish, went from one job site to another hawking sandwiches and beverages.

One constant in the mix of workers who built Atlantic City was the role of "colored folk" (considered the least offensive term for African Americans at the time). These men and women performed servile but critical roles in the building industry; in the case of the men, everything from mixing concrete and hoisting it up in buckets to the bricklayers, to lugging shingles up ladders to the roofers. In the boom era following Richards's narrow gauge railroad, only the most talented and persistent black man was able to work in the skilled trades. Black workers were viewed as a threat because they were willing to work at skilled positions for lower salaries than demanded by whites. As a result, they were generally only granted positions unwanted by whites in the building trades. As with the building of the railroad, if construction work entailed the three Ds, black workers were the first assigned. Regardless of a person's role, *everyone*, black or white, scurried about constantly, days blurring one into another, working at a feverish pitch from sunrise until after sunset.

Year after year, from early spring through late fall, Atlantic City was a beehive of activity swarming with workers living in tents, sleeping on cots, eating in makeshift chow halls, and working seven days per week. Workers signed on for the season, knowing they'd work every day until the weather turned. For nearly three decades, from the latter part of the 19th century into the second decade of the 20th century, "Tent City" rose up from the sand every spring, pitched at different locations, following the growth of the resort. The residents of Tent City were mostly itinerant laborers and tradesmen, sometimes with their families, usually not. These crews of workers were brought to town by Philadelphia contractors and established businesses looking to get in on the action at the shore.

Black workers were excluded from Tent City. Those who had the means pitched a tent of their own near their worksite. Those who didn't were forced to live in stopgap flimsy housing—often abandoned bathhouses or small shacks they constructed themselves—or rent from a family that had established itself in the resort. Regardless of their race or living circumstances, there were few idle people. Many tolerated horrible living conditions just for the chance to earn decent wages, greater than anything they could hope for in farming or domestic work.

The several decades of Atlantic City's growth in this period formed the town's permanent character. With "the season" a small fraction of the year, the merchants lured to town by the second railroad knew that, in order to make a return on their investments, they had to cater to the wants of their customers. It was inevitable that the resort would acquire the tastes and assume the character of its patrons. With merchants migrating from throughout the Northeast region leading the way, Atlantic City became a resort for the working class. Thousands of hoteliers, restaurateurs, building tradesmen, and laborers came to town looking to cash in on its growth and many remained, making it their home.

Between the years 1875 and 1900, Atlantic City's year-round population increased from less than 2,000 to nearly 30,000. By the turn of the century, the only city in South Jersey having a greater population was Camden, which had an important port and thriving industries. But in the summer, the resort became a major metropolis, its population ranking in the top dozen cities in America. "In-season," the city's daily population exceeded 200,000, with weekends hovering at nearly 300,000. Compare that with the 1900 census figures for Newark, with 246,000; Jersey City, with 206,000; Camden, with 76,000; and Trenton, with 75,000.

First- and second-generation Irish, Italians, and Jews, most by way of Philadelphia and New York, came to town and brought their citified ways with them. During the same time frame, the African-American population increased from less than 500 to nearly 7,000, representing more than 23 percent of the town's population. Thousands more black workers came each spring, living with friends and family, or sleeping in makeshift quarters in hotels for the season.

At the turn of the 20th century, there was no community like Atlantic City anywhere in the country. In New Jersey, and particularly the South Jersey region, it was an oddity. The resort was unlike any of its neighboring towns and unlike any place the people on the mainland had even heard of. The surrounding villages were sparsely populated, primarily by white Anglo-Saxon farmers and fishermen, while the resort was an ethnically diverse, populous city visited by strangers from far and wide. The tastes and desires of Atlantic City's visitors were far from "proper" in the prevailing view of its neighboring communities. For many, gambling and drinking on Sundays made it a wicked place, a modern day Sodom and Gomorrah.

Also setting the resort apart was the scale of the construction that was occurring. Hunting waterfowl and trapping small game on Absecon Island were no more. Hundreds of train cars carrying lumber, bricks, and gravel arrived each spring. Intense development was occurring on a barrier island that neighboring farmers understood all too well was merely a large sand deposit created by the tides. The "Further Island" that had captured Jonathan Pitney's imagination was little more than spindles of sand rising up from the ocean floor. The process by which the island was formed is ongoing. The only *constant* feature of barrier islands is that they are subject to the whims of nature: Waves, currents, tides, winds, storms, and sea level change, all with the potential to wreak havoc. Atlantic County's farmers understood the island's character. It's possible that Richard Osborne, the engineer who prepared the first city map, did as well, but you wouldn't know that from his development plans.

Parceling the island into neat squares and rectangles, the street grid designed by Osborne created many narrow lots ideal for small homes and boardinghouses. These early structures were built in rows, sometimes with meager side yards, often with common walls. No one on the mainland could conceive of living in such a manner. In addition to modest residences and boardinghouses, outlandish structures were being built. Hotels, five to ten stories high, were erected in a region where barns had been the tallest buildings for as long as anyone could remember. Atlantic City's piers were built *not* for fishing, but instead for entertaining visitors atop the ocean. The island's only protection from the Atlantic Ocean, a natural system of sand dunes, was leveled and a wooden walkway constructed, all for the pleasure of visitors. Add to the mix as many as 50 or more trains a day roaring through mostly farm fields and forest—where everyone traveled by horse and wagon—and one can see why residents of nearby towns were stunned by what was going on in Atlantic City. Making things even more unsettling in the minds of its neighbors was the city's booming black population. During the last decade of the 19th century, more than 90 percent of Atlantic County's African-American residents lived in the resort.

To its neighbors, Atlantic City was a marvel and a mystery. In relation to the rest of the county and South Jersey, it was a world unto itself. Within a single generation after Samuel Richards's second rail line, Absecon Island had transformed from a quiet beach village that shut down at the end of each summer into a socially complex, bustling, and—as we shall see—morally conflicted and politically corrupt city with an economy based solely on tourism.

Nationally, the tourism industry was in its infancy. In that era, there were only a handful of vacation spots, and they were reserved for the wealthy. Outside of cities, the hotels that existed were generally large guesthouses, which welcomed people only for lengthy stays. They weren't geared toward working class patrons. Atlantic City was a sharp contrast to the norm. Cheap transportation, coupled with affordable rooms, meals, and attractions to suit a broad range of tastes, made the resort a favorite not only of Philadelphia's blue-collar workers but of the newly rich, as well, many of whom were looking for excitement.

Atlantic City understood its role well. Its mission was twofold: to provide lodging for thousands of vacationers and to keep them entertained the entire time they were in town. The many thousands of diverse people who flocked to town during the summer months shared a unique community of feeling unlike anything else that existed in the United States at the time: *They were there to have a good time.* The new "city" that had evolved out of Pitney's beach village stands alone in American history: It was the first dedicated principally to pleasure—social experimentation on a grand scale. Unlike all other U.S. cities that had come before it, Atlantic City had a singular purpose: to provide leisure-time activities for vacationers. The city's very existence was dependent on money spent by out-of-towners, and resort merchants had something for everyone.

As the *Philadelphia Press* reported in the summer of 1904, the resort's 50th anniversary, "There is no one that can visit Atlantic City, from the King of England to the $10 a week clerk, who will not find accommodations to suit his taste and pocketbook." The article noted that the same was true for entertainment. "As to amusement, there is no place in the world where amusement is reduced to the exact science that it is here ... and should a new form of 'shoot the shoot' or toboggan slide turn up in England or Africa, it would be set up here within the same week. Here amusement is carefully studied by the proprietors of the different places as is fashion by the moditiate."

Pioneering amusement rides began shortly after construction of Samuel Richards's second railroad. These mechanical devices had three principal forms, still familiar today: the merry-go-round, the Ferris wheel, and the roller coaster. All three rides were popular in Atlantic City as early as the 1880s. What's hard to grasp today is the excitement these rides generated and how important they were in making the resort a popular destination. Whether for factory workers or farmers, shopkeepers or professionals, a ride on a Ferris wheel or roller coaster was excitement beyond anything experienced in their daily routine. At the time, Philadelphia was the largest producer of mechanical amusement rides in the world, with more carousels manufactured there than in any other city. Atlantic City provided nearby manufacturers with an opportunity to experiment and display the latest models. Thrill rides were erected all over town, some in clusters and others—particularly the very large ones—free standing. Each ride had a storied and sometimes fanciful history and was promoted as a wonder of the modern age. The principal element they shared was the use of modern technology for pleasure instead of work. Rather than making *things*, these machines were designed to make people happy.

Maintaining the original mechanical amusements was dirty, difficult, and often dangerous work. Countless gears had to be greased, nuts and bolts tightened, and cables kept taut without frays. It was more than hard work. A careful eye had to be kept to ensure the safety of the riders. Generally, it was African-American workers who tended to these tasks behind the scenes, while white workers greeted the riders and collected their tickets.

Amusement rides were just part of the entertainment package evolving in the 1890s. Within the first decade of the 20th century, Atlantic City was the largest city in the world dedicated exclusively to entertaining the traveling public, annually hosting more than 3 million guests. It was estimated that by 1903, the typical visitor was spending $25 per week and that the resort's annual revenue exceeded $100 million. Within five years, the annual receipts were estimated in excess of $200 million. Although some of those receipts may have been from "kings," most was spent by "clerks."

Most amusements, whether for royalty or ordinary folk, were found near the Boardwalk. An Atlantic City first, the Boardwalk began as a means to keep tourists from tracking beach sand all over town. First constructed in 1870, it quickly became a busy street with hundreds of businesses facing the beach. By the dawn of the 20th century, there was nothing like the Boardwalk anywhere in the world. It quickly evolved into the town's central nervous system, with grand hotels and storefronts lining it on the land side and piers on the ocean side.

Businesses along the Boardwalk helped to foster an emphasis on retail sales that would characterize Atlantic City for years to come. Every foot of the Boardwalk was dedicated to assisting its strollers to part with their money. Atlantic City played a major role in fostering the illusion that spending money was a pleasure unto itself. Some social historians believe that Boardwalk merchants introduced the concept of the "spending spree" into American culture.

For many first-time visitors, Atlantic City was a fantasy island and the Boardwalk was Main Street, a wonderland of glitz and cheap thrills. "The Boardwalk was a stage, upon which there was a temporary suspension of disbelief; behavior that was exaggerated, even ridiculous, in everyday life was expected at the resort. The rigidities of Victorian life relaxed, permitting contact between strangers and the pursuit of fantasies." Atlantic City's grand promenade created for its strollers an illusion of social mobility that couldn't be found at other resorts. Coinciding with the emergence of the Boardwalk was an explosion of affordable clothing. The recently invented sewing machine made it possible for the working class to afford stylish garments "off the rack" without having to hire a tailor. Ready-made clothing blurred class lines and, for most of the resort's patrons, the Boardwalk became a showcase for their new clothes. A trip to Atlantic City was an excuse for getting dressed up. Strolling on the Boardwalk made visitors feel they were part of the "upper crust."

If blue-collar workers and their families were to spend a weekend in Atlantic City, not just an afternoon stroll on the Boardwalk, they needed places to stay that were within their means. Boardinghouses were the answer. Historian Charles E. Funnell has estimated that between 1880 and 1920 boardinghouses accounted for more than 60 percent of all rooms for tourists. For a modest investment, one could be up and running in a few months. Construction on dozens of small, wood-frame hotels and boardinghouses began in the early spring and were completed in time for the summer season. Surviving the *second* season was the key to making it. Lacking the glamour of the beachfront hotels, boardinghouses made it possible for middle-class families to have an extended stay at the seashore. Without boardinghouses, most of Atlantic City's visitors would have only been able to afford daily excursions. Typically, the accommodations were simple to the point of monotony, but they were clean and comfortable, which was more than what most of the visitors had at home.

Boardinghouse owners and their patrons were a critical mainstay of the resort's tourist economy. With the rates charged by boardinghouses, a whole new cross-section of Americans found that they could afford a vacation. Factory workers, office clerks, postal employees, government workers, and teachers realized that they, too, could vacation in Atlantic City.

Key to success for Atlantic City's tourism industry was to give visitors what they wanted. The shortness of the season demanded repeat business. Visitors had to leave happy. If they didn't, they might not return. Atlantic City measured the tastes and whims of its patrons and found that a significant portion wanted to be able to drink on Sundays, enjoy the pleasures of the flesh, and take a chance at gambling. As one longtime resident opined, "If the people who came to town had wanted Bible readings, we'd have given 'em that. But nobody ever asked for Bible readings. They wanted booze, broads, and gambling, so that's what we gave 'em."

"Booze, broads, and gambling" are precisely what many of the guests staying in boardinghouses wanted. Vice—on a scale unlike anything available to vacationers during that era—quickly became an important part of the local entertainment package. The resort was booming in large part because of its commitment to making visitors happy, regardless of what the law allowed.

By the turn of the 20th century, the state's "Bishops' Law," which prohibited the sale of alcohol on Sunday, was being flaunted, houses of prostitution could be found in most neighborhoods, and gambling rooms were run in a wide-open fashion. With the arrival of spring, brothels bloomed and those that didn't pay police protection ran the risk of being shut down. One such instance was reported in the local press with the headline "Police Wipe out House of Ill Repute." The front page article reported, "A locally notorious house of ill repute in this City was wiped out of existence by the police yesterday … despite the vigilance of the police, places of this kind sometimes flourish without their knowledge … The conditions which the police found in the place were shameful and of such a repugnant nature that it was unfit for publication even in a police court, where ordinarily everything goes." Generally, such arrests were for show and had two purposes: to keep up appearances with law-abiding citizens and to get the message out that the only brothels permitted were ones that paid a portion of their income to the local political powers.

As for gambling rooms, they were run in a similar fashion and the *Atlantic City Daily Press* reported on them frequently. One such article complained, "Persistent rumors are heard to the effect that extensive gambling houses and club rooms are being operated in the city … One is on the Boardwalk, in the very center of the city where thousands of visitors are passing daily. These places, we understand, are not simply little quiet card games that no one would seriously object to, but fully-equipped gambling houses where players can be accommodated with almost any game they desire." In a short time, the resort became known as the place to let loose, the spot to go for a hell-raising good time.

Word spread quickly, and Atlantic City became popular throughout the Northeast. In addition to being a place for hell-raisers, the resort's hospitality industry gained a reputation as a destination where vacationers were treated well. Regardless of their financial means, upon arrival in Atlantic City guests knew they would be pampered. But it took large numbers of servile employees to do the pampering. By the first decade of the 20th century, with a summertime population of 250,000 to 300,000 (of which only 35,000 were year-round residents), many unskilled workers were needed for everything from greeting guests and carrying bags to cleaning rooms and preparing and serving meals. Desk clerks, bellboys, waiters, cooks, dishwashers, chambermaids, laundresses, and janitors were in constant demand. These demands created a problem for Atlantic City.

Atlantic City couldn't compete for white workers in the economy of the late 19th and early 20th centuries. In that era, there were few "career fields" for whites in the slowly emerging national hotel industry. Although nearly all hotels were owned and managed by Caucasians, the number of hotels was few and guest services were virtually nonexistent. Those who could afford to travel and to stay at a hotel often brought their own servants with them, limiting the career opportunities for people as servants in the hotel business. But the resort's growing popularity changed everything.

Atlantic City created a whole new array of opportunities for black people eager to escape the "Jim Crow" South. For nearly three generations after the Civil War, as America was shifting from an agriculture-based economy to a manufacturing economy, racial prejudice excluded black people from industrial employment. During the years between the Civil War and World War I, the only occupations realistically available to the American Negro were either as a farm laborer or domestic worker. Domestic work was thought to be peculiarly "Negro work," and the attitude of most whites was that "Negros are servants; servants are Negros." If Atlantic City's hotel industry was to flourish, "servants" were needed.

Service was critical to making visitors feel like royalty. Resort hoteliers understood that to make their guests happy, many hands were needed to do the pampering, and the more helpers, the better. This was true not just in the large hotels and busy restaurants but especially so for boardinghouse operators. Most boardinghouses were owned by sole proprietors; some were the classic "mom and pop," and others were investor-owned and operated by a hired manager. Some lived at their properties year-round; others left in the fall and returned each spring. Getting ready for the season was no small task. The entire property had to be cleaned and repairs made before the influx of visitors began.

Once the season started, rooms had to be "turned" for each guest. Given the class of clientele that stayed at most boardinghouses, some left behind headaches for the cleaning staff. Sheets had to be changed and washed and sometimes mended, as did rugs and furniture. Most boardinghouses served breakfast and dinner—it was part of their attraction. Meals had to be planned, food purchased and prepared, and everything washed and dried and made ready for the next meal. Some properties provided livery service from the train station, and carriages and horses needed tending. Then as now, the hospitality business was very hands-on. The problem for Atlantic City's businesspeople was where to find so many hands and strong backs.

Atlantic City's solution was unique for its time. The hotel industry reached out to the Upper South and recruited people who had been marred by slavery. The many service positions necessary to keep the resort running smoothly were filled mostly by former slaves and their descendents, coaxed to the North during the three generations following the Civil War. With an inner strength forged in adversity, these migrants quickly became a major asset to the resort economy.

Black hotel workers added to the town's mystique among the tourists streaming out of Philadelphia. There was no better means by which to reinforce the illusion of being part of the upper crust than to be doted over by obliging "colored servants" dressed in uniforms. While the money required to transform a quiet beach village into a bustling city based on tourism was supplied by eager out-of-town investors, the muscle and sweat needed to create a full-fledged resort were provided by African Americans. Black workers were the indispensable ingredient in making Jonathan Pitney's and Samuel Richards's experiments a success. The black experience in Atlantic City, and the contribution African Americans made there, stand apart in American history.

2

Working, Not Being Worked

Being worked meant degradation; working means civilization.

—Booker T. Washington, educator

"Boy! You there, boy. Come get these bags!" Mid-summer, Monday morning, Atlantic City, the train station—as ever, it was pandemonium. Several middle-aged black men dressed in uniforms looked in the direction of a young white man hollering on the crowded platform, then looked away.

Attired in a light-color suit, starched collar, tie and hat, the gentleman was surrounded by his wife and children, dressed equally well. Piled next to them was their luggage, enough for a week at the beach. Staring intently in the direction of an elegant horse-drawn carriage with the name of the hotel emblazoned on the side, he bellowed again, "The Mansion House, here, *please!*" A second later, the visitor made eye contact with the carriage driver, and a wiry black man came scurrying to gather up the suitcases. Fawning over his patrons, the black man apologized repeatedly, bowing and nodding his head, speaking softly, "Yes suh, yes suh." Dressed smartly in a formal black suit and cap, wearing white gloves, the driver politely requested his guests follow him. With passengers and bags aboard, it was off to the hotel.

First crawling, then stumbling, finally off and running, Atlantic City at the turn of the 20th century was a *must* for vacationers of America's Northeast. And those visitors expected first-rate service. At the prompting of hoteliers, the resort became a mecca for black men and women seeking hotel work. Between the years 1880 and 1920, thousands of blacks left their homes in the Upper South and relocated to the resort in search of opportunity. Atlantic City historian Richlyn

Goddard has identified the blacks who came to the town as belonging to three distinct groups: the southern-born—the largest segment—who migrated primarily from Virginia and Maryland's eastern shores; free black persons born in New Jersey and its bordering states, notably Pennsylvania; and Caribbean immigrants, including many from the British West Indies—the latter comprising a small but tight-knit enclave of black migrants who had come to the resort when work ended on the construction of the Panama Canal. Regardless of origin, these individuals inevitably brought with them emotional baggage from their experiences at the hands of white society.

At the beginning of Atlantic City's boom period, the scars on the American psyche from the conflict over slavery remained raw. The freed slaves who had come north to make a new life couldn't escape the shadows cast by the old one. Slavery haunted them. Brimming with opportunities, Atlantic City was the rare place where African Americans were wage earners, not sharecroppers or servants. Many jobs in the new resort offered responsibility with a chance at dignity. But the experience of slavery couldn't be extinguished. Its legacy lingered. Laden with an inferior status imposed by racism, many black people were plagued with a deep insecurity beyond their control.

Bondage for a dozen generations, spanning more than two centuries, had left its mark on black America—wounds that white America has never fully grasped. For the nation, and Atlantic City, slavery's history became a prism through which relations between the races were viewed. Blacks saw the images clearly—whites did not. Getting a handle on the psychological baggage of slavery is a prerequisite to comprehending the black experience in Atlantic City and across the nation.

American history fondly evokes the experiences of the early settlers who populated the New World and the hardships they overcame. Routinely ignored is the fact that slave labor was essential to building the infrastructure upon which American society was founded. Utilizing slaves in the same manner as oxen or horses, many more tracts of colonial lands were opened for settlement than could have been possible had real wages been required to be paid. Through their labors, African Americans developed skills essential to the colonial economy and, for many segments of society, their labor became indispensable. If slavery hadn't been part of the colonial period, the American economy would have developed at a crawl.

"Life, liberty and the pursuit of happiness" as defined by the Founding Fathers was a whites-only proposition. Black people didn't fit into the freedom scenario espoused by their masters. Passionate patriots such as Thomas Jefferson, James Madison, and James Monroe were able to compartmentalize their thinking, demanding freedom for their fellow Americans while continuing to defend slavery. Jefferson gave us "All men are created equal"—arguably the five most important words in the American lexicon—yet his vision excluded African Americans.

Advocates of slavery justified it by persistently arguing two points: First, they suggested an inequality of rights based upon Christian religious teachings; second, they argued for an innate difference, namely, the *inferiority* of people of African descent. According to the slave masters, slavery was grounded in the Holy Bible, and Old Testament scripture was frequently quoted in support of the institution. The second prong of the pro-slavery rationale was that the African race was different, namely, less than human. African Americans were inferior to persons of European descent. Black people were "baboons" brought to civilization from the "jungle." Slavery's advocates stigmatized an entire people, and their success in tarnishing the African persona did not end with abolition.

Although racism has been a strong force throughout American history, scholars have noted that, despite the Union victory of the Civil War, during the last generation of the 19th century—the era in which Atlantic City was emerging as a major resort—race relations developed rigid patterns. It was a critical stage in our nation's history. As part of a bargain to hold onto the White House following the disputed Hayes-Tilden election of 1876, in which he lost the popular vote, President Rutherford B. Hayes withdrew the last federal troops from the South, restoring home rule. "The compromise of 1877," as it became known, stripped African Americans of voting and other rights and fanned the flames of the white supremacy movement.

Failure of the "Reconstruction Era" saw a wave of segregation laws adopted by Southern state legislatures in the 1880s and '90s. These "Jim Crow" laws institutionalized a harsh separation of the races. Every aspect of life was affected. "Schools, restaurants, trains and all forms of transportation, theaters, drinking fountains—virtually all public and many private facilities practiced total separation of the races. The state of Florida went so far as to require *Negro* and *white* textbooks and in South Carolina black and white cotton-mill workers were prohibited from looking out the same window." Mr. Jim Crow prompted the migration of many thousands of black people to the north.

Migrating to the North, freedmen found that the mind-set of the South had become the national attitude. A series of events—all negative—came together at the end of the 19th century to destroy any progress made in race relations following the Civil War. These events would freeze race relations until the rise of the American Civil Rights Movement in the 1960s. Those societal currents were: (1) the refusal of Congress to fund the Freedmen's Bureau, the agency envisioned by Abraham Lincoln as the bridge to equality for former slaves; (2) the failure of Congress and several presidents to enforce two amendments to the U.S. Constitution, namely, the 14th, which guaranteed all citizens "equal protection of the laws," and the 15th, which guaranteed that the right to vote shall not be "denied or abridged" by reason of race; (3) court decisions upholding racist laws, prohibiting any meaningful integration, most notably *Plessy v Ferguson*, which enshrined into American law the concept of "separate but equal," not to be removed for three generations; and (4) popular entertainment through the medium of the minstrel show—musical theater in which white performers donned blackface and staged parodies about "coons" filled with racial hatred. This form of bigoted, nitwit entertainment held sway for nearly a century. One of its many negative legacies was "Mr. Jim Crow." As recounted by historian Juan Williams,

> The name Jim Crow was first heard by the American public in 1832 when Thomas "Daddy" Rice, one of the first whites to perform comic representations of blacks, danced across the stage of New York's Bowery Theater and sang the lyrics of the song that would become America's first international hit:
>
> *Weel a-bout and turn a-bout*
> *And do just so.*
> *Every time I weel a-bout*
> *I jump Jim Crow*

Rice's portrayal of the lame black man soon became a standard comic character of minstrel shows. By the middle of the 19th century, the name Jim Crow had evolved into a synonym for blacks and their "comic" way of life.

But there was nothing comic about the consequences of the currents flowing through American society in the last half of the 19th century. Society produced an entire generation of educators, clergymen, journalists, businessmen, politicians, and lawyers who, without any hesitation, advanced the intellectual rationalizations for white supremacy. By the last decade of the 19th century, most Americans "believed that for the good of all, the naturally superior whites should rule over the baser races. They heard or read little to the contrary." For many whites, North and South alike, they *knew* it in their bones, they *knew* it from their Bibles, they *knew* beyond all debate that black people were inferior and not worthy of equal treatment. The tragic injustice of racism had prevailed in both popular culture and the law. The Southern Way had become the American Way.

Making their way to Atlantic City during the latter portion of the 19th century, former slaves and their children found both opportunities for work and a more sophisticated form of racism. Although there were no segregation laws, there were limits—not always pronounced but real just the same. The African Americans who came to the resort understood early on that all they could ever hope to be were servants. Their existence was precarious. They learned quickly that, in order to survive, they had to "stay in their place."

When freed black tradesmen were thrown into competition with white workers, there was often open social conflict. They were a serious threat to the status quo. Despite the fact that many freedmen had gained skills on southern plantations valuable to the growing industrial economy of the Northeast, racial prejudice barred them from working at their trades. Thousands of black tradesmen were forced to abandon finely honed skills to become servants. African-American historian E. F. Frazier found that at the end of the Civil War there were approximately 100,000 skilled Negro tradesmen in the South as compared with 20,000 whites. Between 1865 and 1890, the number of black artisans dwindled to a relative handful. Without opportunities for work in their trades, skills were lost. That such a large reservoir of talent was wiped out by racial prejudice bespeaks an ignorance few modern societies can match.

For those blacks who had come north in the hopes of working at crafts, what most found was a choice between domestic work and farm labor. According to the 1890 and 1900 U.S. Census, more than two-thirds of all African Americans living in the North Atlantic region earned their income in domestic work. In addition to employers' fears of violence from white workers, another major reason so few blacks were hired as skilled workers was the refusal of labor unions to admit black tradesmen. Skilled black workers had extreme difficulty securing positions in their trade. Between 1886 and 1892, the American Federation of Labor (AF of L) was affiliated with craft unions all across the country, comprising more than one-quarter of a million members.

Notwithstanding the fact that the AF of L declared that it stood for the organization of working people "irrespective of creed, color, sex, nationality or politics," it permitted the local unions to manage their own affairs as they saw fit. For most, that meant blacks would not be admitted. When forced to choose between racial integration and expansion of AF of L through the support of white-only locals—many of them in New Jersey—union leadership invariably chose the latter, abandoning equal rights as a condition of affiliation.

Reports published by the New Jersey Department of Labor and Industries in 1903 reveal how racial prejudice worked to prevent most African Americans from becoming members of craft unions. A questionnaire was submitted to approximately 300 union locals throughout the state to determine the extent of black membership and union members' sentiments "toward the Negro as a workman and co-laborer." A majority of the 196 locals who responded stated they favored equal opportunity and were willing to enroll workmen of good character who were properly qualified, but it seems they weren't able to find many. The reasons given for exclusion of blacks revealed that "racial prejudice was based upon a derogatory assessment of their intelligence, character and personal habit that was interwoven with the desire to protect wages."

Among the reasons stated in reply to the state's questionnaire were: "Blacks are not sufficiently intelligent; they are lazy and lack ambition; they are undesirable associates for white men; they are not clean in their habits; they have disagreeable personal characteristics; and they are deceitful, dishonest, and untruthful." One of the machinists candidly admitted, "If they were to become machinists

in numbers, wages in the trade would go down through their competition." The glass bottle blowers stated, "White men would not care
to use blow pipes that Negroes had in their mouths." The cigar mak-
ers claimed, "Smokers would generally refuse to smoke cigars made
by Negroes because of the disagreeable odor thrown off by them
when they perspire."

Patterns of discrimination revealed through the state's study held
true in Atlantic City. The experience of the black artisans and skilled
workers who came to the resort mirrored state and national patterns
of exclusion. Ironically, in 1919, the AF of L met in Atlantic City and
talked about equal opportunity. At the convention, AF of L members
discussed several resolutions dealing with the rights of blacks to
become members. The resolutions included petitions for separate
charters to permit African Americans to organize themselves and the
appointment of black organizers. This was necessary because white
union organizers refused to recruit black workmen. Reporting on the
resolutions, the AF of L acknowledged that there were some unions
affiliated with the federation that rejected black workers but looked
forward to "the day when these organizations will take a broader
view of this matter." The committee handling the resolutions recom-
mended that in those cases where blacks were barred, the federation
should organize black workers under separate charters. The AF of L
did what many institutions in America did—it created *separate* facilities and called them "equal."

Skilled black workers in Atlantic City saw little immediate gain
from the resolutions of the 1919 AF of L convention. Although a few
craft unions in the resort admitted black workers without discrimination, this was a sham. Membership fees were beyond their reach. For
example, the electrical workers union had an admission fee of $200
(think $5,000 in today's dollars), which few black workers could
afford. During the various construction boom periods in town, one
being 1920 to 1925, blacks did find work as plasterers, hod carriers,
and bricklayers. One bricklayer, Oscar Smith, who eventually opened
a candy store in the resort's African-American community, explained
how he was discriminated against by the Brick Masons and Plasterers
International Union of America, Local 33, when he was a member:

> I was a contractor in 1920–26 in Atlantic City, and a
> member of the local union. At that time I worked on any

job that was available and employed laborers. As soon as the white mechanics knew of a Negro mechanic on a job, they would immediately refuse to proceed with construction of the job regardless of the location.

When I came from New York in search of work, I met Harry Jump, a white contractor, who informed me that "if you are alone and in dire need of work, I can give you something to do but not with the mechanics, because they will not work with you." Later I went to work on private jobs for myself and needed support from the union, which I was denied. They refused to furnish me with men, forcing the curtailment of several jobs.

Many whites would sooner shut down a job than work beside blacks. The prevailing attitude across white America generally—and Atlantic City consistently—was that black people weren't fit for skilled labor. For most whites, African Americans were there to do the chores they wouldn't do. Any job that involved the three Ds (dirty, difficult, or dangerous) or that was generally unpleasant was viewed as "nigger work"—a term that prevailed in American society for nearly 100 years after the Civil War. In rural areas, this meant farm labor, often behind a plow or wielding a shovel, cleaning up after animals, and harvesting crops. In urban areas, it typically meant domestic work.

Blacks hired to work in a white household were generally servants. Routinely, a family hired a single domestic servant who was required to be a cook, a waitress, and a housekeeper. Common "Help Wanted" ads of the day read: "Colored girl wanted for general housework" or "Neat colored woman must be good cook, private family." The typical general servant worked a 12-hour day and was responsible for maintaining the household seven days a week. Days off were at the whim of the employer. Holidays, including the Christian ones such as Christmas and Easter, didn't begin for domestic servants until after all the needs of their employers were met. Domestic service was a field of work sought out of necessity rather than choice. For most freed persons, the menial work of a domestic servant was only a small step up from slavery.

But the menial employment in Atlantic City was different. Hotel work was an attractive alternative. There were crucial differences between the work experience of black people in Atlantic City and those of other cities at the time. The work opportunities were more varied and stimulating. The hotel and recreation economy had many types of positions requiring strong backs and quick hands and feet. To keep the resort running smoothly during its peak season, hoteliers, restaurateurs, Boardwalk merchants, and the amusement operators relied heavily upon the affordable labor provided by black workers. Employment in the hotel-resort industry was often demanding, but a worker was part of something bigger and more dynamic than were blacks hired to work on farms or to perform domestic work in private homes.

While the wages of a domestic servant in the wealthier homes of most northern cities were comparable to that of hotel employment, work in a hotel was easier than domestic service and considerably more exciting. Equally important, hotel employees were working for a salary, not being worked by someone akin to a master. For many, working as a general servant was synonymous with social inferiority; not so with hotel work. Unlike in other occupations, the hotel worker himself was hired—not his labor. In Atlantic City, African Americans were not *servants*, they were *employees*.

The variety and pay of hotel-resort positions, and, consequently, the social structure of Atlantic City's black community, differed greatly from those of other northern cities, both large and small. Generally speaking, hotel work in the resort paid more than domestic service in other cities, not only because of higher wages, but also because black hotel workers earned gratuities through their contact with tourists. "Tips" were a vital supplement to hotel workers' incomes. Whites avoided work where their take-home pay depended on tips, believing that such positions hurt their social standing. Black workers had no such aversion and pursued jobs where they knew patrons were generous. The competition to work at popular hotels or restaurants was intense. Where one worked could make a huge difference in take-home pay. Additionally, at the better properties most employees were provided with daily meals, an important added benefit.

Unlike many other forms of employment in which African Americans were engaged, there was a hierarchy of positions within the hotel-resort industry, giving black workers the opportunity to advance from one type of job to another. Such upward mobility in the Atlantic City workplace was generally unavailable to "colored folk" elsewhere, and a result of this phenomenon was the development of a black social structure far more complex than that of other northern cities. By virtue of their higher income, property ownership, and greater responsibility attached to their hotel positions, a substantial number of Atlantic City's black residents were, by comparison to blacks nationally, part of the middle and upper class.

The social class structure among African-American workers in Atlantic City during the first half of the 20th century broke down roughly along these lines:

> *Upper:* Hotel keepers, boardinghouse keepers (and owners), headwaiters, stewards, cooks, head bellmen, and rolling chair managers—these were critical positions. There was discretion in supervising others and responsibility for both the contentment of patrons and the profitability of the business.
>
> *Middle:* Wait staff, chambermaids, elevator operators, desk clerks, musicians, entertainers, and performers—people in these positions took direction from others but played a key role in making guests happy. Charm and appearance counted for much.
>
> *Lower:* Bellmen, busboys, porters, dishwashers, kitchen help, and rolling chair pushers—all these jobs were very "hands on." The work could be hard and the days long. Tips, both direct and shared, were essential to making a livable wage. This lower stratum was particularly vulnerable to any type of economic downturn. They were the first to bear the brunt of a bad season.

Implications flowed from the existence of these strata. The members of the upper stratum were mostly from what we call "nuclear families" today and were usually literate. They possessed skills and poise, making them valuable to a resort operation, and because they were paid relatively well, they were able to save. This translated into home ownership as well as the chance to succeed in business as the black community grew. The first widely available business opportunity was as a landlord or boardinghouse operator, providing housing to other black workers who arrived in late spring and left in early fall.

Income from regular employment, combined with revenue from renting out rooms, made it possible for their children to remain in school and, in many cases, to go on to higher education at historically black colleges and universities (HBCUs).

Workers in the middle stratum were sometimes literate, often not, but tended to be from intact families that could give them a solid start in life. They were generally renters and worked hard to get themselves well-positioned with predictable, if seasonal, income, meaning their living situations were relatively secure and their children weren't forced to go to work at tender years. They might never own homes or businesses, but if they were frugal, they didn't have to live in fear of losing the roofs over their heads or worry where the next meal would come from. Over time, some of them found their way into year-round employment in Atlantic City's municipal government or with the railroad.

Members of the lower stratum lived a sad existence. They struggled to survive. These illiterate, unskilled workers were last to be hired at the beginning of summer and the first to be terminated as the season wound down. They were often the children and grandchildren of families destroyed by slavery. Broken in spirit, many of them remained intimidated by the world upon becoming freed persons. The Jim Crow South had seen to it that there was no bridge from slavery to a stable existence as free people in white society.

Time and again, these people were tied so tightly to the land as sharecroppers that they couldn't leave the South. Generation after generation lived only one step removed from slavery until the Civil Rights Movement of the 1960s. Those who did flee to the North at the end of the 19th century were often so severely handicapped in terms of the education and social skills needed for employment in a resort economy that they were paid the most meager salaries and relied greatly on tips. Their living conditions reflected abject poverty: a single set of clothes; one pair of shoes; no furniture; and no place to put it if they had it. Only after years of struggle could they hope to attain steady employment and establish a secure household.

Experience, intelligence, and personal initiative counted for much in the hotel-resort economy. Unlike many other cities where black workers were simply servants, those in Atlantic City had a realistic chance for advancement in the tourist economy. Opportunity could present itself at any time. On any given day, someone might fail to appear for work, be fired, or get promoted. Those workers who did their job well and had made it a point to know something about the job of the person ahead of them could be tapped for promotion.

As the resort economy grew and the numbers of hotels and boardinghouses increased each summer, the town's black population increased proportionately. The 1880 U.S. Census reported 763 black people in residence in Atlantic City. By 1890, the black population had increased to 2,113, and by 1900, it reached nearly 7,000. But these figures don't tell the whole story. There were many workers who came to town only during the summer months; some estimates put the summer head count at more than double the census figures for the year-round population. It was common for hotel workers with permanent ties in the community to encourage relatives and friends from other parts of the country to come to the resort during the summer, assuring them of a place to stay and work. To the community's dismay, the presence of these temporary workers in large numbers diminished the bargaining power of black workers. Their weak status to negotiate wages and conditions is demonstrated by three unsuccessful strikes during the early years of Atlantic City.

In the summer of 1893, the Hotel Windsor was the scene of the first such incident. A small but well-appointed hotel, the Windsor was viewed as a cut above most small- and medium-sized properties. Noted for its service and its elegant courtyard, the hotel had a certain decorum that would not be disrupted by its employees. One of the waiters, unhappy with the food provided to him and his fellow workers, picked up a menu and boldly ordered himself a meal from the kitchen. When the order was rejected, the entire staff went on strike. The Windsor's response was swift and final. All the waiters were fired on the spot and replaced immediately with the hotel's chambermaids. By the next day, the dining room was staffed by a new force of black waiters.

Six summers later, there was a similar confrontation at the Albion Hotel in August 1899. At the height of the summer season, the workforce of the hotel's restaurant staged a walkout in an effort to secure better wages and working conditions. The Albion's owners were outraged at their staff's ingratitude and, as with the Windsor years earlier, the response was quick and harsh. The hotel manager discharged all the strikers immediately. As for the few workers who lingered, management sent for the local police to have them removed from the premises. The *Atlantic City Daily Union* reported that, "The managers greatly deplored the occurrence and received the sympathy of the guests who realized the dilemma they were in."

Despite an elegant veneer, the management of the Marlborough-Blenheim—the scene of a third strike, in 1906—was ruthless. That year, work was completed to connect the Blenheim and the Marlborough by means of an elevated walkway constructed over Ohio Avenue. What led to the dispute was management's demand that the waiters transport meals across the walkway between the two buildings. The waiters' wages were $20 per month in the winter and $22 per month in the summer. Combining the two hotels meant many extra steps for the waiters, who sought an increase to $25 per month. The hotel deflected their pleas, making temporary adjustments to get through the summer. By the end of the season, every one of the black waiters had been replaced by a white counterpart. Black waiters would not be employed by the Marlborough-Blenheim again until 1940.

Loss of a position at a hotel like the Marlborough-Blenheim was particularly painful. The patrons of such a hotel were generous tippers, and the gratuities inevitably exceeded salary. As one old hotelman recalled, "I have been tipped more money for waiting on a party than that particular party paid for his board at the hotel." The ruthlessness of hotel management in dealing with workers who dared to question conditions sent an unmistakable message to the resort's black workforce: *You're here on our terms. Play by the rules, nigger, or you'll be replaced.*

Although many hotel workers did well in Atlantic City, a significant percentage of the black workforce was callously exploited. Generally, wages were at the sufferance of the employer and competition for the better jobs was intense. The position of black hotel workers who were year-round residents was undermined each summer by the influx of transient workers. An example of one such summer worker is a student of the historically black college Lincoln University.

William Ashby worked in the resort several summers in the early 1900s. During the day, he was employed in a small hotel, and at night, he waited tables at the Ilesworth, a hotel known for its spacious cabaret, a popular waterhole and place to meet. Ashby was on duty on July 4, 1910, a night black America would savor for years.

That evening, Jack Johnson knocked out Jim Jeffries to retain his title of Heavyweight Champion of the World. Johnson had gained the title by defeating Canadian boxer Tommy Burns in 1908. One of white America's greatest nightmares had come true. After years of asserting the inferiority of the black race, one of their numbers had become champion of the world!

Brash and controversial, in large part because of his open fondness for white women, Jack Johnson constantly reminded white society of his superiority as a boxer. Word went out for a "Great White Hope" to regain the championship. Jim Jeffries was urged out of retirement, but it was a mistake. Jeffries was 34 years old, out of shape, and no match for Johnson. The fight went all 15 rounds (some believe Johnson toyed with Jeffries), and the older fighter took a terrible beating. His corner ended the fight after several knockdowns in the final round. African-American poet William Waring Cuney captured the exuberance of black America in his poem, "My Lord What a Morning":

> O my Lord
> What a morning,
> O my Lord,
> What a feeling,
> When Jack Johnson
> Turned Jim Jeffries'
> Snow-white face
> to the ceiling.

White America's reaction to Johnson's victory wasn't pretty. The huge disappointment felt by many whites turned into anger and resentment toward an entire race. News of Jeffries's defeat ignited numerous incidents of white violence against blacks. Bigoted white boxing fans took out their rage on every black person they encountered. By the following day, in response to their celebration of Johnson's victory, scores of blacks were killed or injured throughout the nation. There were many communities in which black people had to maintain a low profile for weeks—expressing their joy at Johnson's victory only in the privacy of their homes—until the rage among racist white boxing fans had subsided. Fears of inciting more race-related violence dampened the spirits of promoters who had filmed the fight. The film was never released for public viewing.

Ashby recalled what happened in Atlantic City that Fourth of July: "The patrons were in an ugly mood. Jeffries had let the whole white race down ... by letting that nigger beat him up." The black waiters bore the brunt of the crowd's anger, with Ashby's patrons calling him "ugly, profane, and degrading names." According to Ashby, the Johnson-Jeffries fight was not an isolated incident. An educated person, he was attuned to racism, both blatant and subtle. For some guests, being waited on by obliging black servants dressed in uniforms wasn't enough. They needed to show their supposed superiority by demeaning the workers. He recalled that the humiliation of black waiters in Atlantic City was common sport. "We suffered from rude or half-drunk guests who called us degrading names because of our color." Such treatment had to be suffered in silence, but there were opportunities for revenge:

> We could in a way always get back at them. We could spit in their soup or in their beer. This was sometimes done but this was a vicarious triumph. They would never know of our repulsive act ... rebellion caused us to think of ways to get even the very minute we stepped on the floor.

Getting to work on the floor of the Ilesworth had its own price. Every waiter had to purchase a towel for 25 cents from the headwaiter. It was a common practice throughout the town, condoned by white management, and one that "no waiter would dare challenge." According to Ashby, his summers at the Ilesworth were like "being in a jungle." Management and the workers were out to cheat the patrons and one another. On hectic nights, items such as silverware, plates, and glasses were often in short supply. Competing with one another to satisfy their patrons in pursuit of tips, waiters stole from one another. Ashby recalled that there were many fierce fights.

Without its black workers, Atlantic City would have been in its own fierce fight for survival. The hotel-resort industry relied on black labor much the way the plantations of the South had prior to the Civil War, and the workers weren't appreciated much more than the slaves of the old South had been. The local tourist economy could never have flourished without the cheap labor provided by black workers, yet the fact that they were the mainstay of the city's workforce did little to deflect racism.

As the black presence in Atlantic City grew, whites—residents and visitors alike—began to see their numbers as a problem. In the summer of 1893, the *Philadelphia Inquirer* asked of Atlantic City:

> What are we going to do with our colored people? That is the question. Atlantic City has never before seemed so overrun with the dark-skinned race as this season ... the Boardwalk and Atlantic Avenue fairly swarm with them during bathing hours, like the fruit in a huckleberry pudding ... of the hundreds of hotels and boardinghouses which stud the island from one end to the other, it is probable that not a dozen could be found in which white help is employed. And when to the thousands of waiters and cooks and porters are added the nurse girls, the chambermaids, the barbers and boot blacks and hack drivers ... it is easy to see what an evil it is that hangs over Atlantic City.

The *Inquirer* was among the most influential newspapers read by Atlantic City's visitors at the time, and local black leaders viewed this article with alarm. Adept at dealing with bigotry, one-on-one on a daily basis, racist comments in a major newspaper were more troublesome. Community leaders, black and white alike, worried that such reports could discourage vacationers and undermine the economy upon which they depended. They needed to counter these comments promptly. One week after the *Inquirer* article appeared, the *Philadelphia Tribune*, an African-American newspaper, sent a reporter to Atlantic City to investigate, and his findings were reported by a local newspaper, the *Atlantic City Daily Union*:

> He found no serious "problem" agitating the public. His people were here in great numbers because they were needed and had been sent for as servants. As a rule, they kept in their places becomingly, and did not intrude to offend those who were oversensitive as to race prejudice. The colored people are natural born servants, taking

bossing more meekly and gracefully than white help, and
for these and other good reasons, generally preferred.

Black people had little choice but to accept "bossing more meekly
and gracefully." They appreciated their status in the resort and their
first rule was survival. Although Atlantic City was far from the
"Promised Land," it was an important foothold for blacks in the
urban North and both the *Tribune* and the *Daily Union*—obviously
for different reasons—felt obliged to mute the attack made by the
Inquirer. But from another perspective, the *Inquirer*'s reporting
reveals that Atlantic City had yet to impose any serious measures to
exclude African Americans from the Boardwalk or beach. More
importantly, there were no limitations on where African Americans
could reside.

By the late 19th century, black people lived throughout the entire
city, from one end of town to the other. They were gradually establishing a permanent presence in the community. And it was a struggle. After years of families and individuals "doubling up" to save on
living expenses, many workers were gaining a secure position for
themselves and their families, finding homes and rental units. There
was no pattern to where the resort's African Americans lived other
than what they could afford and was convenient to their place of
work. There were no "white" or "colored" neighborhoods. But that
was about to change. Throughout American history, the mixing of
races has been a complicated process. Many "enlightened" white
communities have grown less tolerant as the number of blacks living
in their midst has increased. So it was with Atlantic City.

In the early years, even after the second railroad, many residents
were seasonal. Employers and employees alike might call Atlantic
City their home, especially for voting purposes, but a significant percentage lived and worked elsewhere during the off-season. As the
number of year-round blacks increased and whites found themselves
living next to blacks, whites felt the need to separate themselves.
Through landlords charging unreasonably high rents, anonymous
acts of violence by neighbors and family members, and, finally, the
help of lawyers and real estate agents, blacks were forced out of
neighborhoods they had lived in for years. White neighborhoods
developed, and blacks were pushed into a ghetto that became known
as "the Northside."

Trying to make sense of what makes people move from one place to another and congregate as they do is a challenge. Studying demographics can usually tell us what a given population does but not always *why*. Why Atlantic City's white residents, who had so much in common with its black residents—the most dominant being their insular experience and status as captives to a seasonal economy—felt threatened by their increase in numbers will never be fully understood. Racism alone is too simplistic an answer. The explanation lies in an emotional brew comprised of folk history, religion, sexual taboos, and myths of the old South concocted in the slavery era, together with the fallacious dogma of white supremacy. It's a part of the American psyche that historians have yet to fully explain. Despite the superior position of whites in Atlantic City society and politics, they *feared* blacks; while the fear had no basis in reason, it was real just the same, especially when it came to living in the same neighborhoods.

Fear prompted change, and the consequences were dramatic. Between 1880 and 1915, the pattern of residence in Atlantic City's residential areas underwent a radical shift. In 1880, more than 70 percent of the black households in the resort had white neighbors; by 1915, that percentage shrank to less than 20 percent. In a single generation, the population had diverged. White society had spoken loud and clear, and the message was that whites refused to live beside blacks.

Researchers familiar with urban housing trends have discerned what is referred to as a "tipping point." People who study demographics believe that the level that makes blacks comfortable in a given neighborhood is probably about the point at which whites begin to get nervous. Statistics from the 20th century show that the tipping point at which white neighborhoods feel threatened by the presence of black residents is 8 percent to 10 percent. When that tipping point is reached, whites begin demanding change. As the number of black faces reached the tipping point in Atlantic City's neighborhoods, they began to look dominant to white eyes and whites grew fearful. There was an elemental fear of the growing numbers of black people in the resort that brought out the worst in the town's white community. In Atlantic City, as across the nation, citywide integration would never be achieved.

Discrimination visited upon Atlantic City's black population didn't bring out their worst; on the contrary, it brought out their best. Despite the degrading experience of being exploited for their usefulness in the workplace and then being shoved out of neighborhoods that whites wanted for themselves, blacks refused to be humiliated. African-American community leaders recognized that when one door closes— or is slammed shut, as in this case—another one opens. Shunned by the white world, black people understood that they hadn't been vanquished; rather, they'd been forced to do things on their own. Over the long haul of American history, there is no group more resilient or resourceful than the African-American community. They are the most persistent survivors in our nation's history.

With ghettoization thrust upon them, their survival instincts took over. Deprived of their own written history, African Americans had a strong tradition of oral history, recounting family by family many of the hardships their enslaved ancestors had overcome. Regardless of the brutality suffered or the travails weathered, black people had endured. They were a permanent part of America *and* Atlantic City, no matter how uncomfortable that made some white people.

There was a sense of pride emerging among black people. They had withstood the horrors of slavery and were now weathering institutionalized racism and discrimination against their entire race. They had *survived* and felt good about themselves. As poet Langston Hughes expressed it:

> This is our own, our native land,
> And I'm mighty glad that's true.
> Land where my fathers worked
> The same as yours worked, too.
> So from every mountain side
> Let freedom's bright torch glow—
> Standing hand in hand with democracy
> I'm America's Young Black Joe!

Atlantic City's African-American church and civic leaders preached the message that the prejudice encountered in Atlantic City was just one more obstacle to be overcome in the march toward equality. Over time, the network of black churches in Atlantic City would play a crucial role in creating an identity for the resort's black community. Forced to contend with segregation, senior members of the community reminded their neighbors that, when it came to inflicting hardships through discrimination, Atlantic City's white power structure didn't have sharp teeth. It was a toothless dragon compared to slavery or the "Jim Crow" institutions that arose in the South after the Civil War.

Presciently, the leaders of the black community in Atlantic City recognized that their numbers were large enough to establish an urban center of their own, yet small enough not to threaten the white power establishment. They would create their own city in miniature form, a city within a city. In time, the Northside would become essentially self-supporting, delivering most of the basic necessities to residents and providing them with a nurturing society of their own. In time, this miniature metropolis would even create its own *resort within a resort*, attracting both white and black visitors. Black leaders knew that making their community thrive would require planning, finesse, and discipline. They accepted the challenge and turned rejection into opportunity.

Taking shape at the end of the 19th and beginning of the 20th centuries, this African-American enclave was literally on the north side of the railroad tracks that brought visitors to town, away from the Boardwalk. At that time, it was common in many American cities to find communities divided by railroad tracks, often with a section known as "the other side of the tracks" where real estate values were lower and people of lower economic means resided. So it was that Atlantic City came to have its "Northside," with the division based on race.

Sprawling and shifting over time, the boundaries of the Northside generally comprised the area bounded by Absecon Boulevard to the north, Connecticut Avenue to the east, Atlantic Avenue to the south, and Arkansas Avenue to the west. One also knew the boundaries by the change in street names. On the Northside, it's Baltic Avenue; in white neighborhoods, it's Fairmount Avenue on one end and Madison at the other. The same was (and remains) true of Mediterranean Avenue, which on the white side of town becomes Melrose Avenue and Arctic Avenue and then Grammercy Place. These street name changes created subtle boundaries that were observed by both races, especially blacks, who knew they weren't welcome in white neighborhoods except as workers.

Other color lines weren't so subtle. In 1904, a "local reform group," the Citizens League, posted a bathing notice signed by hoteliers, restaurateurs, and other wealthy businessmen. This notice established a prohibited area, designating the beach between Massachusetts and Arkansas Avenues as off-limits to black bathers. For several seasons, black beachgoers acknowledged the ban but still violated it by congregating at the Indiana Avenue beach. But when several new hotels were built—none of which catered to African Americans—the ban became more stringent. Blacks were shooed away by the hotels that wouldn't permit their guests to be offended by having to mix with "coloreds" on the beach. In short order, black people were relegated to the "colored beach" between Mississippi and Missouri Avenues, which became known as "Chicken Bone Beach." In time, Chicken Bone Beach blossomed into a popular destination for vacationing African Americans throughout the Northeast and was, undoubtedly, the liveliest and most interesting of all Atlantic City's beaches.

Boardwalk merchants also practiced discrimination. One small but poignant example involved soda fountains. While the seating in such shops wasn't segregated per se (though black patrons were encouraged not to sit near the entrance), there were separate sets of glasses for blacks and whites. These "Jim Crow" glasses, as they became known by the local black community, were larger, thicker, and held slightly more liquid. But the extra soda pop didn't make black customers feel any better knowing they were forbidden from drinking out of the same glasses as whites. Much the same as had occurred generations earlier in the South, formal mechanisms of discrimination were put into place. Although there were no "Black Codes," Atlantic City's white establishment was determined to deal with "the problem." Beginning in the summer of 1904, blacks were ordered off carousels and other amusements on the Boardwalk. After 1904, the color line, while still unofficial, was enforced with vigilance by white business owners. They made certain blacks "knew their place."

An example of "keeping coloreds in their place" occurred in 1906. That summer, a notice was posted in the employees' sections of scores of hotels and restaurants throughout the city. This notice called attention to the resort's increasing southern patronage and read, "We therefore request that you, our colored employees, and your families and friends, not bathe or lounge in front of our respective properties ... feeling sure that you will appreciate the appeal and the spirit in which it is made and that its observance will benefit both yourselves and ourselves."

Driving home that "spirit" was a statement that "there would be fewer colored employees" if blacks continued to "bathe or lounge" in front of the hotel properties. Encouraging acquiescence to the hotel's demands, the *Atlantic City Gazette* noted bluntly:

> The colored man is dependent on the white man for his living, and when the white man says it is necessary for the colored man to join him in improving business by a little self-denial, he should promptly agree to the request. For years, a colored bather has been an issue on the ocean-front. Hints that he was not wanted were of little consequence. Until the southern man arrived, the hotelmen were disinclined to force the issue, which to them would look like discrimination. When it reached the issue of dollars, the hotelmen acted.

Many blacks were "dependent on the white man" for more than their wages. While, over time, the number of hotels operating year-round had increased and some black workers found employment beyond the summer, many more did not. By the first decade of the 20th century, thousands of hotel employees had made Atlantic City their permanent home, with the hope of finding year-round work. Unfortunately, things didn't go that way for most of them.

3

The Off-Season

The Negroes dwell in a state of intermittent prosperity. Always living from hand to mouth and with rents in arrears, they take refuge in the morrow. In the winter they reason with cheerful philosophy that it is the city's duty to take care of them.

—Margaret Brett, sociologist

Wheelbarrows were available in nearly every neighborhood. If there wasn't one on the block, people brought tow sacks. They made do. It just meant a few more trips. Shoving or fighting for the last shiny black rock didn't occur. People knew there would be a new pile of coal as often as required until the last frost in the spring. The same was true of food. For those down on their luck, there was usually a church, fire hall, or storefront where soup, bread, and, if needed, blankets were dispensed. There were no homeless but hundreds of "underhoused," and it was a chronic condition, forcing many to double-up with relatives and friends. Come cold weather, entire families of seasonal workers hunkered down, praying for a short winter. The burden of more people occupying a home than it was designed for created dilapidated housing throughout the Northside.

As the days grew shorter, much of Atlantic City took on an eerie quality. Scores of restaurants were shuttered. Row upon row of boardinghouses went dark. Anything the wind might catch was tied down or stored away. Amusement rides, covered with canvas, dotted the Boardwalk, with piers like sentinels standing guard against the fierce winds of the North Atlantic.

Before central heating and the use of modern insulation in constructing buildings, winter was no fun in Atlantic City. The winter of 1905 was brutal. The city's Overseer of the Poor was overwhelmed by pleas for help, many from the Northside. City government was more about jobs than social services, and the budget for relief to the unemployed was meager. Private organizations filled the void. The Republican clubs in all four voting wards pitched in to meet the shortfall, with local politicians distributing gallons of soup and hundreds of loaves of bread each day.

Work was even harder to come by than food. Year-round employment was scarce, even for longtime white residents. For the city's African-American population, it was rare indeed. Any job, including part time, that extended beyond September was coveted. The only people—black or white—who were certain of work through all four seasons were either self-employed or held positions in local government. The competition for a job in City Hall was fierce, and any person of color who landed one was someone special. Not only must he be a leader in his neighborhood and able to round up votes, but, all things being equal, the white person got the job; to have a chance at it, the black applicant had to be more qualified than any competing white candidate and have the support of the established powers. For the great majority of Atlantic City's residents, the ability to earn income was at the whim of nature. A rainy Fourth of July or the washout of an entire week in August—known to occur when the remnants of an early hurricane moved through the region—could spell disaster, dashing any hopes a worker had of squirreling away enough cash to get through the off-season. That made winter very long. The person who had income 12 months a year was the envy of his neighbors.

Living conditions on the Northside were studied by sociologist Margaret Brett, who reported in 1912 that, "Irregularity of employment, the most serious problem of modern life, reaches its apex in Atlantic City." The recruitment efforts of the resort's hoteliers had been successful; what they left out of their pitch to early freed persons migrating from the South was the fact that both housing and off-season work opportunities were sparse:

> "In-season" relatives and acquaintances are urged to come to El Dorado, and come they do in battalions, happy with the vision of picking up like shells from the beach gold that the visitors waste. And then they wake up. "Out of season" a city of 300,000 all of a sudden in the moisture

of a cold wave has dissolved to 100,000, and in two weeks the recently arrived are paying room rent with promises and subsisting on sea breezes.

Rooms for rent weren't always easy for newly arrived black people to find. In the years after the second railroad, as freed slaves and their children thronged to town in search of jobs, little thought was given to housing this population of newcomers. Housing for black people was entirely a catch-as-catch-can proposition. The numbers of persons, especially during the summer months, overwhelmed the supply of safe, sanitary, and affordable housing. Black workers lived wherever they could and very few of them could afford to purchase homes. In 1905, the percentage of black households that owned their homes was less than 2 percent. What little decent housing there was available for rent to African Americans was so expensive that households were forced to "double-up." Many of Atlantic City's black tenants dealt with high rents by taking in boarders with "privilege of the kitchen" during the summer season. It was a practice that grew each year. For the more enterprising, it was an opportunity to save a few extra dollars and accumulate capital to buy a home of their own and, over time, possibly convert it into a boardinghouse. As the black population swelled, the percentage of household heads who took in boarders increased from 14.4 percent in 1880 to 57.3 percent in 1915.

Growth of the black population, combined with racial discrimination in the form of higher rents, created a chronic condition of crowded, substandard housing. Habitually over-occupied homes produced a deteriorating housing stock—a problem that plagued the Northside continuously. Newcomers who couldn't find a space of their own to rent or suitable arrangements for subleasing were forced to live in whatever makeshift housing their employer or fellow workers might provide—everything from warehouses and storage sheds to out-of-service train cars and tents. The "lucky" ones lived in worn-out abandoned homesteads and poorly constructed houses without baths or modern fixtures of any type, many of which were neither sanitary nor waterproof, and most of which were owned by rapacious landlords.

Some workers were forced to live in cramped quarters at the rear of luxurious hotels, crowding into dirt-floor storage rooms and windowless shacks behind their place of employment until they were able to save a little money and find better accommodations. The accesses between many of these improvised "dwellings," all to the rear of commercial buildings, formed a labyrinth of alleys that would have been a startling sight to any modern-day fire inspector. Some of the worst living conditions were found among the families of the fishing boat helpers. Their work was not only hard but often dangerous. Their employers permitted them to live in houseboats tethered in the marshes, most with ceilings so low that it was impossible to stand upright and so cramped that parents and children had to sleep together in a single bed.

Squalid housing and the lack of any type of community health services took its toll on the quality of life. In an era in which there were no workers' compensation laws for the injured, hospital emergency rooms to treat the sick or injured, or mandatory health exams for school-age children, most health-related problems of the working poor festered. Tuberculosis took black people's lives at a rate more than four times greater than that of the resort's white residents, and the infant mortality rate on the Northside was double that of white children. But it wasn't just the lives of African-American babies that could end abruptly.

"The season" could be ruthlessly short and the off-season dangerously long, endangering the entire family. For many of the blacks who were transplants to the resort, picking up and leaving wasn't a viable option. With little to no savings and poor work prospects in other northern cities beyond domestic service, those who could afford to return to the Jim Crow South weren't anxious to do so. In returning, the best they could hope for was sharecropping or domestic work, both of which were only a small step removed from slavery.

Atlantic City's early black residents were determined to tough it out. For the vast majority of the resort's black population, as for African Americans throughout the United States, their economic goals were defined in terms of *survival*. Failure wasn't an option. They had to make a place for themselves. "Three months to hurry and nine months to worry" is how historian Richlyn Goddard has characterized the local African-American experience. As noted by Goddard, Atlantic City's year-round residents generally worked two jobs, plus any odd jobs they could snare during the three months of summer. They worked tirelessly during the summer in order to "get through" the balance of the year until the season began again:

> Labor Day sounds the death knell for hotel employment and there is a general exodus of all guests and help the very next day. The change that comes over Atlantic City at this time of the year is startling in its abruptness. One day the resort is teeming with guests and help. The very next day it is the direct opposite. The hotel worker is now the victim of this annual depression in Atlantic City. He is first given days off, then weeks off, and soon he only works during holidays.
>
> The few that remain employed barely make enough to subsist on. The "tips" are gone and the wages are very meager. Since the "tips" that people give are not very large, the average hotel worker doesn't get an opportunity to save as much as he once did. Consequently he spends the winter getting into debt and the summer making his credit good.

Getting through this "annual depression" was, for most unemployed black workers and their families, a daunting task. Winters in Atlantic City can be harsh. Some years, winter comes early and stays late. Although snow isn't frequent and rarely lingers, there are weeks when it seems the rain will never stop. Wind blasting off the mighty North Atlantic can make rain spew horizontally. Together, the wind and rain are bone-chilling and—for those unprotected from their fury—lethal. Death from exposure is a fear of any sensible person. Talk of the "soothing gulf stream" is nonsense when a nor'easter hits in November. March storms are just as nasty, and the months between can be damp and miserable for weeks on end.

Miserable weather was only the half of it. Without income and with winter wearing on, many working-class families, black and white alike, struggled to put food on the table. An injury that didn't heal, a fracture that made it impossible to do one's job, or a sickness that lingered could spell disaster. With no unemployment payments, welfare, rent vouchers, food stamps, Social Security, meals-on-wheels, free school lunches, or social programs whatsoever, most of urban America's working poor were vulnerable any time they were out of work. But Atlantic City was different. Long before FDR's New Deal in the 1930s or the expansion of those programs during the "Great Society" of the 1960s, the resort had its own private welfare system, though the people responsible for it weren't exactly philanthropists.

Charity had little to do with the assistance doled out on the Northside. Votes were what mattered. Beginning at the end of the 19th century and continuing for nearly five decades, the local political organization, nominally Republican but having a single-minded purpose—success of Atlantic City's tourism economy—provided the means for many unemployed to make it through the off-season. It was an organization the likes of which few cities have known.

The founder of the local Republican organization—which has been termed the "Boardwalk Empire"—was a hotelier and entrepreneur, Louis "the Commodore" Kuehnle. The Commodore's family was from Germany and made it to the resort after a successful stay in New York City, where Louis Sr. had done well as a chef. In 1858, Louis Sr. brought his wife and three sons to the mainland community of Egg Harbor City, 12 miles northwest of Atlantic City. Essentially a creature of the Camden-Atlantic Railroad, Egg Harbor, in its early days, was primarily a settlement of German immigrants. Within a short time, the Kuehnle family established the New York Hotel. It was a huge success, and so was Louis Sr. He was elected mayor of Egg Harbor several times and served on the County Board of Freeholders. From his experiences as an immigrant in New York City, Louis Sr. gravitated toward the Democratic Party and held both offices as a Democrat.

Deciding to branch out in 1875, the Kuehnle family opened a second hotel in Atlantic City at the southwest corner of Atlantic and South Carolina Avenues. The hotel was under the management of 18-year-old Louis Jr. The son had grown up in the hotel restaurant business, and the father was confident he could manage the family's new investment. Kuehnle's Hotel was an easy walk from the train station and was built in anticipation of the arrival of Samuel Richards's second railroad. It was a typical mid-range "hotel" for its day, namely, a large, well-appointed boardinghouse with guests who were primarily working-class vacationers. It also featured a bar and restaurant popular with local residents. The younger Kuehnle never married. He was married to the success of his hotel, and he spent his early days totally committed to growing his business. When the Pennsylvania Railroad acquired the Camden-Atlantic Railroad, the new train station was constructed across the street from the hotel. It was a blessing to the hotel's business. The hotel became an adjunct to the train station waiting area, especially for those who wanted a drink before returning home. For most Philadelphia-bound patrons, the chance of buying a drink in their hometown, particularly on a Sunday night, was virtually nil. "Its sixty-foot bar was constantly filled with travelers waiting to entrain, and departures were announced by conductors who ran into the building to yell, *all aboard*."

The railroad also brought Kuehnle the opportunity for notoriety and to make a name of his own. He had a flair for public displays, and the railroad played into his hands during one of its many construction projects. "In 1890, Kuehnle waged a legal fight with the Pennsylvania Railroad over a property encroachment and became something of a local hero when, backed by one hundred citizens, he faced down a railroad work crew who attempted to remove curb stones from his hotel sidewalk."

Kuehnle worked at staying in the public eye and had a knack for drawing attention to himself. On one occasion while he was seated in a barber chair, one of his liquor salesmen from Philadelphia—who, as the story goes, was every bit equal to Kuehnle's 250 pounds—taunted him about his hefty physique. "Kuehnle challenged him to a footrace, and each man put up one hundred dollars. The race was staged with great ceremony, and Kuehnle was ahead until a Saint Bernard dog jumped in his path. Kuehnle lost the race, but the Philadelphia man spent the better part of his purse treating spectators at the bar of Kuehnle's hotel." To ensure contact with his patrons, the Commodore always worked the "front of the house." He often tended bar and waited on tables himself. Year-round, Sundays were special. The Commodore positioned himself at the front door collecting half-dollar coins for his popular "fifty-cent family dinner." It was a weekly tradition that continued for many years, with most "regulars" being nonpaying customers. It was his way of treating local families to an affordable meal, many stopping by for afternoon supper following church.

One of the few hotels remaining open the entire year, Kuehnle's Hotel featured a large porch, which soon became a popular meeting place for local politicians of both parties. It was known by everyone as "the Corner." It was here that the Commodore received his education in politics.

The Corner was where the three Republicans whose views counted most began meeting in the 1890s. This leading group was comprised of County Clerk Louis Scott, Congressman John Gardner, and County Sheriff Smith Johnson. With Scott serving as the unofficial leader, the three of them planned the strategy for the Republicans. As late as 1896, Kuehnle was nominally, like his father, a Democrat, but the events of several political campaigns worked to drive him *and* the black community into the Republican fold.

Records aren't available to confirm when Kuehnle switched parties, but reports show that he had become part of the Republican inner circle sometime before 1900. It's believed that he was prompted by opportunity to become the party leader, enabling him not only to play a role in the community but also to expand his business interests. Favorable circumstances combined with lack of any direction by the Democrats, except negative—they opposed most efforts at modernization, including street paving, and seemed quite content with Atlantic City remaining a beach village—likely pushed Kuehnle to become a Republican.

Negative political campaigns are central to American history. Politicians know that voters are far more motivated to vote *against* a candidate or issue than they are to vote *for* someone. Appealing to voters' prejudices has been a successful tactic on many occasions in American politics. Looking back over two centuries of American political campaigns, it is apparent that some appeals to prejudice are subtle, others blunt, but few politicians have hurt themselves by appealing to their constituents' baser instincts. The Atlantic City municipal election of 1892 illustrates this tenet well. Although it's unlikely it was fully appreciated at the time, that election set in motion the eventual demise of the local Democratic Party.

Featuring races for both mayor and city council, the municipal election of 1892 was an important one. The Democrats had the ardent support of one of the local newspapers, the *Atlantic City Daily Union*. Together, the Democrats and the *Daily Union* waged a campaign that won the election but helped forge a permanent relationship between the emerging Northside community and the Republican Party. Like many American election battles, it was all about race.

Democratic candidate Willard Wright had served several terms as mayor years earlier. His Republican opponent was Robert Stroud, an incumbent councilman. For city council in the Third Ward (the voting district in which many blacks resided), the Democrats backed Somers Doughty. His name alone revealed his heritage: "Somers" was a prominent local name because of the naval war hero, Lieutenant Richard Somers of Somers Point, who had fought in the Battle of Tripoli. "Doughty" dated back even further, to the American Revolution, when Colonel Thomas Doughty commanded a fort at the mouth of the Great Egg Harbor Inlet. In the 19th century, Enoch Doughty was a brother-in-law of Jonathan Pitney, a supporter of Pitney's efforts to establish Atlantic City, and an investor in the first railroad. The Doughty family had been prominent in both Absecon and Atlantic City from the beginning.

Somers Doughty was best known for his racial hostility. He operated a saloon at Indiana and Atlantic Avenues and made no effort to hide his feelings toward people of color. One observer described him as a "man of mean and contemptible spirit" and in the spring of 1892, the *Philadelphia Bulletin* reported:

> Last summer a party of colored gentlemen, representing the best culture, standing, and education of Philadelphia, entered Mr. Doughty's place on their way to the beach and were charged a double price for everything they ordered. Upon one of the gentlemen remonstrating, he was told, "The boss of this place does not care for nigger trade, so I hope you will all keep out of here."

Doughty's opponent was Samuel B. Rose, a three-term incumbent who, as the *Bulletin* noted, had "shouldered a musket in the Great Rebellion" (the Civil War) and was a consistent friend of Atlantic City's black citizens.

Daily Union news articles set the tone of the campaign. It reported on each party's meetings preceding the election, informing its readers of the racial composition of the organizations in the Third Ward. At the Republican meetings, "The number of colored men that attended the Republican precinct caucuses last evening surprised the whites." As for the Democrats, "The large attendance of white men was the special feature of the Democratic caucuses."

White supremacy remained the principal theme of the national Democratic Party and—unlike other urban Democrats—Atlantic City's rank-and-file were right in step. In other northern cities, Democrats were determined to woo European immigrants arriving in New York, Philadelphia, and Boston. Those Democratic organizations were shedding the racist mantle, appealing to all minorities, including African Americans. But Atlantic City's Democrats would have none of that, and candidates like Doughty represented the true values of the party.

Playing the race card was something the Democrats did well, and the Republicans knew they'd get nowhere trying that tactic. Even if they had the inclination to do so, which they apparently did not, there was no way they could "out-nigger" the Democrats. Nationally, the Republican Party presented itself as "progressive." The philosophy of Lincoln—"It's the duty of government to do those things for the people which they can't do themselves"—had been a large part of the original national Republican agenda. Following the failures of the Reconstruction Era, many Republicans lost their zeal for uplifting African Americans. The children and grandchildren of the abolitionist movement hoped to avoid conflict over race, but unlike the Democrats, Republicans remained nominally committed to the principles of equality for all people. They may not have always exerted themselves to that end but neither did they attempt to institutionalize racial politics as the Democrats had done throughout the South with Jim Crow laws.

Locally, the Atlantic City Republicans aligned themselves with the business interests of the hotel-tourism industry. They promised to build up the town—one big issue was street paving—and to do whatever it took to make the local economy grow. The Republicans were looking to the 20th century. It was a natural fit for Louis Kuehnle, and the election of 1892 helped him arrive at his eventual destination.

The race-baiting during the campaign was so ugly that it caught the attention of the Philadelphia daily newspapers. As reported by the *Bulletin*: "The colored people are taking more than usual interest in this election because of the well-known antipathy to their race on the part of several of the Democratic candidates." Thomas Swann, "the well known colored journalist and [Democratic] politician" from Philadelphia, supported Republican Stroud's candidacy. As quoted by the *Bulletin*, Swann exhorted African Americans to vote for Stroud:

> Mr. Stroud has always been alive to the best interests of the city, and at the same time has never forgotten that they [African Americans] too were a part of the municipality. They are well aware of the prejudices that exist here against them, and have nothing to hope from his opponents.

Prejudice prevailed in 1892. Somers Doughty won a seat on city council by a margin of 24 votes, and Willard Wright was elected mayor by a mere 12 votes. Another Democrat won a seat on council by the same margin as Wright, and the last two seats were won by Republicans, both with slim majorities. The community was polarized along racial lines but the Democrats were in control. The *Daily Union* celebrated the victory, proclaiming that "the coons and gamblers no longer control Atlantic City."

Relying on their racist message, the Democrats retained control for the remainder of the decade. The next critical election came in 1900. That year, the popular incumbent Democratic mayor, Joseph Thompson, chose not to seek re-election. Leadership of the party went to attorney Clarence P. Cole, "who was tainted locally because he had represented a reform group in a recent crusade against commercial vice." Moral crusaders never fared well in Atlantic City, and Cole and the Democrats went down to defeat. The absence locally of any of the Northeastern urban Democrats' new allies, such as organized labor or newly arrived ethnic groups (other than the blacks, whom they had alienated) "who might have coalesced into an effective Democratic opposition, meant that the business-dominated Republicans had a clear field."

That same year the field cleared for Louis Kuehnle. County Clerk Scott died. Neither of Scott's cohorts, Congressman Gardner and County Sheriff Johnson, had the youth or the desire to assume control. Within a short time, the Commodore became the unchallenged leader not only of the Republicans but of the city's entire political structure. After Scott's death, Kuehnle was *Boss*. He wielded a hammer wrapped in velvet, and nothing was done without his OK. Every candidate, employee, city contract, and mercantile license required his nod of approval.

Politicians can't always see the big picture, but the Commodore did. Historians and political philosophers know that the social and political structures that develop in a community are influenced by much more than the form of government chosen. Enduring institutions evolve organically. Factors such as climate, commerce, the sources from which residents earn income, social customs, religion, traditions, and the particular history of a populace all play a role in how people organize themselves politically. Explicitly or implicitly, every community of like-minded people arrives at an understanding of how their world should be ordered. Seen from this perspective, every government is the natural product of a people's experience. What counts is what works. What *is* is right—if it weren't, it wouldn't be. Legal mechanisms and labels are secondary.

History also teaches that people living on an island see the world differently. They tend to have an insular mentality—"there's us, and then there's the world"—that pervades the entire experience of being physically separated from the "mainland." The island—in this instance, Absecon Island—becomes a world unto itself and is the center of the universe for the people living there. The final, and possibly most potent, ingredient in the experience of residents on Absecon Island was the shortness of "the season." It created a sense of urgency unlike anything other communities could understand.

Kuehnle comprehended the unique chemistry that had brought Atlantic City to where it was at the turn of the 20th century. He knew that his town could only be successful if its political and social institutions took into account its singular purpose: to provide leisure-time activities for vacationers. The Commodore's mission was to cultivate the resort's entertainment package and grow both the town and its economy.

Success of the season was everything to local residents. With tourism as the only means by which to earn income, the months of June, July, and August were crucial. Nothing could interfere with the visitors' happiness or they might stop coming. The last thing merchants needed was some reformer tampering with the accepted entertainment package. The Commodore knew what was needed for Atlantic City to prosper. Instinctively, he perceived that Atlantic City's businessmen and residents would gladly sacrifice the "ideal" of honest government for a profitable summer, and he gave them what they wanted.

Bending the law to protect "booze, broads, and gambling" from prosecution, Kuehnle worked with the tourist industry to ensure its success. He forged an alliance that comprised hoteliers, racketeers, and ordinary citizens. Success of the local economy was the one true creed. In exchange, the community let him call the shots. As expressed by the *Atlantic City Daily Press*, a newspaper owned by Walter Edge, who would later become governor of New Jersey, this was a beneficial arrangement. In one of Edge's editorials, he stated:

> Boss rule in most communities is regarded as an afflic-
> tion, if not a curse. But it will be the salvation of Atlantic
> City. There will be no great and enduring progress, and
> fixed, unalterable prosperity in this town until a practi-
> cally autocratic government is created.

Boss rule as delivered by Kuehnle proved to be Atlantic City's "salvation." The Commodore was an autocrat, but he advanced the town's agenda in what was nearly universally believed to be a positive direction. While he profited from his many businesses, Kuehnle used his power to help transform a rustic beach village into the beginnings of a modern 20th-century city.

With a foresight that can safely be described as enlightened, the Commodore understood the need for making investments in public facilities to accommodate the growth generated by Atlantic City's increased popularity. He believed the resort needed a larger and permanent Boardwalk and saw to it that one with steel pilings and girders was constructed. Resort residents, in particular the hotels and shops, were the victims of a telephone monopoly. Kuehnle shattered it by starting an opposing company with reduced rates. The city's electric lighting was inadequate and expensive; the Commodore backed a competing utility and prices fell (that electric company eventually became today's Atlantic City Electric). The natural gas supplier had a monopoly, so Kuehnle organized a competing company, which resulted in lower prices. The local trolley system, important to the convenience of both tourists and residents, was a mess. Kuehnle organized the Central Passenger Railway Company, and soon residents and visitors alike had first-rate street-railway service.

Kuehnle was corrupt, but he had a vision for his town's future, and he worked the levers of power to make that vision a reality. Vitally important, the Commodore realized that without a secure and abundant source of fresh water, the island community would never become a true city. His foresight was the driving force behind the purchase of several large tracts on the mainland that were used as sites for wells for Atlantic City's water system (a portion of this acreage would years later become the site of the Atlantic City International Airport). It was also his regime that established the city's first modern sewage treatment facility. Additionally, street paving, or the lack of it, had been a sore point ever since the resort was founded, with visitors and locals constantly having to dodge potholes and mud puddles. Kuehnle went into the paving business, and, in a short time, the resort had safe, clean, and modern paved streets. Within a single decade of his assuming leadership, the town had been transformed.

There was nothing like Atlantic City *anywhere* in the United States. There were no island/beach cities to compare with the resort. What had been a wilderness barrier island in the era of Jonathan Pitney and Samuel Richards had, over the decades, been evolving and, with a final push from the Commodore, was now a bona fide full-fledged "city." Under Kuehnle's reign, all the elements for the infrastructure of a modern city were put in place.

Having control of Atlantic City politics wasn't enough. If the Commodore was to catch the attention of the state Republican organization, he needed to become totally dominant. To achieve that, he had to run up election margins in a big way. A key ingredient to his strategy was the manipulation of the resort's African-American voters. The message of Atlantic City's Democrats to the residents of the Northside was clear: "Stay in your place, nigger." From the time of the Civil War until the election of Franklin D. Roosevelt during the Great Depression, the overwhelming majority of black people who voted in this country voted Republican, the party of the "Great Emancipator," Abraham Lincoln. The presence of such a substantial minority, with a predictable voting pattern, made the voters of the Northside a pawn in Kuehnle's rise to power. They were ripe for the picking, and the Commodore exploited them for every vote he could and more.

Employment of a large black workforce in his hotel and several businesses gave Kuehnle an appreciation of their plight during the winters. The Commodore was known for his philanthropy before becoming a power broker, and, once in power, he and his lieutenants created their own network for providing relief. Under Kuehnle, the Republican Party saw to it that Atlantic City's hotel workers had coal for the furnace, food for the icebox, warm clothing for the children, and doctor and pharmacy bills paid. This "private social service system" made the Republican organization extremely popular. "The Commodore would personally hand out turkeys on the Northside. And not just at Thanksgiving. Turkeys are big birds, and you can make a second meal and a third if you made soup stock from the carcass. The colored people loved Mr. Kuehnle." But this generosity had a price. In exchange, the Commodore demanded their loyalty in the voting booth.

Prompted by Kuehnle, hotel and boardinghouse owners required all of their employees to register to vote. Any African-American worker who failed to register was harassed until he did. On Election Day, Kuehnle's lieutenants went into the neighborhoods on the Northside and rousted black voters out of their homes. Groups of about 20 blacks at a time were taken in wagons from ward to ward, voting repeatedly. Republican Election Day workers stood outside the polls with their pockets crammed with $2 bills. They each had a list of deceased and fictitious voters whose names appeared on the voter registration rolls. As the African-American voters entered the polls, they were assigned a name and given a sheet of carbon paper, the size of the regular ballot, together with a sample ballot. The voter then took his carbon and the sample into the booth with him and marked the regular ballot on the carbon over the sample ballot. When he returned outside, if the markings were right, the voter received his $2. Voters who wanted a second try at the same poll waited for another black voter and exchanged a hat or an overcoat and then received another name by which to vote.

Purchasing votes wasn't confined to locals. Many out-of-town, seasonal hotel workers were registered in Atlantic City, and they were paid to come to town on Election Day. Hundreds of African-American workers—registered at local businesses—who spent the off-season in cities such as Baltimore, Washington, D.C., and Philadelphia returned by train to vote each fall at election time.

These voters were referred to by Kuehnle's people as "floaters," and Election Day poll workers had lists of people for whom they would pay train fare plus a little something extra after they had cast their ballot. If someone failed to show, his vote was cast anyway by another black person from another voting district. The practice, known as "colonizing" voters, was so widespread that it could not possibly have occurred without the cooperation of hoteliers and boardinghouse owners.

Losing Democrats were enraged. In one election, the losing candidate complained bitterly that the Republican candidate had won with fraudulent black votes. The charges heard by the state legislature, to no avail, pointed to illegal registration of black workers. The process was described thus:

> Such fraudulent registration being in many cases from empty houses and from vacant lots; and in some instances of as many as eight negroes from one small two-story house which had been occupied for several years continuously by but one family, containing only one man ... And in another instance as many as nineteen negroes being registered by a negro Republican from his own home, a small two-story building, with the lower floor being used for a cigar store, kitchen and dining room, and the upper floor for sleeping apartments; said negroes being said to belong to a Republican club having its meeting place there ... and did register and vote from somewhere else during the election ... yet, so registered, were in many cases voted on from said house by negroes.

"Nineteen negroes ... registered by a negro Republican from his own home," whether or not they lived in town, all voting for his candidates, pleased the Commodore more than words could say. While Atlantic County's relatively small population kept his machine from being a major influence in a statewide general election, it was often a decisive factor in his party's primary. Over time, the ability to crank out lopsided votes made the Atlantic City Republican organization a key player on the state level. Politicians respect votes no matter how they're gotten, and Kuehnle was wooed by every Republican seeking statewide office. Before the end of the first decade of the 20th century, the Atlantic City machine was one of the key political organizations in New Jersey, able to influence the selection of candidates for governor, senator, and congressman. Kuehnle's stature as a statewide leader increased his power at home. But not everyone was a fan of the Commodore.

Reformers never fared well in the resort. In time, there was no Democratic Party. For more than 60 years after the Commodore, when it was convenient in state or national politics for someone to be a "Democrat," the organization chose someone. Regardless, there was a small vocal group made up of the owners of family-oriented businesses and the large hotels along the Boardwalk. Some of the large Boardwalk hotel owners, like the White family of the Marlborough-Blenheim, were from Philadelphia with Quaker backgrounds. This class of hotelier saw the world differently than the average Atlantic City boardinghouse owner. They detested Kuehnle, opposed his tactics, and resented his manipulation of the black vote. They felt that African-American voters were being exploited and that the Commodore was too clever by far in orchestrating voter turnout on the Northside to his own ends. Additionally, the Quakers wanted to see Atlantic City become a middle-class family resort that did not rely upon "booze, broads, and gambling."

Allied with the Quakers were a handful of "progressives" who continued to dream of Atlantic City as a genteel resort for the upper crust, as Jonathan Pitney had envisioned it. They included prohibitionists who saw alcohol as an evil that needed to be eradicated from society. Both the Quakers and the dreamers felt things had gone too far under the Commodore. They wanted the resort cleaned up and made themselves heard through the *Atlantic City Review* and its editor, Harvey Thomas, a hard-hitting muckraker. Thomas and his allies viewed Kuehnle as a power-hungry bully and wanted him out of authority. Their chance to launch an attack on the Commodore came in the New Jersey gubernatorial election of 1910.

The election of 1910 was a milestone for both Kuehnle and New Jersey. The Republican candidate for governor was Vivian Lewis, a favorite of the Commodore. Kuehnle was friendly with Lewis and knew his candidate could be counted on to overlook the way things were done in the resort. The Atlantic County Republican organization was the first to endorse Lewis's bid for governor. Lewis's opponent was a scholarly reformer, Woodrow Wilson, president of

Princeton University, who campaigned on a pledge to wipe out corruption at all levels of government.

Wilson was the son, grandson, and nephew of Presbyterian ministers. Although a religious background was common among politicians of his day, Wilson was a crusader who saw things in black and white. To make things worse for the Commodore, Wilson was a teetotaler and a supporter of the movement that eventually produced the 18th Amendment to the U.S. Constitution, banning the sale of alcoholic beverages. He was also a dynamic campaigner. Sounding much like a fire-and-brimstone preacher, Wilson pounded away at Vivian Lewis's weaknesses and his ties to corrupt political bosses. He reminded voters that his opponent had been handpicked by the Republican machine and would be no more than a caretaker for the special interests. Wilson campaigned against the boss system and asserted he would break it up, holding out the promise of regenerating state government.

During his campaign, Woodrow Wilson appeared in Atlantic City before a group of prohibitionists and reformers. The rally had been organized by Harvey Thomas. Speaking before a crowd of 2,000—mostly out-of-towners—Wilson promised that one of the first places he would root out corruption and bossism was in Atlantic City.

The Commodore saw this preacher's son for the very real threat he was. Kuehnle knew that a zealous moralist in the governor's office would be trouble for Atlantic City. The Republican organization pulled out all the stops in an effort to defeat Wilson. In less than six month's time, there were 2,000 new voters registered in Atlantic City. The turnout on Election Day was a record one, with Vivian Lewis carrying the town handily. Much to the Commodore's dismay, however, Wilson was elected together with Democratic majorities in both houses of the legislature. Upon checking the election returns in Atlantic City, Wilson noticed that his Republican opponent had received more votes than the city had registered voters. That spelled trouble for Kuehnle.

Wilson had the legislature form a special committee to investigate election fraud, focusing on Atlantic City. The committee held 19 sessions at which it took testimony of more than 600 witnesses, producing more than 1,400 pages of sworn statements. The committee's findings could have served as the basis for another treatise by Wilson, who was a published author on political science. To no one's surprise, the committee learned that votes were purchased on a broad scale, primarily in the voting precincts on the Northside. One witness called by the committee testified about his confrontation with a Republican poll worker who was doling out cash to black voters outside one of the voting places. "You are getting that man to vote in somebody's name. Every one of you ought to go to prison." To which he was told, "If you don't get out of here they [referring to the blacks] will trample you to death." The dialogue continued, "I said, 'Before they trample me to death there will be a few dead negroes here.' He says, 'Don't call them niggers.' I said, 'I didn't call them niggers, I called them negroes, but if you are buying your votes you are worse than a nigger for buying votes.'"

There were key players on the Northside (most of them on the city payroll) who were part of Kuehnle's organization. One such poll worker was discussed before the investigative committee. "So after that, men came out from the polls and would hand the man a slip; he was a very well-dressed darkey, a dude, rather, he was too well-dressed for his color, he walked up the street with them and he would take out his roll and give them money. I saw him do that time and time again." In all, there were approximately 3,000 fraudulent votes cast in Atlantic City in the election of 1910, most of them coming out of the Northside's voting precincts.

Called before the committee, the Commodore was asked what he knew of "the padded registration in Atlantic City last fall." In response to a question concerning his involvement in voting fraud, Kuehnle replied, "Why, my instructions to the workers was that we didn't want any padded lists, because we had enough Republican votes in Atlantic City and County to win the election at any time." Despite the Commodore's testimony, the investigative committee had more than enough evidence to prove widespread voter fraud in both the city and county.

Indictments returned by a special grand jury named more than 120 defendants, many of whom held positions in city government or the Republican organization. There was Kuehnle, Sheriff Enoch Johnson (son of Sheriff Smith Johnson, one of the regulars at "the Corner"), Mayor George Carmany, City Councilman Henry Holte, City Clerk Charles Donnelly, Building Inspector Al Gillison, Health Inspector Theodore Voelme, President of Atlantic City Electric Lyman Byers, and on and on. These indictments all dealt with election fraud. It was, however, naive for Governor Wilson to expect an Atlantic County jury to return guilty verdicts against officials of the Republican Party. Nearly everyone was acquitted, including Kuehnle, but Wilson was determined to put the Commodore out of business.

Simultaneous with the investigation into election fraud was an inquiry of official corruption in Atlantic City's government. It was no secret that Kuehnle and his lieutenants had been personally benefiting from municipal contracts. The Commodore was a shareholder in the United Paving Company, one of many firms he had formed over the years to obtain government contracts. United Paving was profitable from its inception and in a short time had contracts totaling $600,000. It was successful on every municipal project for which it competed. There might be lower bidders, but they were never able to comply with the bid specifications, so United Paving got the jobs.

Everyone knew that the Commodore was personally profiting from these contracts, but no one cared because they were so relieved to finally have paved streets. As for the residents of the Northside, United Paving was an important employer. The hot, dirty, and backbreaking work of laying asphalt pavement was, like the construction of the railroad, principally the work of African Americans (by this time, the Irish had moved into the mainstream of society). Ironically, the last neighborhoods to be paved—and as we shall see, some streets never quite made it onto the Commodore's list—were on the Northside.

Contracts to install new timber water mains from the mainland to Absecon Island were let out for bid by city council in 1909. The work plan was known as the Woodstave Project. Then, as now, Atlantic City received its drinking water from artesian wells on the mainland, some seven miles over the meadows. For years, the water had been pumped into the city in small pipes. To accommodate Atlantic City's growth, it was now necessary to install one large water main. United Paving hadn't bid on the project because Kuehnle was a member of the Water Commission, and there was an obvious conflict of interest. Instead, a dummy bidder, Frank S. Lockwood, a clerk in United Paving, was awarded the contract at a bid price of $224,000. On the same day the bid was awarded, Lockwood assigned his contract rights to a firm called Cherry and Lockwood, Cherry being William Cherry, the Commodore's partner in United Paving. The Woodstave Project only partially involved paving, but Kuehnle and Cherry wanted the entire contract. Their greed caused the contract price to increase beyond $300,000 with all of the extras being approved by Kuehnle as chairman of the Water Commission. The commission's records showed that of the 15 vouchers submitted for payment, 12 of them had been personally approved by Kuehnle.

Governor Wilson and his attorney general needed no more. An indictment was obtained, and Kuehnle went to trial before a jury that had been carefully screened to prevent any of his cronies from sitting, as had occurred in the election fraud trial. The jury had no choice but to return a guilty verdict. The Commodore's conviction and the success at exposing the widespread corruption in the resort made a valuable trophy for Wilson on his march to the White House.

Appeal of his conviction got the Commodore nowhere and by the time the final ruling came down upholding the verdict, Wilson had gone on to become president in 1913. Kuehnle was sentenced to a year of hard labor and a $1,000 fine. His sentence began in December 1913 and, before going to jail, he made arrangements for several thousand Christmas gifts of food and clothing to be given out on the Northside.

No complaints were heard from the Commodore. He served his time and, upon release from jail, he went to Bermuda for a lengthy vacation and then for an extended visit to Germany, his parents' homeland. Nearly two years after leaving for prison, Kuehnle returned to the resort, tanned and rested. He soon learned things had changed during his absence. A new leader, former County Sheriff, Enoch "Nucky" Johnson, had emerged as the boss of Atlantic City's Republican Party. Nucky was seen by many as the Commodore's protégé. He was also battle-tested, having won acquittal at the election fraud trial. Nucky was the heir apparent when Kuehnle went off to jail and quickly took control of the Republican organization. One thing he changed involved the flow of cash to the organization. Under the Commodore, bribes had been paid in line with a "gentleman's agreement" between the Republican Party and the vice industry. Under Nucky, protection money paid by Atlantic City's racketeers became a major source of revenue for the business of politics. "With Nucky, it was all business. There was nothin' voluntary about the payments. You paid or he shut you down."

After the Commodore's return, he and Nucky had several skirmishes, but there was no doubt who was in control. Finally, they reached an accommodation, with Nucky agreeing to support the Commodore for city council. Kuehnle was elected in 1920 and re-elected each time his four-year term ended, until his death in 1934. To the end, he was active in both city government and the community. A tribute to his popularity was the naming of a major local street in his honor. Kuehnle had the undying affection of the public, but Nucky Johnson had the power.

Throughout the nearly 30 years that Nucky was boss, he lived the life of a decadent monarch, with the power to satisfy his every want. Six-four, trim, and broad-shouldered, Nucky was a ruggedly handsome man with large, powerful hands, a glistening bald head, a devilish grin, friendly gray eyes, and a booming voice. In his prime, he strode the Boardwalk in evening clothes complete with spats, patent leather shoes, a walking stick, and a red carnation in his lapel. He rode around town in a chauffeur-driven powder-blue Rolls Royce limousine, maintained several residences, hosted lavish parties for hundreds of guests, used the local police as his private gendarmes, had a retinue of servants (mostly African Americans) to satisfy his every need, and enjoyed an untaxed personal income of more than $500,000 per year. As we will see, one of Nucky's more lucrative sources of revenue—the citywide "numbers games"—was started on the Northside by enterprising black businessmen who had mastered the gambling business. Money from the "numbers" play and other vice-related businesses were used to keep voters on the Northside loyal to the Republican organization.

As with the Commodore, while Nucky was boss, he chose not to seek elected office. He believed that a boss should never be a candidate. Nucky had learned much from Kuehnle, and he believed that "running for election was beneath a real boss." Crucial to his power and the control of the Republican organization, he learned how to manipulate Atlantic City's black population. He continued the Commodore's private welfare system, but the assistance he gave blacks went beyond anything Kuehnle had done. Come winter, he was their savior.

Nucky understood that the long stretches of unemployment in the off-season could be devastating to poor black families. He saw to it that every needy person on the Northside had food, clothing, coal, and medical care. "If your kid needed a winter coat, all you had to do was ask—maybe it wouldn't fit but it was warm. If the grocer cut off your credit, the ward leader told you where to shop on the party's tab. The same was true if someone needed a doctor or a prescription filled." A far more flamboyant personality than Kuehnle, it was common for Nucky to stroll through the Northside's neighborhoods, frequenting businesses at which he left large tips, peeling off $20 bills and handing them to people with a handshake or a slap on the back. He never failed to get a shoeshine while on his walks and always tipped well. In return, he was loved by the Northside's residents and looked upon as a "white god." Nucky owned the black vote, and, when a large turnout was needed to produce the right election results, they never failed him.

Nucky, as the Commodore before him, used his power to forge what some historians have termed a "compact" between the Republican Party, the hotel-resort businesspeople, and the racketeers who furnished the "booze, broads, and gambling." The Republican organization could count on a steady cash flow. Legitimate businesses were assured they would not be harassed by inspectors from City Hall, and the purveyors of illicit thrills—who paid most dearly, but had the income to warrant it—were guaranteed that the police wouldn't disrupt the fun and games. It was a profitable partnership for everyone involved.

Taken for granted in this community-wide scheme were local African Americans, both as workers and as voters. They were the cornerstone of the local economy, earned a respectable wage, and were a critical bulwark of the local organization's ability to crank out large majorities. They played a pivotal role in generating fraudulent votes enabling the local Republican Party to have influence beyond its true worth or numbers. Yet blacks were forced to live in substandard housing, hired to perform tasks whites refused to do, barred from restaurants and amusement piers, denied shopping privileges by most stores on the Southside, admitted to hotels only as workers, shoved into segregated parts of the hospital, and permitted to bathe in only one section of the beach.

In Atlantic City and throughout the nation, the world of the white man brought slights, insults, and humiliation to black people on a daily basis. No matter how hard working, attentive to hotel guests' needs, well-spoken, or professionally attired, black people were ultimately judged by their skin color. There was no escaping racial prejudice in American society, but there was another society in which people of color in Atlantic City found refuge—their church.

4

The Disinherited

The striking similarity between the social position of Jesus in Palestine and that of the vast majority of American Negroes is obvious ... The basic fact is that Christianity as it was born in the mind of this Jewish teacher and thinker appears as a technique of survival for the oppressed.
—Howard Thurman, philosopher, poet, mystic

Dry eyes were not to be found. The soft sound of weeping was heard throughout the church. It was a cold, rainy morning, and nearly every pew was filled. As the choir members took to their feet, their weariness showed. It was too soon since they had last sung over a miniature coffin. They were relieved this would be the final hymn. The untimely death had taken its toll on everyone. Funeral prayers and blessings concluded, it was time for a closing song of hope to comfort the grieving family members. On cue of the pastor, the congregation rose in unison, singing a spiritual most knew by heart:

Why should I feel discouraged
Why should the shadows come
Why should my heart be lonely
And long for heavenly home
When Jesus is my portion?
My constant friend is He
His eye is on the sparrow
And I know He watches me
His eye in on the sparrow
And I know He watches me

I sing because I'm happy
I sing because I'm free
For His eye is on the sparrow
And I know He watches me

Nothing is more heartbreaking than burying a child. The off-season could be deadly for the old and young alike, and many Northside babies didn't make it through the winter. At such times, the churches on the Northside provided sanctuary of the most basic sort. The only balm that eased the pain—ever so slightly—of those left behind was the loving embrace of fellow church members who shared their faith.

Christianity was woven tightly into the fabric of Atlantic City's African-American community. The history of the resort's network of churches dates from the migration of freedmen journeying north after the Civil War. The freed black people who came to town as part of the initial construction effort in the early days, and during the boom period that followed the second railroad, were hardworking, devout, and generally of limited education. They brought their faith and the need to share it with other freed people. These pioneers worshipped together wherever they could gather in privacy.

Most churches on the Northside had their start as missions. Launched with the blessing of established churches, they provided food, clothing, song, and prayer to all in need. Living Christian teachings, they were missionaries in the true sense of the word. Most of these early missions congregated in homes. Others met in hotel storage rooms, storefronts, and sometimes the tents of traveling evangelists. They were humble and Christian, profoundly so. The "how and where" of black people gathering to worship is preceded by the "why." The odyssey by which African people and their descendants came to embrace the Christian faith is central to the black experience in America and Atlantic City.

African Americans did not adopt the Christian faith. Rather, they *adapted* Christianity to their unique circumstances. From the time of their arrival as involuntary guests on European slave ships and their gradual, forced acceptance of Western culture, the religion of the original African peoples and their offspring "has been something less and something more than what is generally regarded as Christianity." It could not have been any other way.

Professing their devotion to Christianity, the people who brought Africans to the New World in chains were hardly role models for the teachings of Jesus Christ. Although there were Christians who objected to slavery—principally the Quakers—by and large, "the church" in the American colonies and Europe was complicit with the trafficking of humans and the exploitation of their forced labor.

Ironically, the spread of modern free market economies, which originated with the creative energies of the Age of Enlightenment in
Christian Europe, led to the denial of freedom for others. Rather than
pay wages to the workers needed to exploit the promise of the New
World, merchants went to Africa and bought people who had been
kidnapped by neighboring villages. In time, one of every seven
Americans was owned by another.

Most Africans understood slavery. It was an ancient institution,
established in West Africa centuries before the Europeans arrived.
While African slavery could be harsh, it was uncommon for masters
to have the power of life and death over slaves as did the plantation
masters in America. In many African kingdoms, slaves owned personal property, chose their spouses, and knew their children would
be born free people—not so for slaves brought to the New World.
Only in the Americas did people become property.

The American colonies lived by the rule of law and, in the 18th
century, the position of slaves was clear: They were the chattel of
their masters. In advertisements, they were classified with cows,
horses, farm tools, and household items. Slaves were barred from
testifying against whites in a court of law, but their testimony was
routinely forced on charges against other slaves. By law, they could
not receive alcoholic beverages, possess firearms, assemble in
groups, or sell any goods without their masters' permission. Finally,
there were systematic efforts to de-Africanize slaves. They were forbidden to use their original names, speak their native languages, or
practice the religions they knew in Africa. They were often forced to
become Christians by slave masters who used Christianity as a tool
of control. They were told that God loved all his creatures and that
they could have eternal life by accepting Jesus Christ as their savior
and being obedient.

The words of white clergymen on the need for obedience to attain
salvation rang hollow. One former slave who refused to be obedient
was Frederick Douglass. In *The Narrative of the Life of Frederick
Douglass*, the abolitionist and orator condemned the southern
church, saying, "I assert most unhesitatingly, that the religion of the
south is a mere covering for the most horrid crimes—a justifier of the
most appalling barbarity, a sanctifier of the most hateful frauds, and
a dark shelter under which the darkest, foulest, grossest, and most
infernal deeds of slaveholders find the strongest protection."

Christianity as professed by most white people in the Americas was an institution blacks could do without. One didn't have to be educated to see the sanctimonious sham slave masters had made of Christ's teachings. If that was Christianity, then black people wanted no part of it. Instead, early Africans looked to the teachings of Jesus himself.

Many slaves were intrigued by the bits and pieces they had learned about this man "Jesus of Nazareth." As a result, they refused to accept the pious preaching of obvious frauds. They rejected white pastors, because they didn't trust them to teach this new religion centered on the words of one man. The early Africans in slavery were taken with the apparent power of Christ's humility and wanted to learn what *He* had to say. Their appetite for knowledge of Christ's teachings was strong, but language and reading skills were major obstacles to learning more. Not taught in American history classes is the fact that teaching slaves to read was a crime in most southern states. The poet Frances Harper expressed it well:

> Our masters always tried to hide
> Book learning from our eyes;
> Knowledge didn't agree with slavery—
> 'Twould make us all too wise.
>
> But some of us would try to steal
> A little from the book,
> And put the words together,
> And learn by hook or crook.

Regardless of southern laws, circumstances required a small segment of the slave population to be educated. A plantation was more than a large farm. It was a business. Many things had to be kept track of. On each plantation, a limited number of slaves was provided with enough schooling to make them useful in managing things. Over time, there evolved a class structure, which, put simply in the language of the era, was comprised of the "house nigger" and the "field nigger." Gradually, and always secretly, educated slaves taught others how to read and write, and passed on their newly acquired skills to as many other slaves as possible. A significant part of this process involved one of the few books widely available in southern society, namely the Christian Bible.

The King James Version of the Bible was challenging for many literate white Americans of the 18th and 19th centuries. For most African people, learning to read the English language by means of the Bible was tough going. As a result, the learning curve was tortuously long but steady. With true freedom a virtual impossibility, slaves had a strong need for a spiritual answer to their condition. Seeing little hope for happiness in this world, the African people forced into slavery turned instinctively to find comfort in one another. They needed to know that *somehow* all would be made right for them. First with extreme caution and curious skepticism, then finally with fulsomeness unlike anything most whites had ever experienced, black people embraced Jesus Christ and his teachings.

Christ's view of life and his teachings on how to cope with a hostile environment found a receptive audience among African people. Despite the centuries and continents that separated their histories, Jews and blacks shared a common experience. Each had been enslaved and subjected to a harsh oppression that denied their humanity. Each was a pawn in other men's social order: For the Jews, it was first the Egyptians, then the Romans; for the blacks, it was American slave owners. Rome (the institution of slavery) was the enemy. Rome (slavery) symbolized total frustration and was the great barrier to peace of mind. And Romans and their might (slave masters and the laws supporting them) were everywhere. How to cope with such a harsh daily reality? No Jewish (black) person could deal with the "how" of his personal life, his family, his vocation, or his place in society, until he first resolved deep within himself the answer to this critical question.

"This is the position of the disinherited in every age." What should be the attitude toward those who control one's political, social, and economic life? This was the question of the slave, and later freedmen, in American life. Until black people faced and settled that question, they had neither direction nor could they be at peace with themselves.

There is nothing more devastating to a people than to have it impressed upon them daily that they do not count; to know that the only level at which they figure into the social order is through their toil. The "striking similarity" between Jews and blacks was discussed by African-American scholar Howard Thurman in his powerful work, *Jesus and the Disinherited*. As Dr. Thurman noted, black people in America have spent most of their history fighting for survival, and "Jesus' teachings are in large part instructions for survival ..." As was true for the Jews in ancient times, so it was for blacks in slavery—resisting their oppressors was not an option. Musical expression can reveal the essence of people's yearnings more eloquently than any historian, and the lyrics of a popular spiritual echo Dr. Thurman's thesis:

> When Israel was in Egypt land: Let my people go,
> Oppress'd so hard they could not stand: Let my people go.
> Go down, Moses
> Way down in Egypt land
> Tell ole Pharaoh
> Let my people go.

Teachings that enabled the oppressed to endure—in the hope that some day their masters would let them go—were welcomed among the early Africans in slavery. Deprived of all dignity and self-worth, slaves had little choice but to accept their plight or be murdered. Accept they did, yet an inescapable consequence was humiliation, the likes of which no other class of immigrants to the Americas has suffered. The "dead weight advantages" of the social order that controlled the environment of Jews in the age of Rome (and earlier, Egypt) and blacks prior to the American Civil War was gravely humiliating, making it impossible to think of freedom without the intervention of some other force.

Christ taught that the ointment for humiliation was humility and asked his people to learn from him, "For I am meek and lowly in heart; and ye shall find rest unto your souls. For my yoke is easy, and my burden is light." He counseled the oppressed that their kingdom was not of this world and that their survival could be found by worshipping God and loving their fellow man, including their enemies. As characterized by Dr. Thurman, "The basic fact is that Christianity as it was borne in the mind of this Jewish teacher and thinker appears as a technique of survival for the oppressed." No one in American history needed a "technique of survival" more than African people sold into slavery.

The early spiritual leaders or "African priests" among the slaves who came to the American colonies understood that their primary task was the survival of their brothers and sisters. They were joined in their efforts by medicine men or "shamans." Together, they represented the traditional religions and cultures of Africa. These religions were generally animistic, derived from the Latin word *anima* meaning "breath" or "soul." Animism is one of mankind's oldest answers to the mysteries of life. For millennia, African religions taught that the entire universe was sacred and that a soul or spirit existed in every living thing. In a future state, this spirit would exist as part of an immaterial soul. Thus, newly arrived Africans tangled in the web of slavery believed that the spirit of every living creature was sacred. Performing their spiritual duties in virtual anonymity, the priests and shamans among them worked to ensure that these and other traditional beliefs and traditions were not lost. It was no easy task.

Bondage in a strange land was the dominant reality in the lives of the people brought to the Americas in chains. For the Africans, it was immensely disorienting. The traditional reference points that had guided their civilizations through the years remained in Africa. Entire villages had been kidnapped from the sacred earth in which their ancestors were buried and "where the gods of their fathers walked and talked with men and women." Families were ripped apart, boarding different ships to the Americas, never to see one another again. Treated as cargo, when they reached colonial ports, they were locked in cages until they were looked over—much the way a farmer might examine cattle—by purchasers at public auction. Some slaves tried to escape upon reaching shore, but most were too weak to try.

Torn from their communities, these men and women had lost everything familiar in their daily routine. Gone were family, home, social status, and individual identity. They had to adjust to an alien environment, diet, and climate, and conform to the routine established by those who had purchased them. Defenseless against random violence from any white person they encountered, and with virtually no chance of escape, slavery robbed Africans of all those things that gave them their identities, including their names. Naming slaves was an important first step in the process of controlling them. Upon being purchased, slaves were given new names by their owners. Biblical names were often used.

Thousands of miles from the roots of their culture, the first several generations of Africans clung desperately to the faiths of their homeland. The priests and shamans were a critical link with the past and crucial to preserving community identity. These spiritual leaders and medicine men brought to Christianity perspectives unique to their experiences—some in agreement and others at variance with the faith as taught in the American colonies. First traditional African priests and shamans, and later black Christian ministers, became the trusted advisers and leaders of their communities. It was from them that slaves learned about Jesus Christ and came to passionately embrace Christianity.

Most relevant to the experience of slaves, these spiritual leaders recognized the relationship between "bad magic" as practiced by whites who professed to be Christians and the dehumanizing condition in which black people found themselves. They saw that the Christian religion was being used as a tool for oppression. They supplemented Christian teachings with ingredients from the African religious past. According to the prominent turn-of-the-century African-American leader and historian W. E. B. Du Bois, "The Negro Church is the only social institution of the Negroes which started in the African forest and survived slavery." In support of his conclusion, Du Bois argued that the transplanted African priest "early became an important figure on the plantation and found his function as the interpreter of the supernatural, the comforter of the sorrowing, and as the one who expressed, rudely, but picturesquely, the longing and disappointment and resentment of the stolen people." Reinforcing Du Bois is Joseph R. Washington Jr., who eloquently summarized the African-American religious experience:

> Born in slavery, weaned in segregation and reared in discrimination, the religion of the Negro folk was chosen to bear the roles of both protest and relief. Thus, the uniqueness of black religion is the racial bond which seeks to risk its life for the elusive but ultimate goal of freedom and equality by means of protest and action. It does so through the only avenues to which its members have always been permitted a measure of access, religious convocations in the fields or in the houses of worship.

Black historians including Du Bois and Washington have noted that the first established black churches had only "a veneer of Christianity." Over the years, black people found in evangelical sects, such as Methodist and Baptist, a set of beliefs and an opportunity for emotional expression relevant to their everyday experiences in slavery. For the slave owners, African people's espousal of Christianity was fine as long as they continued to be property of the white man. Blacks were free to develop their versions of Christianity, taking from white churches those practices and tenets they found relevant to their unique condition and cultural roots. Gradually, a church encompassing the black experience evolved.

The "invisible institution" is how some African-American historians have characterized their church in slavery. Many black religious practices were forced to remain "invisible" because whites feared the "heathen" rituals of the early slave church, viewing them as "black voodoo." As a result, the religious services of slaves were often, of necessity, conducted in secrecy. The upheaval in southern society caused by the Civil War disrupted the "invisible institution." With Emancipation, the black man's world had been turned upside down. The social disorganization resulting from the collapse of the plantation economy was overwhelming.

Defeat left white Southerners a "bitterly hostile people hating with a deepening despair." White supremacists vented their rage. In the months and years following the Civil War, an orgy of violence swept the South. "Judge Lynch" ruled the day and despite the presence—for a time—of the Union Army, there were beatings, rapes, lynchings, and mob violence by whites on blacks with no provocation. Most historians view it as one of the ugliest chapters in our history.

But through it all, the many black congregations that had surfaced after the Civil War would not be suppressed. They refused to worship in secrecy any longer. Many of the early black churches were burned, and outspoken ministers who looked too much like potential social activists ran the risk of lynching. But these freed persons were not to be denied the right to worship. Out of this turmoil, the "invisible institution" became visible.

Black religious leaders began moving closer to mainstream Christianity by affiliating with existing independent Negro churches in the North. Initially, the most prevalent denominations with which they joined forces were the Methodist and Baptist organizations, often creating their own "Negro" church societies. The new black churches that grew out of slavery, both prior to and following the Civil War, were, in large part, a result of black people being barred from participating with white congregations. Over time, these and other denominations grew rapidly, and the church became the glue of black society throughout the country. The U.S. government had abandoned the commitment implicit in Emancipation. With Reconstruction a total failure and most of white society—in the North as well as the South—at best indifferent to their plight, African Americans clung to the church. It was the only effective institution for helping black people to cope with racial prejudice and build their own society. Its growth was a product of necessity as much as religious fervor.

The critical importance of the role played by African-American churches—city or rural, large or small, grand or humble—cannot be overstated. "The black church has no challenger as the cultural womb of the black community. Not only did it give birth to new institutions such as schools, banks, insurance companies, and low income housing, it also provided an academy and an arena for political activities, and it nurtured young talent for musical, dramatic, and artistic development." The development of a separate network of black churches, between the Civil War and World War I, was shaped not so much by Biblical teachings as by the collective experiences of their isolated social world, first as slaves and then as freed people.

Bigots know no limits, and some of the early church-related experiences in Atlantic City reinforced the need to establish separate churches. One dark page of the resort's history tells of a three-day period in late August 1873. As reported in "Current Drifts," a daily *Atlantic City Review* column reporting on "colored folk," local blacks had organized a "camp meeting." The meeting was well attended not only by local African Americans but by whites, though for different purposes. The whites were there to create trouble.

As reported by the newspaper, "A colored camp meeting is in progress on Illinois Avenue and it has naturally attracted great crowds of people. There is associated with efforts of this character a peculiar excitement which appears to be indispensable to the natures of our colored citizens, and we have no doubt the meeting will be productive of great good among them. All such religious gatherings should be encouraged by the people."

In a letter to the editor that appeared a short time later, the writer commented on the white people who attended this religious gathering. "The persons having charge of the colored Camp Meeting are justly complaining at the disorder of the white people. Their benches have been repeatedly broken down, and the services are constantly disrupted by loud talking and laughing. While the colored folks are pleased to see the white folks in attendance, they respectfully ask that common respect be shown while engaged in their religious exercises." These disruptive fools could hardly have been viewed as representative of the entire white community; nevertheless, they underscored the vulnerability of black people, even when trying to worship.

Through no choice of their own, those blacks who decided to make Atlantic City their home became socially isolated. Of necessity, these new residents banded together in their churches, which became the center of social life in the emerging Northside. It was only here that black people could freely express themselves through worship and attain status and recognition by participation in the hierarchy and social organizations of their churches. It was common during the off-season for blacks to combine both religion and recreation on Sundays. Families and friends frequently met at their common place of worship, bringing along picnic lunches or uncooked meals. At the conclusion of religious services, they walked to the beach, gathering firewood, and camped at the shore for the remainder of the day, cooking over open fires and spending the afternoon talking, singing spirituals, and playing games.

African-American scholars who have studied the development of their churches in northern cities have argued that there was a relationship between black social classes and church affiliation. The upper class usually formed the majority of the relatively small Episcopal, Presbyterian, and Congregational churches; the middle class primarily comprised the more numerous Methodist and Baptist churches; and the lower class gravitated toward the small and numerous "storefront" churches that arose as part of reform movements.

The first traditional black church in Atlantic City was the Bethel African Methodist Episcopal (AME) Church, founded in 1875. Bethel AME's development gives it a special place in the resort's history. Little more than 20 years after the founding of the resort, while Atlantic City was still very much Jonathan Pitney's idea of a village—there were no paved streets, electricity, central plumbing and heating, or any of the things taken for granted once the resort was fully developed—a group of the faithful reached out to Bishop James A. Shorter of Philadelphia. They asked for help in organizing a "religious society."

Bishop Shorter dispatched a young minister, the Reverend Jeremiah H. Pierce. Although the precise date is unknown, the ceremony performed by the Reverend Pierce to found this new church of Methodists in Atlantic City was conducted with the help of a white Protestant congregation, Union Church, on Delaware Avenue between Arctic and Baltic Avenues. The new religious society of devout Methodists was called the Bethel AME Church of Atlantic City. Following the initial organization, the worshippers held services in the dining room of a hotel, the Ocean House, at the corner of Maryland and Arctic Avenues.

Bethel AME, like the rest of Atlantic City, was "seasonal." For the first several years, the church didn't meet year-round. By the fourth year, in 1878, the first permanent church building—a small, one-story structure—was built on Baltic Avenue near Maryland Avenue, on land donated by Mrs. Louvenia Showel, daughter of Ryan Adams, one of the early settlers of Atlantic City. The pastor was the Reverend George Jones, and his congregation consisted of 25 members. Services were held at this location from 1878 to 1884, during which time the church was served by five different pastors.

In 1884, the Bethel AME was renamed St. James AME Church in honor of one of the 12 apostles. According to the New Testament, St. James and his brother, John, were called the "sons of thunder" by Jesus. When Jesus asked the brothers to follow him, they dropped everything and left their family and business behind. The founding members of St. James possessed this same religious fervor. They were led by their pastor, James T. Rex, who oversaw the relocation of the church from Baltic Avenue to its present location at the corner of New York and Arctic Avenues. The church was reconstructed and renovated several times over the years, each time weaving its threads more tightly into the fabric of the Atlantic City community. There's no doubt that the original founders of Bethel AME would be proud of what has come of their efforts.

The evolution of the AME Church illustrates the path traveled by black Americans in the effort to establish their own religious identity.

Its roots can be traced to the Methodist movement of early 18th century. The original Methodist Church began as a "Holy Club" of students at Oxford University in the mid-1720s. Led by John and Charles Wesley, this small group of Episcopalians developed their own methods of worship and service, seeking to minister to the needs of London's poor. The Wesley brothers were soon overwhelmed. Although they hadn't started out to found a new church, the enthusiastic response they received from the people, combined with rejection by the Anglican Church, eventually resulted in a separate Protestant denomination. Over time, the Wesleyan movement made its way across the Atlantic, and by 1784, at a conference of the movement's American leaders, the Methodist Episcopal Church was formed.

From the outset, this new church was well received by the lower classes and, in particular, by black people in the American colonies. The poor welcomed the emphasis on religious experience: a "warm heart," in stark contrast to the austere intellectualism of the Puritan churches and the Episcopalians. Blacks embraced Methodism not merely because of the message, but equally important, because of the church's stance on slavery. In the original "General Rules" set forth by the Wesleys in England, then ratified by the American church, members pledged to work toward the abolition of slavery. African Americans were among charter members of many Methodist societies in the colonies, including Frederick County, Maryland, New York City, and Philadelphia. Of the 287 members of St. George's Church in Philadelphia, 17 were African American.

Despite the Methodist Church's stance on slavery, some of its members were racist and objected to worshipping with blacks. On one occasion in 1787, while worshipping in the Philadelphia church, members Richard Allen, Absalom Jones, and several other black Methodists were "pulled from their knees during worship in a gallery they did not know was closed to black Christians." According to Richard Allen, a former slave who had belonged to a Methodist society in Delaware and joined St. George's after moving to Philadelphia, the insult was more than these adherents could tolerate. "All went out of the church in a body and they were no more plagued with us in that church."

In the spring of 1787, Allen and Absalom Jones formed a mutual aid society in Philadelphia known as the Free African Society, which assumed both religious and social service functions. From its inception, the two primary concerns of the Free African Society were racial solidarity and the abolition of slavery. Within a short time, Allen had established a mission and was holding services in an old blacksmith shop he had renovated. By 1794, the Free African Society had built a separate church and dedicated it as St. Thomas' African Episcopal Church. Allen was asked to be the first pastor but declined because of his commitment to the Methodist teachings. Wishing to remain a follower of John Wesley, a short time later Allen formed a church of his own, the Bethel Church of Philadelphia, which was dedicated by Methodist Bishop Francis Asbury. The Bethel Church became the "mother church" of what was to be a new religious domination, the AME Church. It was this church that lent support in establishing Atlantic City's first AME Church in 1875.

From the beginning, the AME Church was concerned with providing social service relief to the impoverished. Consistently throughout their experience in America, people of African descent, upon gaining a foothold in society, have reached down for their brothers and sisters. This tradition is exemplified in the history of the AME Church. The church's motto was "God our Father, Christ our Redeemer, Man our Brother." The AME's pledge to deliver social services designed to uplift its congregants was matched by an equally strong commitment to education. The leaders of the church "had a clear perception of what education would mean to the interests of the church and to the advancement of the African people then held in abject slavery." They eagerly bought into the concept of education as "social capital." They understood that the most effective means to vanquish the remnants of slavery was through the power of education. Given the era in which the AME Church was being established, their commitment to learning was no small matter.

Southern states had adopted laws against teaching blacks to read and write, but in northern states, few schools, public or private, welcomed African Americans. (Again, the initial exception was the Quakers; over time, other Protestant denominations joined in teaching African Americans.) Educated blacks generally received a suspicious and unfriendly reception from whites in the North, and it required exceptional courage and vision on the part of AME Church leaders to work toward educating their congregations. These leaders were themselves held to a daunting educational standard; after rigorous training, ministers were expected to organize schools in their communities as part of their ministry. A statement from one of the church's early conferences highlights the value the AME Church placed on the education of both its ministers and those they sought to serve:

> We assure you, dear brothers, this is no time to encourage ignorance and mental sloth; to enter the ranks of the ministry, for the education and elevation of millions now issuing out of the house of bondage, requires men, not only talented, but well educated; not only well educated, but thoroughly sanctified unto God.

As was true of most black churches, the AME's doctrines were modeled after the original tenets of the churches founded by whites, whether Methodist, Baptist, Presbyterian, as the case may be. It was the mission of all the early black churches to minister to the needs of those "issuing out of the house of bondage." The founders of these churches generally avoided disputes with the white hierarchy either on matters of faith or the governance of church affairs and were content to worship with their white brothers and sisters. The need for separate churches arose from the failure of the white church to honor its own religious tenets. Sadly, the history of the Methodists in America illustrates this point well.

Early Methodists of the northern colonies professed brotherhood, respect, and love for all of God's children but couldn't live it. Despite the fact that Methodist societies founded by the Wesleys had taken an early stance against slavery and welcomed freed black people as members, things changed as their numbers grew. By 1793, the proportion of black members in the American Methodist churches had risen to more than 40 percent. The resulting tension and discriminatory treatment, combined with the refusal to fully ordain black ministers, sparked the move toward separation. Ultimately, it was prejudiced whites refusing to worship with blacks that forced the creation of a separate network of national church organizations. There were established Methodist churches in both Absecon and Atlantic City when blacks began arriving in great numbers at the end of the 19th century, but neither welcomed them. Atlantic City's St. James AME Church rose up to meet their needs.

The second traditional African-American church in Atlantic City, Price Memorial AME Zion, was founded in 1876 by a group of local residents. As with St. James, AME Zion had its origins in the late 18th century, when a delegation of black members broke away from the white-controlled John Street Methodist Episcopal Church in New York City. Whereas Richard Allen held the services of his breakaway congregation in a blacksmith shop in Philadelphia, the faithful in New York, led by a former slave named Peter Williams, established their chapel in a cabinetmaker's shop.

Initially, the black Methodists in New York worshipped by the same tenets as those in Philadelphia, but historians believe that the two separate churches arose from "an encroachment on their [the New York Methodists'] territorial prerogatives [by Philadelphia Methodists]." Apparently, followers of Richard Allen ventured to New York City to do missionary work, creating resentment among the followers of Peter Williams. The result was the birth of the AME Zion Church, a separate Methodist church dedicated to many of the same principles as its Philadelphia counterpart.

Abolition of slavery was the principal mission of the New York Methodists. Long known as the "Freedom Church," AME Zion was intensely involved in the Underground Railroad. The church claimed such abolitionist luminaries as Sojourner Truth, Harriet Tubman, Thomas James, and Frederick Douglass, who was ordained as an AME Zion preacher in New York.

Atlantic City's AME Zion Church was started by people with strong roots in the local community. Headed by Clinton Edwards, Dr. George Fletcher, and Cora Flipping, the founders were committed to their faith and appreciated their church's heritage. Edwards was the first black person born in Atlantic City, while Dr. Fletcher was the city's first black physician. Flipping and her son, John, operated one of the first funeral homes in Atlantic City to serve the black community. These individuals were not only the leaders of a new church, but community leaders whose stature attracted new members to the church.

The third early Methodist Church to be established in the resort was Asbury United. "Asbury" was Francis Asbury, an original follower of the Wesley brothers and one of the people who brought the movement to America from England. Committed to Christian charity and helping the needy, Asbury United grew out of Bible study meetings held in the fall of 1885 at a home on Delaware Avenue near the bay in a section known as "Fisher's Row." Among the early church leaders were Samuel and Araminta Carroll, Major and Bertha Henry, Lizzie and Ruby Mitchell, Mary Thomas, and Katie Caulk. This eager group of Christians was formally recognized on July 15, 1886, and in the spring of 1887, the Methodist Conference sent Asbury its first pastor, Reverend Thomas Draper. After leaving Fisher's Row, Asbury United had several sites on the Northside, the largest at 1713 Arctic Avenue. In 1998, the church moved to 1213 Pacific Avenue, where it remains an important part of the community.

The next traditional black church in Atlantic City was established by Baptists. The year 1884 saw dozens of Baptist believers migrate to Atlantic City from Virginia. For the first several years, they met in one another's homes and organized themselves into a mission, worshipping from house to house for nearly a decade. In the spring of 1896, local Baptists under the leadership of the Reverend J. D. Hebron, who had been dispatched by the Baptist Council, built the Second Baptist Church, which they outgrew almost immediately, forcing them to rebuild several years later. Some of the early members were William Kline and his family, Ella Hilton, and the George and Thomas Payne families, along with many other families who had made Atlantic City their home year-round.

As the Baptist congregation grew, there were differences of opinion as to the direction of the church and the needs to be satisfied. A second church organization and eventually a third Baptist organization grew out of the original mission. The Shiloh Baptist Church was organized in 1898, prospering under the leadership of its first pastor, Reverend John W. Henderson, who "led the small flock until his death in 1917." Within a decade after Shiloh's founding, the Union Baptist Temple was established in 1907. Although the Baptists may have followed the Methodists in establishing churches in Atlantic City, the Baptists founded the first black churches in America, dating from the antebellum period. The Baptists were the first to carve out a religious space in the midst of the southern plantations.

Like the Methodists, the formal Baptist movement had its origins in England. The first Baptists evolved from a group of Puritans forced to take refuge in Holland, fleeing persecution in England. While in Holland, they met other Protestants and, in 1609, these exiles established the English Baptist Church. They eventually returned to England, organizing a Baptist church in London around 1612. The American Baptist movement emerged in the colonies in the early 17th century and is generally dated from the arrival of Puritan Roger Williams, who was exiled from the Massachusetts Bay Colony because of his fierce opposition to the mingling of church and state interests.

Roger Williams founded Rhode Island and the first Baptist church in America in 1639. As a result of the work of many devout Baptist missionaries, many of whom traveled to southern plantations, the movement spread south. Baptist roots run deep in American history and in Atlantic City, with the first known black churches in America generally acknowledged to have been African Baptist. Of the several Baptist churches in the resort, the Shiloh congregation is notable for its important role in the Northside's network of churches over the years.

"Shiloh" takes its name from an ancient village in Palestine that was a sanctuary for Israelites. The faithful also believe the tablets of the Ten Commandants were once stored there. Atlantic City's Shiloh Baptist Church has provided sanctuary for many Northside residents, serving the community through assistance to the elderly and preschool programs for toddlers. Of the many important events that are part of the church's history, two stand out in particular. In 1958, through the efforts of its charismatic pastor, the Reverend Russell Roberts, Shiloh hosted the Reverend Martin Luther King Jr., who spoke to an overflowing crowd at Atlantic City High School. Several years later, in the pivotal summer of 1964, Shiloh was one of the temporary encampments of a group of insurgent Democrats from Mississippi. Led by a firebrand named Fannie Lou Hamer—who had herself attended Shiloh Baptist in her home state—this group of civil rights activists left their mark on resort history, as will be detailed in Chapter 10.

A third community of Christians that stands out is the Presbyterians. At the end of the 19th century and the beginning of the 20th, a significant population of black Presbyterians came to Atlantic City from Georgia, North Carolina, and Virginia. After meeting for a short time in the home of Mr. and Mrs. Alonzo Ridley, the Presbyterians organized themselves into the Jethro Memorial Presbyterian Church, founded in 1909. "Jethro" was the father-in-law of Moses, and the name means "friend of God." Jethro Presbyterian was certainly a friend of the residents of the Northside, where the church's membership supplied a steady stream of community leaders. Consistent with the philosophy of the entire network of Atlantic City's black churches, Jethro Presbyterian kept itself about the business of helping its members to lift themselves up through the creation of social capital. As detailed in Chapter 5, one member of the Jethro Presbyterian family—Claiborn Morris Cain—ministered to the needs of the entire community. Few people in Atlantic City history left a mark comparable to Cain's.

St. James, Price Memorial, Asbury United, Shiloh Baptist, and Jethro Presbyterian are only several examples of churches that made important, lasting contributions on the Northside. Service was the common thread running through them, first to fellow members and then to the greater community. Atlantic City's early black churches took their role as "mission" very seriously, working not only to recruit new members but to help the disadvantaged, including all those left emotionally crippled by the "house of bondage."

In their own way, the resort's black churches complemented the private social welfare system established by Louis Kuehnle and the local Republican organization. They were much attuned to the hardships brought by the seasonal economy. Each fall, there were scores of new migrants who were effectively stranded, unable to return to their homes in the South after working the summer in local hotels. These people were part of the lower stratum of hotel workers. Their salaries were meager and rarely were they able to save any of their earnings. Sometimes working with, at other times apart, from the Republican organization, the local churches helped the needy make it through the winter months.

Each church's organization was structured to include—almost demand—participation by its members. Whether serving on committees to perform particular tasks such as maintaining the church and its fixtures, volunteering for clubs that raised money or ran programs including those for youth and the elderly, or singing in the choir, *everyone* had a role to play. No one could shirk responsibility as a member of the church. In the process, Atlantic City's black churches were cultivating leaders. By creating a structure that was not only hierarchical but diffused, these churches were building a solid community that could look forward to the continual regeneration of mature, responsible citizens with the wherewithal to play meaningful roles. To this day, Atlantic City's black churches remain a vital force in the community.

Many church organizations took root on the Northside during the two generations between 1880 and 1930. The religious experience of the resort's black community eventually embraced all Protestant denominations and the Roman Catholic faith. Although the resort's Irish and Italian neighborhoods supported several Roman Catholic churches, Northside residents weren't welcomed in any of them. To address the needs of a small number of local black Catholics, the Augustinian Fathers at St. Nicholas of Tolentine Parish worked with Emma Lewis to establish a mission in 1917, originally located in a home on North Delaware Avenue. Several years later, the mission moved to North Pennsylvania Avenue, and in 1949, a church was finally built. St. Monica's remains a vital part of the community.

By 1930, Atlantic City had a total of 15 traditional black church organizations. These traditional churches were mainly patronized by the upper and middle stratum of hotel workers. Numerous storefront churches served the needs of the lower strata of hotel workers, many of whom were desperately poor migrants—with little to no education—newly arrived out of the South with not much more than the clothes on their back. The migration of these black people out of the Jim Crow South to the urban North was a traumatic experience for most. Stripped of the religious practices and social structures they had created in order to cope with their lowly status in southern society, these newcomers were lost in a strange land. Many had come from small farms and sleepy little rural communities with no modern conveniences. Upon arriving in Atlantic City, they found paved streets, electricity, trolleys, telephones, a totally new set of work experiences, and a different type of community morality. The result was an emotional and religious crisis in the lives of black migrants relegated to the resort's lowest stratum.

These people needed churches attuned to their situation. During the first three generations following the American Civil War, there emerged two movements within the Protestant community: the Holiness Movement and Pentecostalism. As noted by African-American theological historians C. Eric Lincoln and Lawrence Mamiya, "Just as Methodism was originally a part of the Puritan movement within the Anglican Church, so did Holiness originate as a reform movement within Methodism." Although both the Holiness and Pentecostal churches started out interracial, black people soon learned there was little room for them. Whether the Wesleyan Church, Bible Holiness Church, Pilgrim Nazarene, or Assemblies of God, African Americans were forced to form separate churches.

In Atlantic City, most of these new religious societies had their inception in storefront churches, side-by-side with row houses and businesses. These small churches, usually located in the poorer neighborhoods, held a special appeal for those who came from small communities where everyone knew his neighbor and where church served as political forum, school, social center, and spiritual guide. As was the case in other northern cities, storefront churches flourished in Atlantic City because they adapted the rural church experience to city life by providing the face-to-face association of a small church. Their existence was due partly to the poverty of their members and the fact that congregants could participate more freely in services.

The first Holiness-type church in Atlantic City was founded in 1911 by Levi and Franklin Allen. From that church, 10 other churches sprang up almost immediately. Although the sermons of their ministers were otherworldly, these tiny sects never lost sight of the hardships their members had to overcome in this world. The Holiness and Pentecostal churches provided material as well as spiritual assistance to help southern migrants deal with urban life. A cornerstone of these churches' doctrines as they prevailed on the Northside was to serve the community by raising funds to help feed and clothe the poor. They were as much devoted to their communities as to God. A fundamental teaching was never to permit a member to be without the basic necessities of food, shelter, and clothing.

A final "necessity" to the experience of all black churches was music. An important part of most North American Protestant services, singing was a special outlet for the creative energies of African Americans. Songs originating in slavery were passed down by word of mouth, from one generation to another. As with their faith, the imprint of Africa was evident in their musical traditions. Sometimes exuberant, the music of African-American churches was always personal and democratic. In comparison with the worship style of whites, Africanized Christianity was lively and often loud. Regardless of the denomination or sect, music was a vital part of every church service. Until a congregation could afford a piano or organ, the main "instruments" for making music were the worshippers' voices, raised together in praise of their God. Negro spirituals provided comfort and eased the boredom of daily tasks, but above all, they were an expression of religious devotion and a yearning for freedom from bondage.

Musically complex, Negro spirituals contain elements of both African and rural American folk music. Most of the more traditional spirituals have their roots in slavery. In the early years of slavery, African people were forbidden to speak their native languages, to play drums, or practice their animistic rituals, which white slave owners viewed as paganism. Because they were unable to express themselves freely in ways they found spiritually meaningful, African people snuck away to clearings in forests, to remote fields, or around isolated ponds, and held secret religious services. These "camp meetings" initially involved ancient African rituals, which included chants and songs.

Over the generations, the services at these camp meetings evolved. The children and grandchildren of the original enslaved Africans created songs that expressed not only their spirituality but their everyday travails. These field songs were intricate, multipart harmonies of faith, forbearance, struggle, and overcoming. Inspired by the message of Jesus of Nazareth, "You can be saved," Negro spirituals were integral to every church event. Unlike conventional hymns of white Protestant churches, spirituals shared the hard condition of being a slave and the yearning to be free. It was common for many devout persons to quietly hum their favorite songs throughout the day.

One special song frequently sung in many black churches was "Just a Closer Walk with Thee." It provided ready comfort to people of faith employed in a white-dominated work place, contending with indignities daily. The verses were known to all:

> I am weak, but Thou art strong;
> Jesus, keep me from all wrong;
> I'll be satisfied as long
> As I walk, let me walk close to thee.
>
> Just a closer walk with Thee,
> Grant it, Jesus, is my plea,
> Daily walking close to Thee,
> Let it be, dear Lord, let it be.

Church brought black people closer to their God and gave them the strength they could find nowhere else. The teachings of Christ comforted and guided them in their daily travails as they walked in the white world of Atlantic City's hotel industry.

Sundays were special, but there were six other days in the week. As important as their religion was, Northside residents needed more. Discrimination deprived them of many essentials taken for granted by the white community. Atlantic City's black citizens rose to the challenge. The people of the Northside drew on the leadership qualities nurtured in their churches and set about the business of creating their own "city within a city."

5

Cornerstones

I saw him build an organization with scant material. I saw him molding the lives of young, underprivileged Negroes whose chances in life were so limited. I saw him instill great courage and higher ideals in the youth of Princeton. They wanted to be like Mr. Cain.
—Christine M. Howell, entrepreneur and civic leader

William Ashby wasn't the only Lincoln University undergrad rooting for Jack Johnson to whip Jim Jeffries that July in 1910. Ashby was joined by a classmate that summer. Morris Cain had journeyed to Atlantic City from North Carolina while still in his teens and worked in the hotel-resort industry several years before enrolling in Lincoln as a divinity student. His trips "home" during the summer and holidays were to earn money for college. After graduation, Ashby moved on, but Cain returned and made the resort's young black people his life's work and the entire city his congregation. Cain's career personifies the social vitality that made Atlantic City's Northside one of the leading African-American communities in the Northeast.

Cain was from a social caste that is sorely missed. The graduate of a historically black college, he came of age in a time when service to one's community was the highest calling an educated person could pursue. Although this was true of white America as well, it was particularly the case for African Americans. Cain and educated black people of his generation were inspired. They brought a sense of urgency to all they did. They were on a mission. Young educated black men of his generation believed that education was the key to lifting up African Americans and destroying the vestiges of slavery.

Claiborn Morris Cain was born March 27, 1883, in Hillsboro, North Carolina. The son of Jerry M. and Agnes Thompson Cain, he was orphaned as a small child. The cause of their deaths, whether illness or mishap, is unknown, but it was not uncommon for black children to be orphaned at an early age. Cain went to live with his maternal grandparents in Durham, North Carolina, where he attended elementary school and graduated from Whitted High School. He then enrolled in the Albion Academy, a Presbyterian preparatory school in Franklinton, North Carolina. Albion was a Bible school for training young black men for the ministry but not a "degreed" college. Although there is no information available on Cain's grandparents, two points can be safely assumed: First, as members of a mainstream Protestant church, they had found their place in post–Civil War North Carolina, and the world was a little less intimidating for them than it was for most freed persons of that era; second, they understood the value of knowledge gained from books and impressed upon their grandson the need to advance himself through a formal education.

After completing all the schooling available to him, and with little-to-no meaningful prospects for a talented young black man in Jim Crow Carolina, Cain migrated to Atlantic City in the fall of 1904. Many southern blacks were making similar treks. More than 20 years into the boom period created by the second railroad, the resort's hotel-resort economy had become a mecca for African Americans leaving the South looking for something more than farm work. But Cain had an edge on most new arrivals: His uncle, the head bellman at the Chalfonte Hotel, found a position for him on his staff, operating an elevator, carrying bags, and performing any chore assigned by his uncle to keep hotel guests happy. The Chalfonte was a prestigious Boardwalk property with patrons who were generally affluent and who tipped well. Better yet, it was one of the few hotels open year-round.

Cain spent the next four years hustling for tips, working at every available job, scrimping and saving every penny, and getting by on the generosity of his uncle—all with the aim of going to college. Although Cain was exceptional, the path he followed wasn't. His story of striving and sacrificing was fairly common for his time. Leading African Americans of the day preached that education was a form of "social capital" that would protect black people from being exploited. They understood that education—first and last—was the path that had to be followed by the children and grandchildren of former slaves if they were to play a meaningful role in American society. They couldn't become part of mainstream America without first acquiring an education. Black leaders of that era stressed that the ability to read and write was an essential tool for interacting with the white world. They saw how easy it was for illiterate people to be swindled out of their earnings and property. Unless they became educated and had a grasp of their rights, black people would remain vulnerable to anyone they came in contact with, whether it be employers, politicians, policemen and merchants, or landlords and realtors.

Pursuing a formal education was the highest calling of a young black man in the latter part of the 19th century and the early part of the 20th century. *Nothing* was valued more highly among African Americans than education, and there was *no one* more frugal or tenacious than a black man of limited means, determined to acquire a degree. Cain had a fire in his belly to uplift his race. Through education, he would become the person his uncle and grandparents knew he could be. Because it was less than a day's ride by train from Atlantic City, he chose Lincoln University as the place where he would begin to build his social capital.

Lincoln University and Morris Cain were a perfect fit. Located in southern Chester County, Pennsylvania, 20 miles south of Philadelphia, Lincoln was a Presbyterian college having its start as the Ashmun Institute. As an early president of the university stated, it was "the first institution found anywhere in the world to provide a higher education in the arts and sciences for male youth of African descent."

The story of Lincoln University goes back to the first half of the 19th century and to the efforts of Ashmun Institute's founder, John Dickey, a Presbyterian minister. "Ashmun" was Jehudi Ashmun, a Presbyterian missionary long respected in his church. Ashmun Institute came into being when two black students whom Dickey knew to be worthy candidates were denied admission to a theological seminary. In 1854, with the support of the Presbytery of New Castle Delaware, Dickey and his wife, Sarah, succeeded in opening the school with the intent of providing a scientific, classical, and theological education to young black men. Unlike some of the schools of higher education that followed Ashmun, the curriculum emphasized the classical and literary over vocational studies.

The institute was renamed Lincoln University in 1866 in honor of Abraham Lincoln. In the first half of the 20th century, it was groundbreaking in preparing African-American students for the professions of medicine, law, education, and the ministry, and a place where black students could grow and develop their talents. (Graduates of Wilberforce University in Ohio, founded 1856, can rightly proclaim that their alma mater was the *first* institution of higher education "owned and operated by African Americans," but although both Wilberforce and Lincoln have a proud heritage, the latter has the distinction of having two alumni honored with commemorative first-class stamps by the U.S. Postal Service: Poet Langston Hughes, in February 2002, and U.S. Supreme Court Justice Thurgood Marshall, in January 2003.)

The story of historically black colleges and universities (HBCUs) like Lincoln University is vital not only to black America but to the development of the Northside. Prior to the Civil War, higher education for African-American students was essentially nonexistent. The few who received schooling, including Frederick Douglass, usually studied in unconventional and sometimes hostile settings. Many were forced to teach themselves with the assistance of friends who had learned to read and write from other blacks or an enlightened white mentor. Some schools for elementary and secondary training existed, such as the Institute for Colored Youth, a school started in the early 1830s by a group of Philadelphia Quakers. A college education was also available to a limited number of black students at schools like Oberlin College in Ohio and Berea College in Kentucky.

The years between the Civil War and World War I were an era of tremendous growth for American colleges and universities. Despite public funding of land-grant colleges by Congress in the Morrill Act of 1862, few of the new colleges accepted black students. African-American higher education was forced down a different path. From the Reconstruction Era through World War I, the majority of black students were enrolled in private colleges. Led by the American Missionary Association (AMA), the philanthropy of African-American religious societies was primarily responsible for establishing and maintaining the leading black colleges and universities.

As ever, the church led the way. From 1861 to 1870, the AMA founded seven black colleges and 13 teaching colleges, then known as "normal schools." The missionary aims of these early schools reflected the ideals of classical liberal education that dominated American higher education in the second half of the 19th century. The curriculum emphasis was on ancient languages, natural sciences, and humanities. Students were given classes to improve their reading and writing skills as well as vocational and professional training in such fields as law, medicine, dentistry, education, the clergy, nursing, and pharmacy—all high-demand professions in Atlantic City as the Northside was taking shape. By the end of the first decade of the 20th century, educated black people throughout the Northeast region recognized that there were opportunities in the resort beyond hotel work. They could earn a living in their professions. Hundreds of graduates from HBCUs found their way to the resort; dozens of them were from Lincoln University.

Morris Cain had a craving for knowledge, and Lincoln was a nurturing yet challenging environment, dedicated to turning out leaders. Cain was 24 years old in the fall of 1908, but his age didn't set him apart. He was hardly the "old man" of the freshman class. African-American college students of that era were often well past their teens, and at Lincoln University, Cain found classmates who were his age and older. Like Cain, many of his fellow students had obstacles to overcome—primarily financial—before enrolling in school. And like Cain, most students arrived on campus with a seriousness of purpose that many today might find quaint. By today's standards, nearly every black man who attended college was a "geek," an "egghead," or a "bookworm." They may have known how to enjoy themselves, but they never lost sight of how critical their education was to achieving success in life.

Failure in college wasn't an option for Morris Cain's generation of students. So much effort went into a young black man's attendance in college—often including the entire family pooling resources to make it possible—that failure was gravely humiliating. Cain could never have faced his uncle had he flunked out of Lincoln University. For the first several generations after the Emancipation Proclamation, most black students had a keen appreciation of their status in American history. Slavery's legacy and the handicaps created by it were still vivid in their collective consciences, and they understood the importance of raising up the African-American community through education. Morris Cain was such a person.

Cain immersed himself in his studies and campus life. He graduated with honors in a time when there were no inflated grades and every "A" was earned. He was one of 14 founding members of Lincoln's Alpha Phi Alpha Fraternity—the first of many fraternal and professional organizations he became involved with. Their motto was "First of All, Servants of All, We Shall Transcend All." The fraternity dedicated itself to defending the rights and promoting the responsibilities of African Americans, especially the down-trodden and uneducated. Its aim was to combine social purpose with social action. Cain and his friends who founded the Lincoln chapter of the national fraternity worked to promote knowledge and achievement not only among fellow students but within the African-American community generally.

Whether because of the values instilled by his grandparents, his years at Lincoln, or his own experience as an orphan, Cain gravitated toward a career in which he could uplift young black men. His role as a "pastor" would not be confined to the members of a particular church; he chose rather to minister to the needs of the entire community. The career path he chose was with the Young Men's Christian Association (YMCA). His first position after graduating from college was with the African American YMCA in Princeton, New Jersey. It was a shortstop internship preparatory to his return to Atlantic City. As noted by Christine M. Howell, "I saw Morris Cain work and apply himself so conscientiously and strenuously to a small position in Princeton before coming to Atlantic City." Howell concluded that his short stay in Princeton of little more than a year had an impact not only on the youth but adults. "The older men of the community were given a new life under his administration. He taught many of them the joy of clean, wholesome diversion and today many in that little town who are enjoying a full life owe it to Morris Cain's efforts and work."

The YMCA movement began in America prior to the Civil War. Its first chapter dates from 1851. Not surprising, black people were excluded. The first black YMCA was organized in Washington, D.C. in 1853 and lasted through the Civil War. After emancipation, black associations were founded in New York City and Charleston, South Carolina, among other cities. The interest of newly freed people and the growth of YMCAs among African-American college students convinced the National YMCA to encourage the formation of all black branches. It met two goals: It extended the Y's mission, and it insulated whites from having to interact with blacks.

The first YMCA in Atlantic City was opened in 1893, and, predictably, local black youths were denied access. By the time the first "Y" was formed, the tipping point in Atlantic City's demographics was becoming a concern, and whites weren't willing to permit blacks to participate in organized recreational activities. Prominent local businessman George Walls, a native of Winston Salem, North Carolina, was disturbed by the discrimination and decided to do something about it.

In 1894, Walls organized a group that conceived a plan for the Northside YMCA. He was a successful entrepreneur and operated the only black-owned business on the Boardwalk. His bathhouse at the foot of Texas Avenue served both races for 25 years. While the term "social activist" had yet to be coined, that's what Walls was. Walls was a dynamic leader who spearheaded numerous causes on the Northside. He lent a helping hand to many blacks in need of assistance in the off-season, frequently with loans to help in starting a business or pursuing higher education. The Northside YMCA was only one of the accomplishments for which he is remembered.

Cain left Princeton and returned to Atlantic City in May 1914, when he was named executive secretary of the Colored Branch YMCA. At the time he came to town, the Northside YMCA operated out of a small cottage on North New York Avenue where it had been founded. In 1930, after 16 years of tireless efforts, under Cain's direction, the Y moved to a new building on Arctic Avenue. It included a gymnasium, recreation room, showers, and dormitory accommodations. Funded entirely through private donations, the Northside YMCA was constructed at a cost of approximately $250,000. (The property is located at 1711 Arctic Avenue. The building remains and is currently the Disston Apartments.) Cain served as executive secretary, doing everything from raising money and recruiting members to managing the finances and training staff. For more than 20 years, the Arctic Avenue branch of the YMCA, or Northside Y as it came to be known, was directed by Cain.

The only interruptions in Cain's tenure at the Y from 1914 to 1936 were a year at the Lincoln University Seminary, where he earned a master's degree in divinity, and 18 months serving in the U.S. Army as a chaplain. After World War I, while on one of his frequent visits to Lincoln, Cain made the acquaintance of a young woman. His stature in the community made him highly sought after to accompany young ladies to social events, and he probably could have had his pick of any number of local women. But Effie Davis, who had ties to his alma mater, was the woman he chose to woo. Several years later, they were married.

The news article from the February 23, 1924, edition of the *Atlantic City Daily Press* reporting on the wedding captures not only the bride and groom but an era when refinement was the standard to which people aspired:

> One of the most talked about weddings of the season was solemnized at 4 o'clock when Miss Effie Nocho Davis, daughter of Mr. and Mrs. John L. Davis of Oxford, Pa. became the bride of C. Morris Cain, executive secretary of the Arctic Branch YMCA …
>
> Immediately following the ceremony the bride and groom entrained to New York City for a fortnight's honeymoon. They expect to visit Boston for several days, during the two weeks. Returning to the shore, the couple will make their home at 1805 Arctic Avenue. The bride, an exceptionally pleasing and charming young woman, up to a few weeks ago when she resigned, was a teacher at the Oxford High School, where she received her preliminary training. She is a graduate of the West Chester Normal School for Teachers, from where she was called immediately upon graduation to teach at Oxford High School.
>
> Interested as he is in every phase of community uplift and being especially zealous of the boyhood of this city, Mr. Cain is one of the best-known and best-liked men in the resort. He has been a resident of the resort since boyhood and long before he was given charge of the Arctic Avenue Branch YMCA, worked as a bellman under his now deceased uncle at the Chalfonte Hotel.

"Community uplift" was the purpose to which Cain devoted his life. The Northside YMCA was his primary vehicle for pursuing his work. By the time he moved the Y into its new quarters in 1930, he was working with a staff of seven full-time assistants and dozens of volunteers. In that year, the program had a membership of more than 250 young black men from the Northside. Cain and his staff put in place a program aimed at strengthening character, mind, and body.

It's not a secret that Cain recruited students for his alma mater. He wanted them to have the same opportunities he had enjoyed, and many young men from the Northside went off to Lincoln University at his urging. During summer recess, Cain's recommendation virtually guaranteed a college student seasonal work in Atlantic City— typically at the top hotels, where the best pay and tips were assured. A large majority of the Lincoln students Cain mentored not only graduated but went on to successful careers in law, medicine, education, and the church.

Through Cain's leadership, the Arctic Avenue YMCA became the headquarters for many black community organizations and clubs. These groups reached out to hundreds of young people, regardless of whether they were Y members. Under Cain's direction, the entire community was uplifted by the activities of the Northside Y.

Thanks largely to Cain's efforts, the Y became a social incubator, stimulating the growth of organizations complementing the efforts of the network of black churches. Many groups got their start after initially meeting at the Y under the tutelage of Morris Cain. Among them were the Northside Business and Professional Women's Club, Young Men's Progressive Club, the Lion's Social Club, the Women's Home Missionary Society, the Lincoln University Alumni Associates, two of Atlantic City's four black Boy Scout troops, and—critical to providing financial "uplift"—the Great Building and Loan Association and the Northside Board of Trade.

The Building and Loan, as it was referred to, was owned and operated by black investors for black patrons. It was one of only a handful that existed in the nation at the time. The Board of Trade likewise made many loans, but the source of those funds was at times somewhat less than conventional. Both of these financial institutions had their start in the Northside Y.

In 1916, the Northside Young Women's Christian Association (YWCA) was founded by Maggie Ridley, an active civic leader who was co-owner of the popular Hotel Ridley and one of the founding members of the Jethro Memorial Presbyterian Church. Cain was a member and one of the unofficial pastors of Jethro. He lent his knowledge and guidance to the effort, and the women's Y was a success. The Northside YWCA operated an employment bureau and provided counseling services to young women. The primary focus was self-improvement through education and training in marketable skills. Young women were taught how to prepare a resume, how to conduct themselves in an interview, and the basics of working with the public, whether it be in an office, shop, or hotel.

Facilities at the women's Y were too small for recreational programs, so young women used the gymnasium facilities at the Arctic Avenue branch of the YMCA. An offshoot of the women's Y was the Northside Business and Professional Women's Club. An inspiration to club members was local businesswoman extraordinaire, Sara Spencer Washington, whose financial empire was headquartered on the Northside. She was a generous contributor and a frequent speaker before the club. In 1930, the club became part of the National Association of Colored Women's Clubs, whose motto was "Lifting As We Climb." The association operated under a five-point program of Education, Employment, Housing, Health, and Legislation. The two Ys and their spin-offs weren't Cain's only contributions to the community.

Most important, Cain and other like-minded college graduates of his generation served as outstanding role models. They demonstrated the crucial role of education in improving the condition of all black people. These educated young men and women accepted the responsibilities of leadership and worked tirelessly to make the Northside a nurturing environment for African-American children. Reminiscent of the ancient African proverb, "It takes a village to raise a child," the Northside was a tight-knit community in which everyone knew their neighbors' children and didn't hesitate to correct them for unsocial behavior. "I remember one time I teased a younger boy by refusing to give back his baseball glove. Mrs. Thomas came off her front porch and gave me a scolding I remember to this day." But Cain understood it took more than disciplining children to ensure their healthy upbringing.

Cain appreciated the fact that a nurturing environment began in the home. But you need a *house* to create a *home*. Most black people in Atlantic City wrestled with the need for safe, sanitary, and affordable housing. It was a constant struggle.

Seasonal income and local banks unwilling to make loans to most black people meant that few were able to purchase homes. Many Northside residents were beleaguered by living conditions beyond their control. They often found themselves at the mercy of out-of-town landlords. For the lower stratum of workers, namely, those employed as bellmen, busboys, porters, dishwashers, kitchen helpers, amusement ride operators, laundresses, and those hired to perform a multitude of menial tasks—the ones last to be hired and first to be let go at the end of the season—the housing needs were urgent. Some were literally stranded in the resort at the end of the summer, having come to town with the intention of merely working for the summer and then moving on with their saved earnings. For those with no savings at the end of the summer, theirs was a hard-scrabble existence in the off-season, many living hand-to-mouth, scrambling to keep a roof over their heads. Cain made it his mission to address their needs. His efforts culminated in the construction of Stanley S. Holmes Village, the first public housing in the state of New Jersey. The story of Cain's successful efforts in bringing about Stanley Holmes requires some background.

Atlantic City has always shown a happy face to the world. To say that the town viewed itself generally, and the precarious financial circumstances of black people in particular, through rose-color glasses is an understatement. The Kuehnle-Johnson regimes and the key players of the "Boardwalk Empire" were in perpetual denial about the state of affairs of the community upon which it relied so heavily. From the perspective afforded by time, it's apparent that maintaining the town's status as a successful resort involved some serious juggling by its leaders. It was a mix of moxie, manipulation, and money spread around that kept things going. Always known, but rarely discussed and never formally acknowledged by the local power establishment, were the miserable housing conditions of the lower stratum of hotel workers who lived in town year-round but worked only seasonally.

Nearly everyone in town with the exception of those employed with the city or the county worked at seasonal jobs. A tax base that yielded revenue year-round, and the demands for service from government being limited primarily to the summer months, meant that the local government payrolls were padded with loyal "no-shows" who were overwhelmingly white. A significant portion of these government employees also had positions in a hotel-resort business during the summer. They could afford decent housing and had the resources to make it through the winter months. Hundreds of white business owners and their managers left town at the end of the summer season. A lucky handful of their key black employees lived at the property in the off-season. Those workers in the upper and middle strata—the class of persons who were employed as boarding-house keepers, headwaiters, stewards, chefs, head bellmen, and rolling chair managers—were able to conserve their funds and make it though the off-season. But for the lower stratum, that was next to impossible. The churches and the Kuehnle-Johnson organization could only do so much. Food, clothing, coal, and occasional cash handouts didn't put a roof over people's heads. The housing available for most of the lower stratum workers was poorly constructed, with no thought given to maintenance. The frequent practice of doubling up—with multiple families living in a residence designed for one—had harsh consequences.

Much of the housing stock existing in the first quarter of the 20th century had been built during the boom period following the coming of the second railroad. In the 1880s to 1890s, there were no zoning ordinances or uniform construction codes. Although there were safety and construction material standards for larger buildings mandated by insurance companies, architects, and engineers, houses were built to standards established almost entirely by the developer. Those standards were anything but "uniform." Any uniformity in construction was more a product of the materials offered for sale by suppliers than by government regulation. In truth, much of the housing erected during the boom period was meant for seasonal occupancy. Moreover, it was intended for single-family occupancy.

Throughout the poorer sections of the Northside, street after street (many unpaved), row upon row, there were erected, slab on grade, strings of narrow clapboard houses, hastily thrown together. These homes were constructed of flimsy materials, the type used for sheds and storage buildings of the hotels and boardinghouses several blocks away. The roofs were made of the cheapest quality sheathing and tin. For most, there were neither insulation nor rain gutters, and the windows rattled noisily during a nor'easter. Live poultry was common, and chickens and ducks had free reign of the streets, leaving behind their feces. Many of the homes were heated with coal in a cast-iron potbelly stove in the main room of the house. The stove was used for both heating and cooking. The smell of the smoldering embers imparted to the home and all its occupants an acrid stench that lingered with both into the late spring. Carelessly installed and poorly maintained privies (a barrier island is no place for outhouses) pocked neighborhoods and were particularly rank during the summer.

"How much rent can we charge?" was the main question on the minds of those who developed housing for employees in the hotel-resort economy. For many of the workers struggling to make a year-round home in Atlantic City, the question was answered, in part, by factoring in money they received from taking in boarders who came to town to work during the summer season. The arithmetic worked well for the landlords and for some of their tenants who engaged in subletting, but the math worked terribly for the structures themselves.

Over-occupancy put severe strains on the Northside's housing supply. Absent any serious maintenance, the properties deteriorated quickly. The decrepit state of much of the housing was like something out of the Jim Crow South. At least sharecroppers had the open space of the land they tilled. The closeness of the living quarters for many of Atlantic City's black population conjured up the cheek-by-jowl conditions of the slave ships. There were sections on the Northside where the squalor and decay were a huge embarrassment to a city that hosted millions each summer. Leaders in the black community, including Cain, had decried the situation for years to no avail. The scope of the problem was beyond their where-withal to resolve.

The housing situation for Atlantic City's black people came into startling focus with the downturn brought on by the Great Depression. Vacations were one of the first things to go when the American economy collapsed in 1929. Atlantic City was no longer a national resort. Philadelphia's working class continued coming, but most were day-trippers coming by train, with many visiting solely to gamble and frequent the city's bars and taverns. The 1930s brought hard times to the resort as it did for the rest of the nation. Many land-lords stopped paying taxes and any maintenance of residential rental properties, whether by owner or tenant, ceased.

Scores of longtime, well-established businesses went under. The survivors had to scrounge to get by. With every hotel, boardinghouse, restaurant, bar, and laundry that closed, the economic condition on the Northside grew more precarious. Nearly all of the major hotels along the Boardwalk were operating in the red, and 10 of the 14 local banks were forced to close, bringing financial ruin to many local investors. By 1938, real estate assessments had shrunk to one-third of their 1930 high of $317 million, and the tax rate was one of the highest in the state, causing many residents to lose their homes at tax sale. The small percentage of black homeowners who survived did so by taking in boarders, which further strained the condition of their properties. City government was unable to make payroll, and the issuance of "scrip money" was how many employees were paid. Merchants who accepted scrip had to hold it until the city was able to redeem it, which was usually many months. "You had to abide by the rules for turning scrip into real money. If you didn't fill out the right forms and get everything in at just the right time, you could be left holding worthless paper." By the end of the 1930s, Atlantic City's per capita debt was not only the highest for its class of 30,000 to 100,000 year-round residents, but it was higher than that of any other city in the country.

Repeal of Prohibition in 1933 made things worse. The resort had been a "wet town," and most observers agree that the period during which the 18th Amendment to the U.S. Constitution was in effect (1920–1933) were Atlantic City's best years. What was intended as a boost to portions of the nation's economy deepened the resort's financial problems. The end of Prohibition stripped Atlantic City of its competitive advantage in attracting conventions, an advantage that it had enjoyed for 14 years and brought home the effects of the Great Depression in very stark terms. As ever, the people hit the hardest by the economic downturn were those living on the margins. Black workers were the first to be let go when the numbers of visitors declined. Complicating things further was the willingness of unemployed whites to work at jobs that had previously been beneath them.

Prior to the Great Depression, many white residents refused jobs in which "tips" were an integral part of the pay. Gratuities for personal services were not looked upon well in white society. Free white workers were paid an honest wage for an honest day's work. Only black people worked for handouts. But hard times made carrying bags and waiting on tables more attractive. An already meager job market tightened further. "Come the Great Depression, more and more white people started lookin' for work in the hotels and restaurants. The season had gotten shorter as it was. Out-of-work white people made for competition the people on the Northside didn't need. The '30s were desperate times."

Housing needs of the unemployed, black and white alike, had become desperate. Help from beyond Atlantic City was needed. In 1933, the Civic Committee for Better Housing was formed. Its aim was to secure financing through the housing division of the Public Works Administration, one of several federal agencies created by Franklin Roosevelt's administration in response to the Great Depression. The committee's goal was for Atlantic City to be the first community in New Jersey to "provide public housing to counteract the ill effects of the unsanitary and unsafe housing that existed in slum areas."

As a member of the committee, Cain was actively involved in its work. The first task in securing the needed funds was to quantify the need. No one appreciated "the wretched conditions of the crowded homes of the Northside" better than Morris Cain. He had been counseling children and ministering to the needs of families from some of the poorest neighborhoods for many years. He understood their plight. Working with officials from the State Housing Authority, Cain and several Northside Y members participated in a study that inventoried the city's housing.

For purposes of the investigation, the city was divided into nine sections, referred to as "housing tracts." The tracts "were economically and socially homogeneous—the dwellings in a single section had similar facilities. Thus, a true picture was obtained of how people in a particular area lived." The study found that "the chief blot" of blighted housing was Housing Tract No. 6. Predictably Tract No. 6 was located in "the Negro section known as the Northside." According to the committee's report:

> Of the 2,843 structures in Tract No. 6, 1,059 needed major repairs and 592 were unfit for use. This disproportion reflected the abysmal lack of sanitary facilities as well as structural defects in the buildings. Almost 40 percent of the structures had only stoves for heating, and 946 had no hot running water. Families in 145 of the units had no running water whatever. Toilet facilities were as bad: 176 units had a partial use of hall toilets, and 609 units

were entirely without indoor water closets. And in this section 949 units had no bathtubs or showers. In 27 percent of the homes oil or coal was used for cooking, and 18 percent did not have electricity ... the site, besides lacking the most rudimentary facilities, was so overcrowded that it gave rise to intense social problems.

The committee's report was a compelling plea. Thanks in large part to the information compiled by Cain, Atlantic City was first in line among the applicants to the newly created Public Works Administration of Roosevelt's New Deal. The request for financing was granted. If there was a city neighborhood somewhere in New Jersey during the Great Depression with a greater need for public housing than the Northside, which was unlikely, it got funded later. An eight-acre parcel of land bounded by Baltic, Illinois, Adriatic, and Kentucky Avenues was selected as the site for what was to be a model for other public housing and a showplace to demonstrate to visitors that the State of New Jersey and Atlantic City looked after their poor. "Before the houses on the site were demolished, fumigation produced bushels of dead rats from the old dwellings ..."

The initial phase of the development comprised "16 two- and three-story fireproof buildings containing 277 apartments of 928 rooms. One hundred and eighty-four are three-room units; 89, four-room; and 4, five-room ... Each apartment contains a living room, kitchen, bath and from one to three bedrooms ... Bedrooms are located to insure privacy and to afford the maximum exposure to light and air ... Grouped around two large landscaped areas, the buildings form eight quadrangles which serve as playgrounds for the children. The large open spaces are in effect a park." (Unfortunately, three generations later, "park" was not the name anyone would use to describe these quadrangles.)

Named in honor of Stanley S. Holmes, first chairman of the State Housing Authority, construction commenced in July 1936. At typical Atlantic City pace, construction went quickly and was completed by spring of the following year. Cain had not only inventoried the dwellings but the people as well and, thanks to his efforts, the State Housing Authority was ready to move quickly in designating eligible tenants. The first tenants moved in on April 16, 1937. The entire complex was rented out by July and a large waiting list showed that the demand had been only partially met. Within a short time, a second phase of 156 additional units was constructed. Closely following the Stanley Holmes project was the development of an apartment complex earmarked primarily for working poor Italian-Americans who could not afford decent housing. "On May 4, 1939, President Roosevelt approved the application for a low-rent housing development for white families." This project was known as Jonathan Pitney Village and was located at Georgia and Fairmont Avenues. The efforts of Cain and the members of the Civic Committee for Better Housing benefited the entire community.

Not surprising, in October 1936, Cain was selected by the city to manage Stanley Holmes. According to Walter Buzby, chairman of the Atlantic City Housing Authority, "The name of Cain was so outstanding that no other citizen was even thought of." Cain resigned from his position with the Northside Y and threw himself into his new position. Living in the penthouse at the nearby Liberty Apartments on Baltic Avenue, Cain spent most of his waking hours not only seeing to the management of the apartment buildings, but more importantly, ministering to the needs of the families living there. He made full use of the community building at the development, creating a satellite Y for both sexes and all ages. Cain helped organize the Village Boys Club, sewing circles, arts and craft clubs, the Father's Club, and discussion groups to deal with problems of raising children. Finally, he launched a credit union, which encouraged savings and provided low-interest loans for the apartment residents.

Shortly after moving from the Y to Stanley Holmes, the Northside community decided to honor Cain. On the evening of May 25, 1938, Arctic Avenue was closed between Illinois and Indiana Avenues. There was a huge street party organized by the churches, civic clubs, fraternities, sororities, and lodges on the Northside. It was an extraordinary event the likes of which the city had rarely seen. The occasion was attended by many hundreds of people, from both the black and white communities, whose lives had been touched by C. Morris Cain. Music was provided by the YMCA Glee Club, and more than 100 voices were heard singing in tribute to Cain. A new neon sign for the Y was unveiled and dedicated to Cain for 20+ years of service to the youth of Atlantic City.

The list of speakers was long and several need highlighting. Dr. Channing Tobias, senior secretary of the Colored Department of the National Council YMCA, delivered the dedicatory address, stating, "The light is placed as a symbol of Christian character and a noble method of recognizing distinguished service for the youth of America." Another speaker that evening was Dr. Walter L. Wright, president of Lincoln University. He stated that Cain was "… honest in business, outstanding in character and an honor to the institution from whence he came." (Several years later at Lincoln's 1940 graduation ceremonies, Cain was awarded an honorary Doctorate of Humane Letters.) Master of ceremonies, Hibberd Smith, noted that throughout his career Cain was responsible for securing summer employment for hundreds of Lincoln students in the resort's hotel-resort industry. Most of these young men were from communities where there were no "summer jobs" for black people other than farming. They could never earn the kind of money they made in Atlantic City. Cain's name as a reference was a sufficient credential for many local hotels. Because of the many students he had helped, Morris Cain was a legend at Lincoln University.

That evening Cain was presented with a gold watch from the entire community, with the formal presentation being made by County Prosecutor Joseph Altman. Many congratulatory notes from distinguished people throughout the country were read by Mary J. Washington. Probably the most touching message was an elegy written for the occasion and delivered by the poet Ira Yemmens. It is titled, "Service." The poem contains 12 stanzas and 48 lines and chronicles Cain's service to the community. As Yemmens delivered his elegy, tears welled in the eyes of many people in the crowd. The poem reads in part:

> So, helping young men in their battle with life,
> While a fourth of a century went by;
> Teaching that fellowship lessens the strife,
> Stood Cain at the head of the Y . . .
>
> There's an art in the giving the best that you can,
> To a world that is rude as can be;
> There's an art in being an unselfish man,
> When so few things in life come free . . .

Cain served as manager and then supervisor of project services at Stanley Holmes for the next 18 years, retiring in 1954. Following retirement, he continued to give freely of his time, energy, and knowledge to the people on the Northside. Cain also remained an active alumnus of Lincoln University. He was responsible for staging Thanksgiving Day football games between his alma mater and Howard University in Atlantic City's Convention Hall and for bringing his university's ensemble to town to sing at special occasions. (The last performance by Lincoln's singers during his lifetime was at the Margate Community Church during National Brotherhood Week on February 18, 1962.)

Using his own funds, Cain created scholarships for worthy Lincoln students and personally shepherded many local youths off to college to begin careers in professions that would nourish their lives and those of other black Americans. An ordained Presbyterian minister, he often served, when asked, as pastor of Jethro Memorial United Presbyterian Church. He was stricken with a heart attack and died at age 79 on March 31, 1962, one day before he was scheduled to deliver the Sunday sermon at his church. Although many wish they could have heard his final sermon, no one believes he left behind unfinished business. He accomplished deeds worthy of a dozen civic leaders.

How significant was Claiborn Morris Cain to his town's history? In terms of touching the lives of those around him, he stands tall. Born two months apart, Morris Cain and Nucky Johnson were contemporaries. Johnson was born in January 1883, Cain in March of the same year. Johnson was steeped in Atlantic City politics from an early age, and from his youth, he had a sense of the town and his entitlement to rule it. Cain was the grandchild of former slaves and grew up determined that he and his generation would transcend that dreadful experience. Their styles were very different, but each had a flair for connecting with people and their careers merit a comparison.

Relying on guile and finesse, Nucky charmed the people of Atlantic City. Using money secured from many corrupt sources and the power to ease the hurt of the off-season by putting people on the public payroll, he bought the loyalty and affection of residents, black and white alike. When necessary, those he couldn't win over were either shunned by his supporters or bullied into silence by the foot soldiers of his organization. Shrewd, calculating, flamboyant, boisterous, and bent on a hell-raising good time, Nucky epitomized the qualities that made Atlantic City a successful resort. Cain was anything but cunning. Dedicated to his community, the people on the Northside admired and loved him for the unselfish way in which he gave of his time and energy to others. He was an educator in the true sense of the word—a very hands-on one who wanted people to have experiences that would enrich their lives and assist them in fulfilling their potential. Proud without being arrogant, ambitious and driven, and always patient, cooperative, and courteous, Cain was the picture of humility. He was a living sermon on the importance of faith, family, hard work, and education. By both word and deed, he inspired his community and led those who followed him to personal independence.

Nucky's legacy has two sides: the memory of good times from Atlantic City's days of glory, and the flip side, a city incapable of honest government. Cain's legacy is more, or less, tangible. As result of his efforts, hundreds of young people had their lives enriched and matured into model citizens; though, alas, over time many of them moved away. Despite the eventual turn of events in the Northside's fortunes, Cain remains a giant of his era. People of his stature are few and far between.

Although it was the job offer of his uncle that initially brought Cain to Atlantic City, what made him return after college was the town's opportunities and his own sense of responsibility to his people. At the time, the resort was the most "black city" in the northern U.S. Because of the varied job opportunities and thousands of positions in the hotel-resort economy, it was a place many African Americans considered a trendsetter for the greater black society in terms of mobility in the workplace.

By 1915, the black population was 11,000-plus, comprising 27 percent of the resort's permanent residents—a percentage more than five times that of any other northern city. During the summer months, the black population swelled to nearly 40 percent. At the same time, blacks comprised a staggering 95 percent of the hotel workforce. Of those northern cities having more than 10,000 black residents, Atlantic City was without any serious rival in terms of percentage of total population.

In addition to hoteliers and businessmen, there was the traditional array of professionals. Atlantic City's black community came of age at a point in time when HBCUs were graduating thousands of students trained in the disciplines of medicine, dentistry, divinity, law, and education. The young graduates were essential to building a city within a city. These eager professionals were attracted to Atlantic City as a place where they knew their skills would be welcomed and, equally important, as a community of black people with a sufficient population base to permit them to make a living at their chosen professions. The town wasn't just a mecca for hotel workers. By 1930, the Northside had in residence 12 medical doctors, five attorneys, three dentists, four pharmacists, five registered nurses, five morticians, 13 full-time clergymen, 85 teachers, and three school principals, plus many businesspeople, all of whom had been educated in HBCUs. That the needs and resources of the community could attract and sustain such a cross section of trained professionals attests to its robustness.

The needs of the Northside community were served well by their professionals. The career of one physician in particular illustrates how important the community was to him. Shedrick LeRoy Morris had heard that Atlantic City needed doctors and, after completing his medical studies, made his way to the resort. Born in Lexington, Virginia, on April 10, 1865, as the American Civil War was coming to an end, he was a graduate of Lincoln University and Howard University Medical School. In 1898, he moved his family to Atlantic City and set up a medical practice the following year. As recalled by Dr. Morris's daughter, Amaza Lockett, "When my father first started, he had a horse and buggy ... they had stables around here in Atlantic City where the horse was kept, and he went from call to call in a horse and buggy." To service the needs of the poor, in 1906, Dr. Morris and his wife opened a 24-hour drugstore on the first floor of his two-story house at 109 North New York Avenue. During the winter months, credit was extended to most customers and nearly all paid their bills come summer. The drugstore also doubled as a "sub–post office" for the Northside, a branch of the main post office, overseen by Mrs. Morris.

Like many young professionals educated at HBCUs, Dr. Morris was civic-minded and used his talents and training for more than making money. He was imbued with the philosophy of service to others and was particularly concerned with the poorest members of the community. Again, Dr. Morris's daughter noted:

> The one thing I remember about him is that he was always deeply concerned; even though he had a good practice here in Atlantic City for many, many years, he was always deeply concerned about the people who did not have sufficient money to hire a physician. He would go out any hour of the night to make calls to these people who needed medical attention—any hour of the night.

In 1910, Dr. Morris was hired by the city to serve as "physician to the indigenous poor"—a position that he held until his death in 1936. Dr. Shedrick Morris played a significant leadership role on the issues affecting the people on the Northside. One of the many needs he tackled was care of the elderly poor.

Confronted by discrimination and forced segregation, turn-of-the-century black leaders began to establish social agencies on the Northside. The first permanent social agency created by black people was a home for the elderly. Dr. Morris and his colleagues, Drs. Walter Fayerman and George Fletcher, played major roles in establishing the home. It's believed that the idea for a home had its origins with Maggie Wayman, co-owner of the Wayman Inn. She worked together with Mary Fletcher, Rebecca Bush, Carrie Morton, Mary Gamble, and others in getting things started. "I knew Miss Fletcher and Miss Gamble as a boy. They were old by then but they were strong-willed women who knew how to get things done. As long as you did what they said, everything was fine. Cross them and you'd have a headache." Under the direction of these ladies, the physicians were recruited and the Old Folks Home and Sanitarium opened its doors at 127 Bay Street in 1898. This group of community-minded persons started their project with little more than several beds and blankets.

The mission of the Old Folks Home was to provide convalescent care for worthy black persons in need, regardless of religion, 65 years or older, at low cost. Their commitment was to provide basic shelter and care for aged persons who could no longer support themselves and had no family to look after them. Throughout the more than 70 years of its existence, it was one of only a tiny handful of homes for the aged in New Jersey neither operated for profit nor sponsored by a religious or fraternal organization. With the help of the community, the Old Folks Home grew and the doctors and the group then rented a small house on Delaware Avenue. The home had the support of Northside residents and was run by a Board of Managers consisting of 15 people who investigated and approved all admissions and established charges depending upon need.

The home's original policy was to guarantee lifetime care to its residents in return for an admission fee of $300. In short order, this proved impractical, and payments from the residents and their families plus contributions from the community and churches were needed to keep things going. The home prospered and grew—having a peak resident count of 38 seniors—moving several times until it bought its first permanent facility at 416 N. Indiana Avenue in 1919 (where it remained until 1957). Renamed the Colored Old Folks Home of Atlantic City, it was managed well and after several successful fundraising drives, on July 14, 1922, the Board of Managers had a formal ceremony at the Price Memorial Church where the mortgage was burned in celebration. The next seven years were for the home—as for Atlantic City—some of its best, but then the Great Depression hit hard. Through the 1930s, the home struggled, and it was only through the dedication of Pauline Bell, matron of the home, with help from wives of several local ministers, that the home was able to keep it doors open. But the elderly weren't the only ones in need of social services.

As the permanent black population increased, numerous other social societies were established. These groups were often "secret societies" akin to the Masonic Order. These societies were among the vehicles used by blacks to cope with their minority status. As early as the Revolutionary period, free blacks found it desirable to join together for social and cultural improvement, economic self-help, and mutual relief. The secret societies provided their members with one of the few opportunities for group expression and cooperation outside of the church. The first such society in Atlantic City was the Masons, with the Prince Hall Lodge being founded in 1881. By 1900, Atlantic City had more than a dozen black secret societies. Besides the Prince Hall Masons and their auxiliary, the Order of the Eastern Star, there were the Independent Order of Good Samaritans, the Grand United Order of True Reformers, and the Elks.

Besides looking after one another and providing a death benefit to the families of deceased brothers, these groups reached out to the broader community. Sometimes working with the Republican organization, often with churches, they helped create a social safety net for the residents on the Northside. They prepared meals for the elderly and poor during the winter months and holidays and lent financial aid to fellow residents who had fallen on hard times. Societies such as the Masons and Elks emphasized moral and social uplift of the black race through the conduct of individual members and provided charity to the less fortunate. The Good Samaritans and True Reformers took the lead in providing insurance and business loans for their members. All these societies met at the Mason's Hall at North Michigan and Arctic Avenues.

Among the more than 80 different social clubs and groups that met regularly (many in one of the Northside Ys) were the American Legion, Veterans of Foreign Wars, Ambassador Social Club, Gentlemen of Sports, Algonquin Civic and Social Club, and four separate chapters of the Parent Teacher Association. It was difficult to find a Northside resident whose life was untouched by one of these groups, whether as a member or recipient of charitable works.

Many of the societies and groups existing on the Northside had their genesis as offshoots of national white organizations. As had occurred with the traditional Protestant church organizations, when the number of black people became too numerous for whites to tolerate, African Americans were forced to start organizations of their own—sometimes with aid from the white national organization, sometimes not.

A vibrant social network was indicative of an economically viable community. The salaries earned by black people in the local hotel-resort economy made it possible for neighborhood businesses to blossom. This critical mass of African-American wage earners created an environment that attracted entrepreneurs, large and small alike. As a miniature metropolis, the Northside provided a full range of businesses such as restaurants, cafés, beauty parlors, pool rooms, barbershops, garages, laundries, funeral parlors, drugstores, confectionery stores, tailor and dress shops, grocery stores, florists, printing shops, butcher shops, boardinghouses, and hotels. One successful entrepreneur of that era stands out. She was extraordinary for her time or any time.

6

Building Blocks

She had tasted power yet remained sober, understood glamour but prized integrity above all, stressed the importance of economic progress for black people—and all people.
—Jim Waltzer, journalist

Wanamaker's was one of the finest department stores in America. An anchor of Philadelphia's central shopping district, it attracted the wealthy and the near wealthy. In its prime, the first half of the 20th century, Wanamaker's didn't cater to working-class people, which naturally included all African Americans—or so thought the foolish young white salesgirl working in the fur department that day as she said to herself, *What is this Negro woman doing here? She must be lost. I'll put her in her place!*

Attired in a silk brocade dress and smartly tailored wool coat, with leather handbag and shoes to match, her coiffure and make-up tastefully understated, the only thing about this customer that didn't fit in at Wanamaker's was the color of her skin. The officious, young bit-of-a-snip had asked her—no, rather *told* her—to wait. Patient at first, this elegant-looking black woman was now doing a slow burn. She had waited, and waited, then waited yet again as the clerk helped several customers who had arrived after her. She decided the salesgirl had ignored her long enough.

"Excuse me."

The clerk looked up from the cash register, where she was busying herself. She responded with a saccharin sweet smile and voice.

"I'm sorry. I'll be with you as soon as I can."

What happened next couldn't have been scripted better had it been a scene in a Spike Lee movie. The fur department supervisor happened to be making her rounds and noticed her longtime customer near the counter.

"Mrs. Washington," the supervisor said warmly. "Back so soon?"

Madame Sara Spencer Washington returned her smile. "I'd like to get one more."

The supervisor sized up the situation quickly. She stepped toward the salesclerk and in a low, icy whisper ordered, "Another mink, my dear—*now!*"

Moments later, after knowledgeably examining several furs, Madame Washington settled on one she liked. Without skipping a beat, she promptly wrote a personal check for the price tag of $4,600. Given the year—1946, when a working person's home in Atlantic City could be had for less than $5,000—the purchase price was equivalent to more than 10 times that amount today. The supervisor knew something the salesgirl didn't: Sara Washington could have written a check to buy most of Wanamaker's fur inventory.

Pricey for certain, but she had made her point, the same as many times before. Once after a waiter had treated her rudely, Madame Washington responded by renting the entire restaurant for an evening and filling it with her friends and employees. Indignant that blacks were not acknowledged in Atlantic City's famed Boardwalk Easter Parade, in 1946—the same year she wrote the check for the fur at Wanamaker's—she launched an annual parade of her own on Arctic Avenue, featuring black women in furs and broad-rimmed hats and men in brightly colored suits with canes and fedoras. Leading her parade that first year was none other than the legendary song-and-dance man, Bill "Bojangles" Robinson, a regular performer in the Northside's entertainment district. To go one better, the parade was followed by a fashion show and a champagne brunch the next morning at the famed Club Harlem. Together, the parade and fashion show became the highlight of the spring season.

Throughout her life, Washington put the white world on notice that she would neither tolerate prejudice nor would anyone consign her to second-rate status. A woman of means and moxie, she was no one to trifle with.

Born on June 6, 1889, in Norfolk, Virginia, the daughter of Joshua and Ellen Phillips, Washington was determined to make her mark in the world from a young age. She attended a public school in Beckley, a small village in Princess Anne County that is now part of the city of Virginia Beach. She then went onto Norfolk Mission College, which, despite its name, offered a full academic program. After graduation, eager to find a profession and start a business to call her own, she studied hairdressing in York, Pennsylvania, and later did advanced work in chemistry at Columbia University. A dressmaker from 1908 to 1913, Washington ignored the urgings of her family, who wanted her to become a schoolteacher. Instead she embarked upon a career in which early innovator and African-American entrepreneur Madame C. J. Walker had made a fortune.

Washington entered what was then the relatively new field of beauty culture. Although Walker had New York City for her headquarters, Atlantic City is where Washington made her mark and the base from which she established a financial empire, making her accomplishments all the more remarkable. Walker's career in business came to an end as Washington's was beginning, but the parallels in their paths to success are unmistakable. Both women were creative, dynamic, and resourceful—marketing geniuses who were determined to be the masters of their own destiny. Fiercely independent, they would never permit themselves to be beholden to the white world.

Washington moved to the resort in 1913 and planted herself on the Northside. In the same year, she started her own hairdressing business and quickly developed a reputation as a trendsetter whose customers always left her shop feeling better about themselves. Working days in her salon and teaching students her profession at the same time, she used her evenings to go door-to-door throughout the neighborhoods on the Northside, pitching her products. In retail sales, it doesn't get much tougher than knocking on the doors of strangers, making cold calls, yet that's how she got her empire started. Her commitment to her business wasn't shared by her husband. Not long after coming to the resort they divorced, though she kept her married surname. Within six years of her arrival, she founded, as sole owner and president, Apex Hair and News Company. She never looked back.

Soon, there was the Apex Beauty College. Its slogan was, "Now is the time to plan for your future by learning a depression-proof business." Opening a dozen beauty colleges in as many locales throughout the country and elsewhere, she educated young women in Atlantic City, New York, Washington, D.C., Baltimore, Richmond,

Chicago, Detroit, Philadelphia, Pittsburgh, Atlanta, the Caribbean Islands, and Johannesburg, South Africa. At its peak, Apex Beauty College graduated more than 4,000 students yearly. Madame Washington believed in her students and helped many of them to find employment after they'd completed their schooling. Her more ambitious graduates who wished to open beauty salons of their own received loans for start-up costs and credit for beauty products on generous terms.

Apex's Atlantic City plant, at Indiana and Arctic Avenues, manufactured more than 75 products. Raw materials were purchased by the railroad boxcar-load and, with her training in chemistry, many of the items produced were of her own formulas. Madame Washington received a patent for a hair curl-removal system and marketed it nationally, mostly by word-of-mouth and her own marketing techniques. "Glossatina" ensured sheen and pomades celebrated a sleek look, while specialized combs and brushes aided in the process. Perfumes, lipsticks, and facial creams of all sorts were also part of her line. Her many products, all directed to African Americans, were shipped out to stores and vendors across the country. She had her own delivery service using a fleet of company trucks and cars. Between production and delivery, she employed more than 215 women and men as chemists, lab technicians, administrative workers, instructors, delivery persons, and drivers, as well as more than 4,500 active Apex sales agents.

A highly inventive marketer, Madame Washington kept her agents and customers informed of what was going on in the lab and in the salon through her own public relations department. She published a journal, *Apex News*, geared to the needs of beauticians and sales representatives, and distributed it nationwide beginning in 1928. Keeping readers abreast of the latest trends in the hairstyling and beauty culture professions, it featured industry news along with "how-to" articles.

Sponsoring seminars and demonstrations for African-American business owners and groups across the nation—many having nothing to do with beauty culture—Washington was not interested solely in profits. A regular speaker at the Northside Business and Professional Women's Club, she was about the business of uplifting her race. What's difficult to appreciate today is that for people of her generation, slavery remained an ever-present memory, and the "uplifting" was about promoting economic self-reliance within the black community.

Madame Washington wanted to share her knowledge and educate African Americans on how to succeed in the business world. She understood well the importance of the social capital created by education. But success in business gave rise to capital comprised of hard cash, and Washington wanted black people to be financially self-reliant. Everywhere she spoke, she preached the importance of African Americans supporting one another and buying from black businesses. At the New York World's Fair in 1939, she received a medal honoring her as one of the outstanding businesswomen in the country. With her expertise in developing products, teaching their use, marketing and delivering them, and ultimately expanding her customer base with loans to start-up businesses, she was a model of the economic term "vertical integration."

Madame Washington didn't let Atlantic City's or America's refusal to accept racial integration stand in her way. She amassed a fortune. By 1946, some of her holdings included her beauty culture colleges, a drugstore in Atlantic City, Apex Farm, Apex Golf Course, and Apex Rest. Apex Farm was an active, 120-acre farm 15 miles outside of the resort in the mainland community of Galloway Township. The farm was purchased originally as a place for resort children to have a chance to learn about nature during the summer. Soon afterward, she acquired the Apex Golf Course in nearby Cologne, New Jersey, making her the first African-American golf course owner in America. The course gave black golfers access to the links and was the scene of numerous social and sporting events.

Located at Indiana and Ontario Avenues in the resort, Apex Rest was a 15-room hotel-resort center, including tennis courts, a dancing pavilion, and a croquet field. It was a grand place to entertain, and Washington never lost an opportunity simultaneously to party and market her Apex brand. Acquired initially for the use of her many employees and agents, Apex Rest was soon open to the public and became another moneymaker. Washington billed it as the "most exclusive, up-to-date hostelry in New Jersey," featuring "cool, clean, comfortable private rooms." She promoted Apex Rest as the "only place of its kind—surrounded by large spacious lawns—bright colored beach umbrellas—lawn service—for select families and tourists." Finally, in yet another example of the vertical integration

economic model, her advertising touted "good home cooking," noting, "all fresh vegetables—fruits—eggs—milk—direct from our
own Apex Farm."

Apex Rest wasn't the only hotel Washington owned. Fearing that
the owners might refuse to sell to a black woman or that neighbors
might try to block her purchase, she concealed her identity when
acquiring the Brigantine Hotel, in the nearby island community of
the same name, through the use of straw parties. In a search of
county records, local historian Jo Kapus learned that at one point the
property was sold to "a group of buyers named Mr. Truth Eternal,
Mrs. Peaceful Samuel, Meek and Lowly Joseph, Seraphim Light,
etc. These individuals were none other than Sara Spencer
Washington." But Washington didn't just use her wealth to acquire
things. She gave back to her community.

Charities, large and small, black and white, local and national all
benefited from Madame Washington's generosity. She contributed to
civic-minded groups of all races and creeds. The two Northside Ys
were among her favorites. She lent support to Horace J. Bryant Jr.,
an aspiring local black political candidate who was the first African
American to run for City Commission in Atlantic City. Washington
donated properties for homes to care for "wayward girls" in need of
a place to stay during their pregnancies and funded a summer camp
for disadvantaged children from Atlantic City and other African-
American communities. During the Depression, she hired an open-
cockpit airplane to fly over the resort and drop coupons good for a
quarter ton of coal. With the outbreak of World War II, she went to
work raising money for U.S. War Bonds and was so successful in this
effort—not to mention that she purchased a $10,000 bond of her
own—that she was flown to Portsmouth, Maine, to crack a bottle of
champagne on the hull of the S.S. *Harriet Tubman*, a U.S. Navy bat-
tleship named in honor of the distinguished former slave and abolitionist leader.

Shortly after the war, Washington had a battle of her own. In 1947,
she was paralyzed by a stroke. She fought back courageously, regaining her speech and eventually throwing away her cane. When death
took her in 1953, she left an estate of more than $1 million, at a time
when only a small fraction of Americans were millionaires. She was
a titan of both American commerce and her community and was so

recognized as one of the first inductees into the "Atlantic County Women's Hall of Fame" in 1997.

Stimulated by efforts such as Madame Sara Washington's, the Northside became an incubator for many businesses, large and small alike. Although few of these enterprises—black or white—experienced the level of success that Madame Washington had with Apex, the critical mass of African-American customers, matched with savvy entrepreneurs who understood their needs and tastes, enabled a dynamic economic society to emerge. The Northside business community blossomed in plain view of the resort's white power structure, which viewed it as a blessing. By 1920, the Northside had a "main street" of its own. Spanning from west to east, from Virginia Avenue to Arkansas Avenue, Arctic Avenue became the spine of commercial activity. Featuring a long string of retail shops, meeting places, boardinghouses, and churches, the avenue was the central nervous system of the resort's black community. The white community was relieved that black people had their own places to shop, eat, and mingle, thereby diminishing the chances of conflict with white establishments.

Today, two generations later, when the prevailing business types known by consumers are national chains and franchises, it's difficult to appreciate the predominance and strength of small businesses owned and operated by people living in the neighborhood. Atlantic City had thousands of independent businesses, and hundreds of them were owned by black people. In its prime, the Northside was a self-contained, vibrant community supporting locally owned firms that ran the gamut. Congregated primarily along Arctic Avenue and several side streets, there were scores of corner grocery stores along with restaurants and bars, gambling rooms, nightclubs, hair salons, barbershops, gas stations and garages, radio repair shops, furniture stores, laundries, funeral parlors, newsstands, tobacco shops, pharmacies, luncheonettes, candy shops, seamstresses and tailors, flower shops, stationery stores, meat markets, fish mongers, boardinghouses, and hotels.

Many of the business owners or their key employees lived above their places of business, making Arctic Avenue the classic mix of commercial and residential uses that was the thread that tied together so many small cities and towns across America in the first half of the 20th century. Today, city planners acknowledge that the loss of such mixed-use "downtowns" and their replacement by "strip shopping centers" hasn't meant progress. "Main Street" provided America, and Arctic Avenue gave the Northside, a *sense of place*. Both the nation and Atlantic City are poorer for the loss of these urban commons.

A partial listing from the 1940 Board of Trades annual publication (alas, neither the board nor any of the businesses remain) illustrates the dynamism of the commercial community that flourished within this miniature metropolis. Some of the business names and how they touted themselves to the public are:

Fanny's Café, 2001 Arctic Avenue: The brightest spot in town—Table service for ladies

Aimee's Streamline Beauty Salon, 1811 Arctic Avenue: Apex system—Only streamline in South Jersey

Winder's Ice Co., 226 North New Jersey Avenue: We deliver—Open all hours

Johnson's Garage, 11-15 North Ohio Avenue: Day & Night storage—Cars called for and delivered

Hotel Ridley, 1804-6 Arctic Avenue: Open all year— American & European Plan

Davis' Lunch Wagon, 1305½ Baltic Avenue: The only indoor Barbeque in South Jersey—Specializing in sandwiches of all kinds

Weeke's Tavern, 1702 Baltic Avenue: Where the goodfellows get together

Brown's Cigar Stores, 135 N. Pennsylvania & 901½ Baltic Avenue: Ice cream—Stationery—Tobacco—News Stand

College Valet Shop, 1623 Arctic Avenue: French dry cleaning—Pressing and repairing—Tailoring and hat blocking

Herb's Hotdog Stand, 303 North Indiana Avenue: Eat, drink and be merry

Emma B. Ferguson Florist, 24½ North Kentucky Avenue: Say it with flowers

Virginia's Variety Shop, 105½ N. Tennessee Avenue: Cigars—Cigarettes—Candies—Soft Drinks

Hattie's Royal Palms Rathskeller, 1915 Arctic Avenue: The Finest Wines & Liquors—Delicious Fried Chicken

The Paradise Club, No. Illinois Avenue: Where colored stars are made—Beautiful, Creole girls

Creole girls were a beautiful diversion, but there were Creole *guys* who were entrepreneurs in their own right. They didn't sell goods or provide services, but their enterprising ways were felt on the Northside and throughout the entire city. Gambling had flourished for years as part of the resort's economy. It finally found a home in the black community. An integral part of the Northside social and economic experience was the "numbers game," also known as the "policy game." It was brought to town by African Americans of West Indian descent.

Gambling was a luxury few people on the Northside could afford. The casinos, card rooms, and betting parlors that arose during the reign of Louis Kuehnle and expanded under Nucky Johnson were an important source of revenue for the Republican organization. These gambling establishments catered primarily to out-of-towners and some locals, but they were generally not open to black people. Although there would eventually be nightclubs that featured cards, craps, and roulette as part of their entertainment package, in the early days on the Northside there were no gambling enterprises per se. That changed with the arrival of the numbers game, or "Nigger Pool" as it was referred to in the urban Northeast.

Walter Greenidge was originally from Barbados. He had gone to work on the Panama Canal and, after the work was completed, in or around 1904, he headed to Pittsburgh. He wasn't there long. Friends—also with roots in the West Indies—told him about Atlantic City. There was a flourishing network of West Indies descendents all doing well in the resort economy. A significant percentage of those black people on the Northside employed in the professions and operating their own business were of Creole heritage. The people of the West Indies had a stronger tradition of literacy and their ancestors had been released from slavery several generations earlier than were many from the American South. The British culture of the "islands" was a far more enlightened one than that of the old Confederacy. Among island black people, education and self-reliance counted for much. Additionally, their family structure was not as fragmented. Those who arrived in Atlantic City—often indirectly from Washington, D.C., Baltimore, Pittsburgh, Philadelphia, Newark, and other northern cities—had formed the "Sons and Daughters of the Islands" and were an important part of the community. Sometime prior to 1920, Greenidge and his family made their way to the resort. Within a short time, he teamed up with his nephew Austin Clark to set up a "policy bank" and began taking bets in the form of a lottery that people could play daily.

The numbers game consisted of players betting on a series of three numbers from 0 to 999. A player won if his or her numbers matched a preset series of three numbers. Each day, a winning number was announced. In a community where many of the residents had little to no expendable income, the opportunity to place a bet for a quarter, dime, nickel, or even a penny enabled the game to catch on quickly.

Bets could be placed in bars, barbershops, cleaners, grocery stores, and other business establishments. Wagers could also be made with "runners" who came to your door. Trust was a key ingredient. Sometimes there were receipts for the number played, oftentimes not. Additionally, unlike today's lottery, bookies could extend credit. A player might ask, "Am I good for a dime?" If the player was a senior citizen, handicapped, or down on his luck, the answer was almost always "yes." Many bettors were regulars and played the same number daily. Without having to advance any money, players could live in the hope that an eventual win would pay off all their back debt and leave them with extra cash they would otherwise never see.

The odds were striking. Payoffs to winners of 500 and 600 to 1 were common. A single penny could yield a payoff of $50 to $60, enough to get most people through a month of expenses. What's more, winners never had to pay taxes. The "policy game" became enormously popular among Northside residents, and even professionals and so-called respectable people, including some of the clergy, placed bets daily.

The profits of the "policy bankers" were large, and several on the Northside in addition to Greenidge and Clark did very well, including Bruce Williams, Festus Braithwaite, Ike Nicholson, and Dutch Campbell, whose operations were primarily in the neighboring community of Pleasantville. (One successful policy banker, Raymond Shepperson, ran into problems with the numbers kingpins of Harlem. Shepperson found out they play rough in the Big Apple—he was murdered and dismembered.) The volume of money, both in coin and bills, created a logistical problem: how to handle so much cash. Two of the local banks helped launder the profits, but a steep premium was charged. Rather than share profits with white-owned banks that wouldn't lend money to black people, the policy bankers became heavily involved with the Northside Credit Union, which not only laundered the money but arranged loans for local businesses and residents. One of the financial architects of the credit union's workings and a key player in assisting the policy bankers in making loans in the community and investing their profits was Horace J. Bryant Jr., who years later became New Jersey's first African-American cabinet member, as Commissioner of Banking and Insurance. For now, suffice it to say that Bryant brought both know-how and integrity to the policy bankers' dealings through the Northside Credit Union.

Integrity of the numbers game was everything. Greenidge and the people who followed him into this new enterprise knew that bettors had to be confident that the daily winning number wasn't rigged. To ensure the game was run fairly, the winning number was always one that could be verified in a daily newspaper. It might be the last three numbers of the total trades of the New York Stock Exchange or the balance of the United States Treasury. After the Treasury began rounding off the balance, most bookies in the urban Northeast, including Greenidge and the other policy bankers on the Northside, began using the "mutual" number. This consisted of the last dollar digit of the daily total handle of *win, place,* and *show* bets at designated racetrack, read from top to bottom. For example, if the daily handle at the Belmont Park Race Track in New York City was *win*— $1,100.5<u>3</u>; *place*—$565.8<u>7</u>; *show*—$25.6<u>2</u>, then the winning number that day was "372."

Greenidge and the other policy bankers on the Northside eventually caught the attention of Nucky Johnson, head of the local Republican organization, who by this time was in complete control of the town's government. Nucky knew easy money when he saw it. Unlike Louis Kuehnle's reign, during which bribes were paid in accordance with a gentleman's agreement between the Republican Party and the vice industry, under Nucky, it was all business. "With Nucky, the payments weren't voluntary. Everything had its price and you paid up or he sent the police out to shut you down." Greenidge and his business colleagues in the numbers game understood that they either accepted Nucky and the Republican Party as their partners or they would be out of business or, worse still, find themselves in jail. The Republican organization controlled the local criminal justice system. Every player in the process, from the policeman patrolling the neighborhoods to the prosecutor filing charges to the judge presiding at trial, was hand-picked by Nucky. Greenidge and his associates didn't dare defy Nucky's organization.

Nucky gave the policy bankers his blessing to continue under two conditions: First, he wanted a portion of the winnings—it was believed to be 15 percent weekly, delivered personally to Nucky in envelopes from each bank; second, he wanted the policy bankers' help in setting up the game throughout the rest of the city. It was agreed that Dutch Campbell would work with Paul "Skinny" D'Amato, owner of the 500 Club and a close ally of Johnson, in taking the numbers game citywide.

D'Amato and the others in Nucky's organization were enterprising people themselves. Within a short time, everyone in town was able to play the numbers game. In a city of 66,000 year-round residents and in a game where the average bet ranged from 5 cents to 10 cents, the enormous volume of play is revealed by the fact that the profits, raked in by the citywide operation made up of many individual policy bankers, averaged roughly $5,000 to $6,000 per day and $1.5 million to $2 million per year. Those numbers are staggering when one considers that the salary of most hotel workers rarely equaled $100 per week.

The numbers game became so popular that there were two plays per day, one for daytime and one for evenings. Years later when the FBI came to town for Nucky, the agents surveyed nearly 1,500 local retail businesses throughout the Northside and the remainder of the city. The agents interviewed the owners, and no one was bashful about what was happening. Of the approximately 1,500 people questioned, 830 signed affidavits admitting under oath that their place of business was used for selling numbers. Another 200 to 300 admitted to writing numbers but were afraid to sign affidavits. "If you went to the corner store to buy a quart of milk, you could get your change or play a number. Nearly everybody who had a business wrote numbers." What started out as an enterprise of two black men from the West Indies had become a major source of revenue for the local Republican Party.

The businesses that benefited from loans made by the policy bankers were all located on the Northside. Because they owned real estate that could be mortgaged, boardinghouse operators were ideal borrowers. As the Northside gained prominence throughout the Northeast region, it became a tourist destination unto itself. Throughout the Northeast was a growing number of black people who had disposable income and free time away from work. The resort's African-American community rivaled New York's Harlem as a stylish place for young urban black people to party. Although the Northside couldn't boast Harlem's range of offerings, it was more affordable and at a less intimidating scale. And conveniently, it was a short ride to Atlantic City by train from Washington, D.C., Baltimore, Pittsburgh, Philadelphia, and Newark.

Once visitors arrived, everything was within walking distance of "Main Street," that is, Arctic Avenue. In addition to frolicking with celebrities from the entertainment world on that portion of the resort's beach assigned to African Americans, "Chicken Bone Beach," tourists could have a meal of some of the best barbecued pork or chicken north of Virginia, place their bet for the next day's winning numbers, take in a show, and while away the evening dancing and drinking at one of many clubs open 'til dawn. And it wasn't just individual vacationers; conventioneers came as well. The Black Masons, Elks, and Shriners—to name only a few—came for annual conventions, as did church organizations and gospel singing groups, each of which found the merchants and hoteliers on the Northside obliging hosts for their gatherings.

The Elks, or the Independent Benevolent and Protective Order of Elks—the formal name—staged its national convention annually in Atlantic City for 72 years, between 1900 and 1972. Typically drawing 20,000+ members from across the nation, the Northside was the place to be in the last week of August. As reported by the *Atlantic City Press* in August 1929, "traffic in this city before, during and after Colored Elks parade was completely paralyzed for more than five hours." Daily headlines in 1932 read: "Colored Elks Stage Parade: Brilliant Spectacle with 15,000 marchers, viewed by 150,000 people." (Please pause to absorb those numbers.) Leading the annual parade in the 1950s and 1960s was local landmark Raymond Harris. Standing 7'7", he towered above everyone and made an impressive drum major. Most years, the parade was comprised of as many as 25 bands and the members of 500 lodges. A beauty pageant, competitions in oratory, and educational programs on racial tolerance, held at the Indiana Avenue School, were all open to the public. It was the local Elk Lodge that coordinated the arrangements to house, feed, and entertain its guests during this week on the Northside. All this meant that there was money to make from vacationing African Americans. Many of these vacationers could have afforded a room "south" of Atlantic Avenue, but nearly all of the white-owned hotels and boardinghouses refused to rent rooms to them. This created an opportunity for black hoteliers.

Most of the Northside's boardinghouses and hotels had their start with property owners who rented rooms to visiting workers during the summer months. After working a full shift at a white-owned business, married couples—the husband typically a waiter or porter, the wife a cook or laundress—turned their attention to their own patrons: in the early years, seasonal black workers, later, tourists. Upon arriving home, these self-made entrepreneurs cooked and cleaned some more, seven days a week. Saving every extra dollar earned, these landlords/fledgling hoteliers were determined to make a place for themselves in Atlantic City. For them, there were no days off from May to September. Two prominent hotels on the Northside, the Ridley and Wright, had their start as boardinghouses renting to black workers for 10 weeks to 12 weeks during the summer. The owners were diligent and frugal, investing their profits back into their properties. With the help of loans through the Northside Credit Union, they eventually were able to create hotels that black vacationers frequented when they visited town to experience life on the Northside. Margaret "Maggie" and Alonzo Ridley were a dynamic pair of entrepreneurs and community leaders. Originally from Baltimore, they settled on the Northside prior to the turn of the 20th century. The Hotel Ridley opened its doors in 1900 and was a mainstay on the Northside for more than 50 years, hosting thousands of guests in the summer months and renting rooms to out-of-town school teachers in the off-season. The annual officers' installation meeting of the Northside Board of Trade was always held at the Hotel Ridley. Aunt Maggie's "Ridley Rolls" were a favorite with everyone in town. The Ridley and Wright are just two examples of successful black hotels during the first half of the 20th century.

With the creation of successful businesses and intense housing patterns, one service sorely needed in the black community that required local government's participation was fire protection. Although the city's tax dollars were necessary to operate the program, the fire safety needs of the densely populated Northside were met by an all black fire company.

Indiana and Grant Avenues was home to "Engine Company #9." The firefighting company had two platoons of firemen who lived and worked together out of their own segregated firehouse. The firefighters were important role models in the community. Each of them had—one way or another—paid their dues to the Republican organization and could now depend on steady employment. With their employment came the opportunity to serve the community. The firehouse became a second home for many local children where they learned important life skills.

Engine Company #9 earned a national reputation for excellence throughout the country. According to longtime fireman and former mayor, Richard Jackson, "The men at Engine Company #9 were amazing! They were some of the most knowledgeable, well-trained, and bravest firemen in the city. I would have matched their skills against anyone's. They were real pros and helped make our town a safer place." Engine Company #9 played a major role in fighting all the city's fires and held the city record for efficiency six years in a row.

Black people had developed their own city within a city in response to the racism of Atlantic City's white population. They had all the ingredients of a societal infrastructure up and running on their own, save two critical components. Despite their efforts, there remained two areas where the people on the Northside were unable to build their own institutions and continued to be the victims of racial prejudice: education and healthcare. To provide context for how both issues played out in the evolution of the Northside, we need to digress briefly.

True to form, there was no discrimination in the school system during the early years of the resort. As long as their numbers remained small, colored children posed no threat. But once a "tipping point" was reached and the white community hardened its stance on integrated neighborhoods, so, too, did it shrink from integrated schools as the number of black pupils grew.

Prior to 1900, the resort had a single school system with black and white children being educated together, entirely by white teachers. In 1881, a successful bathhouse operator and community leader, George Walls, organized a Literary Society among the members of the Price Memorial AME Zion Church and used it as a vehicle to push for improved education for black children. Walls had taken a road less traveled by black people of that era. Little is known of his background. He was industrious and shrewd, becoming the first—and for years the *only*—black owner of a business on the Boardwalk. After becoming secure financially, he sought out tutors and became literate. He knew what he had missed out on as a youth and had a keen appreciation for education as the critical ingredient in creating social capital for black people.

Walls and other successful African Americans of his age understood education to be the primary means for protecting black people from being exploited. For nearly two centuries, it had been illegal in most of America to teach reading and writing to African Americans. Although northern states abolished slavery long before those of the Old South, few were enthusiastic about educating free black people. Many northern whites viewed them as unwanted competition in the employment market, and white politicians weren't going to spend tax dollars to educate black children.

Throughout most of the Yankee states, the prevailing attitude was that African-American children should be taught no more than what was needed for them to perform efficiently as servants. As for the southern states, from which nearly 80 percent of the Northside's residents had migrated, it has been estimated that, in 1865, fewer than one in 10 black southerners were literate to any meaningful extent. This small percentage was one of the legacies of the "house nigger" versus the "field nigger" syndrome of the slavery era. For a significant portion of the African-American population, both in the nation and Atlantic City, there was a limited appreciation for the power of education. That is why role models such as Northside Y director C. Morris Cain, Dr. Shedrick Morris, and the graduates from historically black colleges and universities (HBCUs) were so important to the community. The small percentage of blacks for whom there was a tradition of pursuing education was a huge handicap not just for Atlantic City but for African-American society as a whole.

Educators know that a critical factor in the success of their students is the respect for learning engendered in the home. Children with educated parents are at a decided advantage over those whose parents are not. The only opportunities for black children in the South to receive an education after the Civil War were either in churches or primitive make-shift schools started by courageous pioneering graduates of HBCUs or normal schools (the name for early teaching colleges) who groomed young people to be classroom teachers. For many years, white supremacists in the South used intimidation and violence to discourage schools of any kind for black people. Who wouldn't be concerned by threats of lynching and arson? As a result, few children in the South received an education in the years following the Reconstruction Era. For Atlantic City, this meant that most of the blacks who had come north to work in its hotels in the late-19th century had little or no formal education. As a consequence, they had limited "social capital" to pass on to their children.

Walls understood not only the critical role of education in keeping blacks from being exploited but also the importance of African-American children having role models in positions of authority. Black children needed to see that their race could "make it" in the white world. At the time Walls began his efforts, other than the clergy and a handful of successful professionals, there were few people of color in visible positions of importance. Walls took it upon himself to investigate conditions in Atlantic City's schools. He concluded that white teachers paid little attention to the special needs and problems of their African-American students. At his urging, the Literary Society adopted a resolution demanding the hiring of a black teacher. It was a bold move.

The Literary Society's resolution sent ripples throughout the Atlantic City community, getting the attention of both white and black residents. C. J. Adams, president of the school board, encouraged Walls to present the society's resolution to the board members. According to historian Herbert James Foster, "The issue was debated and the Board voted to hire black teachers. However, it wasn't until the death of Adams fifteen years later, when his son, Clement, became Board President, that Atlantic City's first black teacher was hired in 1896." What happened in those 15 years?

Interestingly, there is evidence that a separate school for some 46 black children was opened in the resort in 1881, but *without* a black teacher. Early resort historian and newsman John F. Hall recorded that this school operated for several years but was closed when "political forces opposed separate schools." It's not known whether the school was opened in response to the Literary Society's resolution or whether the "political forces" that led to its closure stemmed from the bitter dispute that the society's petition ignited in the black community. What is clear is that Walls's actions embroiled him in a heated debate that deeply divided the resort's black community.

Walls wanted black teachers for black children. He was, in effect, promoting an early black nationalist policy of separation of the races, which many black leaders rejected. His demands aroused a controversy over integrated versus segregated education for Atlantic City's children. This was, and remains, no small matter. Blacks favoring integration believed that if the cost of securing black teachers was the loss of integration, then the price was too high. Walls's opponents were influential people in the black community. M. E. Coats, owner of a popular Northside amusement house, and C. L. Williams, secretary of the Literary Society that Walls had organized, were bitterly opposed to the idea. Coats and Williams viewed Walls as an interloper. Again, according to historian Foster, Walls's status as a fairly recent immigrant to Atlantic City from North Carolina created tension among longtime black residents who felt he was meddling, and "interfering with the harmonious affiliation between blacks and whites in the resort." Coats and Williams believed his proposal would do more harm than good.

As the controversy raged, Coats and Williams organized a mass meeting of black residents; according to Foster, Walls might have been physically attacked if not for several articles supporting him in the *Atlantic City Review*. One such article stated:

> This young man is right. The child is at a disadvantage with a white teacher because she does not know his history and environment. She does not have the patience and understanding. When a boy's mother leaves home at six o'clock in the morning, her child is not out of bed, at school time he jumps up, rushes to school without his face washed or his hair combed, a white teacher does not take that boy aside and make him wash his face, she just goes on with the lesson, ignoring that boy, because she does not know that he is not able to get attention from home. If Negro children have Negro teachers, they will have an inspiration, they will have members of their own race, for ideals and not white ideals that are so diligently instructed about in the schools.

The *Atlantic City Review* and its editor, John F. Hall, were respected by the entire community, and over time, tensions subsided and Walls's proposal gained acceptance. Finally, in 1896, the school board hired someone. Hattie E. Merritt, Atlantic City's first black teacher, was born in Jersey City and was a graduate of Jersey City Teachers Training School. To the school board's credit, it took into consideration the objections of Coats and Williams to hiring black teachers to instruct exclusively black students and assigned Merritt to teach an integrated class at the Indiana Avenue School.

Unfortunately, things didn't go well. Miss Merritt found teaching in an integrated classroom more than she had bargained for. Her problem wasn't the children but rather the parents. Many of the white parents demanded that the school board remove their children from her class, and some made her job impossible by standing outside the classroom, glaring at and taunting her as she tried to teach. Merritt complained to Walls, and he in turn went to the school board. Again, Walls demanded black teachers for black students only. This required separate schools, and that's what he got.

The end of the controversy came in 1900, when the school board decided on a policy of separate education for black children and the employment of additional black teachers to instruct them. Although it's not possible to know with certainty, according to Foster, "It is doubtful that in deciding on this course of action the Board was acceding to the demands of Walls's single voice, but rather to the opposition of white parents to the brief experience with a black teacher giving instruction to white children." The fears of integrationist leaders such as Coats and Williams had been realized: Black children were to be educated in segregated schools.

With the school board's decision made, black children were moved out of the regular school rooms and into the basement of the Shiloh Baptist Church, where Miss Merritt taught with the assistance of Miss Thompson, the second black teacher hired. The church basement didn't work out; the following year, all white students were moved out of the Indiana Avenue School, one of the older school buildings in the system, and the building was reinvented as an all-black school. As Atlantic City's population grew, the Indiana Avenue School couldn't accommodate the increasing number of black students. The next move was to expand and then physically divide the New Jersey Avenue school—half for whites and half for blacks.

Unwittingly, Walls had given would-be segregationists an opportunity, and they repeatedly exploited it for all it was worth. With the partitioning of the New Jersey Avenue School, Jim Crow–like signs were installed. So there was no confusion, the entrances were labeled. There was a "white" door and a "colored" door, and separate play yards to keep the children from mingling.

There's little doubt that the white community thought this arrangement was just fine. By 1901, Superintendent of Atlantic City Schools W. M. Pollard claimed proudly that separate classes for black children were a good thing. In his annual report, he stated:

> The employment of colored teachers for separate colored classes has worked very successfully in our city. We employ ten colored teachers. These teachers occupy rooms in the same building where white children attend. The separation is continued as far as the seventh grade, after that the colored pupils attend the same grades with the white children. This plan has been in many respects beneficial for the race.

It's hard to know who was vindicated by the results, George Walls or his critics. Although segregation in public education has produced many negative consequences for our society, there are longtime residents of Atlantic City who believe that African-American children benefited from the experience of being taught by black teachers, separate from white children. "Our teachers made us believe in ourselves. They disciplined us and demanded our best. They kept us from getting out of control and taught us to respect ourselves and our community. They hammered the '3 Rs' into our heads and gave us the fundamentals not only of education but life."

From 1910 to 1960 when the Northside was in its prime, African-American pupils saw few, if any, white children until they entered high school, which was integrated. They also had few, if any, white teachers until they reached junior high and/or high school. In his plans for a new high school, built in 1923, the architect had included a swimming pool in the basement. The pool was built but never opened for swimming. Fearful of black children in the same water as whites, the school administration had the pool covered over, forcing the high school's all-white swim team to practice at one of the Boardwalk hotels. Notwithstanding the waste and silliness of such ignorance at the high school level, this author has encountered longtime residents who believe the days of segregated education during the formative years in elementary school was a positive thing for the Northside community. One present day role model of the Northside who was part of the last generation to receive a segregated education in Indiana Avenue School has said: "By the time I got out of Indiana Avenue School, I knew who I was. I knew I was someone capable of doing whatever I wanted with my life."

Black children had positive role models standing before them in the classroom, and their family, religious, and community values were reinforced on a daily basis. As one retired schoolteacher, herself a product of both the Pennsylvania Avenue and Indiana Avenue schools, recollected:

> I can remember one teacher, and I think everybody in Atlantic City can remember her—Mrs. Ida Gould. When we'd go in her classroom all around the top of the wall there were mottos and you know when children sit in school and begin to look around … there was one motto we used to look at all the time and it said, "Do you think you know, or do you know you know?"
>
> Ms. Theresa B. Robinson was another. I also remember my high school teachers who were just so kind to me. Mr. Arthur Chenoweth, he's now deceased. Another teacher in high school was Mr. Clarence Dyke, English teacher.
>
> But all the teachers I had enjoyed, because they all seemed to be just so very patient with the students, and they made a good life for us, but they made us study. They made us work.

The graduates of HBCUs recruited by George Walls and the school district were no-nonsense educators—*they made us study … they made us work*—who took seriously the need for young black people to begin building their "social capital" at an early age.

Unfortunately, there was no one like Walls to take up the fight on healthcare for the black community. To many whites, including physicians, black people were subhuman. The image of the jungle savage crafted so well during the slavery era and the years following the Civil

War endured. To many of Atlantic City's employers, black workers were little more than beasts of burdens. If they fell ill and were unable to work, they were quickly replaced. The local power structure saw no need to worry about health services for black people, and what was provided was always as segregated and meager as whites could make it. Blacks were not permitted in white doctors' offices, and routine medical services were dispensed out of a separate blacks-only clinic in a back room in City Hall until 1899. In that year, the first public hospital was opened, but it would treat blacks only in wards separate from whites. Things were no better across the nation. One historian has determined that, by 1920, there was one hospital bed available for every 139 American whites, but only one for every 1,941 African Americans.

Although the local hospital hired blacks for cooking and cleaning, there were none to care for patients. Distinguished physicians such as Drs. Shedrick Morris, George Fletcher, and Walter Fayerman were denied the privilege to treat their patients in the Atlantic City Hospital simply because of their skin color. Black people could be found cleaning bedpans and mopping floors or cooking and serving meals, but they weren't treating patients, regardless of their training or education. As late as 1931, nearly 100 blacks were employed as orderlies, cooks, janitors, waiters, and maids, but *not one* as a nurse or doctor.

There were more than a few young women with the ability and desire to learn nursing, but none was accepted into the hospital's nursing program. Qualified applicants for training as nurses were turned away by the hospital's administration, forced to go to other cities for their education. The same occurred with other eager young people who found the boundaries of the Northside confining. With them left valuable social capital, never to return. Racial prejudice produced—on a limited scale—a type of diaspora that, years later following the "Summer of Freedom," would be eclipsed by what some might term the "law of unintended consequences."

At least until the late-20th century, the message of Atlantic City's white establishment was clear: African Americans were second-rate citizens. The average black person—and for that matter even accomplished persons such as Madame Sara Spencer Washington—would never be treated as an equal. Skin color would always be an obstacle. But some people could not be denied, and one province in which talent counted for much was the world of athletics. At the time, America's most popular sport—its *only* sport—was baseball. And the Northside was home to a black man who played the game as few ever have.

7

"Pop"

If you mean in organized baseball, my answer would be Babe Ruth; but if you mean in all baseball, organized and unorganized, the answer would have to be an Atlantic City colored man named John Henry Lloyd.
—The reply of sportswriter Ted Harlow, in 1938, when asked to name the best player in baseball history

Lawnmowers, rakes, and brooms aren't as much fun to handle as bats, gloves, and baseballs. Instead of roaming the infield and batting "clean-up," he was patrolling hallways and cleaning up after children. Playing winter baseball under the Cuban sun and going head-to-head with the likes of Ty Cobb was only a memory—not much comfort when days grew short at the Jersey shore and the winds howled off the Atlantic Ocean. Working anonymously as a school janitor was a far cry from starring on the baseball diamond before thousands of fans, but he accepted his role at life's end with the same grace and dignity he displayed as a champion. "Pop" Lloyd didn't start out in Atlantic City, and his best years as an athlete were spent in other towns—*lots* of other towns—but the resort was his home at the end of the day, and the people of the Northside were proud to have him as one of their own.

Born in Palatka, Florida, on April 25, 1884, John Henry Lloyd lived for baseball. His father died when he was a child, and he and his mom struggled to get by. A tall, angular man, ruggedly handsome with a Dick Tracy chin, he stood 6'1" and through most of his life was a lean and agile 175–185 pounds, even into old age. Discovered on the sandlots of Jacksonville by the legendary black baseball entrepreneur Andrew "Rube" Foster, Lloyd began his playing career in 1905. He played catcher for one of the amateur ball clubs connected with Foster, the Acmes of Macon, Georgia, but he could have easily played any position on the field. The following year, he moved up to the professional level to play second base with Foster's team, the Cuban X Giants of Philadelphia. (The term "Cuban" was used to obscure the team's true racial identity. None of the players was from Cuba.) The highlight of the 1906 season came against Connie Mack's Philadelphia Athletics for a one-game city title. The Giants lost, but Lloyd got four base hits off the As' best pitching and made an enduring impression on the Philadelphia team's owner, who publicly praised him years later as one of the greatest baseball players of that era, black or white. In 1907, Lloyd switched to shortstop, the position that would bring him baseball immortality.

"The quintessential shortstop—great hands, accurate arm, could perform the double play with ballerina grace and slug for average and power," Lloyd threw right and batted left. A line-drive hitter, he batted from a closed stance, usually making contact and rarely striking out. "He held the bat in the cradle of his left elbow, and would uncoil … to unleash a controlled attack on the white sphere. Lloyd ran with long smooth strides, deceiving opponents who did not realize his dangerous speed, until it was too late."

It wasn't until years later, in Atlantic City—where John Henry Lloyd was loved as both a player and team manager—that he would gain the nickname "Pop." As a player, he was "the Jekyll and Hyde of baseball—a fierce competitor on the field, but a gentle, considerate man off the field." Regardless of the situation, he never lost his poise. During his brilliant career, he was also referred to as the "black Honus Wagner" (Wagner, a Hall of Famer, was the first shortstop to excel at both hitting and fielding). Although this may have been a left-handed compliment at the time, it revealed the deep respect students of the game had for Lloyd's talents.

Regrettably, talent wasn't enough to get into Major League Baseball. Lloyd, like hundreds of other black ballplayers, was relegated to the Negro League. Before organizing leagues of their own, black athletes were part of Jim Crow baseball, which included everything from sandlot games played by pick-up teams to talented professionals with stylish uniforms and full-time, professional managers, who traveled around the country, playing for the gate receipts. In the mid-19th century, baseball was the only athletic pursuit available to most Americans. Following the Civil War, many freedmen took up the sport and frequently excelled at "America's pastime." History tells us that, at first, there was a grudging acceptance of black athletes by early white baseball organizations, but the integration of sports would have to wait. Time after time, the period from the end of the Reconstruction Era to the turn of the 20th century saw gains toward equality reversed by racism. As was true of other aspects of American society, the door to baseball opened briefly to black athletes during the first generation following the Civil War, only to slam shut as their numbers increased.

Although it would be a stretch to say professional baseball in the North was "integrated" between the end of the Civil War and 1890, a substantial number of black athletes played alongside white athletes on both professional and amateur league teams during this era. Despite the fact that the original National Association of Baseball Players, founded in 1867, had banned black athletes, some exceptional players built long and solid careers in white professional baseball. There was Moses "Fleetwood" Walker, a star catcher for Oberlin College who signed with the Toledo Blue Stockings in 1883. With a throwing arm like a cannon, Walker made even the speediest base runners look foolish trying to steal second. John "Bud" Fowler, signed by the Stillwater, Minnesota, team in 1884, was so versatile that at one time or another he played every position on the field. And George Stovey, who began playing for Jersey City in 1886, is remembered as the first great black pitcher, winning 30 games a year with regularity.

In both the North and Midwest, the best black players found a measure of acceptance. It's known that many other African Americans were playing for white ball clubs and with independent barnstorming clubs during the 1880s. "Pioneer baseball historian Sol White tells us of the 20 black men who were on white teams in organized baseball when he made his debut as a 19-year-old third baseman with Wheeling of the Ohio State League, also in 1887. With each passing year, however, it became less and less likely that black and white would be found together on a baseball diamond—or anywhere else in American society." Major league baseball would not be integrated until much later.

One word sums up baseball's failure to assimilate people of color and the degraded status of exceptional athletes like Pop Lloyd: racism. But making sense of it is difficult nonetheless. Why would otherwise intelligent businessmen—in this case, baseball team owners—refuse to employ the most talented players after having them in their line-ups and witnessing their abilities firsthand? And why did things fall apart for the generation of black Americans—Pop Lloyd's generation—born 20 years after the end of the Civil War?

As we saw earlier, the 1880s and 1890s were a time in which an array of negative social currents flowed together to create popular support for the depraved notion of white supremacy. The result was institutionalized discrimination. Notwithstanding the abolition of slavery and the guarantee of equal rights for *all* citizens enshrined in the Constitution through the adoption of the 13th and 14th Amendments, blacks were treated as second-class citizens. It was mainstream thinking of white America to view them as inferior and to discourage the "mingling of the races." In the hearts of many Americans, the South had won the "second insurrection." The despicable injustice of racism had prevailed. The *Southern way* had become the *American way.* And the Southern way couldn't condone white fans paying money to watch African-American athletes or, worse still, watching white ballplayers possibly being bested by black players.

Savvy white baseball team owners—interested in profits and caring little about social justice—understood that the cultural neurosis that reared its ugly head in the widespread violence following Jack Johnson's defeat of Jim Jeffries had existed for years. Simmering below the surface of white American society was an anxiety that—given the least provocation—could produce random acts of white-on-black violence. In the South, this irrational violence took the extreme forms of lynchings and torchings. In the North, it could be a kidnapping for a brief period accompanied by threats and beatings. With Johnson's defeat of Jeffries, it took the form of indiscriminate mob violence. Whether in the workplace or on the ball field, many white men had an irrational fear of being outdone by the black man. Team owners refused to permit the possibility of such humiliation. Prior to the 1890 season, without making a formal announcement, a "gentlemen's agreement" was reached among the owners banning black players from Major League Baseball for the next 57 years.

While Fleetwood Walker, Bud Fowler, George Stovey, and others were trying to make a place for themselves in the white baseball leagues, other African-American players were pursuing their careers, too. From about the time of Pop Lloyd's birth in the early 1880s forward, there were more than 200 all-black independent teams that played throughout the nation. Eastern teams like the Cuban Giants, the Cuban X Giants, and the Harrisburg Giants played both independently and in loosely organized all–African-American leagues through the end of the 19th century. For years, it was common for black teams to "barnstorm," or travel from town to town throughout the nation, taking on all comers and entertaining black and white fans alike. In the early 1900s, professional black baseball began to blossom throughout the Midwest and even in the South. The early years of the 20th century saw the emergence of several prominent teams in the Midwest, with Chicago, Detroit, Kansas City, Cleveland, Cincinnati, and Indianapolis all represented. There were also black ball clubs in Memphis, Birmingham, and Austin. Interestingly, most of these clubs were financially successful, attracting loyal fans from their local black populations year after year. Some cities were able to support more than one team.

Regardless of how uncomfortable it made some white Americans, the black community embraced "America's pastime" and made it their own. By the end of World War I, black baseball was the number one entertainment attraction for African Americans throughout the nation. It was at that time that Rube Foster, owner of the Chicago American Giants and black baseball's most influential personality, decided that the time had come for a truly organized Negro league. Under Foster's leadership, in 1920 the Negro National League (NNL) was born. By this time, after 15 years in organized baseball, Pop Lloyd was no longer playing for Foster's team, but rather he was competing against him as a player-manager.

Few people had Lloyd's knowledge of the game. Every place he went, he was a winner. Although there are few "championships" to point to, Pop was rarely on a team that had a losing record. He was a leader both on and off the field, and a big part of that was his ability to *think* baseball and explain his insights on strategy to his teammates. He was coaching most of his career, long before he officially became a manager. Between 1906 and 1918, he played with great teams such as the New York Lincoln Giants, Philadelphia Giants,

Leland Giants, Chicago American Giants, and New York Lincoln Stars. Some commentators viewed him as a "baseball nomad," but this wasn't so much due to his restlessness as to the eagerness of team owners to lure him to their organizations. A team with Pop Lloyd on the roster always had the chance of becoming a winner, and the players on each team he left behind were better for having played with him.

Although statistics can't begin to tell the enormous impact he had on every team he played with, baseball history tells us that Lloyd batted .475 in 1910 and .444 in 1924. His best season was in 1928 when he batted .564, a feat all the more impressive considering that he was 44 years old at the time. What's more, in that year, the NNL had some of the best pitchers ever to play the game, including Hall of Famers Smoky Joe Williams, Bullet Joe Rogan, Ted "Double Duty" Radcliffe, and the immortal Satchel Paige.

From 1918, when he became playing coach of the Brooklyn Royal Giants, through the remainder of his life, Pop Lloyd was a teacher of the game, advising thousands of young athletes. He continued to move from one team to another, playing baseball year-round, wintering in Cuba where he enjoyed the warm, sunny days and cool nights. He played 12 consecutive seasons in Cuba, where he was known by the locals as "El Cuchara"—the shovel—because of his tendency to scoop up handfuls of dirt when charging ground balls.

One season in Havana, Lloyd and his team, the Havana Reds, matched up against Ty Cobb and the Detroit Tigers. Cobb's reputation as both a fearless (some might say vicious) competitor and bigot preceded him, and Lloyd was prepared. He had cast-iron shin guards concealed under his stockings and when Cobb came flying into second base, teeth and spikes bared, Lloyd held his ground, caught catcher Bruce Petway's throw, and made the tag. Pop was not one to be intimidated, even by Ty Cobb. Over a five-game series, Cobb hit .369 but was unable to steal a single base. Pop batted .500, going 11 for 22. Cobb, bitter at being shown up by Lloyd, vowed never to play against black ballplayers again. During his years of playing winter baseball, Lloyd compiled a batting average of .331 and led the Cuban leagues in triples twice and stolen bases once.

Pop Lloyd first arrived in Atlantic City in 1921, joining the powerful Bacharach Giants, which were already well-established. His first stay was short lived. At the end of the 1922 season, the Giants splintered into two factions: One took most of the roster and moved to New York City under the management of Pop Lloyd, while the other remained in the resort. The details of what caused the split are murky, but suffice it to say, there were no hard feelings between Pop and the Northside's sports fans as he was welcomed back enthusiastically several years later.

The Bacharach Giants, and the story of how the team came to town, speaks volumes about the prominence of the Northside community. The Giants were founded in Jacksonville, Florida, as the Duval Giants in or around 1910. The second decade of the 20th century saw a significant increase in the number of African Americans migrating out of the Jim Crow South, and the Giants were part of that migration.

Northside businessmen Henry Tucker and Tom Jackson brought the Giants to Atlantic City in 1916. Recently elected Mayor Harry Bacharach was eager to win support of Northside voters and was willing to lend his name and provide financial backing to the team. The decision to relocate an existing professional baseball team from Jacksonville to Atlantic City illustrates the standing of the Northside in black America. It was a place in which successful black business people were willing to invest. The Northside didn't merely have the entire array of commercial enterprises common to the early 20th century, it had its own professional baseball team with athletes who were written about in the national black press. Then, as now, owners of professional sports teams were seeking cities where they knew they could succeed. It's not only a matter of population but also of residents' enthusiasm for the game, and the Northside loved baseball; thus did the Duval Giants become the Bacharach Giants.

During the next 14 years, the Bacharachs drew record crowds to games, presenting the finest black professional baseball talent from across the nation. They were a top independent team, featuring shortstop Dick Lundy, third baseman Oliver Marcelle, and the pitching greats "Cannonball" Dick Redding and Jesse "Nip" Winters. In 1920, they joined Rube Foster's NNL. Foster was a controversial figure, and there were complaints over umpiring, scheduling, and what some viewed as his heavy-handed influence as league president. Regardless, when Foster and the other club owners extended an invitation for the Northside to be part of their league, Tucker and Jackson accepted.

While the Bacharachs did not compete for the league championship, they played NNL teams extensively, touring the Midwest from 1920 through 1922. Teams from as far away as St. Louis, Kansas City, Chicago, Indianapolis, and Cleveland made their way to Atlantic City. The Northside was plugged into the national sports scene, and residents were able to see first-rate talent up close.

In 1923, the year following the splintering of the ball club into two factions, the Bacharach Giants left the NNL and became charter members of the Eastern Colored League, the second Negro Major League. Soon, Negro Baseball was staging a "world series" of its own, and the Bacharachs were in the thick of things. In 1926 and 1927, the Northside's ball club faced off against Foster's mighty Chicago American Giants in the Negro League World Series. Things didn't go so well for the Bacharachs in either series, but the team made baseball history nonetheless. Baseball historians note that the series of 1926 marked the first no-hit, no-run game in World Series history, pitched by the Bacharachs' ace right hander, Claude "Red" Grier. Don Larsen of the Yankees is remembered for his perfect game in the 1956 World Series, but Red Grier did it first.

Respected in the Negro leagues, the Bacharach Giants were successful on the field and at the box office. Despite the racist views expressed in an editorial of the *Atlantic City Press* that the Bacharachs existed "to keep the colored element off the Boardwalk during the afternoon by providing ball games for them," the team had a loyal fan base of local residents, black and white alike. Having a team of professional athletes lent an added cultural dimension to the Northside. The Bacharachs were comprised of players from around the country, and visiting teams brought players from cities the local residents had never seen. During the summer months, baseball and the Northside's entertainment district created a cosmopolitan atmosphere, the likes of which existed in few American cities at the time.

Many of the Bacharachs' ballplayers were from the South and, like the resort's hotel workers, had escaped Jim Crow for the trendsetting Northside. In season, the players roomed in boardinghouses on the Northside and were part of the community, strolling Arctic and Kentucky Avenues, mingling with the locals, engendering fan loyalty. One of the players, Napoleon Cummings, told of playing for the Bacharachs:

You see, in the first place, we all had guts because we had a lot of experience down in Florida. We all worked in Jacksonville, and we had a lot of experience during the Jack Johnson and Jeffries fight—there were thousands of whites in our part of town ... Of course, we had no chance to play baseball with the whites down there ...

And when we came up here and started playing ball with the white boys, they were more scared of us than we were of them. Because we had such a hell of a ball club; we had a powerful ball club! There were other colored clubs here then but we broke 'em up, we were so strong, and everybody wanted to play the Bacharachs. We played so many ball clubs, and beat everybody, that people came all the way from Philadelphia to see who the Bacharachs were.

It's said that Pop and his wife, Nan, fell in love with the resort the first time around; nevertheless, Pop stayed only briefly, returning to New York City for several years. It was while in New York that Pop made baseball history. He was instrumental in "opening" Yankee Stadium to Negro baseball.

Local lore has it that Pop and George Herman Ruth Jr.—better known as "The Babe"—were more than casual acquaintances. Babe Ruth respected Pop as both a ballplayer and a person, and was not one to permit the racial divide to cloud his vision when he saw a talented athlete. In June 1930, plans were made for a double header between Pop's New York Lincoln Giants and the Baltimore Black Sox. The proceeds from the games were to benefit the fledging Brotherhood of Sleeping Car Porters. A. Philip Randolph, a social activist for civil rights long before there was a "movement," was head of the struggling union and needed an event to raise money and draw attention to his efforts. This was one of his early strokes of genius and would be followed by many more, culminating in the historic March on Washington in August 1963. (The following summer of 1964, Atlantic City would be center stage in the Civil Rights Movement.) But in 1930, A. Philip Randolph was focused on New York and the railroad porters. He needed help.

Key to making Randolph's doubleheader a success was the ballpark in which it was to be played. Even then, Yankee Stadium had an aura all its own. This is where Pop's relationship with Babe Ruth made the difference. As recounted by local baseball historians, including Michael Everett, at Pop's request, Ruth interceded with the Yankee's owner, Jacob Ruppert. "The Colonel," as Ruppert was known to all, had a storied career. He had been a National Guard colonel, a New York congressman, and a brewery owner, in that order, before buying the Yankees in 1915. The Colonel had taken a team that was all but dead and built it into a baseball powerhouse. His own strength as a shrewd businessman with a willingness to wheel and deal was supported by the baseball knowledge of general manager Ed Barrow and the field managing of Miller Huggins and (later) Joe McCarthy, not to mention the talent and charisma of Babe Ruth. The Colonel and his star player were known for their public spats over Ruth's contracts with the Yankees (some things *never* change) but remained personal friends. Pop knew Ruth could make it happen for his Harlem team to cross the river to the Bronx and, at the Babe's urging, Ruppert agreed to make Yankee Stadium available on July 5, 1930.

Advertisements touting the doubleheader began appearing in the leading black newspapers throughout the Northeast. Virtually every large city with a significant African-American population had one or more African-American newspapers, including the (New York) *Amsterdam News*, *New York Globe*, *New York Freedman*, *Philadelphia Tribune*, *Philadelphia New Observer*, *Afro-American Newspaper* (of Baltimore), *Chicago Defender*, *Detroit Tribune*, and *Pittsburgh Courier*. (Very briefly, the Northside had a weekly of its own; it folded after only three editions.) Although it was important for these newspapers to report the news of the day, it was not their primary mission; their cities already had dailies aimed at the general public—these papers existed to provide news with a black perspective.

Beginning several weeks prior to the event, in June 1930, the black newspapers began exhorting their readers to "Fill Yankee Stadium!" The inauguration of black baseball at Yankee Stadium would have been significant in itself, but a benefit for Randolph's union made the occasion doubly special. The event was an enormous success.

As agreed by the promoters, the proceeds of the afternoon's events, which totaled $3,500 (this was the Great Depression when a loaf of bread cost 2 cents and people were lucky to have a job that paid $5 to $10 per week), would be donated to the union's treasury to assist the rank and file in their struggle for recognition by the railroads. Between games, fans chuckled as Bill "Bojangles" Robinson gracefully ran backward to defeat two local youngsters in a footrace. (At the time, Robinson—a nationally known "hoofer" and the honorary Mayor of Harlem—held the record for the 75-yard backward dash at an amazing 8.2 seconds.) They were entertained by the renowned marching band of the 369th Infantry Regiment, better known as the Harlem Hellfighters. Baseball historian Sol White, writing for the *Amsterdam News* said, "Never in the history of the game has an audience left a ball game with a higher regard for its participants. And How!"

From then on, "When the Yankees were on the road, until the integration of the majors in 1947, teams from the Negro Leagues regularly played at the Stadium." Baseball historians report that "Articles about the July 5, 1930, game took special note of several players. A fellow named Pop, the player-manager for the Lincolns who in the twilight of his career was now playing first base, got much of the attention. He stole a base, was credited with a sacrifice, went four for eight, and handled 24 put outs without an error." July 5, 1930, is a special day in baseball history, and Pop Lloyd helped make it possible.

After several seasons in New York, Pop returned to Atlantic City, this time permanently. "In 1931, now 47, Pop finished his career with his old friends, Clint Thomas and Red Ryan, on the New York Black Yankees. He retired the following year with the hometown Bacharach Giants, playing mostly at first base." This time he was here to stay, but the Bacharachs weren't. Attendance at home games had slipped, and there wasn't enough revenue to sustain the team's high-priced roster. Several major trades were made, all with an eye toward limiting payroll. From 1931 to 1933, the team played as an independent and then had a short-lived membership in the NNL in 1934, playing most of its games in Philadelphia in the hope of generating more revenue.

Unfortunately, the Great Depression took its toll on baseball as well as the rest of the economy, and at the end of the 1934 season, the club disbanded. With more than 25 years in professional baseball, and the maturity and patience required to teach energetic but sometimes high-strung athletes, Pop Lloyd continued his career in baseball as coach of the Johnson Stars, a semi-pro team sponsored by local political boss Nucky Johnson.

One of Pop's baseball "students" was Max Manning, a local baseball legend in his own right (Manning was invited to try out for the Detroit Tigers until the team learned he was African American). Early on, while a high school pitching sensation in nearby Pleasantville, Lloyd took Manning under his wing. Every position, especially that of pitcher and catcher, has a mind-set and strategy all of its own, and Pop taught the young star how to *think* baseball. He groomed Manning for big league baseball and for life, and he went on to excel at both.

"Dr. Cyclops" was the nickname given to Manning. Standing 6′4″ and wearing "Coke-bottle glasses," he was an imposing figure on the mound. Starring with the Newark Eagles, in 1946, he went 15–1 and won the clinching game of the Negro "World Series," upsetting the favored Kansas City Monarchs. After baseball, Manning continued his education, graduating from Glassboro State College in 1955 and going on to teach for 28 years in the Pleasantville school system. He touched the lives of many children. Reminiscing after retirement from teaching, Manning spoke of Pop Lloyd for a documentary on black baseball in America:

> John Henry Lloyd contributed quite a bit to my knowledge about baseball, and also to my knowledge and learning about being a gentleman, because that's what he truly was. When I first met Pop he was managing and playing some first base for the Johnson Stars. He was truly a gentle giant, strong in character, an honest man, a wonderful person. It seemed as though adversity would just fall off his shoulders. He would never dwell on adversity. He would always go to the brighter side of whatever might come up.

Equally fitting was a tribute expressed by an athlete who starred in both baseball and basketball and had played for Pop on the Lincoln Giants. With a bit of awe in his voice, Bill Yancey said, "Pop Lloyd was the greatest player, the greatest manager, the greatest teacher. He had the ability and knowledge and, above all, patience. I did not know what baseball was until I played under him."

Pop coached the Johnson Stars until Nucky Johnson went off to jail in 1941. The team then became the "Farley Stars" for its new sponsor, longtime political boss and State Senator Frank "Hap" Farley. The local Republican organization respected Lloyd's popularity in the community, and the money funneled to the team was a wise investment in goodwill among the voters of the Northside. Pop remained coach until 1942, when he turned 58.

Lloyd loved being around young people, athletes in particular, and in his later years, he served as Little League commissioner. The same society that shoved aside talented athletes like Pop Lloyd, forcing them to play with segregated ball clubs, treated him shabbily upon retirement. All but anonymous to white America, many retired black ballplayers found themselves, like Lloyd, relegated to jobs such as school janitor. And at that, Pop needed the nod of Hap Farley to gain his position. Farley was a ballplayer himself and admired Lloyd greatly, so some type of secure job for his senior years was never in doubt. But think of it: A future Hall of Famer pushing a broom. Being a custodian wasn't as gratifying an end to a worthy life as Max Manning would know, but then again, Pop didn't have a teacher like himself to show the way.

Some say that the only place you can find gratitude is in the dictionary, but not so in the relationship between Pop Lloyd and his adopted hometown. On October 2, 1949, as Jackie Robinson was being named the Most Valuable Player in the National League, the people of Atlantic City rewarded their "foster father" with the dedication of a stadium in the Northside at Indiana and Huron Avenues. The stadium bears the name "'Pop' Henry Lloyd" and an inscribed plaque reads: "To a great ballplayer and a fine man." The ceremony was attended by every local person of note, hundreds of well wishers, and dozens of people whose lives he had touched. Overwhelmed with emotion, Pop wiped back the tears and spoke softly in an almost reverent manner:

> I gave my best when I was playing ball, and today I mean to give the best that I have in expressing appreciation of the honor that has been given me this day. I hope the young men, not only of Atlantic City but the entire nation, will benefit from what I have tried to give the youth of America. And I promise that this day, more than

anything else, inspires me to continue to live righteously, so that I may justify the confidence you kind folks have shown in me.

Following the ceremony, a reporter asked whether he felt cheated because his playing days were over before the color line had been broken. Pop replied, "I do not consider that I was born at the wrong time. I felt it was the right time, for I had a chance to prove the ability of our race in this sport, and because many of us did our very best to uphold the traditions of the game and of the world of sport, we have given the Negro a greater opportunity now to be accepted into the major leagues with other Americans."

Pop Lloyd's words express an important reality overlooked in American history. Much is made of Jackie Robinson's career and his courage in thundering through the color line and that is as it should be. Robinson overcame much: Brooklyn teammates who got up a petition to keep him off the team; pitchers who threw at his head; base runners who dug their spikes into his shin; opposition dugouts who hollered for him to carry their bags and shine their shoes; and, yes, even death threats. But would there have been an opportunity for Jackie Robinson to hone his talent as a ballplayer if athletes like Pop Lloyd had surrendered to racial prejudice?

Little attention has been given to how Robinson was "discovered" by the Brooklyn Dodgers. Would he have come to the attention of Dodgers' President Branch Rickey if he weren't playing in the NNL for the all-Negro Kansas City Monarchs? The answer is no.

The Negro League was a response to white society's refusal to accept that black people could excel at America's national pastime. Negro baseball nourished the athletic ability and kept alive the hopes of thousands of ballplayers. Without the determination of pioneering black athletes like Pop Lloyd, Jackie Robinson might never have played for the Kansas City Monarchs and had the opportunity to be discovered by the Dodgers. Thus, Pop and his generation played a pivotal role in smashing the color line.

Ironically, in a sad illustration of the law of unintended consequences, black America's (including Atlantic City) enthusiasm for integrated baseball led to the demise of the Negro leagues. "The big league doors suddenly opened one day," explained sportswriter Wendell Smith, "and when Negro players walked in, Negro baseball walked out." Unfortunately, major league teams refused to embrace the knowledge of longtime athletes and coaches like Pop Lloyd. Many years would pass before there were African-American managers, coaches, scouts, and front office personnel. "In the enlightened age of integration, fewer rather than more African Americans would earn their livelihoods in baseball jobs." Those who knew his talents believe Pop would have thrived as a manager or coach in major league baseball.

After a two-year illness, suffering from arteriosclerosis, Pop died on March 19, 1965, five weeks short of his 81st birthday. His wife, Nan, was the only surviving family member. He was buried in Pleasantville, New Jersey. Max Manning was a pall bearer, and there were dozens of other "honorary" pall bearers. But that's not the end of Pop's story. The next episode involves his induction into the Baseball Hall of Fame in Cooperstown, New York.

At the time of Pop's death, none of the exhibits in Cooperstown even acknowledged the careers of the great athletes of the Jim Crow era and the Negro Leagues. Pop Lloyd was considered Honus Wagner's equal and had bested Ty Cobb in a head-to-head match-up, but you couldn't even find his name in the Hall of Fame. Change, however, was afoot and as the American Civil Rights Movement gained momentum, the inclusion of black players in the Hall of Fame became a controversial subject. If baseball was truly "America's pastime," how could it deny admission of great athletes such as Pop Lloyd to the Hall of Fame?

Some of those opposed to admitting African Americans asserted that because Pop's generation of Negro League players and those before him had never played in the Major Leagues, it wasn't possible to compare the *statistics* of these two different baseball worlds. According to this way of thinking, only Jackie Robinson and those ballplayers who came *after* him were entitled to be enshrined as a baseball great. Anything else would offend the gods of baseball. As for those who played *before* Robinson—they were simply out of luck.

Luck has a way of changing, especially when leaders stand up. One of the more forceful voices to call for integrating Cooperstown was Ted Williams of the Boston Red Sox. The Red Sox was the last team to integrate and not once during his career—all of it with Boston—had Williams objected publicly to management's racist policy. Surprisingly, on July 25, 1966, while speaking at his own induction ceremony in Cooperstown, Williams caught everyone off guard, stating, "I hope that someday the names of Satchel Paige and Josh Gibson can be added as a symbol of the great Negro players who are not here because they were not given a chance." Williams's statement was a clarion call. Within days, it was picked up by several influential sportswriters, and a short time later, the Baseball Writers Association of America lent their support to the move.

Three years after Ted Williams's outspokenness (there's not much *fast* about baseball), Bowie Kuhn, upon becoming Baseball Commissioner in 1969, moved to include black athletes as candidates for the Hall of Fame. He ran into opposition from the old-boy network of baseball, again, obsessed with *statistics*—a minimum of 10 years of play is required to be considered for the Hall of Fame. At first, Kuhn seemed to back off his commitment. He suggested a compromise to the baseball "purists"—a special exhibit acknowledging the athletes of the Jim Crow era. The purists accepted, and at Kuhn's direction, a committee of baseball historians and sportswriters chose Satchel Paige as the initial honoree. But Paige would have none of it.

In many respects, Satchel Paige was to Negro League baseball what Babe Ruth was to the majors: a rare combination of talent and personality that captured the imagination of fans across America. His unique brand of showmanship combined with his remarkable skills on the mound filled ballparks everywhere and kept the fans coming through the turnstiles through even the darkest days of the Great Depression. His unmatched drawing power resulted in his frequently being "loaned" to struggling teams that needed a quick boost in attendance to stay afloat. In hindsight, it seems predictable that he would play a role in breaking baseball's color barrier.

Paige refused to have his long and illustrious career relegated to an obscure corner of the Hall of Fame. He rejected Kuhn's proposal, saying, "I was just as good as the white boys. I ain't going in the back door of the Hall of Fame." His voice was heard loud and clear: He would receive full honors or none at all. Would Cooperstown take a hard line against him? Hardly.

Few baseball fans knew about Kuhn's proposed compromise; most assumed Major League Baseball was prepared to recognize the great black players of the Negro League, and the Jim Crow era generally, as full honorees on an equal standing with white ballplayers.

When Paige's comments hit the mainstream media, they unleashed a firestorm of protest against Kuhn's plan for "back door" honors. The Hall of Fame had to retreat from its position, and on July 6, 1971, Kuhn announced that Satchel Paige would receive full induction honors at a special ceremony.

During the next several years, a special committee appointed by the Commissioner began selecting additional honorees, choosing a player for each position. The goal was to move quickly in establishing the *first team* of all-time great black ballplayers. Following Paige, there was catcher Josh Gibson, first baseman Buck Leonard, second baseman Martin Dihigo, third baseman Judy Johnson, outfielders Cool Papa Bell, Oscar Charleston, and Monte Irvin, and finally, at shortstop, John Henry "Pop" Lloyd.

Twelve years following his death, in 1977, Pop was inducted into the Baseball Hall of Fame in Cooperstown, New York. On hand at the induction ceremonies to acknowledge the honor and speak on behalf of the people of Atlantic City was Assistant Superintendent of Schools, James Usry, one of the many men Pop had mentored in their youth. He spoke of Pop and the honor conferred that day. "Pop was an exemplary player. He was a great coach, a dedicated worker, and above all, a humanitarian ... I accept with profound sadness and regret that neither Pop Lloyd nor his wife, Nan Lloyd, lived long enough to experience this, their fondest dream. I know, however, that he looks down with his warm wide smile. I accept fondly with the deep sense of gratitude, intense gratitude to the selection committee, and to those many others who were instrumental in furnishing information, background material, etc. for this the ultimate award in sports."

Pop's plaque at Cooperstown reads:

JOHN HENRY LLOYD
"POP"
NEGRO LEAGUES 1906–1932
REGARDED AS THE FINEST SHORTSTOP TO PLAY IN
NEGRO BASEBALL. SCIENTIFIC HITTER. BATTED
OVER .400 SEVERAL TIMES DURING HIS 27-YEAR
CAREER. PERSONIFIED BEST QUALITIES OF ATHLETE
BOTH ON AND OFF FIELD. INSTRUMENTAL IN HELP-
ING OPEN YANKEE STADIUM TO NEGRO BASEBALL
IN 1930. MANAGED MORE THAN TEN SEASONS.

Racism couldn't deny Pop this final honor. In the end, he prevailed. But Pop is more than a name on a plaque in the Baseball Hall of Fame. To this day, Pop Lloyd's legacy remains a vital force in the greater Atlantic City community. The John Henry "Pop" Lloyd Committee preserves his memory and that of Negro Baseball, holding an annual awards ceremony to honor individuals who exemplify Pop's service to their community. It's a fitting tribute to such a fine gentleman and role model.

Racial prejudice spawned more than the Negro League. It created another incubator for African-American talent of equal significance. Again, in response to white America's refusal to accept black people as serious entertainers, the black community created a network to showcase singers, dancers, musicians, and comedians. This chain of stages was comprised of everything from churches, impromptu theaters, and restaurants to diners, bars, and juke joints. It came to be known as the "Chitlin' Circuit."

Some prefer the more genteel contemporary term of "urban theater circuit." Regardless, the Northside was a stop on the Chitlin' Circuit, an important stop—so prominent, it can be argued it wasn't part of the circuit but rather a galaxy of stars all its own. Through their own unique resistance to racism, the people of the Northside had created a nationally recognized resort within a resort.

The primary venue for clubs featuring African-American talent was Kentucky Avenue. The pulse was strongest at Kentucky and Arctic Avenues. To many, it was known simply as "K-y at the Curb."

8

"K-y at the Curb"

The blues is truth music started way back after the Civil War. It's the music that blacks brought to America ... because all the rest of it was brought here by Europeans who migrated here. But the blacks, the slaves who came here, gave them truth music. America's only music was given to them by the blacks, and it started with the blues, where they could tell the truth.

—Chris Columbo, musician and raconteur

Hecklers weren't common at Club Harlem. It was a place where bands played through breakfast, and the music roared like nowhere else in Atlantic City. The jewel of the Northside's entertainment district, Club Harlem was one of the most chic and talked-about nightclubs in the Northeast. It was the swankiest, most glittering showplace south of New York City, frequented by stylish blacks and whites from throughout the region and famed for its large and faithful following. The club's patrons were generally well-mannered, if not always sober.

Saturday night was always a tough ticket. Club Harlem was a magnet for visitors who appreciated live music. At the height of the season, the club put on two stage shows daily—three on Fridays and Saturdays—each running an hour and a half. These world-class productions featured a house band, dancers, comedians, singers, and an array of prominent headliners. The stars whose names graced the marquee over the years included Billie Holiday, Sarah Vaughan, Dinah Washington, Sam Cooke, James Brown, Ray Charles, B. B. King, Aretha Franklin, and Sammy Davis Jr. A child star, Davis first learned about the club from his father and uncle who were part of the Will Mastin Trio. His mother, Eliera "Baby Sanchez" Davis, also came to Atlantic City during the summers. She worked as a barmaid at Grace's Little Belmont, a jazz bar across the street from Club Harlem. Mrs. Davis maintained close ties to the Northside in the years following her son's extraordinary success.

On Saturdays, the last show ended around 4:30 AM and was followed by the "breakfast show" beginning around 6 AM. "The breakfast shows were the biggest things at Club Harlem ... The other clubs closed at four in the morning, so the [fans and musicians] would come over to see the breakfast show and sit in and jam. Of course, they really didn't serve breakfast. It was something else." Those making impromptu appearances included not only top black entertainers but white performers like Frank Sinatra, Milton Berle, Dean Martin, and Jerry Lewis. "The breakfast show was a big money maker. Anyone out partying at 6:00 AM would do some serious drinking."

Sid Trusty, a drummer who sat in on many jam sessions at Club Harlem, recalled, "That place had a groove. You'd hear about it and you'd think it couldn't be true. ... Just thinking about the folks that came through the place—Sugar Ray Robinson, Sammy Davis, Joe Louis ... and all the beautiful dancers." Trusty continued, "People were unified in their desire to have a good time. As musicians, we learned to enjoy ourselves being ourselves. Every night was our party, and we invited the world." When the jam sessions ended, "everybody would head over to Lessies' Tea Room for grub, then grab their swimsuits and go down to the Missouri Avenue [Chicken Bone] beach." Much of the chatter at the beach was about who would be performing next at the club.

Seating nearly a thousand, located in the middle of the block on Kentucky Avenue between Atlantic and Arctic Avenues, the club always had a long line of guests outside, all dressed to the nines, weaving from the entrance of the club around the corner. "And one of the great things about the shows at Club Harlem was you would find people standing in line for hours—and the lines would stretch beyond Kentucky Avenue all the way around Atlantic Avenue and they would stand there just waiting to get in to see the shows. Everyone who was anyone appeared there." While it had a dazzling marquee, the club's exterior was fairly routine and provided little clue of the magic inside. But music lovers knew.

Club Harlem was one of the few places in America during the '40s, '50s, and '60s where one would find many white fans waiting patiently to see black performers. This Saturday night was no different. A large number of those waiting in line were returning customers and avid fans, but not everyone would get in to see the show. Many of the men had two $10 bills earmarked—one to be pressed in the palm of the doorman, a gentle giant, 7'7" tall, named Raymond Harris, and a second to be slipped into the maître d's tuxedo suit pocket. Given his extraordinary height, Harris was a local landmark of sorts and was hired to appear at many functions. In addition to Club Harlem, he also worked the door on special nights at Skinny D'Amato's 500 Club. Known around town as "Seven Foot Seven," he had bit parts in horror movies and is remembered by many as the lead majorette in the annual Elks' Parade on the Boardwalk.

The club's patrons came for fiery singers, exciting dancers, and scorching brass and drum sounds. They were rarely disappointed. Inside was an extravagant mirror-backed bar where continuous music was provided by several small bands rotating performances into the early morning hours. To the left of the bar was a door leading to the back showroom, where the main attractions performed.

Working in one of the club's bar bands was a coveted opportunity for aspiring musicians. One tall, athletic maître d', James "Big Jim" Usry, who excelled in basketball and baseball (and was one of Pop Lloyd's "students"), went on to become a school administrator and eventually mayor of Atlantic City. Usry recalled his 15 summers at Club Harlem as "a wonderful job and a real education. I learned a lot about what makes people tick and how to handle them."

Sparkling and glittering, the showroom was full-bore show biz without being garish. It was as fancy as any place you could find in New York City and unlike anything Philadelphia and Baltimore residents had ever seen. Untold numbers of vacationers from all three cities found their way to the club. "It was better than any showroom you had in the casinos, where you're so far away from what's happening that you don't feel it. The seats may be more comfortable in the casinos, but at the Harlem you got an impact of what's happening."

Cutting-edge comedy was woven into the show between the musical acts. It was often raucous, rapid-fire, and risqué, the type seen today on late-night cable television—think Chris Rock. Among the regular stand-up comedians was Slappy White, who had a long and colorful career with many people hearing him for the first time at Club Harlem. He could be irreverent. In one of his routines, he imagined a religious black man questioning God about his physical features:

> And so the black man said to God, "Lord, why is my skin this dark?"
> And the Lord replied, "My Son, it is so that the intense sun in Africa will not burn you."
> And then he said, "Lord, why is my head covered with a large mass of kinky hair?"
> And the Lord replied, "My Son, that is so the mosquitoes and other insects in Africa cannot bite your head."
> So this black dude says, "Then, God, why the f*#k am I in Atlantic City?"

No one ever upstaged Slappy White. He had a powerful stage presence, and few MCs knew how to give him the space he needed to do his thing without letting him dominate the entire show. The master of ceremonies who presided over each performance at Club Harlem was Larry "Good Deal" Steele. He understood the talent he had to work with as well as his audience. Always meticulously groomed, Steele had the voice and poise to match his appearance. Rarely permitting the stage lights to shine on him, he graciously allowed the entertainers to bask in the applause while taking his satisfaction from the perfection of his productions.

Larry Steele was more than a veteran showman; he was an innovator and pioneer in live entertainment. He organized traveling companies of black entertainers and, in addition to working the "Chitlin' Circuit," booked his productions into any white venue that would accept them. He did Las Vegas long before it was a national resort, and some believe his ideas influenced the opulent shows for which the town is celebrated today. One notable accomplishment was his success with *Smart Affairs,* a production that broke the color barrier at the prestigious Cotton Club in Miami Beach.

Always on the lookout for talented female entertainers, Steele helped launch the careers of scores of young women. Everywhere he went, from Atlantic City's Boardwalk and beaches to its churches and bars, he used his recruiter's eye to search for new cast members. He had his finger on the pulse of the music world and knew how to please a crowd, regardless of color. He conceived, produced, and directed show after show featuring beautiful, long-legged women, including *Smart Affairs, Beige Beautes,* and *Sepia Revue.* His goal was to "glorify the beauty, the soul and the talent of the black woman." All of his productions appeared at the club in the summer and toured the country during the off-season. "There'd be a 15-piece band, ten chorus girls, and eight showgirls, and they could dance to the tempo, all moving across the stage like soldiers, never touching each other. You'd wonder how they did it."

The music was nonstop at Club Harlem. Backing up the featured vocalists and all of Steele's productions was the house band led by drummer and master showman Chris Columbo. A homegrown talent, Columbo was born on the Northside in 1902. He gravitated toward music from childhood, growing serious about the drums by the time he reached his teens. While still a teenager, he played at Truckson's Hollywood Grill, a tavern on the Northside. When he was 21, he began playing with the big bands of Fletcher Henderson and Jimmy Lunceford, both of which performed at local dance halls. Columbo later went to work at the Paradise Club and, after a few years there—having gained the necessary "chops" and confidence—moved to New York where he became part of the uptown Harlem scene, performing at the Cotton Club, the Apollo Theatre, and the Savoy. At the Savoy, he played drums for the show *Happy Feet* and helped local performers like Ray Tune, Rufus Wagner, and Art Davis break into the New York entertainment world. Sometime in the late 1930s, Club Harlem owner Leroy "Pop" Williams lured Columbo back to Atlantic City to put together the house band, "Christopher Columbo and his Swing Crew."

For years, Columbo's life had a rhythm of its own. He appeared from June through September at Club Harlem, spending the other eight months in Manhattan and on tour, playing clubs, concerts, and recording sessions. But Columbo wasn't just an accomplished entertainer and raconteur—he was a drummer for justice in the workplace. He fought segregation in the show business world. He traveled widely during his long career, and in each town he visited, he would stroll into the business office of the local musicians' union and apply for membership. More often than not, he met resistance from the union leadership; little did they know that he had a contact "on call" at the U.S. Department of Labor. A telephone call from Columbo to

Washington, a second call to the union office, and *presto*—the local union was integrated.

Traveling and touring for more than 30 years and returning to Atlantic City and Club Harlem summer after summer, Columbo worked with many jazz greats, from Cab Calloway to Duke Ellington and Billy Eckstein to Sammy Davis Jr. His appearances at the club and his own radio show as "Captain Swing" made him into a local celebrity. Usually charming, occasionally brash, he was a born entertainer who thrived on stage. He had the instincts needed to handle an entire audience and any one unruly patron. Blessed with thick skin and a quick wit, on this Saturday night, both traits would serve him well.

Upset with the loudness of the music this evening, a white man began behaving badly. Rising from one of the club's high-backed, art deco–style red-and-black booths to make himself seen and heard, the man rudely registered his displeasure in the direction of the band-stand. The drummer gave him a thrashing. The tale is best told by Chris Columbo himself:

> I only had one man that I ever got angry with what he said to me, and I *should* have been angry. He looked up and said, *Why do you niggers play so loud?* and I said, *Sir, would you like for me to tell you why we play so loud?* and he said, *Yeah*.
>
> So I said, *Well, I'm gonna slow the band down and quiet them down so you can hear*. And I picked up the mike and said, *So that your wife won't hear you asking the broads how much it costs, that's why we play so loud*. Well, he really was messed up. I wasn't angry when he called me a nigger, *Why do you niggers play so loud?* so I just told him why, so that his wife wouldn't hear him when he asked them broads how much it cost. And that's what he was doin.' There was a broad sitting next to him and he was trying to proposition her, and he couldn't get his message across and we were playing. He's sitting right under us and he wanted to know *Why you niggers have to play so loud?* So instead of getting mad, I told him why we played so loud.

The patron was silenced, and the night went on without incident. Club Harlem was a special place, but the story of the Northside's entertainment district is a whole lot more than Club Harlem. Entertainment was a key ingredient in Atlantic City's success in gaining repeat business. "Word of mouth" has always been the best advertisement, and no place in the resort provided more captivating and talked-about live shows than the ones on the Northside. In its prime, the Northside's nightlife was a major draw for the resort. For many visitors who stayed in Southside hotels, it was the beach during the day and the Northside for entertainment at night.

Entertainment had long been part of Atlantic City's hotel-resort package. The railroad's excursion houses permitted traveling singers, dancers, and musicians to perform, after which they would pass the hat. From the resort's earliest days, performers gravitated toward public spaces, primarily the Boardwalk and high-volume street intersections. The same was true for the larger hotels: They had dinner shows and afterhours cabarets, featuring singers and musicians from Philadelphia and New York City. As for the saloons, brothels, and casinos that blossomed under the reign of Louis Kuehnle, there was always some type of entertainment sprinkled in with the "booze, broads, and gambling"—usually someone strumming a banjo, blowing a harmonica, or playing a piano, sometimes accompanied by vocals. The beautiful, sepia-toned working girls of "Chalfonte Alley," Atlantic City's red-light district, also entertained with song and dance. By the turn of the 20th century, there were numerous theaters, burlesque houses, and concert halls staging not only vaudeville shows but serious productions, many using the resort as a "try-out town" before moving on to New York's Broadway. As always, the resort's goal was to offer something for everyone.

Black entertainers didn't have the same access to a stage as white performers, and most of their careers had a different launching pad, namely, their churches. The black church was an incubator for more than civic and religious leaders—it was the place where aspiring performers got a first chance to try out their voices before an audience. In the early African-American churches, there were no musical instruments; pianos and organs came later—*everyone* was expected to sing. As one successful blues/soul/rock songstress recalled of finding her voice in church, "You don't need gimmicks to sing from the heart. Music from the heart reaches the heart." Just as the early slaves adapted Christianity to their unique situation, so, too, did African Americans adapt their musical talents to the opportunities presented. Church was the first opportunity. When one looks at the personal histories of successful black entertainers throughout the 20th century, it's difficult to find one who didn't start his or her career through participating in the musical aspects of their church services. Nothing could have been more natural.

As is true of other cultures, music is a river running through the lives of African Americans. However, what sets African-American music apart from other forms is the number of tributaries that come together to create this stream of expression. The African people who came to the Americas in the 17th and 18th centuries were not an ethnic monolith. The people forced into slavery comprised dozens of different cultures kidnapped out of West and sub-Saharan Africa. In the era in which slavery became a profit-making enterprise for Europeans, the African continent was every bit as ethnically diverse as the continent of Europe, and the number of dialects spoken exceeded Europe's.

Abducted to America beginning in the late 16th century, the earliest African people in America struggled with more than their chains. They were forced to overcome language differences in communicating with one another in much the same way that, hundreds of years later, immigrant Italians, Germans, Poles, Eastern European Jews, and Scandinavians did at the dawn of the 20th century. Over time, English became the spoken language for all. But what about music? It flowed differently. Try to imagine those European ethnics coming together in song; it didn't happen, but it did for African Americans, and the result was extraordinary.

Voices were the first instruments utilized by African slaves in America. Sharing the common experience of oppression, they pieced together words spoken by their masters to create songs reflecting on their condition. Inspired by traditional slavery work chants and spirituals, many of these early songs were coded messages encouraging escape from their slaveholders or dreaming of freedom from their shackles. An early form of blues-like music took the form of call-and-response shouts, which originated with slave field hands. These shouts and hollers expanded into solo songs. Stringed instruments were generally allowed by the slave owners (drums were not), who viewed them as similar to European instruments like the violin.

Slaves who managed to cobble together crude guitars or banjos out of strips of wood, dried gourds, and braided strings of grass were free to play and sing. Over time, the call-and-response tradition evolved into emotional music of voice and guitar sung by a single individual.

Following the Great Emancipation, the opportunities for musical expression expanded. During the latter part of the 19th and the first quarter of the 20th centuries, as the Northside was coming into its own, the music of African Americans evolved and the river widened. Despite the growing sophistication of their music, white America refused to accept black people as serious entertainers. In response, the black community created a network of its own to showcase singers, musicians, dancers, and comedians. This boundless entertainment found an outlet on the Chitlin' Circuit.

What's not taught in high school history classes is that Jim Crow cast a shadow throughout the nation, not just across the South. "No Colored Allowed" signs were more common in the North than in the South. Segregation was the *law* in the South. There was no need for signs. Blacks knew their limits and obeyed them. It wasn't until the Civil Rights Movement of the 1960s that southern businesses began posting "White Only" signs. In the North, there was the illusion of equality, but it was custom and practice for the races to remain separate. Generally, throughout the nation, African-American entertainers had no more access to mainstream white venues than did black baseball players. Throughout the first half of the 20th century, Atlantic City was the rare place where black people performed before integrated audiences.

Neither black entertainers nor their audiences could be denied. The Chitlin' Circuit arose to meet local desires and tastes and, over time, a chain of diverse venues catering to black patrons developed spontaneously across much of the country. It was the only option for touring black entertainers who wanted to hone their talents and gain exposure. Historically, it's believed that Baltimore was the first city on the circuit.

Early venues of the circuit were juke joints offering food, beer, music, and dancing, catering mainly to black audiences. Located primarily in African-American enclaves in small cities east of the Mississippi, these clubs—including several tap rooms on the Northside—were hot spots where locals could enjoy touring black entertainers. The circuit stretched south from Baltimore, bending westward through Texas, extending north to Chicago, and continuing east to Cincinnati, Pittsburgh, Philadelphia, and New York. First the blues, then ragtime, and finally jazz flowed through the circuit and inevitably washed over the greater American music scene. Some say the blues was the root of all other popular American music forms. W. C. Handy, a founding father of the blues, said, "The blues is where we came from and is what we experienced. The blues came from nothingness, from want, from desire."

Blues music made its way to Atlantic City, but the Northside wasn't exactly *part of* the Chitlin' Circuit. It was something more. In the early 1900s, as residence patterns hardened and social forces coalesced, a river of blues, ragtime, and jazz flowed to the resort and found a home in the bars, restaurants, and clubs of the budding black community. Music nourished the Northside and created an attraction that helped set Atlantic City apart from other tourist destinations.

Denied access to the entertainment facilities on the Southside, enterprising blacks created their own places of amusement. The first known amusement house in Atlantic City where blacks could gather to drink and socialize was established in 1879 by M. E. Coats. It had the first liquor license issued to a black person and was believed to have been on Indiana Avenue. Given the era, the featured music was likely the blues, black folk music influenced by work chants and spirituals. Another early café and dance hall was Fitzgerald's Auditorium on North Kentucky Avenue. Built in 1890, and starting out as a dance hall for African Americans featuring ragtime, Fitzgerald's grew in popularity, becoming a bar, restaurant, nightclub, and gambling room. Equipped with its own "race wire," which enabled a type of radio-simulcasting, it was the first gambling joint on the Northside. There was "a pool room downstairs, race horse room in the back, a big wall where you could pull the curtains and you could hear the horses run, *They're off and running.* You could make your bets right there." During the Great Depression, Fitzgerald's fell on hard times, and business declined to little more than dances and roller skating in its ballroom.

Fitzgerald's was bought by Pop Williams and his brother, Cliff, in 1935 and renamed Club Harlem. One of their early benefactors was Madame Sara Spencer Washington. Williams worked with her in staging a special show each year on Easter Sunday, with a spring fashion show the following Monday. It was an elegant affair. When Williams was asked why he named his establishment Club Harlem, he replied, "That's where a lot of black people live."

Club Harlem is remembered today as a vibrant, pioneering showcase for black entertainers from throughout the nation, but that's not quite what it was under Pop Williams. For more than 15 years after Pop bought Fitzgerald's and renamed it, the club's main source of revenue was gambling. Gambling wasn't confined to the Southside and, in fact, the numbers game was born on the Northside. As related by one longtime resident, when Nucky Johnson elbowed his way into the Northside numbers game, he agreed to permit more gambling operations—horse rooms, card games, and mini-backroom casinos—in the black community in exchange for the numbers bankers' help in spreading their game throughout the entire city. By 1951, gambling rooms in Atlantic City, and on the Northside, in particular, were slowly fazing out, and Pop decided it was time to expand the club's entertainment operations. Enter his liquor salesman, Mendel Tischler of Federal Wines and Liquors.

With wheels to match those of Nucky Johnson—Tischler drove a Rolls Royce—Mendel Tischler was extraordinarily successful in business. The foundation of his success was loyal customers who considered him not just their liquor salesman but their banker. Then, as now, New Jersey law prohibited liquor distributors from extending credit to tavern owners. With its seasonal economy, this created a hardship for most of Atlantic City's bars and restaurants, and there were many bills that went unpaid through the winter. No matter, Tischler plugged the gap in the off-season by paying the liquor wholesalers himself and then personally granting financing to all his customers come the fall. When things perked up in the spring and cash began flowing, Tischler collected on his loans. It wasn't legal, but no one seemed to care.

Among Tischler's customers were Pop Williams and Jewish businessman Ben Alten, who had a financial interest in the Paradise Club at the time. When Tischler brought the two men together, brokering a deal in which Alten bought into Club Harlem, he had no way of knowing that the resulting partnership would last a lifetime. For Pop, in particular, the timing was fortunate: He was in trouble with the IRS, and unless he could raise some serious cash, he was looking at a potential jail term. Added to his frustration at being unable to get the IRS off his back, he couldn't afford to make critical improvements to his nightclub. Neither the numbers bankers nor the Northside Credit Union were prepared to handle such a large loan, and the town's white bankers weren't lending to the likes of Pop.

From his involvement with the successful Paradise Club, Ben Alten was able to make things happen for Club Harlem in ways Pop had not expected. First, he secured the needed cash to help Pop satisfy the IRS and upgrade the property. What had been a nightclub seating fewer than 500 was nearly doubled in size by the time Alten finished acquiring property and making the planned addition. He was not only a capable businessman but a *mensch* (Yiddish for someone who "always does the right thing") who was happy to let Pop bask in the club's newfound success.

Alten and Pop made quite a team. Alten ran the business competently but gently, overseeing operations, handling creditors, and making staffing decisions during the day to ensure things ran smoothly at night. Pop was the face of the club to most of the patrons during the evening, working the crowd and creating a convivial atmosphere for customers and staff alike. Any serious problems that came up had to wait until morning. As recalled by Alten's son, Steven, who worked in the business while growing up, "Ben was in his office every morning between 6 and 7 AM. That's when the real business of running the club took place. Ben had great respect and affection for Pop and Cliff Williams, but Pop was not a businessman. He had basically operated the club out of a shoebox until Ben took over."

Alten and Pop both had an eye for talent, and during the off-season, they took trips to New York City together, seeking out and signing acts for the following summer. They spent a great deal of time together, yet never quarreled. They always agreed on who they thought was an up-and-coming prospect to be showcased at the club. Under Alten's direction, Club Harlem was the anchor of K-y at the Curb until the time of its closing in 1986.

Another early nightclub of similar pedigree to that of Fitzgerald's was the Waltz Dream on North Ohio Avenue. Founded in 1903 by a white woman from Philadelphia (remembered only as "Mrs. Thomas" today), the club was a large recreation center and dance hall that provided entertainment in the broadest sense. There were weekly dance contests, wrestling and boxing tournaments, and basketball games, all playing to sold-out crowds. The Waltz Dream was the site of many black charity events; when dances were held at the hall, popular black orchestras played to capacity crowds of more than 2,000, young and old alike.

The Waltz Dream was a favored venue of the legendary James Hubert "Eubie" Blake. Born in Baltimore in 1887, Eubie was the child of former slaves and the sole survivor of their eight children, all his siblings having died in infancy. He grew to love the Northside and first appeared at the Waltz Dream with his band in 1907. He developed a relationship with the people on the Northside that spanned the remainder of his famously long life.

Eubie returned to Atlantic City each summer through 1915. After several years of touring the country, in 1921, he made a triumphant return with his orchestra to perform at the Apollo Theatre on the Boardwalk, playing to sold-out crowds throughout the summer. As recalled by Chris Columbo, blacks were permitted to attend Blake's concerts but "had to go to the back door, climb five or six flights of steps" and were confined to the rear portion of the balcony, "looking down between your knees at the show on stage."

Eubie Blake and his band were described as "the sensation of the season." Over the years, despite his international celebrity status, Eubie continued to make regular appearances at various clubs in the resort. He knew how to give back, too. In August 1923, he performed in a "monster benefit" concert at the request of the St. Augustine Episcopal Church.

Together with his vaudeville musical partner Noble Sissle, in 1921, Eubie Blake wrote, produced, and directed *Shuffle Along*, the first Broadway musical to feature an entirely black cast. The production included the song, "I'm Just Wild about Harry," which years later became President Harry Truman's 1948 campaign song. As Sid Trusty recalled, "I was a young man when I saw Eubie for the first time. He was at the Little Belmont. He had a full orchestra of really talented musicians. What a showman. He was the epitome of class." Eubie Blake was a beloved honorary citizen of the Northside until his death in 1983 at age 96.

It can be argued that Fitzgerald's and the Waltz Dream were stops on the Chitlin' Circuit, as they hosted virtually all the popular traveling black entertainers of the day. Atlantic City was a desirable stop because touring bands such as Eubie Blake's found audiences willing to pay for first-rate talent in the Northside's clubs. But things were different in Atlantic City from the outset. It was one thing for white audiences to pay to see black entertainers in a Boardwalk concert hall, but quite another for whites and blacks to sit together in a nightclub on the Northside. Unlike anywhere else, white visitors came to the resort for the purpose of crossing the racial divide to see black entertainers. The earliest illustration of this may be the Paradise Club.

As the Waltz Dream was growing in popularity, one of political boss Nucky Johnson's key players in the local gambling scene, Ralph Weloff, bought property nearby in the 200 block of North Illinois Avenue. The year was 1919, and Woodrow Wilson had moved on from the New Jersey's governor's mansion to the White House. With Wilson's help, Victorian morality won a major victory with the adoption of the 18th Amendment to the U.S. Constitution. Prohibition, which banned the manufacture, sale, and transportation of intoxicating liquors, was doomed to failure, particularly in Atlantic City. New Jersey was the last state to ratify the amendment, and Weloff bought the property knowing the sale of alcoholic beverages would soon be illegal. No matter—selling liquor unlawfully was nothing new in Atlantic City. Resort tavern owners had violated the state's Bishops' Law for years by serving drinks on Sunday. If they could get away with it one day a week, why not seven? With Nucky's blessing, Ralph Weloff's new business would be pouring drinks regardless of the law.

Weloff, who knew gambling, teamed up with Dave Abrams, who knew black entertainment. The two of them opened a casino known as the Gold Room. There are no surviving photos of the Gold Room, but it is remembered as a large gambling room with card and table games, hard liquor, and quality entertainment. There were many gambling options in the resort and, before long, entertainment became the primary draw and the Gold Room's reason for being in business. The development of the Gold Room represented a phenomenon that would play out all across urban America during the 1930s, '40s, and '50s, namely, Jewish businesspeople operating businesses in black neighborhoods, catering to black people.

History helps to explain this phenomenon. The Jews who fled Russia and Eastern Europe at the turn of the 20th century and the African Americans who migrated North during the several decades following the Great Emancipation had a core attribute in common: Their identities had been forged in oppression. The people of both races had scars on their psyche that few other ethnic groups comprising America's patchwork quilt could appreciate. While Jews didn't live in slavery, at least in the modern era, many lived in constant fear of random violence, something blacks knew firsthand. African Americans had their labor and freedom stolen from them, but Jews had seen their homes and assets stolen any time the government they lived under granted permission for a *pogrom*.

The Jewish and African-American peoples have similar stories. Just as blacks were subject to being ripped from their families and "sold down the river," so, too, were the Jews. The term "pogrom" refers to the wave of anti-Jewish riots (i.e., massacres) that swept Imperial Russia in the late 19th century. The triggering event was the 1881 assassination of Czar Alexander II, for which arch-royalists blamed the Jews. During these pogroms, thousands of Jewish homes were destroyed, with many families reduced to poverty. Young women were raped, and large numbers of men, women, and children were beaten and killed in hundreds of towns throughout Russia, all with the tacit support of the czarist government. These experiences led to a significant Jewish migration, mainly to the United States.

As a noted African-American historian has said, "The black folk said [to the Jews] 'We've been down for a long time. While you were getting your butts kicked in the Ukraine, we've been getting our butts kicked here.'" By the time of the 19th-century migration wave, pervasive Christian attitudes branded both Jewish and black people as less than human—a status the dominant society saw as sanctioned by divine authority. As a consequence, Jews and blacks developed an empathy that existed between no other ethnic groups in America. There were times when this empathy translated into business success.

Ralph Weloff and Dave Abrams were successful at staging elaborate musical productions featuring black entertainers. Apparently, as Weloff saw his investment becoming more of a showroom for entertainment, as opposed to a gambling casino, he opted to sell his interest in the business to Al Branch, an adjacent bar owner and Northside businessman. Abrams remained involved (in time, his son Harold followed him), but Branch was the driving force in joining the two properties together to create a major entertainment venue and casino.

Branch decided to rename the business the Paradise Club. According to Chris Columbo, who played there:

> The Paradise Club was the first nightclub in the world. Before that you had the cabarets and cafés, where entertainers would come right up to your table and sing risqué songs. You don't have that entertainer now, you have stars.
>
> I can remember when the Paradise was owned by a black dude named Al Branch. He kept building and building and soon he had this big, ugly room. But when the lights went off it was the most beautiful place in the world.
>
> The entertainment was 90 percent black. The trade was 90 percent white. They'd all come down from the Traymore at night in rolling chairs like a regular parade. There were so many whites slumming to see black entertainers they just didn't leave any room for us.

Entertainment of a high caliber—along with the freedom to consume alcoholic beverages without fear of police raids—made the Paradise Club a hit with both white vacationers and local residents on the Northside. While the Paradise Club was Atlantic City's first true "nightclub," whether that term was coined in the resort won't be resolved here. What is beyond dispute is that the club was a forerunner of the many nightspots that made the Northside entertainment district so dynamic. It created an environment in which white people could experience African-American entertainers alongside black patrons.

The Paradise Club also encouraged collegiality among visiting entertainers by becoming the place to congregate after hours. Before Club Harlem even existed, "The manager of the Paradise would send telegrams to entertainers all over the city, inviting them to a breakfast show starting at 5 or 6 AM, when the other clubs would be closing up. The show ran until 10 or sometimes noon. It was a performer's chance to be judged by a jury of his peers. Sometimes there would be a million dollars worth of entertainment up on the stage jamming."

Hal Abrams, who followed his father in managing the Paradise Club, spoke of one early morning session. "During one breakfast show Jerry Lewis came over and did a pantomime to some records. He was so awful that we turned the lights off in the middle of his act and asked him to leave. He was pretty indignant, of course. He left, and I believe he went over to the 500 Club to try his luck with Skinny." Hopefully, most readers know how things turned out for Jerry Lewis and Dean Martin at the 500 Club at the encouragement of its owner, Paul "Skinny" D'Amato.

Abrams fostered another tradition at the Paradise besides the breakfast show, namely, the "burial." It was a production in which the performers would close out the season saluting one another's talents. They did this by taking on a part they had never done during the season, as a way of acknowledging their fellow cast members' abilities. According to Chris Columbo, "In black entertainment the last show of the season was called the burial, or the burial of the show. That night all the performers switched roles. At one burial at the Paradise a chorus girl named Carmen McRae sang instead of danced and was advised by the manager, Hal Abrams, to switch her profession to singing. ... He [Abrams] didn't call all the shots right, though. I remember him turning down Billy Eckstein's offer to work for $75 a week and Nat King Cole for $200 a week."

A final note on the Paradise was its strong bond with the community. Living in today's world of neatly defined zoning districts and strict limits between "night life," businesses, and homes, it's hard to conceive what a vibrant and intense mix of uses co-existed side-by-side in parts of the Northside. The Paradise was a vital part of the neighborhood. Surrounded by homes and located a short walk from churches and public schools, residents of all ages on the Northside were happy to have the club as a neighbor and admired the success of the performers. The community enjoyed an atmosphere of respect and civility between resident families and the transient population involved in the entertainment business. As one longtime resident of the neighborhood recalled:

> Club Harlem was preceded by another club that was on
> Illinois Avenue ... that was called the Paradise Club. The
> Paradise Club was a nightclub; it had a doorman and
> beautiful ladies who were hostesses. There were any

number of jazz greats who appeared there before the existence of Club Harlem. There were great dance troupes that performed on stage, besides the jazz artists. So that was the first club, and I can remember my dad putting me on his shoulders so we could look into the side door and watch the performers as they were practicing.

The little girl on her father's shoulders, Joanna LaSane, went on to become a world-class model. She was one of the first people of color to appear in national and international ads of a major corporation, Pepsi Cola, and in the 1960s, toured internationally as a part of Ebony Fashion Fair, sponsored by *Ebony* Magazine. No doubt her conceptions of glamour and style were shaped, to some degree, while propped on her father's shoulders gazing at the performers on stage at the Paradise Club. During its final years, the club was operated by Ben Alten, and when the opportunity with Pop Williams arose, he had a tough decision to make. Once things got going with Club Harlem, he closed the Paradise Club and devoted all his energies to the new venture. Financially, it was a wise decision. The Paradise Club was more or less a stand-alone business, while Club Harlem shared the energy of related businesses on Kentucky Avenue. Regardless, old timers familiar with the history of the Northside's entertainment district will tell you that despite the fact that the Club Harlem name has had far greater staying power, it was the Paradise Club that first established the aura of classy black entertainment and the standard for all entertainers who came to town, making Atlantic City a place to be—and return to—for those who loved music and nightlife.

Kentucky Avenue had an ambience all its own that drew return visitors. Year after year, summer nights between Atlantic and Arctic Avenues had the electricity of a never-ending block party. A significant portion of the guests at this particular block party were white. As one historian of the era has noted, "They went on tour to see, feel, smell, and maybe even touch primitive blackness up close. They went to the Timbuktu, Wonder Gardens, and the Club Harlem to hear black men belt out jazz riffs and to watch black women shake their bodies and to Sapp's, Jerry's Ribs, and Wash's Restaurant to eat southern 'soul' food, plates piled high with crispy fried chicken, smoky tender ribs, and fat wedges of sweet potato pie."

On many nights, the pedestrians were so numerous that they clogged the street, making Kentucky Avenue impassible to automobile traffic. According to local legend and folk historian Sid Trusty, "There was a time when you couldn't see the ground for the people. There wasn't nothing but people on either side of the street. This is where everything happened."

Another musician who became a legend of Kentucky Avenue was "Wild Bill" Davis. His talent was a first on the American music scene. Davis was a jazz organist. "They say you could always tell when Wild Bill Davis was playing Kentucky Avenue ... because Davis's jazz organ would come swinging out of the front doors of Grace's Little Belmont and, right about in the middle of the block, get in a street fight with the music coming out of the Club Harlem, which sat on the far sidewalk."

Davis played Atlantic City 25 straight summers, and people lined up to hear him. Chris Columbo, who played with Davis on many occasions, once said, "He brought the organ out of the church and the funeral parlor and took it into the street. There were no organ players in jazz—it would never have been heard of if not for him." Wild Bill Davis was a virtuoso. He was so respected in the world of jazz that he was invited to play with some of the biggest names, including Duke Ellington and Count Basie. "The Duke is the one who put 'Wild' in front of Bill Davis's name and [Davis] was responsible for developing the arrangement for one of Basie's biggest hits, *April in Paris*."

In the 1930s, William James "Count" Basie became to the Northside what Eubie Blake had been a generation earlier. Born in Red Bank, New Jersey, in 1904, Basie fell in love with Atlantic City as a young man, and the affection was returned. When automobiles eventually replaced horses, Basie's father—a coachman for a wealthy family in Monmouth County—became a groundskeeper and handyman for several families in his home county. Basie's mother was a laundress who played piano at church and taught her son to play while still a child. As a teenager, the Count began accompanying blues singers touring in vaudeville. He picked up the basics of early ragtime from some of the great Harlem pianists and studied organ informally with the legendary Thomas "Fats" Waller, one of the all-time great jazz pianists as well as a master showman with a wonderful flair for comedy. Some believe Fats Waller's influence on the young Basie's stage personality was as critical as the music itself. While still in his twenties, Basie started his own band and was soon touring with many of the popular blues and jazz vocalists of the day. The Count's career spanned more than 50 years and included not only live performances and recorded music but also appearances in numerous Hollywood movies.

The Count first appeared in Atlantic City during World War II at the Paradise Club. He returned many times, appearing at Club Harlem and Grace's Little Belmont, and played a final, farewell concert "on the beach" in 1984. Throughout the 1940s and into the '50s and beyond, when many big bands were falling by the wayside, Count Basie maintained a 16-piece orchestra. The Count and his bandmates exuded an enthusiasm that charmed audiences and sealed the relationship with a rhythm that was contagious. Over the decades, Basie's band featured a long list of inspired soloists who blossomed under his leadership. Jazz legends Lester Young, Herschel Evans, Buddy Tate, and Lucky Thompson all played with Basie and became favorites in Atlantic City.

Basie loved his times performing and staying on the Northside, walking the streets, eating in the local restaurants, and mingling with the locals. He spoke of the resort fondly in his autobiography:

> Our big extended engagement for that summer [1948] was at Club Paradise in Atlantic City ... That gig at Club Paradise turned out to be pretty nice for us.
>
> Everybody did have to take a little cut in pay because we had to reduce our asking price to get in there, but we had a ball even with all those long working hours and all those high Atlantic City living expenses. In the first place, the show itself was a gas. It was what the newspapers used to call "an all-star sepia revue." It was produced by Ziggy Johnson, who was right up there in the same class with Larry Steele when it came to putting on great shows with beautiful chorus girls, singers, and comedians. When it came to big production numbers with fabulous costumes and sets, he was just great. For one feature number with the chorus, they brought an organ in for me. That is what the number "Paradise Squat" is all about.

Basie enjoyed the camaraderie with Chris Columbo and other performers appearing that summer in Atlantic City. Columbo said of
him, "When I look at Count Basie, I think of one thing—a great, big,
beautiful, ripe sweet honeydew melon, and that's what he is. He's
one of the nicest guys."

While the resort's population mushroomed to 300,000 or more in
the summer, the Northside still had a small town feel. Everyone made
the visiting entertainers—none of whom could stay in a Southside
hotel—feel welcome. Count Basie enjoyed "hanging out together"
because, as was the case whenever he came to the Northside, "so
many of our old friends from all over the East Coast were always
dropping down to Atlantic City." But it wasn't all work, and "hanging
out together" included more than breakfast jam sessions:

> As long as our workday at Atlantic City was, the fellows
> still found time to have fun that Summer. [Several band
> members] organized a softball team and played games
> against teams that either had gigs in Atlantic City at the
> time, such as Harry James, Louis Prima, and also against
> local teams; sometimes they were firemen and policemen
> or maybe bartenders. ... We didn't get off until 5:00 in the
> morning, but sometimes there were 2 or 3 games a week
> and I am talking about morning games.
>
> I really think just about everybody enjoyed being at
> Atlantic City that Summer because quite a few guys had
> a chance to have their families with them during that time
> and take the children to the amusement places and the
> beaches along with all the other things that were going on.

Some of the other things "going on" included partying on the
beach. Throughout the Northeast in the 1940s, '50s, and '60s, there
was a network of successful black entertainers, athletes, promoters,
and entrepreneurs who, when big name performers like Count Basie
were in town, beat a path to Atlantic City. They got together to mix
and mingle, to see and be seen on "Chicken Bone Beach."

Barring the mixing of the races in the resort wasn't confined to
housing. On the island, there was no more basic recreation in summer than a day at the beach; as the number of blacks enjoying the
seashore increased, so did the demands of the white establishment

seeking to prevent white hotel guests from mixing with people of color. The beachfront was comprised of several beaches, akin to mini-neighborhoods and representing such groups as the wealthy, seniors, teenagers, the Irish, Italians, and Jews, along with beaches corresponding to neighborhoods of Philadelphia and Camden. The principal beach assigned to black people was at the foot of Missouri Avenue, and blacks who went to the beach were well aware of its confines. The limits of Chicken Bone Beach were generally enforced by lifeguards and beach boys working for the hotels. Although there were instances of unpleasant confrontations between police and out-of-town vacationers, few black people strayed far from the area bounded by Arkansas and Missouri Avenues.

Recollections of most old-timers trace the moniker "chicken bone" to the latter part of the 1920s when the Claridge Hotel opened. Prior to that, the city's unofficial black beach had been at Indiana Avenue. "We used to go bathing at Indiana Avenue, 'til they built the Claridge Hotel and stuff there. Then they would tell the people who worked in the hotels, 'You don't go to Indiana Avenue any longer, because you go making too much noise and disturb the guests.' Then they'd tell you where you go. So we went down to Missouri Avenue."

When the Claridge's hotel guests complained at having to share the beach with colored sunbathers, blacks were forced to move several blocks south. The section of the beach chosen for them by the city was in front of the construction site of Convention Hall, which opened in May 1929. Research yields no one claiming to have coined the name "Chicken Bone Beach," but there's little doubt the term was initially assigned by white residents, derisively, as an expression of their contempt and aversion.

Linking blacks with chicken was part of a time-honored practice among American minstrel performers seeking laughs at the expense of "coons." Beginning shortly before the Civil War and continuing into the early 1900s, minstrel shows featured white entertainers whose faces had been blackened with burnt cork. They depicted blacks as shiftless, lazy, naive buffoons who sang and danced the day away, munching on watermelon and stealing chickens. Two black-face characters nearly always depicted were "Jim Crow," an ignorant country bumpkin ripe for humiliation, and "Zip Coon," a city slicker who always got his come-uppance. The early American film industry exploited these stereotypes and "coons" were featured in popular comedies such as *Wooing and Wedding of a Coon* (1905), *How Rastus Got His Turkey* (needless to say, he stole it), and *Chicken Thief* (circa 1910–1911). The prototypical movie coon was Stepin Fetchit, a slow-walking, slow-talking, self-demeaning nitwit. Cinema historian Donald Bogle lambasted the coon, as played by Stepin Fetchit and others:

> Before its death, the coon developed into the most blatantly degrading of all black stereotypes. The pure coons emerged as no-account niggers, those unreliable, crazy, lazy, subhuman creatures good for nothing more than eating watermelons, stealing chickens, shooting crap, or butchering the English language.

The people who frequented Chicken Bone Beach were hardly stereotypes. They were a cross-section not only of the Northside but of black Americans from throughout the Northeast. There were both local and visiting professionals, including doctors, lawyers, clergymen, and educators taking a day off with their families; singers, dancers, musicians, and bartenders relaxing for a few hours in the afternoon before returning to work on Kentucky Avenue; high-stakes gamblers, numbers bankers, loan sharks, and pimps giving away food and drink, especially to pretty women; and, finally, vacationing working class people who arrived by train and bus as part of an "excursion."

And, yes, many of the excursionists brought fried chicken from home. As recalled by Chris Columbo, "Blacks knew how to fry chicken. Colonel Sanders still don't know how to cook chicken. It's all right long as it's hot, but blacks knew how to cook chicken that … you could wrap up in a towel and put it in one of them cake boxes and eat it for days, without it being refrigerated, and it was always good." And, yes, the occasional chicken bone could be found on the beach at Missouri Avenue. Nevertheless, as recalled by Sid Trusty, "That beach was beautiful. All the black athletes, stars, and showgirls would be on that beach. We didn't get much sleep, but that was the last of our worries. We were pretty young and … we were too busy enjoying it to realize how special it was."

Defying the expectations of the white community was something the people of the Northside did well. Chicken Bone Beach became the most exciting place to be, populated with memorable characters. One of them, recalled by a beach chair concessionaire, was "Champagne" Frank Thomas from New York. "Every day he served champagne in silver goblets. Every day he'd come down, he'd stay here most of the summer, he wore a leopard bathing suit … Everybody would know about the champagne and he would be there handing out the champagne."

Another unique character was Woogy Harris. "He was a big gambler from out of the Pittsburgh area. I'll never forget the time he brought down 19 showgirls. He told me he wanted 20 chairs and I was just getting started … in those days lines were the thing. We had long lines of maybe 70 chairs underneath a canopy, or we'd have umbrellas."

One of the "lines" was special. "There was many a day when we'd have Sammy Davis Jr. and the Mills Brothers and Louis Jordan and maybe Sugar Ray Robinson, and Moms Mabley was there all the time. They'd all be there at one time, and the show girls from the Harlem … and they'd all congregate there and I had a special row. They called it Sunshine Row … That section I had to keep for them, and I wouldn't dare rent it to anybody else. That would just be for them only."

Frequently these celebrities entertained everyone lucky enough to be at Chicken Bone Beach. "They would put on all kinds of skits and all kinds of crazy stuff, and I remember Sammy Davis used to hand one of his help his watch to keep there and on the back was inscribed: *To the greatest little entertainer in the world—Sammy Davis—from Sammy Davis.* He was that kind of fellow, you know."

Sammy Davis Jr. returned to Atlantic City many times, and his career encompassed song, dance, acting, and writing. For this observer, his performance on Broadway in *Golden Boy* was lightning in a bottle. Nothing can surpass it. The acclaim received by Sammy Davis on the stage and Jackie Robinson on the ball field was gradually forcing white America to take notice.

Talented entertainers and athletes had broken the color barrier and, as the 1950s gave way to the '60s, popular culture would never be the same. But opportunities in show business and sports were limited, and serious obstacles remained in employment, housing, education, law, medicine, and government. New pioneers were needed to claim these territories, and in due course they arrived. In the wake of World War II, a new generation of leaders emerged, men and women who looked bigotry in the eye and refused to cower.

The Northside was prolific in turning out courageous leaders in the struggle for equality, years before the birth of the Civil Rights Movement. One man stands out for his intelligence, tenacity, and accomplishments. He was a force unto himself.

9

Breaking Down Barriers

Horace J. Bryant Jr. was a warrior for freedom ... A drum major for justice ... and a long-distance runner for human rights. He left an awful lot of good behind.

He was strong, stubborn, warm, forceful, concerned, justly proud, creative, courageous and effective.

He was witty and nitty-gritty, elegant and down-to-earth, a force to be contended with.

—Gene Robinson, political and social leader

"Lillian, you told me this white boy was smart. He sounds like a dumb ass to me. How'd he get elected to anything?"

"Hold on, daddy, I don't think you understand what we're up against. They've shut us out completely."

"I understand well enough to know there's seven of them on the board and two of you—you and this lawyer—God, I hope he's a better lawyer than he is a politician. Hell, girl ... you got them right where you want them."

"What?"

"You're my daughter and you don't get it? You're as dumb as him."

"What am I missin'?"

"Girl, you can make them squirm. You got the luxury of no responsibility. But you got power! You move, he seconds—he moves, you second. Bam! You've got a motion on the table. Play to the crowd on things they don't wanta do. Hit 'em with resolutions you know will embarrass 'em and let them worry about what to do with 'em. *Expose* them. Do that a few times and they'll cooperate with you."

The lion in winter, counseling political newcomers and inspiring them to take up the fight. While those around him were bemoaning their plight, Horace J. Bryant Jr. was analyzing the situation. Let others complain and vent their rage, Bryant was planning his attack. By the time most people got around to thinking strategy, he had the logistics figured out and was ready to lead the charge. Horace Bryant was a leader all his life. Whether serving in Trenton and mastering the intricacies of finance and insurance, agitating for civil rights and leading protest demonstrations years before Rosa Parks refused to sit at the back of the bus, or running for political office in Atlantic City—and then running again and again when a black man was supposed to know better—he was a born leader.

Compared to others of his generation, Bryant began life in prosperous circumstances. Born June 29, 1909, to Sarah Elizabeth and Horace Joshua Bryant in Lawnside, Camden County, New Jersey, Horace Jr. was the first of eight children (six boys and two girls). It was a noisy and fun-loving household with everyone having their chores but also ample food, clothing, shelter, and the means for education. Theirs was not a hardscrabble existence dependent on seasonal income; Horace Sr. and Sarah were significant players in the local economy generally—not just the African-American community—in a time when that could be said of few black people. They were not to be trifled with.

Horace Sr. had trekked north from Georgia after Emancipation, learning the craft of carpentry. Strong willed and hard working, he began building homes in what's commonly referred to as "central Camden County" in the early years of the 20th century. His success in the construction business led to acquiring vacant land and developing residential subdivisions, not a game for amateurs. His buyers included whites and blacks alike. A drive through the Camden County communities southeast of the city of Camden reveal several Bryant Avenues.

Much like Sara Spencer Washington, Horace Bryant Sr. exploited business opportunities through the economic concept of vertical integration. He saw that a natural outgrowth of homebuilding was insurance. The Bryant Agency was the first black-owned insurance firm in New Jersey and thrived for more than 70 years until it was eventually merged into another firm. Horace Sr.'s business holdings also included a gasoline and service station where several of his children got early training in how to deal with the public. He parlayed his economic success into political clout with the Republican organization in Camden County. He was the first African American named to the position of Clerk of the Assembly in the Republican-dominated New Jersey Legislature.

Horace Sr. was a man of means and influence, and his family held a special place in his hometown of Lawnside. Steeped in African-American history, Lawnside has deep roots in the abolition movement and, then as now, everyone in the community was aware of its important role in the struggle for freedom. Lawnside became a player in that struggle because it was home to a successful free black farmer, Peter Mott, and his wife, Elizabeth. The Motts made their way to New Jersey from Delaware in the 1830s, settling in a free black community, Snow Hill, which later merged with a neighboring settlement, Free Haven. The Motts earned a place in history for themselves, and for Lawnside, because they were willing to make their home a stop on the Underground Railroad.

The "railroad" was a vast network of people dedicated to helping fugitive slaves. It wasn't run by any single organization but rather consisted of thousands of individuals—including many whites but predominantly blacks—who knew only of local efforts to aid fugitives and not of the overall operation. Each year, the railroad carried hundreds of slaves north to freedom. According to one estimate, from 1810 to 1850, the Southern slave masters lost more than 100,000 of their forced laborers to the railroad.

We know this network began not long after the Revolutionary War because of comments made by George Washington himself in 1786. A slaveholder, Washington complained that one of his runaways was helped by a "society of Quakers, formed for such purposes." The system grew, and around 1830, the term "Underground Railroad" was coined. Steam locomotive railroads had entered the American consciousness, and the name was fitting for people on a journey. Organizers adopted railroading terms: Homes and businesses where fugitives could rest and eat were "stations" or "depots" and were run by "stationmasters." Those who contributed money or goods were "stockholders," while volunteers who helped guide fugitives from one station to the next as they made their way north to freedom were the railroad's "conductors."

Running away to the North was difficult and dangerous. Slaves had to rely solely on their wits. The first step was to find the right moment for escaping from the slaveholder. If caught, it meant, at a minimum, a severe lashing and possibly death by lynching or shooting. Sometimes a conductor, posing as a slave, would enter a plantation and then guide the runaways northward. The fugitives generally traveled at night, covering 10 to 20 miles to the next station, where they would eat and rest. Sleeping in barns and other hiding places, such as attics and cellars, waiting for word that the next station was ready, they then continued on their journey. Peter and Elizabeth Mott were stationmasters and, for approximately 20 years prior to the Civil War, their home provided refuge to runaway slaves on their way to Canada. The prevailing attitude in New Jersey toward black people during the first half of the 19th century wasn't hospitable, and for their acts of mercy, the Motts risked scorn, hostility, and financial reprisals from white society. But their courage meant freedom for many.

Snow Hill and Free Haven were renamed Lawnside in 1907, becoming the only ante-bellum, free African-American community to become an incorporated municipality in New Jersey. It wasn't possible for Horace Bryant Jr. to grow up in Lawnside and not have a keen awareness of the struggles black people had endured.

After completing grammar school in Lawnside and high school in nearby Haddon Heights, Bryant enrolled in Temple University in Philadelphia. It was a time when black applicants were scrutinized carefully by mainstream universities, and there were no college loans. Having an affinity for numbers, Horace majored in accounting, graduating with honors in 1929. Although eager to put his education to work, he was rebuffed at every turn.

As recounted by his daughter Lillian, "My father came out of Temple with accounting and real estate as his major, and he couldn't get a job. He was very fair, with hazel eyes. My grandfather had a gas station where my father worked, and people made jokes about having an educated man pumping their gas. Well, he took the civil service test [for a position as junior insurance examiner with the New Jersey Department of Banking and Insurance] and he came out number one, and ... through my grandfather's involvement in the Republican Party my father was considered for his first job."

That first position in 1930—at the height of the Great Depression—had an annual salary of $1,800, and Bryant was glad to have it. Horace Sr.'s financial fortunes were hit hard by the Depression, and he wasn't "hiring," not even his own children. (He did use his political influence to help several of them find positions in government.) Despite Bryant's qualifications, he received a less than cordial reception at the Department of Banking and Insurance. A white co-worker chided him, saying, "You have no future, *ever*, in this department."

Because his position as an examiner was based in Newark and required him to travel to many of the communities of northern New Jersey, Bryant resided temporarily in New York City. In November 1937, he purchased tickets to the Army-Navy game in Philadelphia and asked his brother Isaac to join him. Isaac told him he was bringing a "couple of friends." When they met in Philadelphia, Isaac had two young ladies with him, one of whom was Lillian Weekes, a schoolteacher from Atlantic City. Mischievously lulled into a "blind date" by his brother, Bryant enjoyed Lillian's company enormously, and it wasn't long before he was beating a path to the resort every weekend.

Horace Jr. and Lillian married in 1939 and took up residence with her parents, Reginald and Eva Weekes, at their Atlantic City home on McKinley Avenue. Reginald Weekes and his two brothers hailed from Barbados. The three had arrived in Atlantic City in the late 1890s, had seen the business opportunities of a growing town, and quickly sank roots. Their first business predated the automobile. The Weekes owned horse-drawn carriages, which they hired out to hotels to greet customers at the railroad station. Reginald and his brothers were savvy businessmen and, like many others of West Indies lineage, soon became part of the Northside's entrepreneurial class.

By the second generation after their arrival in the resort, the extended Weekes family owned restaurants, bars, and a large fleet of taxis (the car having replaced the horse). In addition to pursuing new business opportunities, the Weekes—like the Bryants—invested in "social capital," seeing to it that all their children and grandchildren were educated. Their daughter Lillian was a graduate of prestigious Howard University in Washington, D.C., where she majored in education. The Weekes family's reputation was that of tough, shrewd, and honest businesspeople. Their flagship business, which was a major source of revenue for the family for nearly 50 years, was Weekes' Bar at Illinois and Baltic Avenues.

After graduating from Howard, Lillian returned to Atlantic City and began teaching the fifth grade in or around 1932, several years before meeting Horace. "She taught in the same classroom of the same school building [the New Jersey Avenue School] for the next 31 years" and impacted the lives of hundreds of students, many of whom went on to become success stories in their own right.

Lillian was as committed to her life with Horace Jr. and his career as she was to educating the young people on the Northside. Together they had a daughter, also named Lillian ("Little Lil"), who attended Morgan State and later served many years in both city government and with Atlantic County as a freeholder. What the elder Lillian could not have imagined was what an adventure life with Bryant would be.

True to his father's political loyalties, Bryant made an effort to become part of the town's Republican organization. It was a mistake. Local politics were now controlled by Nucky Johnson's successor, State Senator Frank "Hap" Farley. Hap lacked Nucky's charm and when it came to interacting with black people, he couldn't fill Johnson's shoes. Needless to say, things didn't go well for Bryant with the Republicans.

Bryant attended several meetings of the Northside Republicans known as "Hap Farley Standpatters" (that *really* was their name, to indicate they weren't leaving the Republican Party for Roosevelt's New Deal Democrats, as many black voters were doing across America). The explanation for why Bryant and the Standpatters couldn't mesh isn't complicated. Farley and his lieutenants weren't comfortable with independent thinkers, especially an educated black man with a mind of his own, not content to simply go along with the status quo. "My father often remarked about how he came here as a Republican [still the "party of Lincoln" for many African Americans] and was asked to leave the party because he asked too many questions. He was a little too inquisitive and was not going to be told what to do." Hap Farley and his Standpatters had no time for an "inquisitive" black man, especially one with knowledge of how government was supposed to work.

Bryant began to put that knowledge to work for all the people of the Northside when, in the early 1940s, with Joe McQwinn, Ike Nicholson, and several others, he formed the Northside Union League. With early meetings held in the Northside YMCA, the Union League was an early civil rights organization, years before anyone was even using that term.

Every Friday night, the Union League met to spread the word that segregation should not be suffered in silence. Over time, it became an incubator for new leaders on the Northside. Bryant's daughter, Lillian, recalls that the meetings were "part politics, part personal finance, part social talk, and all about uplifting black people and pride in who we are." It wasn't long before Bryant and the Union League members started an offshoot organization, the Northside Federal Credit Union. This is where Bryant showed his true talents as a leader and earned the loyalty of hundreds of Northside families.

Among the more prosperous Northside businessmen were the numbers or "policy" bankers, and Bryant was the accountant for most of them. In the late 1940s, he convinced several of them that they should deposit some of their substantial cash holdings with a credit union that would be used to make loans to the residents on the Northside. Walter Greenidge, Ike Nicholson, and Bruce Williams all agreed to invest cash with the credit union. Then Bryant reached out to the Northside's doctors, dentists, lawyers, clergy, businesspeople (Madame Washington was a supporter), schoolteachers, and city employees (anyone with regular income) and encouraged them to invest as well. In short order, a new financial institution was up and running. And this one lent money to ordinary black families for everything from purchasing homes and starting up businesses to paying for college or hairdresser and barber schools. But Bryant didn't stop there.

Not only did the credit union lend money, it educated borrowers on managing their money and, over time, turned many of them into social activists. Bryant met at the credit union with local residents every weeknight, teaching such skills as how to create a household budget, balance a checkbook, and generally manage a family's funds. His daughter recalled, "Years later I would run into people who told me my father had turned their lives around by teaching them how to handle money."

Ever the agitator, Bryant would encourage more substantial depositors to take a portion of their funds and deposit them in Atlantic City's white-owned banks that refused to lend money on the Northside. After they had accounts there for several months, Bryant instructed them to apply for a loan. When they were rejected, they would reply, "I guess I'll just take my money out of here and go on over to the Northside Credit Union. They'll make me a loan." Their deposits were quickly yanked from the bank, and their accounts closed. This ruse was played out by scores of depositors and gradually local banks got the message. Thanks to Bryant, in an era when there were few parallels in other cities, ordinary wage-earning Northside residents began to have banking options.

At the prompting of the Union League and many of the credit union's depositors, Bryant ventured into politics, running for Atlantic City's City Commission in 1948. There was no "ticket." No one else would run with him. His campaign slogan was "Stand in line, vote number nine and go blind." ("Go blind" refers to voting for no one else, or as is said in local politics, a "bullet vote.") There weren't enough bullet votes out of the Northside. There were still too many Standpatters, but Bryant had sent a message to Hap Farley's organization, and there was much more to come.

Four years later, Bryant took another shot at City Commission, and this time he was part of a ticket. The 1952 commission election featured something previously unheard of: an opposition slate. The "Fusion-for-Freedom Ticket" was headed by former Atlantic County Sheriff James Carmack. He had fallen out with the organization shortly after becoming sheriff in 1941 by failing to clear his patronage appointments with Farley's machine. He was joined by Marvin Perskie, a pugnacious former Marine officer who was also a brilliant, articulate young attorney. Perskie had run unsuccessfully as a Democrat (a died-in-the-wool F.D.R. New Deal Democrat, not a "Farleycrat") for State Assembly three years earlier. Perskie also was so bold as to defend the "Four Horseman," several Atlantic City police officers who had refused to play by the organization's rules. They had demanded a promised raise and, when denied and humiliated, began making arrests for violations of the state's gambling laws. The Republican organization viewed this as disloyalty, and the policemen were brought up on charges of misconduct and crushed by Farley's people.

Marvin Perskie had witnessed the machine's viciousness up close. Perskie raged at the corruption of the local Republican organization and vented that rage at every opportunity. For his efforts to bring honesty to city government, he was treated like a leper by the local power establishment. Shortly after the formation of the Northside Union League, Perskie became a regular at Friday night meetings.

He and Bryant had developed a strong bond. Perskie asked Bryant to join the Fusion ticket, and Bryant couldn't resist.

With Perskie firing most of the salvos, the Fusion ticket made one blistering attack after another against Farley and the Republican machine. Bryant scrutinized the public records he could get out of City Hall, and the Fusion ticket began making its case for change to the voters. Cozy relationships between local contractors and city government were exposed. The payment of insurance premiums and vendors' contracts to local politicians were revealed. The details of the lawyer fees paid for a municipal finance bond ordinance the previous year were also made public. Of the nearly $100,000 in fees paid by the taxpayers, only $21,000 went to the New York law firm that actually did the legal work for the bond issue. The remaining $78,000 was divided among Farley and 11 of his cronies, with Hap himself receiving $9,500 in "legal fees" despite having done nothing at all.

Perskie and Bryant named names and criticized the Republican organization like never before. Bryant also had the financial support of Madame Sara Spencer Washington. Fusion ticket fliers and posters appeared all over town, many being destroyed immediately, then replaced, only to be destroyed again. Madame Washington made one of her limousines available for Bryant to campaign throughout the city. As recalled by Little Lil, who made the rounds with her father, "I can remember sitting in the backseat of Madame Washington's big limousine. Signs with my father's name were taped to the doors. She had her driver take my father all around town. I didn't know anything could be so exciting."

It was an inspiring campaign and grand political theater, but it went for naught. Hap Farley put the fear of God in city workers and the party rank-and-file, appealing to them in terms they understood: If the Fusion ticket won, they would be fired and ward workers would lose their access to political patronage. Farley also brought Nucky Johnson out of retirement and turned him loose on the Northside. Despite his imprisonment and the passage of time, Nucky remained popular with many older voters on Northside. Nucky stumped for Farley's slate in every black precinct, being introduced as "The Champion of 'em all." Farley's strategy worked. The Republican machine slate cranked out the vote, carrying 49 of the 64 voting precincts. Carmack, the "high man" for the Fusion ticket, trailed Tom Wooten, the "low man" on Farley's ticket by nearly 3,000 votes.

Bryant had lost again, but he wasn't beaten. He continued his work with the Northside Union League, the credit union, the newly created local branch of the National Association for the Advancement of Colored People (NAACP), and St. Augustine's Church. He couldn't restrain himself when he saw injustice. He made waves. He annoyed many whites in Atlantic City who viewed him as an "uppity nigger." No matter. Bryant organized parents to demand better school facilities for their children. He protested the segregation of movie theaters. He led residents to picket on the Boardwalk outside Convention Hall when racist groups came to town. Mouths dropped. Bryant persisted. People followed him. No one *dared* interfere.

Bryant also threw himself into his work as an examiner with the New Jersey Department of Banking and Insurance and gained the respect of his fellow employees as the person to go to on a tough problem. By acing every qualifying examination and being patient and persistent, he received several promotions within the department, becoming Assistant Chief Examiner, Chief Examiner, and then Deputy Commissioner. He was appointed to the advisory board of the National Insurance Development Program by H.U.D. Secretary Robert Weaver in October 1968. Eventually, his expertise was recognized by the governor's office.

On January 17, 1969, Horace J. Bryant Jr. was nominated by New Jersey Governor Richard J. Hughes, a Democrat, to serve as the Commissioner of the Department of Banking and Insurance. He would become the first African American to serve in a New Jersey governor's cabinet. Bryant's role in resort politics, especially his confrontations with the Farley organization, was no secret to the media. At the time he made his announcement to the press, Governor Hughes stated, "I have taken care of the amenities," referring to Senator Farley. There are some who believe that Hap Farley would have relished blocking the appointment through exercising "senatorial courtesy," but he was too smart for that. Nevertheless, Farley required that a meeting be held at his office before he would release the appointment from the Senate Judiciary Committee.

Little Lil recalls of her father, "The night before their meeting, he was churnin' and burnin'. *'If he says that, I'll have to say this and if he responds the way I think he will, I might not be able to control myself. Who knows what I might say if I get angry at him—next thing you will know we'll be cussin' one another and it'll all fall apart.'"* But it all worked out. Both behaved and were their savvy selves. "They talked like old friends. Farley was very philosophical and was willing to let bygones be bygones. [Lillian believes it was more likely he didn't want to offend Governor Hughes.] Farley told him he'd be glad to offer up his nomination to the Senate."

Bryant served with distinction as Commissioner of Banking and Insurance and during his term had the pleasure of encountering the fool who years earlier told him he had "no future, *ever.*" Bryant greeted the man courteously, smiled his sweetest smile and thought to himself, "Nice to see you, jackass." In 1972, State Banking Commissioner Horace J. Bryant Jr. retired from state government to take another shot at City Commission. This time he was successful.

Atlantic City's politics were overdue for a major shakeup. The Republican organization had taken a huge hit in the fall of 1971 when Senator Hap Farley and his team were thrown out of office by a newly resurgent Democratic Party. The political machine that had been dominant for three generations was in disarray. The following spring, there was a serious opportunity for a reform/fusion ticket. Bryant was asked to join a slate led by a young banker, Jay Bradway. They ran with three others under the banner "Save Our City." Only Bryant and Bradway were elected from their slate. This time, the voters of the Northside were solidly behind Bryant. He was elected easily, trailing closely behind the two machine-endorsed white candidates. Bradway came in fifth, winning by a mere 55 votes. The remainder of the "Save Our City" slate went down to defeat. Despite the fact that Bryant hadn't made history as he had as member of the governor's cabinet, some people believe his election to City Commission was even sweeter for him.

Bryant served eight years as city commissioner, overseeing revenue and finance. (He was re-elected in 1976 with running mate and protégé Pierre Hollingsworth but was defeated in 1980.) He was a workaholic, arriving before everyone else and working long past the time City Hall closed. From his first weeks in office, Bryant's trademarks were his expertise with budgetary matters and his ability to quickly grasp the governmental and political ramifications of any issue. "There were city employees who expected him to turn their world upside down. They thought he was going to do everything based on skin color and politics. They were surprised. He was all about merit and gettin' the job done."

The commissioner's quick wit, together with a willingness to share his knowledge and to counsel anyone who sought his advice, made him a favorite with employees and the public alike. Even at City Commission meetings, which could be raucous affairs, "He had the ability to quiet an angry crowd with humor. It happened so many times. He always felt that if you couldn't laugh about something, you'd fall." His sense of humor sometimes camouflaged his shrewdness. He could single-handedly engineer a one-man filibuster and defeat unwanted ordinances, all the while cracking jokes and getting even his adversaries to laugh along with him.

Despite his many battles, Bryant never tired of the fight. He never lost faith that blacks would prevail in their struggle for justice. Shortly before his death in 1983, he said, "Most white people know that black people got the shitty end of the stick in American history and we're still gettin' only crumbs from the white man's table. But people know the difference between right and wrong and the right will win out. It's just sometimes they need a kick in the ass to get 'em to do the right thing."

Bryant loved his community and proved it throughout his career as a steward of the people's trust. He set a standard of excellence few can attain. No one elected to City Hall since his tenure as City Commissioner has been his equal.

Horace J. Bryant Jr. stood at center stage of the Northside, but he didn't stand alone. He had a strong and talented supporting cast and their roots were predictable. During the many years in which the Northside's churches had cultivated their congregations, they had produced a bumper crop of leaders. When looking back to the 1940s and '50s, an era ostensibly "pre" the Civil Rights Movement, what is most striking is the number of ordinary people in Atlantic City doing extraordinary things. Everyday role models are the marrow of a community and the quiet leaders who create a healthy society. The core of the Northside had many such leaders. They battled racial prejudice at every opportunity.

Pursuing virtually all professions and career fields, the Northside's leaders involved themselves in every aspect of uplifting their community and breaking down the walls of segregation. In ways large and small, they drove the equal rights agenda forward.

They started businesses not only to profit from their efforts but to create jobs. They went off to World War II and fought for our country in segregated units. Upon their return, many utilized the G.I. Bill of Rights to buy homes and further their education. Other veterans applied and reapplied to the city's police and fire departments until they were accepted and became role models in uniform. They got involved in everything from working to improve the academic, physical, and spiritual well being of children, both in school and at church, to securing college scholarships and job opportunities for promising students. They organized and patiently pushed for reforms, chipping away at malignant workplace barriers, which had metastasized into American society, but they boldly shoved when needed to ensure that blacks who had earned rights in their chosen fields weren't passed over for less qualified white candidates.

Those people today who bemoan the supposed unfairness of "affirmative action" need to know that this country had affirmative action in reverse for many years. For the last half of the 19th century and first half of the 20th century, who your parents were, where you were born, which neighborhood you lived in, what church you attended, and which school you graduated from were the decisive factors in employment and other opportunities. "White Anglo Saxon Protestant," known as WASP, candidates were always favored, regardless of ability. Non-WASP Caucasians—Italians, Jews, and Irish—could generally succeed (within limits) on their merits. Not so for black Americans.

For blacks, skin color was the deciding factor. To even be considered for a position, their abilities had to be superior to those of white competitors. And often that was not enough. The Northside leaders discussed in the following pages (and in the Appendix) were all accomplished individuals. They came of age in a time when the term "affirmative action" had yet to be coined, and when advancements for black people came only after a fiercely determined struggle. It's not possible to name all those from the Northside whose careers as activists overlapped with Horace Bryant Jr.; there were so many noteworthy lives. Acknowledging that there are numerous additional persons who warrant recognition, a partial survey follows.

Margaret Lee Caution was anything *but* cautious when it came to uplifting her people. A member of Governor Alfred E. Driscoll's 1950s task force on civil rights, she worked on legislative issues affecting people statewide as well as advocating on behalf of individuals. In one instance, she successfully appealed a state agency's decision to by-pass a Northside resident who had more seniority and better credentials than other candidates. The resident was promoted to manager of the local State Employment Office.

Caution encouraged Northside residents to take the civil service exam and then prodded the local Republican Party to hire black people in both the police and fire departments. Her confrontations with Public Safety Director William Cuthbert over his failure to hire black residents are legendary. As recalled by Elwood Davis and Ada McClinton, two key players in the "Summer of Freedom" (see Chapter 10), "She barged into his office so often that Cuthbert took to hiding from her. He would leave his office in secret, escaping her by going out the back stairs of the old City Hall. One day Caution was at the bottom of the stairs waiting for him. She had her umbrella in one hand (she took it everywhere with her) and an application of a qualified candidate for the police department in the other hand. Cuthbert was exasperated. He gave up and the person was hired."

Employment wasn't Caution's only concern. She pushed for the adoption of the New Jersey Public Accommodations Act of 1953, which ensured that the resort's Boardwalk hotels could not refuse rooms to people of color. (Prior laws had banned discrimination but there were no penalties for violation.) She got the ear of Governor Driscoll, and the law was changed.

Judge Herbert S. Jacobs wasn't the first Northside resident to become an attorney, but he was the first African-American judge to sit on the Atlantic County bench. A graduate of Dartmouth College and New York University, where he was often the only black student in his classes, "Herb" Jacobs had a keen mind for the law. After several years in the U.S. Attorney's office, he came to Atlantic City and developed a successful practice. Respected by everyone on the Northside and by the Atlantic County Bar, he was appointed to the court by Democratic Governor Richard Hughes, who convinced Senator Frank Farley that it would be a bad move to block the appointment with "senatorial courtesy." Judge Jacobs served with distinction and is remembered by all who appeared before him as a gentleman and a "lawyer's judge."

One story in particular from Jacobs's years on the bench deserves telling. In the early 1960s while sitting in Landlord Tenant Court, the judge received a call from an out-of-county lawyer asking if he was required to appear personally at the "call of the list" in order to secure a default judgment against a tenant he believed was unlikely to appear. Jacobs told him it was his practice to require an appearance. Given his name, the lawyer assumed Judge Herbert Samuel Jacobs was Jewish and complained, "Give me a break, Judge. It's a long ride to Atlantic City. The tenant's a *schvartze* [a Yiddish term used disparagingly to refer to a black person] and I know he won't show for court." The lawyer's comment made Jacobs more determined that his appearance was necessary. To quote the judge, "You should have seen this man's face when I called the list. I was worried he might have heart failure."

Margaret Creswell was another early pioneer in Atlantic County law, namely, the local police department. Born in Greenville, South Carolina, she moved to the resort in 1919 with her husband, Bernard Creswell. Creswell's law enforcement career began in 1929 as a clerk with the Atlantic County Sheriff's Office. She became the first policewoman—black or white—in the state of New Jersey and served as a patrol officer for 40 years from 1924 to 1964. A dedicated servant of humanity, she concentrated her energies on female juveniles and rape victims. Privately, she collected food and clothing for the needy. Active in numerous civic organizations, she took lead roles in the United Sons & Daughters of the British West Indies and the local NAACP. When she retired from the department, she was issued "Badge No. 1" in recognition of her long and distinguished service.

Cora Boggs was a community activist for many years, founding the "Gild the Ghetto" youth development program, which took Northside teens off the street for weekly work, study, recreation, and discussion sessions. A longtime executive committee member of the NAACP, Boggs co-founded the Atlantic City Congress of Community Organizations, an umbrella organization of civic associations around the city. She was one of the early proponents of the creation of an agency to utilize a portion of casino gaming revenues to fund public improvements, which eventually resulted in the establishment of the New Jersey Casino Reinvestment Development Authority.

Joseph Allmond was determined to make his mark in the local police department. A World War II U.S. Army Air Corps veteran, he received a special citation for "extreme courage and heroism under fire" for dragging a wounded comrade 50 yards to safety during a gun battle that left seven officers wounded. Joe Allmond became a rookie police officer in 1947, a beat cop patrolling the Northside on foot. In 1960, he was promoted to sergeant, and eight years later, he was appointed captain. Two years later, he became chief inspector of detectives and, finally, in 1979, was named the first African-American chief of police in the resort's history. He was listed repeatedly in *Who's Who in American Law Enforcement*. He was a member of the International Association of Chiefs of Police, and served on the board of the Northside YMCA, the Westside Convalescent Center, the Atlantic County Criminal Justice Advisory Board, and the Vestry of St. Augustine's Episcopal Church. Throughout his career, Chief Allmond gave back to the community, working with the youth of the Northside and serving as an inspirational role model.

Aleathia B. Ward was a "teacher's teacher" and so much more. Having earned her BA and master's degree from Glassboro State College (now Rowan University), she was a respected innovator in education. Listed in *Who's Who in American Education*, she conducted seminars and workshops throughout the region. A longtime member of the Phi Delta Kappa professional sorority for educators, she was among the founders (including Dorothie Dorrington) of the Iota Chapter in Atlantic City. The sorority's mission is "To foster a spirit of sisterhood among teachers and to promote the highest ideals of the teaching profession." Ward lived that spirit. As part of her female students' education, she taught them about grace and elegance. She was the first chairperson of "The Cotillion," a formal ball at which the young ladies of the Northside were "presented to society." A local institution for more than 55 years, the town has nothing to compare with the Cotillion's enduring grace and style.

James L. Usry was another educator who made important contributions to the Northside. A lifelong resident of Atlantic City, he was born in Athens, Georgia, and his family came north while he was a young child. Affectionately known as "Big Jim," Usry was a U.S. Army veteran, professional athlete, part-time maître d' at Club Harlem (see Chapter 8), and educator. He stood 6′6″ and is remembered as a giant of a man who never raised his voice. A classroom teacher and school principal, Usry rose to the position of assistant superintendent of the Atlantic City Public School System and was a

The First Railroad African Americans provided the labor to build the first railroad to Atlantic City in 1854. Some historians believe slave labor was used. (Photo circa 1900.) [Courtesy of Corbis]

Storm Repairs Work that was dirty, difficult, or dangerous—the "three Ds"—was performed by black laborers. Notice who is working and who is watching following storm in 1898. [Courtesy of ACFPL]

Railroad Accident African-American railroad workers repairing track following a train collision, circa 19[...] [Courtesy of ACFPL]

City Street Work, circa 1950 The "three Ds" again. One hundred years after the first railroad, African Americans were still maintaining the city's infrastructure.

[Courtesy of ACFPL]

George Walls George Walls was Atlantic City's first African-American entrepreneur and a "social activist" before the term was coined (circa 1900). [Courtesy of ACFPL]

Walls and Family Walls was an early civic leader who fought for the right of black children to be educated and helped establish the Northside YMCA (circa 1905). [Courtesy of ACFPL]

Black Vacationers At the end of each summer, the railroads offered their lowest priced
outings. Many black people in the Northeast came to visit relatives and friends working in
the resort. [Courtesy of ACFPL]

Alonzo and Maggie Ridley In 1900, this dynamic pair founded the first Northside hotel, known as the Hotel Ridley. [Courtesy of Mary Ward]

Ready to Serve From 1880 to 1930, Atlantic City's hotel workforce was 95% African American. Remove them from the town's history and the city never comes to be.

St. James AME The thread that bound together the Northside was the church. This was the first church on the Northside. Founded in 1875, the church's motto is "God our Father, Christ our Redeemer, Man our Brother." The church members lived the concept of education as "social capital." [Courtesy of Wendel White]

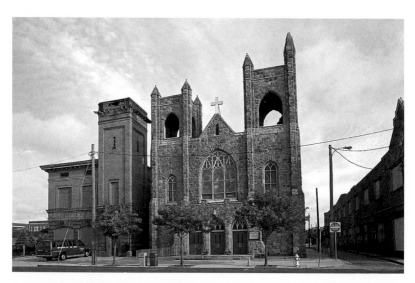

Price Memorial AME Zion Founded in 1876, long known as the "Freedom Church," AME Zion was intensely involved in the Underground Railroad. The national church included among its members abolitionist luminaries Sojourner Truth, Harriet Tubman, and Frederick Douglass. [Courtesy of Wendel White]

Asbury United Methodist Founded in 1885, Asbury United grew out of Bible study meetings at a home on Delaware Avenue near the bay in a section known as "Fisher's Row." [Courtesy of Wendel White]

Shiloh Baptist Formally organized in 1898, this church takes its name from an ancient village in Palestine and grew out of an early church mission in a Northside home. In 1958, Shiloh hosted the Reverend Martin Luther King Jr. [Courtesy of Wendel White]

Union Baptist Union Baptist Temple was established in 1907 as an off-shoot of Shiloh. The church was dedicated to "uplift" of the entire black community. [Courtesy of Wendel White]

Jethro Memorial Presbyterian Starting in the home of Mr. and Mrs. Alonzo Ridley, owners of the Hotel Ridley, the Presbyterians organized themselves into the Jethro Memorial Presbyterian Church in 1909. "Jethro" was the father-in-law of Moses, and the name means "friend of God." [Courtesy of Wendel White]

St. Augustine Episcopal Founded in 1909, St. Augustine's was aided by a "monster benefit" fundraising concert staged by internationally famous musical talent Eubie Blake in August 1923. [Courtesy of Wendel White]

St. Monica's Roman Catholic The Augustinian Fathers at St. Nicholas of Tolentine Parish helped establish a mission in 1917. Located in a home on North Delaware Avenue, it grew and moved to North Pennsylvania Avenue, with a church built in 1949. [Courtesy of Wendel White]

Young Claiborn Morris Cain
Morris Cain was a dynamic
leader from the time of
his youth and headed the
Northside YMCA for
20 years. He personifies
the spirit that made the
Northside a leading African-
American community in the
United States (circa 1910).
[Courtesy of Ralph Hunter]

Lieutenant C. Morris Cain Cain was a patriot and served as a chaplain
during World War I. In this photo, disputed by at least one Cain
authority, he is purportedly shown [center, with bag] receiving training
in protection for gas warfare. [Courtesy of Ralph Hunter]

s Cain and the Elks Cain [third from left] dedicated his life to "uplift." He led many able efforts on the Northside to aid the working poor during the off-season (circa 1940). sy of Ralph Hunter]

Origination of the Northside The site of the Pennsylvania Railroad (today's Bacharach Boulevard) divided Atlantic City (circa 1930). [Courtesy of A.C. Housing Authority]

"The North side" of the Tracks As was true of many American cities, there was usually a sect of town known as the "other side of the tracks" (circa 1930). [Courtesy of A.C. Housing Authority]

POWELL FORSYTHE LUCAS FOWLER ALLEYNE McGUIRE

HARRIS MARSHALL SCOTT HOLMES COLLINS

ATLANTIC CITY MEDICAL ASSOCIATION 1937

1937 Physicians Association The Northside was such a robust community that it supported 11 physicians. [Courtesy of Dennis Burroughs]

The Northside Fire Company Engine Company #9, shown here with Commissioner Cuthbert was the backbone of emergency services on the Northside. [Courtesy of Alma Dobson]

Engine Company #9 This segregated fire company won numerous awards for excellence. In addition to saving lives and property, its members were role models for the community. [Courtesy of Alma Dobson]

Commissioner Cuthbert and "Colored Police" Atlantic City's black people had to overcome many barriers to gain entry onto the police force. [Courtesy of Alma Dobson]

John Hollinger and His Staff This undated photo was originally captioned: "John R. Hollinger, General Manager of the Hotels Madison, Jefferson, Monticello, Devonshire and Boscobel, is not only a large man physically but is a great admirer of all mankind in a broad perspective [surrounded here by a few of his employees]. Directly in back of Mr. Hollinger is his chief aide de camp, Daniel Gibbs." [Courtesy of Ralph Hunter]

Nucky and Friends On one of his frequent visits to the Northside, Enoch "Nucky" Johnson [right] poses with Robert Chase and Josephine Johnson—described in a newspaper article as his "intimate friends." [Courtesy of Ralph Hunter]

Original Site of Stanley S. Holmes Village This is the overcrowded and blighted property that was to become Stanley S. Holmes Village under the vision and leadership of C. Morris Cain. [Courtesy of A.C. Housing Authority]

Housing of Lower Stratum Workers As shown in the latter three photos, of the 2,800+
es in "Tract No. 6" (the poorest neighborhood), nearly 60% were either unfit for
ation or in need of major repairs. Theirs was a hardscrabble existence that led to high
of infant mortality and tuberculosis. [Courtesy of A.C. Housing Authority]

Morris Cain Discussing Plans for Stanley S. Holmes Village Cain [left] took the lead on the application made to the Roosevelt administration to gain the needed funding during the Great Depression. Stanley Holmes was completed in 1937. [Courtesy of A.C. Housing Authority]

Northside Board of Trade The annual installation dinner was held at the Hotel Ridley, one of key places for such social events. [Courtesy of ACFPL]

Northside Board of Trade The Executive Committee was a dynamic group of entrepreneurs owned and operated dozens of successful Northside businesses. [Courtesy of ACFPL]

Northside PTA, 1939 The Indiana Avenue School was the heartbeat of the Northside. It had very active Parent Teacher Association. [Courtesy of Alma Dobson]

Indiana Avenue School Drama Club Northside children learned the "3 Rs" plus gained poise and confidence through school performances (circa 1945). [Courtesy of Joanna LaSane]

diana Avenue School Student Leadership Council Northside children were groomed to be aders. Many of the children in this photo went on to graduate from historically black lleges and universities [HBCUs] (circa 1935). [Courtesy of Joanna LaSane]

ation Bible School of Union Baptist Church All of the Northside's churches worked to instill es and to create leaders through uplift and education. [Courtesy of ACFPL]

Sara Spencer Washington Madame Sara Spencer Washington was Atlantic City's most successful entrepreneur. She became a multi-millionaire through the sale of hair styling products. [Courtesy of Royston Scott]

Apex School of Beauty Culture Graduation Class of 1946 The caption on this promotional piece from 1946 advises prospective beauticians that they can "Earn $50 to $75 weekly after learning the APEX SYSTEM of Scientific Beauty Culture." [Courtesy of Ralph Hunter]

Madame Washington Receiving an Honorary Degree Madame Washington received many honorary doctorate degrees for her cosmetic innovations and philanthropy.
[Courtesy of Royston Scott]

The One and Only Madame Washington was an entrepreneur who demanded and earned respect from everyone she encountered.
[Courtesy of Royston Scott]

John Henry "Pop" Ll...
Pop Lloyd was one of
the greatest ballplay...
of his generation an...
is an inductee to the
Baseball Hall of Fam...
in Cooperstown,
New York. [Courtesy of
Michael Everett]

**Pop Lloyd With
Nucky Johnson**
Political boss
Nucky Johnson
[center, shaking
hands with Pop]
was an ardent
sports fan and
admired Pop's
talent greatly.
[Courtesy of Michael
Everett]

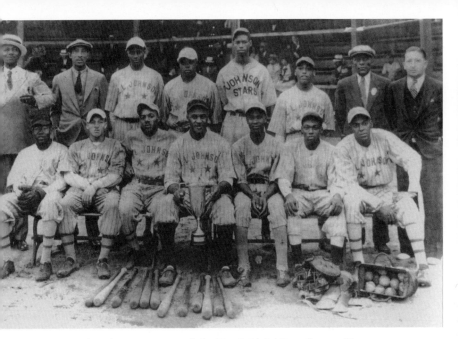

nson Allstars Nucky Johnson sponsored the Northside's Negro League Team. [Courtesy of ael Everett]

and Hap Dedication ceremony of Northside stadium in honor of Pop Lloyd on October 2, 9. Pop was a patient teacher of baseball and an excellent role model as a gentleman. His s an inspiration and a lesson in humility. [Courtesy of Michael Everett]

The Paradise Club This is the only surviving photo of Atlantic City's (and possibly America's) first nightclub (circa 1930). [Courtesy of A.C. Housing Authority]

Ziggy Ziggy Johnson was the creative genius behind the Paradise Club, which some people believe was America's first "nightclub." [Courtesy of Ralph Hunter]

The Founders of the Paradise Club Black entertainers and Jewish businessmen devised the formula for successful nightclubs. Shown here are Ziggy Johnson [right], Harold Abrams [center], and popular entertainer Peg Leg Bates. [Courtesy of ACF]

e Duke Duke Ellington, sitting at the piano, was a master showman and a longtime favorite the nightclub scene at "K-y at the Curb." [Courtesy of ACFPL]

ie Blake Eubie
ke was a musician
raordinaire who
ied international
brity status but never
d of appearing in
thside nightclubs.
s award-winning
ting is by Edward
es who was born on
Northside.

The Count
Count Basie was a legend in his own time for his musical innovation and superb sense of swing. He was a huge draw on the Northside.
[Courtesy of ACFPL]

The Count With Band Members
The Count [left] and his orchestra loved performing in Atlantic City. They often brought their families and "hung out" on the Northside.
[Courtesy of ACFPL]

Chris Columbo Chris Columbo learned to play drums in his youth and never stopped until the day he died. He was a longtime favorite at Club Harlem. [Courtesy of Ada McClinton]

s Columbo
His Band

imbo [right]
t his
mers at
Harlem in
ntic City
his winters
ew York
's Harlem,
toured
y nightclubs
ughout the
try. [Courtesy
McClinton]

Club Harlem "K-y at the Curb" was ground zero for top-notch entertainment in Atlantic City for many years, attracting both white and black patrons. The Northside never recovered from the gun fight at Club Harlem on Easter 1972. [Courtesy of Ralph Hunter]

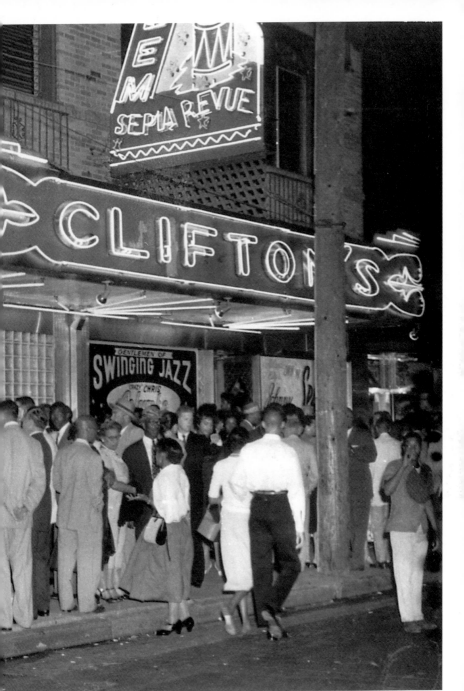

Sid Trusty Sid was a true Renaissance man and a folk historian to whom the author is indebted. He was the "conscience" for the writing of this book.
[Courtesy of ACFPL]

Sid at the Drums Sid did many things well, but he loved music the most.
[Courtesy of ACFPL]

:ken Bone Beach Missouri Avenue was the most exciting and glittering portion of
ntic City's beach, attracting entertainers from around the nation. Sammy Davis Jr.
a regular. [Courtesy of Ralph Hunter]

Northside Easter Parade Rebuffed by the racism of Atlantic City's Boardwalk merchants, Madame Sara Spencer Washington started her own Easter Parade on Arctic Avenue. [Courtesy of ACFPL]

Join the NAACP Atlantic City's chapter of the NAACP was a vital part of the national organization and played a key role in the 1964 Democratic National Convention. [Courtesy of AC?]

taste that beats the others cold!

Why do so many people who start out with a thirst end up with a Pepsi? Because there's nothing quite like Pepsi-Cola! Open a Pepsi and you've opened a world of cold. Pepsi is made for the cold. Made to taste better, pour livelier... crisp, clean and delicious. Put it to the taste!

The Real Pepsi Difference Joanna LaSane was the first African-American model to appear in a national advertising campaign. The story of how it came to be is an Atlantic City original.
[Courtesy of Joanna LaSane]

An Elegant Lady
LaSane was acclaimed internationally as a model and sought after by fashion designers and magazines.
[Courtesy of Joanna LaSane]

The LaSane Family Karlos LaSane Sr. was the first African American elected to City Council. Karlos Jr. is now an executive in the casino industry. [Courtesy of Joanna LaSane]

"Dr." Joseph Herbert Jacobs
Joseph Jacobs was a musical impresario who taught thousands of Atlantic City students about music and life. He was a founder of the "Mu Lit So Society."
[Courtesy of Joseph Jacobs, Esq.]

The Honorable Herbert S. Jacobs A graduate of Dartmouth College and New York University Law School, and son of Dr. Jacobs, Herbert Jacobs was Atlantic County's first African-American judge.
[Courtesy of Joseph Jacobs, Esq.]

nny Lou Hamer This feisty little lady energized the 1964 Democratic National Convention th her nationally televised speech to the Credentials Committee. Atlantic City was center ge during the "Summer of Freedom."

ned Car at the 4 Democratic ional vention

Mississippi
edom
nocratic Party
ught to town
replica of the
mobile in
ch three civil
ts workers
murdered.
tesy of Jo Freeman]

Demonstrators at the 1964 Democratic National Convention Thousands of Civil Rights activists marched on the Boardwalk throughout the entire convention. [Courtesy of Jo Freeman]

Martin Luther King Jr. at the Convention Atlantic City was the place to be for Civil Rights activists in the "Summer of Freedom." [Courtesy of Library of Congress]

race J. Bryant Jr. A born leader and a longtime itator for equal rights, Horace J. Bryant Jr. was : first African American to serve in a New Jersey vernor's cabinet. Few people can match his pluck d wisdom. [Courtesy of Lillian Bryant]

Election Night 1972 Bryant with his family, Big Lil and Little Lillian, following his historic election to City Commission in May 1972. [Courtesy of Lillian Bryant]

nt Leading a Protest on the Boardwalk, 1952 Bryant was leading demonstrations for equal ts years before Rosa Parks refused to sit in the back of the bus. He enjoyed making bigots mfortable. [Courtesy of the Schomburg Library and Vicki Gold Levi]

Captain Hank Tyner Hank Tyner is shown here with President Richard Nixon. Despite their body language, this really was a friendly meeting.

City Commissioner Pierre Hollingsworth Pierre Hollingsworth was a warrior for freedom his entire adult life. [Courtesy of Ralph Hunter]

Hollingsworth and Julian Bond Hollingsworth [right] worked at every level for equal rights and was respected by national leaders of the American Civil Rights Movement. [Courtesy of Ralph Hunter]

Pierre and Soundra Two talented and beloved Northside leaders on their wedding day. [Courtesy of Ralph Hunter]

Ada McClinton
Longtime Civil
Rights leader and
mentor to hundreds,
Ada McClinton [left]
is shown here with
Governor Florio and
Joseph Jacobs, son of
Judge Herbert Jacobs.

James Usry World
War II Buffalo Soldier,
professional basketball
player, Club Harlem
maître d', longtime
educator, community
leader, and the first
African-American
mayor of Atlantic City.
[Courtesy of ACFPL]

Casino Executive Redenia Gilliam-Mosee
Redenia Gilliam-Mosee played a critical
role in the original licensing of Bally's
Park Place Casino Hotel.

Gilliam-Mosee and Her Family
Gilliam-Mosee, shown here
with brother, Latha, and her
mother, Vera Mae, who was
the most important influence
in her life.

bs Family Terrace Groundbreaking Gilliam-Mosee spearheaded acquisition of the land,
approval process, and construction, and arranged financing for the buyers in creating
bs Family Terrace.

"Little Boo" The Honorable James L. Jackson, JSC, as a child at age 5. His nickname was given to him by his mother.

Jim and Conrad on Jim's Wedding Day Judge Jackson [right] and his brother, Conrad, were very close. He learned lessons from Conrad he could learn no place else.

JAMES L. JACKSON, J.S.C.

The Honorable James L. Jackson, JSC Judge Jackson shown here with two attorneys discussing a pending matter. [Courtesy of Wendel White]

visionary of the Martin Luther King Jr. School Complex. Ultimately, he would become the town's first African-American mayor.

Big Jim was a soldier in World War II, serving in the famous segregated unit, the "Black Buffalos." An outstanding athlete, he was one of the first African-American basketball players to play professionally, with the Harlem Renaissance, and he later played briefly with the Harlem Globetrotters. He was a graduate of Atlantic City High School and Lincoln University, and received his master's degree from Glassboro State College. Usry devoted most of his career to education. As a teacher and school administrator, he touched the lives of thousands of local children. He was a community leader for years prior to making his first run for political office in 1982. In that election, he lost to Democrat Michael Matthews in a bitterly contested election. Following Matthews's indictment on corruption charges as a result of an FBI undercover operation, Usry was elected mayor in the recall election of 1984, then re-elected to a full term in 1986.

As the *Press of Atlantic City* reported at the time of Usry's death in 2002:

> His legacy is found in the daycare facilities, the youth centers and the new housing complexes that dot the city … even though many of those improvements were built after he left office—he was the one who sent the message: Atlantic City's residents cannot be passed by.

Usry's tenure as mayor was marred by bribery charges arising out of the COMSERV investigation in 1989. COMSERV was a seriously flawed state "sting operation," long on press releases and short on hard evidence. Usry eventually pled guilty to a minor campaign finance violation and was defeated in his re-election bid in 1990 by James Whelan. Notwithstanding the circumstances of his time and political life, Usry is remembered as a role model who, for three generations, positively impacted the lives of the children who passed through the Atlantic City school system.

The Tuskegee Airmen were groundbreakers. At the beginning of World War II, there were *no* African-American pilots in our nation's armed forces. Following a series of legislative moves in Congress, the Army Air Corps was forced to form an all-black combat unit. In an effort to thwart the plan before it could get started, the War Department set up a system that put unreasonable (and presumably impossible) demands on candidates in terms of education and flight experience. To the surprise and chagrin of some white officers, the Air Corps received applications from many men who met or exceeded the daunting requirements. In 1941, the 99th Fighter Squadron was formed at the Tuskegee Institute; its pilots would come to be known, famously, as the Tuskegee Airmen. Four of the 900 qualified candidates made Atlantic City their home. **William C. Walker**, **Pedro Alexander**, **David Charman**, and **Tom Gill** served our nation proudly as members of the 99th, along with many other veterans who lived on the Northside.

Henry "Hank" Tyner was a trailblazer in local government. After returning from World War II, he applied repeatedly to the Atlantic City fire and police departments, but despite acing the civil service tests, he was passed over every time. No matter, he kept taking the tests each time they were offered and, in the meantime, worked at everything from cab driver to soda jerk to bartender. At the recommendation of his subward leader, Charlie Petillo—the black counterpart of the Republican ward leader—Tyner joined the Third Ward Republican Club. He attended rallies, paid dues, went to meetings once a month, and appeared in photos with Republican candidates. (A popular, handsome black war veteran was helpful to a white candidate wooing Northside voters.) Finally, after four years of persistence, Tyner was hired as a fireman. He served for eight years and then, with the encouragement of Republican leader Dick Jackson, applied and reapplied to the police department. After scoring at the top of the list on the police exam a second time and following a one-on-one meeting with Hap Farley, Tyner attained his goal. He was hired as a policeman.

Once in the police department, Tyner rose through the ranks from patrolman to sergeant to detective—despite the fact that he wouldn't pay "ice money" to the Republican organization. He prided himself on "knowing every street corner on the Northside." He had "reliable contacts in all the neighborhoods. People I could count on to slip me information because they knew I'd never reveal my source." High-profile crimes seemed to find their way to Tyner, and he was always up to the task.

One memorable incident in the 1960s involved a serial burglar known as the "1:30 Bandit." There had been five heists in eight days, all occurring between one and two in the morning. Tyner was on patrol when the bandit made his sixth attempt at a liquor store at Ohio and Arctic Avenues. The bandit drew a gun but Tyner fired first, killing the man. Eventually, Tyner was recognized by the State Attorney General's Office, receiving a Valor Award for stopping the 1:30 Bandit. Locally, he received no recognition; the man he'd killed worked at the local hospital and was the brother of a police department employee. The incident strained relations within the community, though no one ever questioned Tyner's professionalism in handling the matter.

Throughout his career, Tyner was interested in the Northside's children. He was one of the founders of the Boys' Club and was involved in establishing its initial headquarters in a warehouse donated by the *Atlantic City Press*. It was in part because of his outstanding reputation as a police officer that the *Press* agreed to donate the building.

From 1982 to 1986, Tyner served as a member of City Council and was the first council president under the current form of government. He found that he'd rather chase criminals than consort with politicians. Leaving City Council after one term, despite the likelihood of his re-election, he returned to the police department with the rank of inspector. Tyner had overcome every obstacle thrown at him. His career is an inspiration.

Dr. Charles Wilson lived an inspired life. Among the many hats he wore throughout his long career: U.S. Army veteran, barrier-breaking business executive, beloved Northside physician, elected official, philanthropist, and family man. He excelled in every endeavor. Born in 1926, "Charlie" Wilson was orphaned at age eight. He and his sister were raised by his grandmother (who had eight children of her own) in Crisfield, Maryland, where he was introduced to oyster shucking at an early age. "I can't remember when I didn't have a job. I did everything from shuck oysters, clean fish and wash boats, to build fences, sweep floors and make ice cream sodas."

While still in his teens, Wilson traveled to Atlantic City. Several of his aunts and uncles worked in the hotels and lived on the Northside. He visited them and worked at odd jobs available to children during the summers. He knew early on that Atlantic City would be a suitable place to pursue his ultimate career.

Wilson was an excellent student who recognized that working in hotels was just a stepping stone. His plan was to become a doctor. After graduating from high school, he enrolled in the Hampton Institute in Virginia (now Hampton University). In 1944, at the end of his freshman year, he was drafted into the Army. "I was humiliated in the Army more times than I can remember but I got all the schooling I could, everything from topographical drafting to flying an airplane." Upon his discharge from the Army when the war ended in 1946, Wilson returned to Hampton and completed his studies, graduating with honors. But medical school was not to be the next step: Money was scarce, and he needed to work and save for the opportunity to study medicine. Shortly before graduation in June 1949, Hampton's president introduced him to a representative from Pepsi-Cola, there to recruit for a program that groomed African-American executives who could successfully market Pepsi to the black community. It proved to be a history-making adventure involving not only Charlie Wilson but another notable Northside resident.

Wilson was hired by Pepsi as part of a team of 12 young black men whose job was to crisscross the nation to sell cola. They were soon on a mission to educate corporate America on the need to take a whole new look at black people. Long before the term "niche marketing" was coined, Wilson and his colleagues at Pepsi worked at ways not only to pitch their products to black customers but to elevate the image of black people. Prior to their efforts, typical advertisements depicted blacks as one-dimensional characters, frequently in the "Uncle Ben" and "Aunt Jemima" molds. At the prompting of its upstart team, Pepsi took a different approach and began portraying African Americans as the accomplished middle-class professionals and homemakers they were fast becoming. This novel approach included using black models for the first time in a national advertising campaign, among them a native of the Northside by the name of Joanna Forenan LaSane.

From Wilson's perspective, at least in the beginning, the relationship with Pepsi was chiefly important as an opportunity to secure a scholarship and save money for medical school. Yet the breakthrough that occurred wouldn't have been possible without him and his colleagues. Their story, beyond the scope of this chapter to detail, is covered in Stephanie Capparell's 2008 book, *The Real Pepsi Challenge: How One Pioneering Company Broke Color Barriers in 1940s American Business.*

Wilson's work for Pepsi brought him to New York City, where he spent his spare time tracking down every possible source of funding for his studies. "Affirmative action" wasn't even being imagined in 1952, and the chances of a young black man receiving a scholarship to medical school were slim to none. On a lark, one afternoon Wilson paid a visit to the Swiss Consulate in Manhattan to inquire about schools in Switzerland. They put him in touch with the Swiss Educational Conference and, after reviewing his college transcripts and conducting a placement exam and interview, he was on his way to becoming *Doctor* Charles Wilson.

Wilson was granted a full scholarship and studied at the University of Geneva Medical School for the next five years. He asked his longtime sweetheart Mary Shelton to join him and she did. They married and their first child was born in Switzerland. Imagine—an oyster shucker from the eastern shore of Maryland studying biology, chemistry, and anatomy in French at a Swiss University. Wilson not only did it, he graduated with honors.

Dr. Charles Wilson returned to Atlantic City in 1957, and it wasn't long before he had established a successful medical practice. It is recalled that his love for people and his concern for his patients shone as brightly as his smile. Over his long career, "He made house calls when no one was making house calls and he went to neighborhoods where no one would go." In addition to his patients, Wilson found time for family, church, charity, and traveling. He even became involved in politics and was elected as a Republican member of the Atlantic County Board of Freeholders. If that wasn't enough, he also served as ring doctor for hundreds of boxing matches, retained as a medical examiner by the New Jersey Boxing Commission. As one longtime employee of the commission who was friendly with him said, "When Doc Wilson said a fight was over, it was over. No one ever questioned his call that a fight should be stopped. Everyone respected his opinion."

Considering the positive impact Dr. Wilson had on so many people's lives, his own life deserves a more extensive biography than can be provided here.

Joanna Forenan LaSane's history-making career, and the positive turn her life took largely due to the efforts of junior Pepsi executive Charlie Wilson, gives new meaning to the term "serendipitous." At the same time Wilson was pushing the Pepsi-Cola Company to feature people of color in its advertising, LaSane was an aspiring actress, dancer, and model with the talent, charm, and looks to excel at any or all of them. In 1953, following her graduation from high school, she left Atlantic City for Montclair College and a year later was off to New York City to pursue her career. She took voice lessons, studied dance and acting, and performed in several shows in New York.

LaSane was a striking young woman. Elegant and poised in appearance, she was as gracious and beautiful on the inside. One feature that set her apart was her hairstyle: It was natural, much to the consternation of her mother—a graduate of Madame Sara Washington's Apex Beauty College. "My hairstyle caused a great deal of tension," LaSane recalled. Yet she refused to straighten her hair, and in this case it appears that daughter knew best.

While attending a cocktail party in New York, LaSane was approached by a freelance photographer who was looking for models for Pepsi's new ad campaign. The rest, as they say, is history. She was invited with 300 other candidates to audition at Radio City Music Hall, making the final cut of only a dozen models. She went on to be featured in Pepsi's national advertising campaign, then to travel the country and the world with fashion shows sponsored by *Ebony* magazine. In addition to appearing in *Ebony*, she graced the pages of *Vogue, Redbook, Look, Life,* and *Glamour,* and was the first black model to be featured in a primetime, national television commercial.

After years of travel, LaSane returned to Atlantic City and settled into teaching dance and giving voice lessons to children on the Northside, which she continues to do today. Many hundreds of young people have been exposed to the arts because of her efforts. She has served on the Board of Directors of the Atlantic County Cultural and Heritage Commission and the Atlantic City Arts Commission. She is listed in *Who's Who Among Black Americans* and has received numerous honors including the New Jersey State Senate Cultural Arts Award. In 1996, she was inducted into the Atlantic County Women's Hall of Fame.

Pierre Hollingsworth didn't have the high profile of Dr. Charles Wilson or Joanna LaSane, but he was a soldier for justice his entire adult life. A veteran of the U.S. Army during the Korean War, he served with the 584th Medical Corps. He was also a vocal member and executive of the NAACP, serving as the organization's president for 24 years. He worked tirelessly on behalf of the people on the Northside. He championed many issues, from equal opportunity in employment to housing and education to honest government, voter registration, and community development. Hollingsworth's work with the NAACP and his employment with the Atlantic City fire department were mainstays in his life. Together, Hollingsworth, Marvin Beatty, and John Jasper, known as "The Big Three," rose to become chiefs in the department. In tribute to his long and dedicated service, Fire House No. 3 at Indiana and Grant Avenues is named in his honor.

Hollingsworth was a member of City Commission from 1976 to 1980, and some believe the primary reason he wasn't re-elected was his commitment to sound planning in redeveloping the resort, including the use of eminent domain, which was opposed by many residents. Hollingsworth brought a keen sense of fairness to all his dealings. Despite his many successes, he never came off as pretentious, but rather he was known for his self-deprecating sense of humor. His life's story reveals him as a protégé of Horace Bryant in the best sense of the word: a champion of the people until the day he died. The integrity he brought to city government is sorely missed.

Hollingsworth was one of the leaders who bridged the decade of the 1950s to become an important community leader with Bryant through the 1960s and beyond. As America entered the 1960s and African Americans waged battles for their civil rights nationally, many Northside voters followed the examples of Bryant and Hollingsworth, abandoning the party of Lincoln. A major shift was underway, but it wasn't until several years into the new decade that Hap Farley and his organization grasped what was occurring. It was a rude awakening, one that forced them to do the unthinkable.

The 1960s were a tumultuous decade. One year in particular—1964—was pivotal. Upheaval was afoot for both Atlantic City and America. Some knew what was on the way. Most didn't. A portion of those who knew labored mightily to hold off the change they saw coming but to no avail. The winds of history are unrelenting, and after they blew past the Boardwalk that August, the world was a different place. It would be billed as the "Summer of Freedom," and Atlantic City would take center stage for a grand political drama, the impact of which is felt to this day.

The story begins with the nomination of a president against the backdrop of people fighting for equal rights.

10

The Summer of Freedom

A man came to me after the students began to work in Mississippi, and he said to me the white people were getting tired and they were getting tense and anything might happen. Well, I asked him "How long he thinks we had been getting tired?" ... All my life I've been sick and tired. Now I'm sick and tired of being sick and tired.

—Fannie Lou Hamer, civil rights activist

Television was still a luxury for many of America's working poor. And for some of the young black women who changed the sheets and cleaned Atlantic City's hotel rooms, work was their only chance for a glimpse of TV. The faces on the screen were all white, all the time. Not surprising, there were few shows that captured black America's attention. As a diversion from the tedium of their work, most women turned on the TV as they entered the room. Others were content to be alone with their thoughts, while scouring toilets and emptying ashtrays. But this week was different. The TV—in the hotel rooms that had one—was on, and it was not for entertainment. The chambermaids were watching their hometown on national television. The Democratic Party was in town to nominate a U.S. president, and black people were making history on the Boardwalk.

Presidents had visited Atlantic City in the past, but the summer of 1964 was different. With the Vietnam War consuming ever more of his attention, President Lyndon Baines Johnson wanted a site for the Democratic National Convention that was within an hour's ride by helicopter from the White House. He chose Atlantic City. It was convenient for the national press corps and gave LBJ the freedom to come and go without disrupting his work in Washington. In addition, he had a close ally in New Jersey's progressive Democratic Governor Richard Hughes and knew he would be in friendly territory.

But that summer, while Americans were fighting in Southeast Asia, there was another conflict raging in America's southern states. What LBJ hadn't bargained for was that a fearless group of civil rights activists led by a gritty little black woman from Mississippi would make the trip to Atlantic City and steal the spotlight from him.

At the dawn of the 1960s, Mississippi stood out. Even in the American South, where only 40 percent of eligible black citizens were registered to vote, Mississippi was the exception. Of its nearly 500,000 black voting-age residents, only 6.4 percent were able to overcome the obstacles of literacy tests, citizenship exams, poll taxes, and, finally, relentless violence and official intimidation, the likes of which we cannot fully appreciate today. Because the literacy tests were subjectively administered by white voter registrars, even college-educated blacks had been refused registration on literacy grounds.

One incident that illustrates the vicious shenanigans of that era involved a young professor at Alcorn State, an HBCU. When he went to register to vote, he was given a literacy test. After he had aced a series of questions on U.S. history, English literature, math, and science, plus the State and Federal Constitutions, he was presented with a document written in Ancient Greek and asked to translate it. He looked at the document for a moment and replied, "I understand very well the meaning of this document. It says black people don't vote in Jefferson County," to which came the reply, "You got that right, boy."

As one civil rights worker recalled, among Mississippi's black residents, the fear of even attempting to register to vote was "a highly rational emotion, the economic fear of losing your job, the physical fear of being shot at. Domestic servants know that they will be fired if they register to vote; so will factory workers, so will Negroes who live on plantations." Notwithstanding President John F. Kennedy's professed commitment to equality, he was fearful of antagonizing southern Democrats and consistently refused to enter the fray, permitting southern states to administer their own affairs. This meant that the rights guaranteed by the U.S. Constitution had little meaning for blacks living in the South.

Things began to change in 1963 when a 29-year-old math teacher from New York City named Bob Moses decided to make the plight of Mississippi his mission. Inspired by the wave of lunch-counter sit-ins that had engulfed the South in early 1960—a spontaneous movement involving some 70,000 students—Moses traveled to Atlanta to serve as a volunteer in the start-up office of the Student Nonviolent Coordinating Committee (SNCC). He quickly realized that the most pressing need was in Mississippi and that was where he headed. Moses was promptly named SNCC's field secretary for the state. "The work was dangerous, lonely and hard." Sleeping in the homes of local activists, Moses spent his days walking from house to house, trying to convince local sharecroppers and service workers that it was both their right and their obligation to register to vote. "He was beaten by local police and harassed by white citizens; some of the people who took him in lost their jobs and even their lives."

Working with local black residents throughout the state of Mississippi, the idea was forged to create the Freedom Vote project. The strategy as formulated by Moses involved two mock-elections. The first was staged in November 1963, in which some 80,000 black citizens turned in mock ballots electing Mississippi National Association for the Advancement of Colored People (NAACP) president Aaron Henry as governor. The vote meant nothing, but it wasn't meaningless. It demonstrated that black citizens wanted to participate in the political process.

Next came a mock primary to select delegates for the 1964 Democratic National Convention in Atlantic City. Hundreds of volunteers from universities and law schools in northern states converged on Mississippi, supporting SNCC and Moses in their efforts. A new political entity was created, the Mississippi Freedom Democratic Party (MFDP), and every black and white citizen of voting age was invited to participate in caucuses throughout the state for selecting delegates to go to Atlantic City. "The MFDP followed Mississippi election law to the letter, acting as though it were, in effect, the state Democratic Party. Since most black citizens were artificially disenfranchised and since the MFDP opened its delegate caucuses to people of all races, the new organization would argue that it, not the regular state party, held rightful claim to Mississippi's slate of convention delegates."

On June 22, 1964, not two weeks into the Freedom Vote project, the world learned that three voter registration workers had *disappeared*: James Chaney, a 21-year-old black man from Meridian,

Mississippi; Michael Schwerner, a young white New Yorker; and Andrew Goodman, a white volunteer from Queens College in New York City. The three men had gone to investigate a church burning that had occurred days earlier. The Mt. Zion Church in Philadelphia, Mississippi, had been burned to the ground after its congregation agreed to permit the church to be used as a center for voter registration efforts.

The FBI later determined that Chaney, Schwerner, and Goodman had made it safely to Mt. Zion Church but had been arrested for "speeding" by Neshoba County Deputy Sheriff Cecil Price on their return journey. They were held in jail for several hours, released, stopped outside town—again by Sheriff Price—then turned over to the Ku Klux Klan. The three men were never seen alive again after their arrest on June 22. Mississippi Governor Paul Johnson dismissed fears that the men had been murdered, saying, "Maybe they went to Cuba," a reference to Communist ties—a tactic frequently used by bigots for smearing civil rights activists. Johnson's personal sentiments regarding equal rights were a matter of record: In 1962, while serving as lieutenant governor, he had played a leading role in trying to prevent James Meredith, a black man, from enrolling in "Ole Miss" (the nickname for the University of Mississippi) by physically blocking federal marshals escorting Meredith to the university.

About six weeks after the disappearance of the three voter registration workers and following a massive and well-publicized federal manhunt in which state and local authorities took no part, the men's bodies, along with those of several unidentified black men, were found beneath an earthen dam. Both Goodman and Schwerner had been shot twice. Chaney had been shot several times and mutilated. That summer, the Mississippi KKK was responsible for at least 35 shooting incidents and six murders, the burnings of 65 homes and churches, and the beatings of at least 80 volunteers. By August, in the wake of this orgy of violence, SNCC organizers and MFDP convention delegates were of little mind to walk away with anything short of a total victory in Atlantic City.

On August 7, at Chaney's funeral, state field secretary for the Congress of Racial Equality (CORE) David Dennis delivered an angry, impassioned eulogy that concluded, "If you go back home and take what these white men in Mississippi are doing to us …

if you take it and don't do something about it … then Goddamn your souls!"

In the midst of all this turmoil and violence, LBJ had been overseeing more than the war in Vietnam. He had been shepherding major legislation through the Congress guaranteeing rights for African Americans. As a former senator from Texas and senate majority leader, LBJ had brokered compromises on two major civil rights acts in 1957 and 1960. Throughout the spring and summer of 1964, Johnson spent countless hours on the phone persuading House and Senate members, both threatening and sweet-talking Democrats and reminding Republicans that "You're either the party of Lincoln or you ain't." John F. Kennedy could talk the talk about civil rights, but LBJ walked the walk. As noted LBJ biographer Robert A. Caro has said:

> Lyndon Johnson cared—cared, and helped. And the compassion had … been combined with a rare capacity to make compassion meaningful, a startling ability to mobilize the forces of government to fulfill what his father, an idealistic, populist legislator had said was government's most important function: to help people "caught in the tentacles of circumstance," to help them fight forces too big for them to fight alone.

Little more than a month before the Democratic National Convention in Atlantic City—following an 83-day Senate filibuster, the longest in American history—LBJ signed into law the Civil Rights Act of 1964. A century of legally enforced segregation was over. The act banned discrimination in *all* places of public accommodation and outlawed racial discrimination in both private and public sector employment. Blacks could now ride on the same buses, eat in the same restaurants, and sleep in the same hotels as whites. Moments following his signing of the Civil Rights Act, LBJ told his aide Joseph Califano, "I think we've delivered the South to the Republican Party for your lifetime and mine."

The delegates selected by the "regular" (all-white) Democratic Party in Mississippi were unhappy with LBJ, they were unhappy with the MFDP, and they weren't exactly happy being in Atlantic City. To be forced to go North with all those damn Yankees, and of all places, to New Jersey—home of pointy-headed Ivy League liberals, good for nothing nigger lovers, and the mafia—was more than some of them could abide.

Lest there be any mistake about how the Mississippi "regulars" felt about seating the MFDP, the chair of the Mississippi delegation, Governor Paul Johnson, infuriated northern Democrats by saying that "The NAACP stands for niggers, alligators, apes, coons and possums." He sure had a way with words. As noted by historian Theodore White, Johnson had been elected governor by running "on a platform of segregation and race hatred so inflexibly extreme as to satisfy the most violent white segregationists." Against this backdrop, the stage was set for the Democratic National Convention.

On Friday, August 21, 1964, several days before the convention's opening gavel, busloads of black Mississippians arrived in Atlantic City. A reporter watching them assemble for a prayer session saw "a hymn-singing group of dedicated men and women, who feel as though they had temporarily escaped from a Mississippi prison and who think they may be jailed when they get back." The people from Mississippi included schoolteachers, preachers, small-business men, domestic workers, and sharecroppers. They even brought props, including a replica of Michael Schwerner's burned-out station wagon. They put pickets on the Boardwalk outside Convention Hall with enormous banners bearing likenesses of the three slain civil rights workers.

Longtime Northside resident and civil rights activist Ada McClinton remembers convention week well. Working at both the Northside Y and the Union Baptist Temple, she was responsible for registering people coming into town and coordinating places for them to sleep and eat. "It was orderly, yet exciting. This was a first for Atlantic City. We had never seen anything like it. In the weeks before the convention, we never thought it was really going to happen. When it did, we were all thrilled. It changed everything and how we viewed our role in the community."

McClinton continued, "I don't think the Democratic Party expected the local black community to mobilize the way we did. This was a resort. We were thought of as a laid back town by many people. Everyone was here to relax and have a good time. But we surprised them—did we ever."

Another longtime Northside leader and civil rights activist, Elwood Davis, recalled how local churches made it all possible. "We knew what was coming and word got out fast. It was the churches that mobilized to get things ready. You had Shiloh Baptist, Union Baptist Temple, Christ Memorial, AME Zion, Asbury United Methodist Episcopal, St. James AME, Second Baptist, St. Augustine, Hamilton Memorial United Methodist, and Jethro Presbyterian. Everybody had a role to play. Local Pastor Matthew Neil was acquainted with Ralph Abernathy of the Southern Christian Leadership Conference [SCLC] and worked with them in coordinating their efforts locally." Abernathy was the number two person at SCLC behind the Reverend Dr. Martin Luther King Jr. and a national figure in his own right. Together with Dr. King, Abernathy had organized the bus boycott in Montgomery, Alabama, after Rosa Parks refused to move to the back of the bus in 1955.

As recounted by Davis, "Reverend Neil was contacted by Abernathy and that set the local churches into motion. Many of the people from the South who came to town to demonstrate on the Boardwalk were told to bring sleeping bags and backpacks. Our churches were used as both dormitories and dining rooms. The main dining halls were at St. Augustine and Union Baptist Church. As a community, we knew we would do whatever was needed."

Davis continued, "Besides the several hundred people who stayed in churches and the Northside Y, there were hundreds more who stayed in people's homes and local hotels and boardinghouses on the Northside. The churches were also involved in transporting people using their vans and buses to shuttle them back and forth to Convention Hall. Things started happening the Friday before the convention and every day through the weekend into Monday you could feel the excitement building."

As recalled by Davis, the other organization involved in leading the overall effort was the NAACP. "Maceo Turner [a local attorney] was friendly with Cecil Moore, the leader of the Philadelphia NAACP and a man known by just about everyone in the Civil Rights Movement. His people made sure that the picketers had signs, posters and banners while demonstrating on the Boardwalk." Moore, like many African-American veterans, bristled at the thought that a man who had risked his life as a U.S. Marine fighting in World War II was looked upon as a second-class citizen when he returned home.

A graduate of Temple University Law School, he was a no-nonsense lawyer who fought aggressively on behalf of poor black people on a whole range of issues, from integration of schools and trade unions to increased political and economic representation. Fannie Lou Hamer and the MDFP were Moore's kind of people.

Both McClinton and Davis believed that convention week "energized the Northside." The event began a massive voter registration drive to get all the people on the Northside registered for the 1964 election. Under the Farley regime, black people in Atlantic City were discouraged from registering. Although Atlantic City's black people didn't have the same obstacles as those in Mississippi, many found it difficult to register and were often turned away because they didn't have driver's licenses, utility bills, or property tax records to prove their identities to election board workers.

After the summer of 1964, local black leaders were committed to fighting any and every obstacle to voting. They were inspired, and one of the people who inspired them most was the spokesperson for the MFDP.

Fannie Lou Hamer, remembered as the lady who was "sick and tired of being sick and tired," was determined to be heard at the Democratic Convention. Little more than 5' tall, dark skinned, with stubby little fingers that jabbed like bullets, her eyes alternated between twinkling and glaring. Hamer's body was bent by polio, but her message went as straight as a ramrod into the belly of bigotry. Her left eye permanently injured from a beating by a Mississippi sheriff, her vision for the future of black America compared to that of Dr. King, even if her eloquence did not. The youngest of 20 children, born to sharecropper parents, Hamer had only six years of schooling—a year of schooling for black students consisted of just four months at the time—but that didn't hold her back in her pursuit of equal rights.

Hamer began her career as a civil rights activist in 1962, when at the age of 45 she learned that black people had the right to vote. When members of the SNCC came to Ruleville, Mississippi, and asked for volunteers to go to the courthouse to register to vote, she was the first to raise her hand. Her decision had consequences. Jailed and brutally beaten several times, she later noted, "The only thing they could do to me was to kill me, and it seemed like they'd been trying to do that a little bit at a time ever since I could remember."

Consistently weaving humor, songs, and Biblical stories into her organizing efforts, Hamer showed that "professional" skills weren't necessary to be an effective civil rights leader. She preached that every person could contribute regardless of class or education, saying, "Whether you have a PhD, DD, or no D, we're in this bag together." On one occasion, she urged blacks to depend on themselves to bring about change, saying, "You can pray until you faint. But unless you get up and try to do something, God is not going to put it in your lap."

By now a legend in her home state, Hamer had worked closely with Bob Moses in forming the MFDP. As a result of her leadership and charismatic presence, MFDP expanded its voter registration efforts, challenging the legitimacy of Mississippi's "regular" Democratic Party. Hamer and the MDFP members arrived in Atlantic City determined to unseat the official Mississippi delegation.

Hamer was a lightning rod and attracted attention everywhere she went. Days before the convention was to begin, national newspapers ran photographs of her arm-in-arm with the family of Michael Schwerner, keeping vigil on the Atlantic City Boardwalk. The Democratic Party's Credentials Committee was flooded with telegrams from across the nation, urging that the MFDP be seated.

Initially, Hamer and the MDFP were hopeful they would succeed in their efforts. They had caught the attention of the national media and, with the help of the SNCC, NAACP, and SCLC, thousands of people had been mobilized in support of their efforts. As recounted by Ada McClinton, "Hundreds of people were on the Boardwalk from early in the morning 'til past midnight. They carried placards and signs, all demonstrating peacefully. The state police erected a fence separating the Boardwalk from the Convention Hall entrance but they really didn't need it. There wasn't one ugly incident. We were all proud of the role we played in supporting the efforts of the demonstrators."

As Pierre Hollingsworth, longtime Northside leader, recalled, "It was an amazing time. All those years of frustration finally had an outlet. All those years of being ignored were over. All those years of being told to be patient a while longer now looked silly. There were hundreds of black people picketing on the Boardwalk, and TV cameras were letting the world know this was Atlantic City and that black people weren't going to be silent any longer. I never saw the people on the Northside so energized. There was no reason to wait for the crumbs to fall from Hap Farley's table. We could do it on our own. We understood that the power to change our lives was in our hands."

Ironically, bringing the Democratic Convention to the Boardwalk was something that Hap Farley wanted. Despite his position in the state and national Republican Party, Farley's relationship with Democratic Governor Richard Hughes was quite cordial. When Hughes made it known that LBJ was thinking of staging his nomination for the 1964 presidential election in the resort, Farley assured Hughes that the town would roll out the red carpet. That Farley believed his town was up to the task speaks volumes about how out of touch he was with what had happened in America—and Atlantic City—since World War II. Little did he realize how shabby Atlantic City's red carpet would look in the eyes of the national media.

Arrival of the Democratic National Convention was the impetus for early completion of the Atlantic City Expressway. Farley made sure that the delegates flying into Philadelphia from around the nation would have a new road to Atlantic City. The Atlantic City Expressway was ready on time, but the resort wasn't. As Hollingsworth stated, "I can remember Horace [Bryant] saying, 'Can you imagine, Farley wanted this convention. He thought it would be good for the town. Little did he know.' Oh, yeah, what a surprise he got that summer."

Things didn't go as planned for either Farley or LBJ. The MDFP and Hamer sent ripples across the nation. Hamer demanded that the convention seat her delegation. She challenged the "regular" Mississippi delegation as a sham, unrepresentative of her state and an affront to the principles of the Democratic Party. Word of her planned remarks got to Johnson before the committee began its hearing, and he quickly pre-empted her with an impromptu presidential press conference. To no avail, Hamer's testimony to the Credentials Committee was taped and televised nationally by the three networks, later that evening in prime time.

Hamer blistered the committee members, saying, "If the Freedom Democratic Party is not seated now, I question America. Is this America? The land of the free and the home of the brave?" She told the committee how black people in Mississippi had been prevented from voting, from attending precinct meetings, and from the most basic forms of democracy, and how she had been brutally beaten for wanting only to vote. Offered a compromise of two seats for her delegation, she rejected it saying, "We didn't come all this way for no two seats when all of us is tired."

Hamer left Atlantic City smoldering but not before she had fractured the Democratic Party. By demanding equality as a player in the process, she became a catalyst in reshaping national politics. The "Solid South" of the Democratic Party would sooner leave the party than yield to the demands of black America. Proud whites weren't going to share power with "some little nigger woman." As one political observer has recently noted, "For most of the post–Civil War era, the Grand Old Party survived in the southern popular imagination as the Yankee enemy, eager to conspire with the newly enfranchised slaves to overturn the entire southern way of life ... the idea of [the South] delivering its [presidential] electoral votes to the party of Lincoln would have seemed outrageous before the 1960s—before, that is, the national Democratic Party made a commitment to the enforcement of civil rights for blacks."

The Republican Presidential candidate, Barry Goldwater, didn't share LBJ's commitment to civil rights. Despite the support of Senate Minority Leader Everett Dirksen, Goldwater opposed the civil rights legislation. One of the new southwestern Republicans, the GOP's identification as the "Party of Lincoln" was irrelevant to Goldwater, who cared little that his opposition to the Civil Rights Act of 1964 offended black voters.

On Election Day, Johnson swept to victory but lost Alabama, South Carolina, Louisiana, Georgia, and Mississippi. The Mississippi "regulars" had backed Barry Goldwater. In the following election of 1968, upon the invitation of Richard Nixon, and later, Ronald Reagan, southern Democrats opposed to integration and equal rights for African Americans crossed over and found a home with the Republicans. The Nixon and Reagan administrations did little to enforce civil rights laws, "while appearing publicly to endorse them. That move would soon be enshrined by the press as the 'Southern Strategy.'"

Two generations later, the genesis of today's "Red State" solid Republican South can be traced to the confrontation over race at the 1964 Democratic Convention. It was the first plank in the bridge that realigned American politics. The two-party system hasn't been the same since Fannie Lou Hamer's appearance in Atlantic City. (One can only imagine what Hamer and Mississippi's Governor Johnson would make of the 2008 election of President Barack Obama, who carried Virginia and North Carolina—two of the old "Solid South" states.) In the brief time Hamer was in town, she and her delegates left their mark. She became a heroine on the Northside that summer. Pierre Hollingsworth recalled, "She was one feisty little woman who wouldn't take 'no' for an answer. She had a powerful presence. She didn't make many white people happy that summer, but everyone respected her."

A lot of people were unhappy with what occurred during the Democratic Convention. The local power establishment had been mugged by the modern world. Two ugly realities had been bludgeoned into the town's psyche: First, from a public relations perspective, the convention was a grievous, self-inflicted wound; second, the political fallout was irreparable—the genie was out of the bottle.

In the first case, the impact on Atlantic City's image as a national resort was an unmitigated disaster. The 15,000 delegates, newsmen, and technicians found a town unable to meet their needs. Hotel services broke down under the demands of the convention. "By midmorning switchboards would collapse and the flustered operators refused to take messages for political guests whose message-mating and communication are of the essence; promised television sets did not work, and promised air conditioning proved nonexistent."

It didn't help any that several weeks earlier the reporters covering the convention had attended the Republican National Convention in San Francisco. What a contrast: San Francisco was polished and sophisticated. The hotels and restaurants in the "City by the Bay" were first rate. By comparison, Atlantic City was grungy. The journalists reeled from culture shock and couldn't wait to get out of town.

To make matters worse, local hotels and restaurants jacked up their prices during convention week. Out-of-town politicians and media people had never been favorites of Atlantic City. Resort businessmen viewed convention week as a chance to grab a few extra dollars from people they would never see again. Their greed had its price—most of the delegates were outraged at being exploited. Short-changing someone in a position to spread news of poor treatment is foolhardy. For Atlantic City, it was fatal. The news media transmitted the delegates' tales of contempt for the resort to the entire nation. One reporter dubbed it "the original Bay of Pigs." Presidential historian Theodore White observed, "Never had a town and a Chamber of Commerce made a greater effort only to end by exposing themselves to ridicule."

Following the Democratic Convention, criticism of Atlantic City became derisive and widespread, with the national media ridiculing the resort at every opportunity. Whether it was a snafu at the Miss America Pageant, a weekend visitor ripped off at a Boardwalk auction, or a disgruntled Elk, Moose, or businessman in town for a convention, the criticism found its way onto the wire services. *TIME* magazine reported that, "Today aside from the conventioneers, the typical Atlantic City tourist is either poor, black, elderly or all three—and the change has depressed almost every aspect of the city's economy ... the picture which emerges is one of steady physical, economic, and social deterioration." After the convention, virtually all national news about the resort was negative, and it had a corrosive effect on everyone's spirit, regardless of skin color.

A sense of foreboding infected the town's psychology, it was plain to see. Atlantic City had lost its swagger. A town that for generations had audaciously promoted itself to the world had lost its voice, as well as its reputation as a great and unique destination for vacationers. Perhaps not surprisingly, the Northside's entertainment district endured as one of the few aspects of the resort still capable of drawing and engaging visitors. Kentucky Avenue continued to lure patrons seeking the best in song, dance, comedy, and soul food. It was among the few remaining bright spots in town and continued generating jobs and income for Northside residents. With the exception of the Miss America Pageant, which ran for only one weekend each year, not much besides Kentucky Avenue was bringing in people with money to spend.

The impact of the Democratic Convention on local politics was profound. The entire Northside was tuned in that summer. All its nerve endings were exposed, all its synapses charged. Everyone on the Northside knew what was occurring just a few blocks away on the Boardwalk at Convention Hall. Black people were making history. They wanted to be part of it.

For many local activists, convention week marked the point of no return. Fannie Lou Hamer and her delegates from Mississippi weren't the only black politicians in town for the event. The delegations of several other states included African Americans—some of whom held positions of power in their home sates. They were very visible role models. "It was somethin' to see ... meet and talk to black people who had real power. We met Democratic politicians and NAACP leaders from across the country. It was inspiring. They made us believe we could do it, too."

The resort's African Americans found hope for meaningful political involvement in the Democratic Party. Some would remain Republicans, but for most politically engaged people, Hap Farley's organization represented the past. Northside voters were now beyond the control of the "Boardwalk Empire." The bond forged three generations earlier by the Commodore with their grandparents and great-grandparents had disintegrated. Nucky Johnson had strengthened that bond and exploited the Northside for every vote he could squeeze out on Election Day, but his successor didn't have the same charm. "Farley could never cultivate the blacks the way Johnson had. When Nucky went to jail everyone in the black community assumed he'd eventually come back as the Boss. They never really accepted Farley." With Nucky Johnson all but a memory, and with social service programs set in motion during FDR's administration having replaced Republican Party handouts during the off-season, blacks could no longer be herded to the polls and their votes taken for granted as they had been for nearly 75 years.

Aggravating the Farley machine's plight was the change in Atlantic City's demographics. The population base was eroding. With the local economy sagging and the country's growing love affair with the automobile and a "home in the suburbs," the resort was no longer an attractive place for many residents coming of age in the 1950s and 1960s. More and more whites were abandoning the town.

"White flight" hit the resort hard. Some left the region; others headed down beach to the southern end of Absecon Island to the communities of Ventnor, Margate, and Longport, while many more relocated to the Shore Road communities of the mainland. The outmigration of the city's white population was significant, nearly doubling every 10 years. Between the years 1940 and 1970, the percentage of whites in Atlantic City declined from nearly 80 percent to 50 percent. During the same time, the total population dropped from 64,094 to 47,859. The 1960s were economically devastating, as the resort lost a full one-third of its white population.

It was a new ball game for the Farley machine, and Hap and his crew moved to minimize the damage. They did the unthinkable. In 1968, they recruited a black man to run for City Commission. He was supposed to represent a new beginning in resort politics, but his career had the same old ending.

Karlos LaSane was married to Pepsi-Cola model Joanna Forenan LaSane, which was just one of the things he had going for him. Bright, handsome, and articulate, LaSane had been a "people person" all his life. The captain and star of his high school basketball team, his hopes of becoming a physician were dashed in 1952 after his freshman year at Lincoln University, to which he had been guided by Morris Cain. He was forced to drop out of college to care for his ailing grandmother. Despite the fact that there was no one else to care for her, he was drafted into the Army. The military was not for him. When his service was up, he returned to Atlantic City where he became licensed to sell real estate and worked for various firms. In 1956, he married Joanna, whom he had known since childhood. Both had traveled far and wide, but the Northside was home.

With the local real estate market hitting hard times, LaSane went to work for New Jersey Bell Telephone Company in 1964, becoming the company's first African-American customer sales representative. In a short time, he was promoted to personnel manager with offices in Camden and Atlantic City, dealing in special projects involving minorities. LaSane had witnessed his town's deterioration and wanted badly to play a role in uplifting the community. He envisioned many things that could be done for the Northside but didn't dream he'd ever be in a position to accomplish any of them. Then the Farley organization came calling, making an approach to the leaders of the NAACP.

The NAACP's initial choice for a black candidate was Elwood Davis. He had been approached by City Commissioner Arthur Ponzio (a Farleycrat—a Democrat in name only), and both Ponzio and the NAACP wanted Davis as a candidate. Davis said "no" to both and later told Mayor Dick Jackson the same. Davis conceded that it was difficult to refuse the mayor's offer. Dick Jackson had been a friend of the Northside for a long time, and Davis had great respect for him. "Dick Jackson was a total gentleman. His word was good with the people of my community." When asked why he declined Jackson's offer, Davis said, "The real Democrats were rising. Governor Hughes was like our godfather in Trenton. He worked locally through Horace Bryant. I didn't want to be part of anything that would sidetrack the real Democrats from gaining a solid position. I didn't want to be part of the Farleycrats."

After Davis declined the nomination, the NAACP—eager to have one of its members in city government—tapped Karlos LaSane. "I didn't seek that thing. It sought me. I was hesitant." LaSane would be the first black candidate to be part of the "nonpartisan" machine slate for City Commission. His hesitance proved well-founded.

Like most children growing up on Absecon Island, LaSane had learned how to swim—but he hadn't learned how to swim with sharks. Unlike nearly everyone elected before him to City Commission, LaSane had not "worked the chairs" of the Kuehnle/Johnson/Farley political ward system. He had been anointed. He was a novice swimming with cagey veterans who knew the waters a whole lot better than he did. The faces in City Hall changed frequently, but one constant was the culture of corruption. Upon election with the machine slate, LaSane entered City Hall with little knowledge of what was in store for him. That was dangerous.

LaSane's concern for the people on the Northside was genuine. As a commissioner, he moved quickly on his agenda. Among the projects he initiated were a comprehensive recreation program for children, a program to open schools at night for tutoring children and adults alike, the application for Model Cities funds that led to creation of the Uptown Complex, and the first free live neighborhood summer concerts at no cost to the city. He was also instrumental in securing, through the federal office of Housing and Urban Development, seed money for building the Martin Luther King Jr. Complex, helping to make one of Jim Usry's dreams a reality. Boasting classrooms, a swimming pool, gymnasium, library, auditorium, cafeteria, senior citizens lounge, and day-care center, nothing of this kind had ever existed on the Northside. In addition to working the levers of power in City Hall for the people of his community, LaSane played by the rules of power established long before he arrived.

Kickbacks, bribes, and extortion were a tradition in Atlantic City. Corruption had been the norm for so long—and so many people benefited from it—that no one knew anything *but* dishonest municipal government. As an example, the municipal recreation programs championed by Commissioner LaSane required purchasing new playground equipment. But the children on the Northside weren't the only ones to benefit from the purchase—big people did, too.

Every vendor dealing with City Hall had to share 10 percent of its receipts with the Farley organization. If they didn't, they were blacklisted. The grease needed to keep the wheels of the local Republican Party working was cash, delivered in envelopes to the official in City Hall overseeing the particular program. Now part of the local power structure, LaSane soon learned there was income to be made in addition to his salary as commissioner. He went along, holding his hand out and demanding payment from his vendors, which he then shared with the Farley machine. He could have said no. But he didn't.

During LaSane's second year in office the town's only newspaper, the *Atlantic City Press*, ran a series of investigative articles, researched by two aggressive reporters. The reporters found plenty to write about, and the *Press* decided to shine a bright light on the Farley organization. Unfortunately for LaSane and his fellow commissioners, resort residents weren't the only ones reading the news. One of the reporters, Jon Katz, had a contact in the U.S. Attorney's Office in Camden, and he turned over damning information to staff counsel and FBI agents.

LaSane found himself in the glare of a more menacing investigation. His initial term as commissioner wasn't completed when the FBI launched one of its periodic inquiries into municipal corruption in the resort. (Occasional investigations by the FBI remain a tradition in Atlantic City to this day.) Its probe in quest of indictments was about as challenging as shooting fish in a barrel. Vendor invoices, City Hall payment records, employee bonus statements, and tax returns all told the tale.

For as long as anyone could remember—dating back to the Commodore's era—it was a routine cost of doing business for vendors selling goods or services to city or county government to kick back a percentage of the invoiced amount to the Republican power brokers. Throughout most of the 1950s and '60s, the going rate was 10 percent. This levy paid to the politicians was merely factored into the sale price, and everyone was content. The required 10 percent kickback was enforced on every transaction—from police cars, fire-fighting equipment and sanitation trucks to office furniture, paper products, and playground equipment. If someone refused to pay, they received a call from Jimmy Boyd, clerk of the County Board of Freeholders—the organization's enforcer and Hap Farley's right-hand man. They paid or soon found themselves removed from the list of eligible vendors.

Press reporter Jon Katz gathered documents creating a paper trail leading directly to City Hall. The brazenness of the organization's "S.O.P." was in plain sight. Invoices showed the amount paid by the city to vendors. Bonus statements equaling a straight 10 percent—often to the penny—paid to the salesmen handling the accounts with the city confirmed the amounts kicked back. Tax returns of the salesmen, absent their "bonuses," created a serious tax liability and cooperative witnesses. Following the issuance of subpoenas for documents, court orders compelling testimony, and threats of prosecution for income tax evasion, the FBI and the U.S. Attorney's Office had all they needed.

Working out of the Newark office rather than Camden to ensure secrecy, it wasn't long before the government had ample facts to obtain indictments against Commissioner LaSane and six others in City Hall. One question that could have been asked then, and remains unanswered today, is: Why only seven indictments? A raft of people in city and county government were involved in extorting payments from vendors, most of whom were far more sophisticated than LaSane and had been at the game much longer.

As one member of the investigation team recalled, "Karlos LaSane was a novice. He was in *way* over his head. He was foolish enough to be lulled into thinking the Republican organization's S.O.P. somehow made it all okay, as if they were above the law. He wasn't venal. He was naive." The fact that LaSane was playing by local rules did him no good with the U.S Attorney's Office; he was indicted as one of the "Atlantic City Seven" and eventually pled guilty to charges of extortion in 1972. Like so many before and after him, his time in local government ended with a stint in prison. The bright political career that could have been, never came to pass.

But the Northside had bigger problems than its first elected official going off to jail. In the same year Karlos LaSane was dealing with his troubles, an incident occurred that slashed the black community's spirit like a knife plunged into the heart. Of all days, it happened on Easter Sunday.

11

Unintended Consequences

Segregation was planned real well . . . Integration wasn't planned at all.
—Sid Trusty, historian and Renaissance man

Five dead. Five dead and 25 wounded. Five dead, 25 wounded, and 700 nightclub patrons terrorized by gunfire. It was a nightmare beyond all words horrible. How horrible? Five *dead*, 25 *wounded*—shot down gangland style. Atlantic City had never seen anything like it. In an instant, everything changed. Vicious thugs had struck a fatal blow to "K-y at the Curb."

Mayhem had arrived. A barrage of bullets had shattered any hope of escaping a world spinning out of control, crazed by drugs and violence. That night, an entire community was robbed of its peace of mind. "Bloodbath" best describes what went down at Club Harlem in the early morning hours of Easter Sunday in 1972. To be precise, it was 2 AM, and the last act, R&B singer Billy Paul, was on stage. As he reached the end of "Magic Carpet Ride," three men with guns—professional assassins—opened fire in a near-capacity showroom and murdered the magic of Kentucky Avenue.

Targeted by the hit men (purportedly led by Sam Christian, a gun-for-hire out of the "badlands" of North Philly) was Philadelphia drug lord, "Fat" Tyrone Palmer, aka "Mr. Millionaire." Palmer had just returned from vacation in Bermuda and was sitting stage side with his entourage of women and five bodyguards when he was shot in the face at point blank range. Before his gunmen could react, Mr. Millionaire was shot twice more as he was falling backward.

Responding to an anonymous call, the local police arrived at the club to find hundreds of well-dressed patrons pacing about in the middle of Kentucky Avenue. As recalled by Hank Tyner, "It was bedlam—

sheer hysteria." As the patrol cars arrived one after another, audience members were running from the building to escape the horror inside. Others were calling out for loved ones, some wailing in disbelief. The policemen fought their way through the crowd, and once inside, they were greeted by gunfire. The stench of gunpowder, spattered blood, shattered glass, and the groans of the wounded filled the room. Several couples left stranded under tables clung to one another, trembling in terror.

"Unable to spot the assailants amid the crying, screaming, and moaning, police held back their fire." One of those moaning victims who later died from a gunshot wound was a 25-year-old pregnant woman. Her husband, a Vietnam veteran, told a reporter, "I survived Vietnam and now I have to come home to this crap. It doesn't make sense." A gangster's bullet shattered his life. But there would be no retribution. Several people were arrested on parole violations and outstanding warrants, but the assassins were never caught. Days later, it was learned that Club Harlem had been made a battleground by the Black Mafia. "Warring gangs from Philadelphia were the culprits, drugs their focus."

Violence on such a scale in the heart of the resort's prime entertainment district had previously been unthinkable. A generation earlier, hoodlums like the ones who shot up Club Harlem would have left their guns at home. For decades on end, Atlantic City had the aura of an adult playground, not a battleground, and even the mafia types respected that. They knew that violence wasn't part of the resort's *anything goes* mentality. But as the economy sank and the town lost its luster, assassinations were no longer taboo.

Despite the town's sinking fortunes, the nightclubs of the Northside remained a powerful draw for black and white tourists alike. The town's nightclubs were one of the few enticements for people to spend any serious money in Atlantic City. But the shoot-out was an ugly gash in the smiling face the resort was struggling to show the world, and even diehard fans were intimidated by gun battles between Black Mafia drug lords. After that Easter Sunday, it wasn't long before Kentucky Avenue found itself sliding into oblivion. Within a few years, Club Harlem was no more.

Atlantic City was sliding, as well, in ways all too painful to behold. The flaws that came to light during the 1964 Democratic National Convention discouraged other conventioneers and visitors generally. By the early 1970s, Atlantic City was scrambling for customers. Few businesses were holding their own. What once was a prosperous and bustling seaside resort was now a beaten down town by the sea struggling to get by on a hollow reputation. No one who knew better, or who could afford to go elsewhere, would choose Atlantic City as a place to vacation.

Making sense of the collapse of the resort economy entails understanding one of its key components. During its peak years, when the resort was the most popular vacation destination of the Northeast region (circa 1885–1935), there developed a "core area" within the city, which traditionally had an 8-to-10-month economy. The area bounded by the Boardwalk and Virginia, Atlantic, and Arkansas Avenues contained a heavy concentration of family-owned and -operated hotels, boardinghouses, restaurants, and shops. The resort had a virtual monopoly in the minds of millions of middle-class vacationers as the number one destination on their travel list. It wasn't happenstance that the most popular board game of the 20th century was *Monopoly*.

When Charles Darrow conceived his game in the 1930s, he chose Atlantic City to base it on because it was the best-known vacation town in America. For his game to be a success, he needed guideposts and identifiers that the average person would recognize immediately. The most expensive real estate in *Monopoly*—the Boardwalk, Park Place, and Pennsylvania, Pacific, and North Carolina Avenues—all lie within the core area. Darrow knew that regardless of whether a person had visited the resort, it was likely they knew the names of the places on his game board. The core area was the most vital section of the town and a prime center of employment for Northside residents, most of whom were able to walk to work.

Within this 20-square-block portion of the city were hundreds of prosperous family-owned businesses. Many of these families were people who had invested in Atlantic City's hotel-resort economy at a time when "tourism" was thought of as a novelty in most American business circles. The owners relied heavily on the Northside to staff their boardinghouses, small hotels, and restaurants. In fact, about 95 percent of the "staff" was African American. White business owners had developed relationships with many longtime black employees, entrusting them to run their businesses in their absence and to look after their properties in the off-season.

The core area was the backbone of the economy, providing a majority of the jobs on the Northside and paying the bulk of the real estate taxes to City Hall.

With the hindsight of more than four generations, the heyday and the ultimate demise of the resort and its core area come into focus. Following World War I, Philadelphia's factory workers were flush with cash. Universal ownership of the automobile was still a dream, so each summer millions of vacationing travelers boarded the train in the City of Brotherly Love and headed for Atlantic City. The hotels, boardinghouses, restaurants, and shops in the core area prospered and so did their black employees, many working at 8- to 10-month jobs. A year after World War I, in 1919, America took leave of its senses by adopting the 18th Amendment to the U.S. Constitution, which banned the sale of all alcoholic beverages. "Prohibition" reigned from 1920 to 1933 and yielded unintended consequences of its own, not the least of which was organized crime. But for the resort, it was an unexpected blessing. With the adoption of Prohibition, Atlantic City—and with it, the Northside's entertainment district—was off and running.

Selling liquor unlawfully was nothing new in Atlantic City. Throughout the closing decade of the 19th century and the first two decades of the 20th, resort tavern owners ignored the state's Bishops' Law requiring Sunday to be "dry." The town's response was basically, *Whataya mean no booze on Sunday? Hell, that's our busiest day of the week.* If resort taverns and restaurants could get away with selling alcoholic beverages one day a week, why not seven? To quote former mayor Richard Jackson, "Prohibition didn't happen in Atlantic City."

Prohibition marked the zenith of the resort's economy. While other cities had speakeasies and private clubs, the sale of alcohol in the resort continued as usual in bars, restaurants, hotels, and nightclubs. This gave Atlantic City's clubs and gambling rooms a tremendous advantage over those in other cities in northeast America. Prohibition was an unexpected godsend, and the Northside's entertainment district *roared* throughout the '20s. As we saw in Chapter 8, the Paradise Club got its start when all of America was supposed to be "dry."

Prohibition's first 10 years—1920 through 1930—were the town's true golden years. Over the decades since, urban historians and the news media have spun pseudo-intellectual explanations decrying the decline of the "Queen of Resorts." Some have pointed fingers at corrupt politicians. Others have blamed greedy hoteliers who refused to make investments to upgrade their properties. Some commentators have said Atlantic City had a "black problem." None of these explanations is correct. It's much simpler. The repeal of Prohibition was the beginning of a long, slow, downhill ride for Atlantic City, and especially for the Northside. That decline was only halted temporarily by World War II.

As the country geared up for war, Republican boss Frank "Hap" Farley and other Atlantic City powerbrokers gambled on the resort's future. They made the calculation, correctly, that the war effort would cut into tourism and essentially turned the town's hotel rooms over to the U.S. military. Throughout most of World War II, Atlantic City was used as a training center for tens of thousands of American G.I.'s. It was a boon to the resort economy. The large hotels and Convention Hall were ideal temporary facilities—they were mostly empty anyway because of the war—and Atlantic City became a basic training center for the Army Air Corps. The Army leased Convention Hall, and its main arena and meeting rooms were transformed into a training facility. Thousands of recruits did calisthenics and received briefings daily at the hall and trained for maneuvers on the beach. Off duty, many of the troops partied, and the Northside's businesses flourished.

For many servicemen, basic training in Atlantic City was a pleasant surprise. Their accommodations were far better than those of the average G.I. who trained at a military base like Fort Dix. Many of the soldiers enjoyed their stay so much they returned with their families after the war. For Boardwalk merchants, shopkeepers, barbers, bartenders, and restaurant owners, the Army and its seven-days-a-week visitors were a blessing. The Army's presence helped many Northside businesses survive the days following the repeal of Prohibition, but when the war ended, America raced into the future, leaving Atlantic City behind.

Following World War II, the owners of the hotels and boarding-houses within the core area witnessed a gradual but steady decline in revenue. The years following World War II saw major changes in American society. Increased car ownership, affordable air travel, the development of new resorts, air-conditioning, and homes with swimming pools all chipped away at Atlantic City's visitor base. Vacationers from the Northeast region now had options beyond taking the train down to the seashore. Besides, once a family had a car of its own, a trip on the train seemed passé. Summer after summer, it was easy for mainland communities to witness the decline in train traffic. Many people in the region assumed the resort was hosting the same number of visitors, now arriving by car, but the core area's businesses knew better.

A large percentage of the core area's customer base was made up of repeat visitors who enjoyed returning each summer to the familiar surroundings of their favorite hotel. But the world changed and Atlantic City didn't, and as the first wave of baby boomers reached adulthood, they began to view the resort as second-rate. As core area businessmen noticed the decline of repeat customers, they grew uneasy. When things didn't improve, they panicked.

By the late 1950s and into the '60s, as their customer counts dwindled, many boardinghouse owners and hoteliers decided to sell out before things got worse. Within a short time following the 1964 Democratic National Convention, the rush was on. This time, it was headed off island. Within a single generation after World War II, the core area no longer enjoyed a year-round economy. The backbone of Atlantic City's economy was broken, and residents on the Northside found it increasingly difficult to find reliable work.

The land of Jonathan Pitney's dream was becoming a squalid, decaying embarrassment. Beginning with battered, towering hotels along the Boardwalk, sloping to grungy boardinghouses on the side streets, the profile of the beach block resembled a garbage pile. Continuing across Pacific Avenue, the streets were lined with abandoned churches, rundown boardinghouses, discount liquor stores, and greasy-spoon eateries that closed by dark. Crossing Atlantic, Arctic, and Baltic Avenues into the heart of the Northside, the buildings blurred into a huge gray pile of rubble. Generations of "doubling up" and decades of neglected maintenance by absentee landlords had taken its toll. Street after street, there were hundreds of row houses needing painting and repairs, some occupied, many vacant, interspersed with the charred remains of burned-out buildings that had once been homes.

The spirit of the community was burned out, too. Off-season, the town was dead. There were days between September and June when a bowling ball could have rolled from one end of Atlantic Avenue to the other without hitting anything. The city was rife with street crime. Corner groceries, bars, restaurants, sandwich shops, and family-owned clothing, jewelry, and hardware stores closed as robberies gobbled up their profits. Barbers and beauticians retired, and no one took over their shops, leaving "For Sale or Lease" signs all over town. Movie theaters closed due to a lack of customers and rampant vandalism. Every office building in town had space for rent.

Deterioration of the resort's social fabric was a citywide phenomenon, but it was especially severe in black neighborhoods. Changes in society have a way of evolving unpredictably, and history is full of surprises, both good and bad. Looking back at the American Civil Rights Movement, an irony bubbles up. The forces of change unleashed in the 1960s had the effect of standing the dynamics that created the Northside on their head. Just as racial discrimination was a catalyst for building a self-contained society, so, too, the mobility afforded by advances in civil rights helped bring about the unraveling of the black community's tightly woven social structure. As often happens in history, the better grew out of the worse, and the worse grew out of the better. The threads that bound the Northside together were fraying beyond repair. Religious, social, and fraternal organizations that had been mainstays for five generations were losing a sad war of attrition. The miniature metropolis was collapsing.

As explained by folk historian Sid Trusty, "This town was goin' down the drain anyway and the Northside was goin' with it. But the Civil Rights Movement created problems nobody saw comin'. It got some people thinkin' about their options and yearnin' to see what life was like beyond this little island. It's a big world out there and once some of them saw it, there was no coming back. Younger people who had the bucks or the brains to get out of here did, and their leavin' put a hurt on this town. They took our future with 'em."

People had the freedom to move, and many did just that. Morris Cain and his generation of leaders could never have imagined such unintended consequences as institutional racism was collapsing. Neither could early civil rights activists like Margaret Lee Caution, Horace Bryant, Joanna LaSane, and Dr. Charles Wilson have foreseen such a turn of events at a time when they were breaking down doors and smashing racial barriers in the pursuit of their careers in the "white world."

Flight from Atlantic City's sinking fortunes wasn't limited to white residents. (Nor was it unique to Atlantic City: The 1960s saw the flight of citizens from cities across the nation, with unfortunate consequences for urban America.) Many of the young black Baby Boomers born of parents who were part of the traditional upper and middle stratum of the hotel workforce, together with the children of black professionals and government employees, were fleeing the island. Although the goals of the American Civil Rights Movement were a long way from being achieved, progress had been made and opportunities existed that hadn't been thinkable a generation earlier. These black Baby Boomers had not only the means, but the motivation to leave town. What was there to keep them home?

Surrounded by the gloom of unemployment, deteriorating neighborhoods, and the desperation of a growing drug culture, in a city led by corrupt politicians stuck in the past, many black Baby Boomers looked elsewhere and saw reasons for hope including college education, military training, the chance to perform on stages beyond Kentucky Avenue, year-round employment at factory and construction jobs, and many more. There were far greater opportunities awaiting them throughout America—and as close as South Jersey—than could be found on Absecon Island. As they left, important building blocks were being removed from the Northside's social infrastructure.

Precious social capital was rapidly becoming depleted. Vital assets, deposited over five generations, were being withdrawn from Atlantic City's community account. When solid citizens flee, it spells trouble. Family by family, as people packed up and left, the Northside's leadership base was crumbling. Abandoned by hundreds of potential role models, the marrow of the black community's skeletal system was drying up, and one need look no further than the high school to recognize it.

Hundreds of talented young black people graduated from Atlantic City High School in the 1960s and '70s, never to return. As they moved on, longtime institutions of the Northside withered away. Fraternal and social organizations such as the Masons, Elks, Good Samaritans, both the "Y's,'" and the Northside Union League saw their ranks ebb until they were forced to dissolve. The same was true for many churches. Congregations shrank. Some resorted to busing in congregants from the nearby community of Pleasantville, to which many Northside residents had fled.

The 1960s and '70s also witnessed the demise of dozens of black-owned businesses. Fanny's Café, Winder's Ice Co., Johnson's Garage, Davis' Lunch Wagon, Brown's Cigar Stores, Virginia's Variety Shop, Hattie's Royal Palms Rathskeller, College Valet Shop, and, yes, Club Harlem—to name just a small number—all became memories. One of the few to find new life on the mainland was Wash's Inn. Known for its fried chicken and tangy ribs, the famed eatery had opened at the corner of Illinois and Arctic Avenues in 1937, during the height of the Depression. It relocated to Pleasantville in 1974—another Northside institution gone.

Watching helplessly was the once mighty Northside Board of Trades. As Wash's Inn and other businesses closed their doors or left the city, its membership dwindled to a handful. Before the 1970s were over, the Board of Trades was forced to disband.

For more than a generation, Atlantic City's leaders were helpless in dealing with the deterioration. From 1950 to 1974, tourist income shrank from more than $70 million annually to less than $40 million; thousands of hotel rooms were torn down or boarded up, reducing the rooms for visitors from nearly 200,000 to less than 100,000, of which few could be considered modern. "How could you get anyone to stay in a hotel where the mattresses were 40 years old and guests had to share a bathroom?"

As the grand hotels were pulled down, they left gaps along the Boardwalk as startling as missing teeth in a smile. Each closed hotel meant dozens—sometimes hundreds—of jobs lost on the Northside. Instead of a grand promenade and showcase for popular culture and industry, the Boardwalk became home to schlock houses, gyp-joints, and panhandlers, many of whom were unemployed Northside residents.

At the dawn of the 1970s, the resort was a bleak place. The unemployment rate exceeded 25 percent for nine months of the year, with a full one-third of the population on welfare. Of the nine New Jersey cities included in the Federal Model Cities Program, Atlantic City had the highest percentage of families earning less than $3,000 per year: 33.5 percent. More than 90 percent of the housing stock had been built prior to 1939, the majority of which was substandard. Many of the houses on the Northside weren't built for year-round habitation. Constructed of substandard materials, the type used for storage buildings, they had tin roofs, and no insulation or rain gutters. Lack of maintenance by out-of-town slumlords who viewed their properties as a sinkhole of repairs had predictable results.

Entire blocks of homes sank into blight, tugging their unemployed residents into utter hopelessness. A report prepared by a local anti-poverty group in 1972 disclosed that the resort had the highest divorce, venereal disease, tuberculosis, and infant mortality rates of any city in the state. According to the FBI's Uniform Crime Report, among 528 American cities in the 25,000 to 50,000 population group, Atlantic City had the highest total number of crimes in the seven standard categories. The criminals were mostly poor people stealing from one another.

Atlantic City was no place for investors. No new money of any kind was coming to town. There had been no major construction for nearly a generation. The only activity on the rise was arson. With no prospect of a turnaround, despair was the dominant mood. As the grand hotels, amusement piers, motels, restaurants, and theaters were abandoned, torn down, or torched, and boardinghouses converted to year-round living units for the elderly and poor, the resort's service jobs disappeared. If not employed by a city, county, state, or federal agency, those Northside residents without the wherewithal to move on to another town had little choice but to scurry for what few jobs were available during the summer and then hunker down come winter.

Hopes given birth during the Summer of Freedom were now lost in the wreckage that prevailed in Atlantic City. It's said that, "a rising tide lifts all boats," but a sagging economy leaves many workers stranded. As the town's fortunes declined, longtime Northside residents who had worked their entire lives in the resort-hotel economy found themselves caught in a city that had no use for them. The descendants of black workers, who played such a crucial role in building Atlantic City into a national resort and who were the indispensable ingredient in the town's once successful experiment in tourism as the basis of the local economy, were now the object of scorn. Job opportunities continued to dwindle, and competition for work was fierce. Black people knew they'd be left out of the better paying positions. Many Northside residents felt trapped in a town that had no future.

In an attempt to revive the resort's sagging economy, advertising agencies for some of the hotels tried promoting Atlantic City as a "family resort." The wide-open days were gone, and Atlantic City was now supposed to be a place where Mom and Pop could bring the kids. Sid Trusty, a veteran of Kentucky Avenue's glory days, looked back over the resort's earlier success. "Family resort, my ass. You gotta be kiddin' me. It was hot music, pretty women, gambling and good eats that brought people to this town, *especially* Kentucky Avenue. Families vacationed here but this town was never a family resort the way Ocean City was and never will be." People like Sid Trusty knew their town could never compete as a family resort. There had to be another solution.

As early as 1958, the resort's Women's Chamber of Commerce, at the urging of local hotel owner Mildred Fox, had gone on record in support of legalizing gambling in Atlantic City. A feisty little redhead with an Italian temperament—she was Fox née Logiovino—Fox was forever banging heads with the local power establishment. Politically active, Fox, like Marvin Perskie before her, was a genuine Democrat, not a Farleycrat. Atlantic City was her home, and she wasn't leaving. Plucky but savvy, she pushed the idea of legalized gambling to anyone who would listen. "It was our only hope for saving the city. We were on our way to becoming a ghost town."

By the late 1960s, the back-room gambling operations were gone. It was tough to find even a card game. To make things worse for the Northside, state government had destroyed the numbers game that had flourished for many years. The "policy game" created by the numbers bankers was replaced by the New Jersey Lottery. It raked in money for state government but took revenue out of the Northside that for decades had been recycled back into the community through the Northside Credit Union. To the Northside's economy, the New Jersey Lottery was akin to a bloodletting.

Gradually, among the people who made up the local power establishment (some living in town, others not), there developed an approach that argued that if Atlantic City were ever to regain stature as a national resort, it needed an edge, the only logical one being casino-style gambling. Las Vegas had casinos and look what it was able to do in the desert. Think of what could be done with gambling in a town with the ocean and the Boardwalk, or so the logic went.

Legalizing gambling required an amendment to the New Jersey Constitution. That wouldn't be easy. Despite the resort's long-practiced talent at marketing itself beyond its true worth, the audience needed to win approval wasn't listening and cared little about Atlantic City's decline. It was just another tired town desperate for a bailout. New Jersey was becoming increasingly suburban, and the state's ailing cities were being left to fend for themselves. The perception of the resort held by many voters living in the suburbs was that it was just one more depressed city pulled down by troublesome black people. The only difference was its location on the ocean. Some cynical commentators dubbed the resort "Camden by the sea." A bigger question than *how* was *who* might launch the effort to change the State Constitution?

Hap Farley was gone from the political scene. During nearly 30 years as leader of the majority party of the Senate, Farley had made alliances, which transcended partisan politics and any one governor's term in office. On many issues, he had virtual control over the legislative process. Few in Trenton dared challenge the senator from Atlantic County.

Farley's defeat for re-election in 1971 (in large part assisted by defectors from his party) left Atlantic City without a strong voice. Swept from office, the Republican legislative team was replaced by Democrats who were neophytes in the ways of Trenton. Led by Joseph McGahn, an obstetrician/gynecologist turned politician, and Steven Perskie (Marvin's nephew), a brash but brilliant young attorney not long out of law school, it didn't take much time to persuade the legislature to permit a public referendum at the 1974 election on a proposal that would have authorized publicly owned and operated casinos throughout the state. The problems with the proposal and its presentation were obvious and, in the end, insurmountable. The voters of New Jersey resoundingly rejected the idea. The only good thing that came out of that debacle is that everyone learned from their stumbling.

For those people serious about rebuilding Atlantic City, there never was a thought of abandoning the quest for casino gambling. That they succeeded a short two years later is a marvel.

Turnarounds of the sort that occurred between 1974 and 1976 don't happen often. The best explanation is the town's obsession with regaining its former glory. There's the hunger that comes from yearning and the hunger that comes from need, and then there's the hunger that comes from desperation. There was no town more desperate than Atlantic City in late November 1974.

The second effort commenced immediately, this time with research and reflection. That was especially true on the part of the young lawyer, Steven Perskie, who had forged a bond with the governor's office. Perskie's relationship with Brendan Byrne played a pivotal role in securing another bite at the apple. Remove Perskie's relationship with Byrne from Atlantic City's history and the second referendum would never have occurred. The weeks and months following the 1974 defeat were spent analyzing the campaign, and, in a short time, the legislative team realized what had gone wrong. Senator Joseph McGahn and Assemblyman Steven Perskie (being Marvin's nephew didn't hurt—particularly with Northside voters) had struck a compromise that came back to haunt them. McGahn and Perskie had yielded to several legislators' demands that the referendum language include a "local option," which would have conceivably permitted any community in the state to have gambling. Nevertheless, polls taken following the election revealed that was what voters feared most, namely, the potential of gambling everywhere. New Jersey's voters had visions of slot machines in drugstores and gas stations in every community, and they were turned off by the idea. They wanted gambling, if approved, restricted to Atlantic City.

Another misconception dealt with the private ownership of casinos. It was thought that by proposing state-owned and operated casinos, voters would have more confidence they'd be run honestly and efficiently. The voters knew better. They didn't want bureaucrats running casinos and believed the only people who would invest any serious money in Atlantic City were private developers. By narrowing the focus of their new question to Atlantic City alone and permitting private development of casinos, the legislators felt that the resort would be able to face the state's voters a second time on more favorable terms. But McGahn and Perskie knew that these changes weren't enough.

For several months prior to the 1974 referendum, New Jersey's clergy went to their pulpits each Sunday and preached against the evils of gambling. The ministers and priests were tough adversaries, and their dire warnings of moral decay had a heavy impact, especially among senior citizens, most of whom went to the polls to oppose casinos. The second time around there was a sense of urgency like nothing else in Atlantic City's history, and the supporters of gambling knew that the churches and senior citizens had to be neutralized. Longtime resort residents viewed the 1976 referendum as a life or death proposition—and it was. This was their town's last hope to avoid virtual extinction. If Atlantic City failed again, there wouldn't be a third chance. The resort's legislative team had to pull out all the stops.

McGahn and Perskie decided to use the senior citizens, along with people with disabilities, as a rallying cry in selling the second referendum. They wrote language into the ballot proposal requiring the tax revenues generated from casinos to be earmarked for a special fund to be used exclusively for subsidizing the utility bills and prescription medicines of senior citizens and disabled persons throughout the state. The second time around, a vote against casino gambling would be more than a vote against moral decay and special treatment for Atlantic City; it would be a rejection of benefits for old widows living hand-to-mouth and the "crippled guy" injured in the war. It's too bad the Commodore and Nucky Johnson didn't live to see it. They would have appreciated such a wonderful concoction. Some viewed it as cynical manipulation, but it worked.

Did the Northside figure in on all the machinations to bring casino gambling to Atlantic City? Simple answer: in the short run, yes; in the long run, no.

Admittedly, the votes of black people were part of any stratagem for approval of the referendum. Dozens of community and church leaders from the Northside were recruited to network with their counterparts throughout the state and to pull them into the referendum campaign. The pastors of New Jersey's many African-American churches were critical to any effort. They had to be brought on board and, through the activism of the local clergy, they were.

Everyone was working from the same playbook and delivering the same message. The main pitch was to voters' pocketbooks—what casinos in Atlantic City would do for people all over New Jersey. The campaign slogan was "Help Yourself—Casinos Yes." Months prior to November, repeat visits were made to Newark, Paterson, Elizabeth, Trenton, Camden, and other cities with large black populations. Many of those visits were on Sundays to permit local speakers to address black congregations. The weekend before the election, buses to the same cities carried people who canvassed black neighborhoods, knocking on doors, distributing flyers, and pleading for votes.

Finally, it was Election Day. One last measure of insurance, "street money" totaling $170,000 (the amount *reported*) was paid to get out the vote. (Think $750,000 to $1,000,000 in today's dollars.) Street money is a tradition in New Jersey politics; without it, voters in some areas don't get to the polls. In many neighborhoods, it takes paid Election Day workers on the street to bang on doors, drag people out of their homes, drive them to the polls, and, when necessary, buy them lunch, give them a bottle, or slip them a few bucks. The campaign's supporters saw to it there was enough money on the streets of every major city in the state to guarantee that when those voters finally did get to the polls, they pulled the right lever. By the end of the referendum campaign, insiders viewed the vote as a formality. Atlantic City was to going to have casino-style gambling.

New Jersey's African-American voters threw their weight heavily behind the gambling referendum. Again, the efforts of black people figured heavily in the resort's success. But was the Northside to benefit directly from this "unique tool of urban development"? The answer is "no," as the price of admission into the new city to be reborn through casino gambling was beyond the reach of African-American entrepreneurs.

For starters, applicants for a casino license had to submit a nonrefundable $200,000 application fee *and* fund the investigative and licensing process (frequently resulting in costs exceeding $1 million), *plus* guarantee construction of a 500-room hotel. Realistically, anyone wanting to become a player—even 30 years ago—had to think in terms of a total financing package in the range of $15 million to $25 million. As reflected upon years later by Sid Trusty, "Probably one of the few people on the Northside who could have thought seriously about a gambling casino was Reggie Edgehill. He knew the kind of people who could have got something going on the Northside. But as clever as Reggie was, he couldn't ante up that kind of cash. Think of it, more than a million dollars just for a license. Not even a shovel in the ground. We were dealt out before the game began."

Only corporate America would open casinos in Atlantic City. The demands of the casino legislation created a situation making it extremely difficult for anyone but a publicly traded corporation to ante up the required front money. Given the resort's hoary tradition of political corruption, it's not a surprise that the legislators viewed tough regulations as a key to credibility in attracting investors. People can differ over the public policy supporting such a costly threshold for entering the casino business, but there's no denying the consequences. There was no chance casinos would revitalize the Northside's entertainment district. As time would tell, the development of casinos in Atlantic City was *first* about money and *second* about people. Atlantic City's and America's past being what they are, it could have been no other way.

Appreciating why it could be "no other way" requires a step back for a broader view of American history. The character of a nation, and a city, are generally molded by their founders. The "tone" established early on lingers and permeates its culture. The character of a people is revealed in the things to which they aspire. This is true of both Atlantic City and America.

Few observers have understood the American psyche and the culture that grew out of it as well as a Frenchman who visited here in the 1830s. Twenty years before Jonathan Pitney began his travels to Trenton in quest of a railroad, Alexis de Tocqueville was traveling throughout America recording his impressions of the new nation. Many historians believe that de Tocqueville's insights into the American character remain as valid today as they were 170 years ago. His profile of the American persona pertains to Atlantic City, as well, and helps explain the local power establishment's constant indifference to the condition of black people.

Ostensibly, the purpose of de Tocqueville's visit to America was to study the prison system and report on it to the French government. What fascinated him most, however, and, which he expressed so well in his remarkable book, *Democracy in America*, was how the ambitious temperament of the migrant differed from that of the average European and how that difference was an advantage in the development of the United States. "In Europe, we habitually regard a restless spirit and immoderate desire for wealth, and an extreme love of independence as great social dangers," he wrote, "but precisely these things assure a long and peaceful future in the American republics."

American culture was shaped—and continues to be—by the migrant experience. The popular ideal of what it means to be an

American is to be a striver, to be impatient with the status quo, to believe that commitment to a goal and determination to succeed will prevail in the end. Americans want to move on. *Somethin' troubling you? Get over it. Pull yourself up by your bootstraps. Forget the past and go from here.* When it comes to white Americans and their thoughts about the black experience in American history, the attitude of many can be expressed as follows: *Why should something that's been over for more than a hundred years affect us today? Let's get real. Everyone's ancestors went through hard times. They all suffered. Slavery happened a long time ago. We didn't have anything to do with it. What good can come from talking about it?* Most Americans don't stop to realize that no other ethnic group has been a slave on American soil, or that our history made the black man's skin color a stigma, or the debt owed to a people whose forced labor during 240 years helped build this country.

By and large, Americans are too impatient and uninformed about our history to give any thought to how past events affect today's world. Our popular culture is one in which most Americans "still believe that anybody can become rich and live the good life. All it takes is desire, hard work, a little luck and the right timing." Alexis de Tocqueville captured our culture's essence. He believed Americans were born merchants.

When it comes to aggressive commercialism, the people who carved out Atlantic City from a wilderness island are a high-octane version of America. From its inception, the town was a speculation. As we have seen, the first time around, the resort was founded by merchants who had migrated to Absecon Island. Whether they operated the large Boardwalk hotels or boardinghouses, managed restaurants, amusement arcades, Boardwalk shops, gambling rooms, brothels, or gin joints, they shared a common trait: They were dedicated to the town's credo of earning a "fast buck" by giving visitors what they wanted, epitomized by *booze, broads, and gambling.*

No one better exemplifies the buccaneer spirit of the entrepreneurs who built Atlantic City than Samuel Richards and the Philadelphia and New York businessmen who streamed to town after his second railroad. Some speculated successfully, cashed out, and left town, replaced by people of similar mind-sets. Others developed businesses, sunk permanent roots, and became an essential part of the resort's economy for many decades. When the bottom fell out in the 1960s, very few of the heirs of those migrant merchants remained. They got what they could for their properties and moved on. But the great-grandchildren of the people who provided the muscle and sweat to run those businesses were left behind to fend for themselves.

Now, instead of Samuel Richards, fast-forward 100 years and think Donald Trump and company. With the approval of casino gambling, the rush was on again. People of the same ambitious, impatient, striving mind-set came to Atlantic City in the years following the 1976 referendum. They knew nothing of the town's history and the indispensable role the Northside had played in building the hotel-resort economy. They came to deal themselves in on the new town that everyone hoped would rise from the rubble.

Migrants, then and now, are special people. "The migrant is the maverick who runs at the edge of the human herd. Migrants are a self-selected band of seekers—those of adventurous and curious mind—who in their restless approach to life lie at the extreme of the bell-shaped curve of behavioral distribution, and because of this eccentricity, given that America [Atlantic City] is a nation [city] built almost entirely on the energy of migrant individuals, some important questions arise." Can Atlantic City flourish without yielding to the demands of migrant merchants? Will corporate America, that is, the casino industry, and the community ever develop a meaningful partnership? Finally, can a homogeneous enclave of African Americans prosper in the new Atlantic City? Events since 1976 reveal that it's difficult to get to "yes" on any of these questions.

"Diaspora" does not overstate what the Northside has experienced as a consequence of the Civil Rights Movement and legalized casino gaming. Two people from Atlantic City High School's Class of 1966 were part of that original dispersion. They each left town with little thought of returning for anything more than to visit family. Their stories are informative of what the Northside was, what it has become, and what it may yet become.

12

Embracing the Future

*Think about this type of child. He's basically homeless.
He doesn't know where he's going to sleep tonight or
where his next meal is coming from, yet we want him to
learn algebra.*
    —James L. Jackson, New Jersey Superior Court Judge

"Mr. Weinberger, talk to me straightforward. Just say whatever it is
you need to say—just between the two of us."

"I never worked with a broad in the casino industry before."

"I appreciate that. Well, guess what? I went to an African
Methodist Episcopal school in Ohio and gambling was not on the
curriculum. So we've got to figure out why the Lord has thrust you
and me together. There's some purpose here; I don't know what it is.
Where did you work before you worked at a casino?"

"Well my family had a catering business in Cleveland, Ohio."

"Okay, you worked in a kitchen."

"Yes."

"I've worked in a kitchen. Now we have a common denomina-
tor. We have both worked in a kitchen. Now we just have to grow
from here."

Working in kitchens, vacuuming guest rooms, and operating eleva-
tors in Atlantic City's hotels gave her a deep appreciation for university life. Excelling in the classroom as both student and professor, the
Northside's Redenia Gilliam was poised for a career in the academic
world. But the 1976 Referendum was a game changer in Gilliam's
life. It brought her home, taking her from the college classroom to the
corporate boardroom. No surprise. She excelled there, too.

Achieving meant overcoming, and Gilliam was used to that. She
was raised in a family in which excellence was expected. Although

245

hardly idyllic, her childhood was filled with experiences—and one important role model—that rooted her in her family, faith, and community, and provided her with the moral compass to make her way in life. In truth, the goings-on in her household weren't all that different from most families on the Northside or, for that matter, throughout America. In looking back a little more than two generations, what's striking is how swiftly the circumstances of families have declined across America. Today, too few children are encouraged to *excel*, and many grow up in an environment where excellence in education isn't expected the way it was for Gilliam and her generation.

When asked who the most influential person in her life was, Gilliam would tell you, "It's my mother. There's no other way to talk about anyone else." Vera Mae Gilliam, *née* Donalson, was the product of a Quaker education, a graduate of the Allen Normal School in Thomasville, Georgia. "So many [black] people in the South went to schools that had been created by Quakers. They were based on excellence—learning the same kinds of subjects that were provided for anyone."

At the encouragement of her aunt, Katie Schuler, Vera Mae headed north as a young woman in 1929. Despite the fact that she had been a teacher in a segregated Georgia public school, upon her arrival in Newark, New Jersey, she found that there were no teaching positions open for a black woman. Her Aunt Katie had done domestic work, and soon after arriving, Vera Mae took the only work available to her, as a seamstress. Not long after, she met James "Jim" Gilliam, who hailed from Virginia. Gilliam was smitten. Following a brief courtship, he wrote to Vera Mae's father, the Reverend Mitchell Donalson, pastor of the Pilgrim Rest AME Church in Bainbridge, Georgia, asking permission to marry his daughter. It was granted, and Jim and Vera Mae began their lives together, raising four children: James Jr., Lorenzo, Redenia, and Latha.

Vera Mae understood the value of a well-rounded education in creating social capital. Denied the opportunity to teach in a classroom, she used her knowledge to educate her own children by supplementing the instruction they received in school. "We all learned to play piano," Redenia said. "My mother expected her children to be articulate and, so, at church [St. James AME] we would memorize pieces … and recite them. She always emphasized how we should be able to speak with people on all levels." In addition to classical literature, Vera Mae introduced her children to the work of noted black poet and author Paul Lawrence Dunbar, who employed the southern African-American vernacular in some of his writing.

Tragedy brought the Gilliam family from Newark to Atlantic City. Jim Gilliam was a skilled machinist working in a factory in neighboring Clifton, New Jersey. Fair-skinned with straight hair, he was sometimes mistaken for an Italian, while Vera Mae was chocolate brown. One day following a workplace visit by his wife, mean-spirited cat calls began as Jim's white co-workers taunted him, asking, "What's it like to sleep with a colored woman?" The relentless verbal abuse either led or contributed to a devastating stroke suffered by Jim that day.

Shortly after Jim's stroke, he, Vera Mae, Redenia, and the youngest son, Latha, headed to Atlantic City to live with relatives. At the time, James Jr., who would later pursue a career in medicine, was serving in the Army, while Lorenzo—who like Latha would eventually become an attorney—was attending Howard University.

The Gilliams moved in with Vera Mae's two aunts, Lillie Mae Johnson—a graduate of Sara Spencer Washington's Apex Academy and the owner of a beauty salon on Illinois Avenue—and Redenia Donalson, a schoolteacher and graduate of Glassboro State College, for whom Redenia had been named.

Not long after the Gilliams arrived in Atlantic City, they were joined by the younger Redenia's great aunt, Katie Schuler. "We always had at least three generations living in our house growing up." As a child, Redenia was known as "Sister Baby" to distinguish her from her Aunt Redenia who was called "Sister." Redenia was 10 when she moved to Atlantic City, and by age 12 she was working in hotels. "No one asked me how old I was … so I started working as a chambermaid—I made 22 rooms a day, two double beds—for $30 a week."

Redenia's years as a chambermaid forged her character and gave her insights that stayed with her throughout life. "In working at cleaning rooms, I learned a lot of things from the women I worked with. I learned teamwork; I learned the aspect of respect that no matter what job you did, it didn't matter. What really mattered was what kind of person you were. I learned that many people who came into hotels talked down to you because you cleaned—by the job you performed they decided almost whether or not you should breathe *their air*. They felt you were so much below them because you were cleaning."

Hotel work occasionally involved more than cleaning for Redenia. During the summer of 1964—the "Summer of Freedom," when the Democratic National Convention was in town—she was operating the elevator at the Ambassador Hotel, the site of today's Tropicana Hotel Casino. The story of what occurred one morning during the convention is vintage Redenia Gilliam.

"I had Bobby Kennedy, Pierre Salinger [Press Secretary to President John F. Kennedy], and one other person on my elevator during the '64 Convention ... Pierre Salinger was smoking a cigar and I had to ask him, *'Sir, please put that cigar out, we cannot have that.'*" She told the story to her mother, who asked her, "Did you know who he was?" Redenia replied, "Yes, I knew who he was, but he still wasn't supposed to have a cigar in the elevator ... But when the doors opened there were all these lights and cameras and it really frightened me because I wasn't expecting it." Imagine, nearly 50 years ago, a 16-year-old black girl telling the president's press secretary to put out his cigar!

After she'd related this story to her mother with a tinge of awe and bewilderment at being in the presence of such powerful people and in the glare of the lights and cameras, Vera Mae replied, "*My* daughter deserves to be in television lights! Those men are no better than you. How did they put their pants on this morning? Did they do it like you, one leg at a time? And if they did, then that means that you're equal. Now you just go on from there and you do the best you can."

Vera Mae taught her children that "your word is your *word*," and that "you can never let other people bring you down ... you must never let people win over you." She once told Redenia, "When you're sure that people are talking down to you and it's clear that they're being racist toward you, that's when you talk very specific and just don't have anything to do with them ... and when they're not respectful to you, then you continue to be respectful ... you will be measured by how you interact with other people and how you treat other people."

When Redenia wasn't working in hotels or around the home, she was busy at school. Despite a hip injury and surgery, she excelled in sports, receiving the highest honor for women in athletics, the coveted Alumni Statuette Association Award at Atlantic City High

School. She was also selected to play the mammoth organ in Convention Hall at the graduation ceremony for her class, following in the footsteps of her cousin, Ronald Fluellen, and preceding her brother, Latha. No other family of musicians has ever been so honored at the school.

After graduating from Atlantic City High in 1966, Redenia went on to study economics and political science at Wilberforce University in Wilberforce, Ohio, a historically black college and university (HBCU). Wilberforce traces its origins to the Ohio Underground Railroad and is located on the site of one of its stations. The nation's oldest private HBCU, it was named to honor the great 18th-century abolitionist, William Wilberforce, a member of the British Parliament who, in the early 1800s, campaigned exhaustively for the end of slavery.

During her junior year, as a result of her outstanding academic achievement, Redenia was awarded a scholarship to study economics at the prestigious University of Hull in East Yorkshire, England. East Yorkshire was the birthplace of William Wilberforce and, during the school's centennial, the Lord High Mayor of East Yorkshire had visited the campus in Ohio. He was so taken with the school that he encouraged his city to establish two annual scholarships for students from Wilberforce to attend Hull University. After attending Hull for a year, Redenia returned to the U.S. and graduated with honors. After Wilberforce, she continued her studies at Rutgers University, obtaining her master's degree in city and regional planning.

Before coming home to Atlantic City, Redenia taught for eight years at Livingston College on the New Brunswick Campus of Rutgers University and received the first Blumberg Award for Excellence in Teaching. While at Livingston, she taught a course, Urban Poor, for the school's Department of Urban Studies and Community Development, as well as a senior seminar. She also taught at Stuart Country Day School, a prep school in Princeton. One assignment she gave to both her college and prep school students was a comparative shopping analysis that required them to shop in nearby Princeton and then in downtown New Brunswick. The steeper prices paid for consumer goods by the urban poor was an eye-opener for her students.

Far removed from the Northside, Redenia had made a place for herself in the world of education. And that's how she expected it would be. "When I was growing up many of us were weaned on leaving—that in order to make a better living and to make your mark, so to speak, you had to leave Atlantic City." Little did she know. Cloistered away in academia, Professor Gilliam never imagined the change in careers she was about to make or the importance of her role in bringing credibility to a major corporation badly in need of it.

Bally Manufacturing Corp. was a giant in the slot machine, pinball, and jukebox businesses. In the early 1970s, Bally dominated the slot manufacturing market, having a stranglehold on a number of Nevada casinos. While the slot machine business was profitable, President and Chairman William T. "Bill" O'Donnell had tired of making machines for others. He wanted a casino of his own. After a trip to Atlantic City following the 1976 Referendum, O'Donnell decided the resort was the place to be. He entered the market by acquiring a long-term lease for an aging hotel on the Boardwalk.

O'Donnell's choice was the Marlborough-Blenheim, one of the few remaining palatial Boardwalk hotels. The marriage of two grand old buildings—the quaint Marlborough, a wood-frame hotel with deep red shingles and a slate roof, built in the Queen Anne style, and the Moorish-style Blenheim, a poured-concrete sand castle—the Marlborough-Blenheim was an architectural gem. Unfortunately, the aging hotel wasn't adaptable for use as a casino and had to be demolished. O'Donnell and Bally's then bought the neighboring Dennis Hotel and combined the two sites. The Dennis was gutted and renovated to provide the required 500 hotel rooms, while new construction on the site of the Marlborough-Blenheim housed the casino, restaurants, and convention space. Upon completion, it became Bally's Park Place Casino Hotel.

While Bally's main base of operations was Chicago, O'Donnell was no stranger to New Jersey. The company's biggest distributor of pinball machines and amusement games, Runyon Sales, was based in New Jersey. Runyon was owned, in part, by one of the state's more notorious mobsters, Gerardo Catena, an underboss in the Genovese crime family. In performing its background check on O'Donnell, the New Jersey Division of Gaming Enforcement (the agency that investigates casino applicants) learned that during the 1960s, funds skimmed from Las Vegas casinos "were ultimately funneled from Las Vegas to New Jersey where they were shared by, among others, Gerardo Catena." O'Donnell's ties to Catena through Runyon Sales proved fatal to his license application. The taint of dealing with the mob was too much for the New Jersey Casino Control Commission. While O'Donnell's fate hung in the balance, the situation at Bally's was fraught with uncertainty. The publicly traded corporation had made an enormous investment in Atlantic City, but its leadership was in turmoil. The years during which Redenia Gilliam was re-establishing herself in her hometown, 1979–1980, were critical ones for the new gaming company. Bally's Park Place Casino Hotel Chairman and CEO Bill O'Donnell was forced to resign and was replaced by a successful Wall Street investment banker named Richard Gillman. Gillman called on Billy Weinberger, a successful casino operator in Las Vegas who O'Donnell had hired, to run the day-to-day operations of a company struggling with an image problem.

At the time Gillman tapped Weinberger as president of Bally's Park Place Hotel and Casino, in early 1979, he had already lured Redenia Gilliam from Rutgers, but he wanted Weinberger to think hiring her was his own idea. He arranged to have the two spend a great deal of time together, getting to know one another as Redenia introduced the new president to Atlantic City. Within weeks, Weinberger realized that Redenia was the "broad" he needed on his team in order to assure Bally's success. Her first task was to monitor the Casino Control Commission hearings on the application of Resorts International, Atlantic City's first casino. She attended all 23 hearings on the application and wrote summary reports of each day's events, identifying for her board of directors issues that Bally's would need to address at the hearing on its own application.

Bally's executives understood that, unlike Las Vegas, Atlantic City wasn't vacant land. The concerns of an existing population needed to be addressed. Fortunately, Gillman and Weinberger appreciated that Redenia had the poise, credentials, and roots necessary to garner the respect of the community. She exuded strength, competence, and warmth. She made it clear to Weinberger at the outset that "People will expect me to do certain things and we [Bally's] will be measured by how we interact with the community." For many people, she would become the face of the corporation and, because of her integrity and unswerving devotion to her hometown, she lent Bally's instant credibility. Gillman and Weinberger had chosen wisely.

Gilliam's title was vice president of Government Relations and Planning. Sound straightforward? Anything but. She wore so many hats (one was awarding nearly $500,000 in grants annually—not as much fun as one might think), interacted with so many people, and juggled so many tasks that most executives would have been overwhelmed. She was not.

Redenia's days were often spent navigating mine fields. A sword and shield would have been useful equipment for dealing with some of the personalities she encountered. On any given day, she might interact with needy people in her own North Maryland Avenue neighborhood, casino employees looking for guidance on handling workplace problems, casino executives seeking advice on how to deal with employees, city hall officials with oversized egos and hidden agendas (requiring no-nonsense street smarts to avoid being unwittingly drawn into one of their schemes), state legislators whose loyalties and alliances shifted like beach sand, and governors who viewed the casino industry as a cash cow to be milked regularly.

The tasks that found their way to her desk ran the gamut. They included issues that resounded to her core: the need for safe and affordable housing; child care for parents struggling to get ahead in the workplace; education in the broad sense of the term to uplift her community; land use questions requiring the balancing of private property rights with the need for planning with vision; and legislation affecting Bally's and the entire casino industry. In addition to resuming her role as a professor in order to educate lawmakers in Trenton that Atlantic City wasn't a piggy bank, she had to show Bally's shareholders and corporate directors how to make their way in the new Atlantic City, with sensitivity to both the historic role of the Northside community and the desire of black citizens to be part of the city's future.

Redenia understood that the biggest part of the Northside's future was its children, and one notable career accomplishment was getting Bally's to "adopt" the Indiana Avenue Elementary School. As a result of her and Principal Rita Krall's efforts, Bally's sponsored an annual gala honoring those students, and their families, who earned citizenship awards for their achievements in the classroom and the community. For most of these children, it was the first time in a fancy hotel with someone waiting on *them*.

The most important chapter of Redenia's life after returning home was far too short. In 1974, her father passed away. While home from Rutgers for the funeral, she spent time with another church member and trustee, Israel Mosee. Mr. Mosee, 18 years Redenia's senior, had mentored her as a young woman and was a longtime admirer. Despite their age difference, the two had more in common than any of their friends knew.

In addition to his membership at St. James AME Church, Mosee—like Redenia—was a graduate of Wilberforce University with a passion for uplifting his community. A dynamic speaker with a powerful presence, at times he was also a controversial public figure. He never shirked an opportunity to speak out against injustice. While Redenia was in junior high, Mosee was participating in the Mississippi Freedom Rides. Although he didn't work directly with Fannie Lou Hamer, their cause was the same: fighting for equal rights.

Following her father's funeral and two years of friendly courtship, Mosee proposed marriage to Redenia. Taken aback at first and uncertain how to respond, she replied, "I need to think about it." She "thought" for nearly 12 years, all the while going about her life and seeing Mosee frequently, both in church and socially. Under circumstances best described as revelatory, while Redenia was hospitalized with a misdiagnosis of diabetes (Mosee *was* a diabetic), she got to thinking of a passage from the Bible's Book of Jeremiah (Chapter 29, Verses 10–14: "For I know the thoughts that I think toward you … thoughts of peace, and not of evil …"). She understood in a flash that "Things can change in an instant, and you need to know who the people are you want with you to work through things when adversity comes your way." She grew at peace with the idea of spending her life with Mosee and soon after accepted his proposal.

Redenia and Mosee were married in 1988, with a storybook wedding at St. James AME. Twelve-hundred people attended the service, divided between St. James and neighboring Second Baptist Church. Sixty people were in the wedding party, including Hall of Fame baseball star Willie Mays. The reception and dinner were held at Showboat Hotel Casino—Bally's couldn't accommodate the required parking, and Redenia's favorite chef was at Showboat. It may have been the grandest wedding ever in Atlantic City. Guests speak of it to this day. Redenia and Mosee were soul mates, but their time together was too short: They had 15 years together as a married couple before he succumbed to diabetes.

During her 27 years with Bally's, Bally's Grand (The Hilton), and Caesar's, Redenia always reported directly to the president and was a trusted advisor to the board of directors, wisely guiding Bally's in its involvement with the community. She had her share of successes in these years. Two that she remains particularly proud of are Jacobs Family Terrace and the Atlantic City Boys and Girls Club. (As we will see, the "and girls" part in the club's name came at her insistence, with the addition occurring in 1982—10 years before the national organization formally accepted it.)

Housing for many Northside residents has always been problematic. Redenia was determined to lead the way on this critical need. If she had anything to say about it, her corporation wasn't going to wait for government to act. She nudged Gillman and Weinberger, and, under her leadership, Bally's began urban renewal on the Northside.

Redenia found a parcel of land among Bally's acquisitions, at Baltic and New York Avenues, and after conferring with the Jacobs family and various community leaders, the name "Jacobs Family Terrace" was chosen in honor of the late Atlantic County Court Judge Herbert Jacobs. It was her project. The selection of the site, planning, coordinating, and logistics all fell to her. She reveled in the opportunity, shepherding the application through the maze of agencies that govern the New Jersey land use process. By the fall of 1983, she was ready to put a shovel in the ground. Next came the work of qualifying buyers for the 72 condominium units and securing loans. It's a wonderful story best told by Redenia:

> So when we got ready to do mortgages for Jacobs Family Terrace—and I was talking with the banks that we had— I said, *Look, just because someone doesn't have a credit history doesn't mean that they're all drug runners. It just means that culturally they pay differently. Many pay by cash and get a receipt, others pay by money order. That's just the way they do it.* So what I did was to negotiate so that Bally's would do the credit checks when people were interested in the housing project. Once applications were signed and we were given approval to pull a credit check, I would obtain one through the casino floor. That meant

the housing applicant didn't have to pay $150 for the credit report—then possibly be told they weren't eligible. Bally's helped tremendously by supporting this procedure. It also allowed me to *school* the applicants about the importance of a credit history and what *housing equity* could mean to their lives.

Finding applicants was one thing, qualifying them in a tight financing market was quite another. Redenia persisted. "It took me 800 applications to qualify 72 people. ... My goal was to get the middle income people out of the low-income housing, because when I came back to Atlantic City there were a lot of people who lived in public housing but they paid market rate—because there was no middle-income housing. So, by developing the 72 units, the goal was to free up as many of the low-income units for the people to have them. And I'm just so proud of the people who live there." Jacobs Family Terrace continues to be a cornerstone of what many hope will be a rejuvenated Northside.

Many of the children residing at Jacobs Family Terrace found their way to Redenia's other pet project, the Atlantic City Boys and Girls Club. Not long after her return to Atlantic City, she was asked to attend a banquet to raise funds for the local Boys Club. She had only been a board member of the association for two months when, at the dinner, she was asked if she would be willing to serve as president. Henry "Hank" Tyner had been president for 18 years, and he was preparing to run for City Council. She agreed, but with a condition:

> The first thing was they had to agree to make it a boys *and* girls club. It was a boys club at the time. And I was really struck by the number of girls who had baby carriages and were pregnant. It was like they wear fashions—they're outdoing each other in baby carriages. And my thinking was—well look at the opportunities I had to travel and see so much of the world. If you choose to be pregnant, that's one thing, but certainly one should know about the opportunities and those willing to help you. And, if you get pregnant, then continue on, for there are enough women and people in this community who've had obstacles to

overcome that they can help you succeed—it just takes the will to get it done.

So, Redenia became president of the Atlantic City Boys and Girls Club. At the outset, she made it clear they had to "get rid of the boxing ring, because there wasn't anything in there but a boxing ring. And we had to prioritize educational programs and we didn't have any money. All we had—through the generosity of the United Way of Atlantic County—was $25,000 for an executive director." Redenia worked patiently with the board and staff and the club grew. One of the people she got involved was Arthur Goldberg, chairman of Bally's Park Place Casino Hotel, who by this time had replaced Gillman. She had spoken about the club to him on many occasions and finally took him to see it. Goldberg said, "So this is the place you've been talking about. We need to do something about this." As Redenia tells it, "So it took a total of 20 years for it all to come together [at her urging in 2000, Bally's contributed $3.5 million to build a new facility that was completed in 2002] and that was my goal when I came home—to have an impact on the lives of people from my community and to keep myself based in the reality of day-to-day and not to get lost in all the hype and glitter of the Boardwalk."

Redenia's distinguished career in the gaming industry ended with her retirement in July 2005. She never did get lost in the hype and glitter and always remained active in St. James AME Church and the Boys and Girls Club. Looking back at her life, "uplift" is what Redenia Gilliam-Mosee was all about. Every person she interacted with and every organization or situation in which she was involved was elevated by her presence. In 2010, she left us. It was too soon.

Much like Morris Cain and the Northside "Y," Redenia Gilliam's success in transforming the former Boys Club has touched many lives and helped hundreds of children to begin the process of accumulating social capital. Sadly, not all children on the Northside find their way to the nurturing environment of the Boys and Girls Club. Far too many have found themselves in the courtroom of one of Redenia's high school classmates. The story of his career is inspiring.

Judge James L. Jackson is the embodiment of wisdom, grit, and humility. Thorough in his analysis, meticulous in his reasoning, with extraordinary patience and finely tuned instincts for sizing people up, there is no one better suited to handle youthful law breakers entangled in the legal system.

"Boo" Jackson is a product of the Northside who knows his hometown's troubles because he sees them every day. His path to the Superior Court bench was the road less traveled. One might say his journey in life began standing on a wooden box, shooting pool in Gibson's Pool Hall on Arctic Avenue.

Jackson was born at home on June 29, 1948. His family lived on the 600 block of North Ohio Avenue; the doctor who delivered him, Dr. Robert Powell, had an office on the 400 block. The family sent word, and Dr. Powell walked to the house to deliver the baby. In 1948, the chances were slim-to-none that Jackson's mother would deliver in the Atlantic City Hospital. Generally, black babies were born at home.

Jackson's parents were "hustlers," as the term was understood in the first half of the 20th century—that is, they worked tirelessly to provide for their family. His mother, Eva, and his father, Plass, were both from Georgia. Eva was from Columbus, and Plass was from Ft. Gaines. Plass left home at age 15 and never returned, his roots ripped out and never spoken of again. No one in the family ever learned what went down during Plass's days in Ft. Gaines. Life teaches that some things are better left unsaid.

Plass and Eva met in Columbus, Georgia, where job prospects were sparse. Eva had a cousin in Atlantic City, and they came north together in 1942 looking for work in the hotel-resort economy. Her cousin worked in the Marlborough-Blenheim Hotel, and initially they both found work there. Eva worked as a maid, Plass as a heating boiler operator. He eventually made his way to the Dennis Hotel where he was promoted to supervisor of maintenance.

Plass also worked in other hotels. On occasion, he manned the front desk at the Seagull Hotel on South Kentucky Avenue, which was a big thing at the time. In those days, there weren't many black faces behind the front desks of Southside hotels. That the Seagull permitted Plass to greet guests speaks volumes about his poise and competence. Eva was a "nurturer" who held her home open to an extended family of cousins and friends, most of whom lived within a three-block radius of Ohio and Caspian Avenues. "When she wasn't at work she was helping other people. My mom was there for everyone."

Jackson's parents had the most stable household of their circle of family and friends, in large part because both of them managed to find work nearly all year-round. When friends of the family came to town, or had problems, or needed a place to stay, or something to eat, it was Eva and Plass who took them in. "Sometimes it seemed like my mom was in perpetual motion—cooking meals, cleaning up, washing clothes—for people who came to our home. My father took it all in with a smile and never was bothered by the commotion." Eva and Plass were exemplary role models and loving parents.

It was Eva who gave her son the nickname "Boo," a term of endearment that has stayed with him among close friends and family members; many others just call him Jim. Eva died at age 51 in 1969 while Boo was in college. His memories of her continue to guide him. He recalls his father as "frustrated by his situation. ... My dad was an intelligent man and an avid reader. He sought out all the black newspapers of the day. One of his favorites was *The Pittsburgh Courier*. When I look back on it, I know he was frustrated with having to deal with a very low glass ceiling." Plass died at age 71 in 1989 but lived to experience the pride of seeing his son achieve success as an attorney.

Asked to name the biggest influence in his life, Jackson pondered the question before naming his older brother, Conrad. Despite a 13-year age difference—or maybe because of it—Conrad made a lasting impression on Jim at a young age, teaching him valuable lessons he could learn nowhere else.

Between leaving high school and enlisting in the Army, Conrad and Jim spent entire days together over many months. Not yet four years old, little Boo would go with Conrad when he was making rounds on the Northside. One frequent stop was Gibson's Pool Room. The two of them became regulars at Gibson's, and it wasn't long before Boo had learned how to handle a cue stick. Conrad rigged up a wooden produce box with a rope tied to it. With drooping pants, bright eyes, and stubby fingers, little Boo would pull the box around the pool table, standing on it to make his shots. He felt at home shooting pool but quickly learned that Gibson's was an intricate social environment.

Many of the older guys hanging out in Gibson's were involved with drugs in one way or another. As Atlantic City's economy sank and young men returned home from the military (and later the

Vietnam War), they brought drug habits with them. Over time, illegal drugs would infect the Northside and all of America. Conrad taught Jim early on that drugs were to be avoided and made him understand that it was easy to get in trouble by going along with your friends. While at Gibson's, Conrad would explain to Jim why some of the men were sleeping on the benches and told him drugs are "something you don't want to do." Jim recalls, "I knew what a junkie was before I was 5 years old and knew I would never be one."

By the time Jim reached his teens, he had graduated from Gibson's Pool Room to Brody's Pool Hall on Kentucky Avenue, across the street from Club Harlem. A savvy pool player, he was able to play with some of the older men, many of whom were professionals, such as Dr. Frank Doggett and Dr. W. Oscar Harris. Another "professional" who hung out at Gibson's was "Baby" Coles, a Northside pool shark who "gave lessons." All one had to do was watch. Boo also met Detective Pete Nelson and Captain Ben Anderson, both successful members of the Atlantic City Police Department and two of the people Margaret Lee Caution had fought with City Commissioner William Cuthbert to hire. Years later, after he had attained stature in his profession, Jim would frequently encounter friends from the neighborhood who said to him, "You used to hang out with us and when we got ready to do something kind of funky, you would leave."

Jackson credits his brother Conrad for giving him the maturity to walk away from things that could do him harm. He was "exposed" to things without the need to "experience" them. He knew the downside of drugs and felt no need to try them for himself.

In addition to his parents and Conrad, a large part of Jackson's development was his experience at Indiana Avenue Elementary School. Most of his teachers were from HBCUs, such as Morgan State, Lincoln University, and Howard University. They "taught us about who we were." But as he explains it, the people responsible for his education included more than his teachers and parents. The entire neighborhood was involved in the process.

"There was a close communication between the school and the parents. If I misbehaved, my parents would know about it right away. Most of my teachers lived in the Northside community as did several police officers. They were a natural reinforcement mechanism."

One example pointed to by Jackson that illustrates the depth of the community's involvement in their children's education was "report card day." As he recalled, "On report card day you had to run the gauntlet. Everyone knew when report cards were coming out. Walking home from school we would be asked about our grades by adults on the street. If a child did well, there were words of praise. If not, there were words of encouragement. There were some local businesses that even gave children rewards for receiving good grades." Success in school meant a great deal to everyone on the Northside. "Having good students in the neighborhood was a source of pride, and they let us know that they were proud we had done well on report card day."

There were other events during Jim's school years that reveal how dramatically the Northside, and the world, has changed just in his lifetime. One that stands out occurred in fourth grade. His fourth grade class sponsored weekly school-wide dances. They charged admission and sold refreshments. *All* the money after expenses was saved and used to finance overnight trips for the entire class. That year, 1957, relying on their own resources, Jim's class visited New York City, Baltimore, and Washington. "Those were important learning experiences. We didn't just see the world. We learned teamwork and self-reliance. Can you imagine that happening today?"

Jackson refers to Indiana Avenue School as an "incubator"—a well-conceived incubator that understood its mission, namely, to create mature young people able to deal with the world. As he tells it, "By the time I got out of Indiana Avenue School, I knew who I was. I knew I was someone capable of doing whatever I wanted with my life." Jim recalls that after leaving Indiana Avenue School, "There were people who tried to undo all that, but they couldn't. When I got to junior high and high school, I got different feedback from the teachers but nothing that occurred there could undo the foundation built by my teachers in elementary school."

After graduating from Atlantic City High in 1966, Jim chose to go to North Carolina College at Durham (an HBCU known today as North Carolina Central University). When he left town for college, "I knew at that point there wasn't much here for me. It wasn't what it was anymore." During his college years, Jim returned to Atlantic City in the summer, working in hotels as a doorman, car jockey, and waiter. The best summertime job he ever found was loading trucks at a Pepsi-Cola distributor on South Carolina Avenue between Adriatic and Sewell. In part because of the creative marketing strategy of young Charlie Wilson (later, Dr. Charles Wilson), Pepsi was a popular drink in Atlantic City. Most of the summer workers at Pepsi were college students. Jim was the only black man loading the trucks.

Jim frequently worked two jobs during the summer; for the hotels during the day and for Pepsi at night. "The Pepsi job was union. It was the best job I had ever had. There were a lot of occasions when I got to work overtime and I would say to myself, *Wow! What is this? They're giving away money.*" One hotel where Jim had the opportunity to work frequently was the Seaside. He had a standing offer from the superintendent of services, Monroe Taylor, to work there during spring break and holidays. Reporting to the Seaside as soon as he arrived home from college, he always found work as a bellhop, doorman, or car jockey. This type of standing offer wasn't made lightly by employers in the resort, especially to young black men, and Taylor's confidence in Jim speaks to his superior work ethic and maturity level.

Jim's days as a student at North Carolina were imbued with the same philosophy that he absorbed at the Indiana Avenue Elementary School. "The professors there were very bright people, interested in you as a person, and they wanted you to learn what you needed to know to deal with the world. You didn't just learn history, but the threads of life. You were given a perspective on where black people fit into history." It was in college that Jim met his future wife, Kaye Dove—today Kaye Jackson, Esquire, a respected attorney and executive officer with the Federal Aviation Administration, with whom Jim has two children, Adam and Jaimi.

In recounting his education, both at Indiana Avenue School and at North Carolina College, Jim said, "I knew that I was going to make something of my life. My education gave me the confidence to go out into the world. I believed I could do anything I set my mind to but I also learned there were certain moves I wasn't going to make and also there were certain things no one was going to tell me about myself, especially what I could or could not accomplish." What he decided to do was to pursue the law.

Jim traces his interest in the law to reading a book in junior high school. The text contained an extensive biographical sketch of Bernard Baruch and his many business dealings. Jim was impressed with the role played by lawyers in advising powerful people. This planted the idea that he wanted the knowledge to advise people. A local role model whom he saw succeed in the practice of law was Maceo Turner. Turner confirmed in Jim's mind that being a lawyer was something he could do. While at North Carolina, Jim was approached by a visiting professor from Duke University with contacts at Rutgers Law School in Newark. He encouraged Jim to apply there and he did, graduating and passing the bar exam in 1975.

Upon graduating from Rutgers Law School, Jim went to work with the Essex County Public Defender's Office. It was baptism by fire. He represented everyone from prostitutes, pimps, and rapists to drug dealers, burglars, and murderers. Several years into his career as a public defender, in the summer of 1978, he was in the chambers of an African-American judge, Herbert H. Tate Sr. They started talking, and Judge Tate asked him, "What are you doing here? They have casinos where you were born. You've got more of a future there than you will ever have here." Jim considered the advice and, not long after, transferred from the Essex County Public Defender's Office to the Atlantic County Public Defender's Office, replacing another African-American attorney, Bruce Weekes. Jim was with the Public Defender for several years before opening a private practice in Atlantic City.

During Jim's career in private practice, he represented a range of private and public clients. Two public agencies worth noting are the City Council of Atlantic City and the Board of Education of Pleasantville, a neighboring community. Those who read the local newspapers have seen how both public bodies have brought needless trouble and turmoil to their towns over the past several years. At the risk of stating the obvious, *no one* from either elected body was indicted during James L. Jackson's tenure as solicitor. What's more, *never* did a meeting at which he presided turn into a free-for-all. Jim's mere presence—and when needed, his stern but wise advice— kept everyone's head screwed on straight.

Jackson and his confidential aide, Kristine Brady, have been together so long—27 years—that like a lot of lawyers and their assistants, there are times when they can communicate without speaking a word. Brady recalls many of Jackson's clients from his years in private practice. "The public clients always wanted a "yes" when the answer was "no." Jim would just say, 'Here's the information and here's the result.' Lots of times they were unhappy, but they always respected his advice. He represented the Pleasantville school board for 18 years and City Council for 10 years. No matter how difficult some of our clients were, he always stayed calm and his voice was soft, but he never sugar-coated anything."

Since his appointment to the Superior Court in June 1998 (which, sadly, his brother Conrad didn't live to see, passing away several days before the swearing in ceremony), Judge Jackson has had the responsibility of overseeing the many hundreds of cases that come before the Juvenile Court in Atlantic County each year. His tenure is the longest continuous service as judge of that court in the county's history. There's no way to sugarcoat the challenges he faces daily.

Juvenile Court, a division within the Superior Court, Family Division, is not "kiddy court." In the 37 years since the shoot-out at Club Harlem, the Northside—and, indeed, the entire nation—has witnessed violence by teenagers on a scale unimaginable on Easter Sunday in 1972.

As one attorney who has handled juvenile matters for many years recalls, "When I began appearing in juvenile court, most of the defendants were there for petty thefts, such as stealing a bicycle. Now they steal a bicycle to do a ride-by shooting, fighting over turf for the sale of drugs." Violent crimes among Atlantic City's youth have spiked dramatically during the past 10–15 years. Consistent with the experience of other urban areas throughout the nation, juveniles account for approximately one-third of all "index offenses" as defined by the FBI. Such offenses include murder, rape, robbery, aggravated assault, burglary, larceny, motor vehicle theft, and arson. Often, indexed crimes involve handguns, with far too many children having access to guns.

One lawyer who has appeared in front of Judge Jackson vividly recalled an incident involving a 14-year-old offender. The juvenile stated to the lawyers, "Having a gun is no big deal. Put me back on the street, and I'll have a gun in half an hour." When told of this incident, Judge Jackson stated, "All it takes is a second for this kid to go from having a gun to looking at many years of jail time."

There's a disturbing cycle at work in urban America, and Judge Jackson and the attorneys who handle the youth offenders see it play out regularly. As one lawyer noted, "Recently in looking through a file, I realized I had prosecuted this young man's mother 15 years ago. Obviously, the system didn't make much of an impact on the family. Almost invariably, when I read a name in the newspaper for a violent crime, it's someone—either perpetrator or victim—who we saw in juvenile court years earlier." It's grim business but through it all, Judge Jackson maintains his composure. "I've watched him work with some of these kids, and frankly you can see that the frustration factor runs high, not just with the children but with some of the state agencies we work with in trying to help these kids. Through it all, he has the patience of Job and never loses sight of the big picture."

There's no such thing as a "routine day" in Juvenile Court. The cases run the gamut from petty theft, disorderly conduct, and possession of drugs to assault on a parent or grandparent, armed robbery, and murder. The agencies involved in trying to deal with this onslaught of youth offenders read like an alphabet soup. There's everything from CMO (Case Management Organization), DCF (Division of Children and Families), DYFS (Division of Youth and Family Services), FCIU (Family Crisis Intervention Unit), and FSA (Family Service Association) to JISP (Juvenile Intensive Supervision Program), JJC (Juvenile Justice Commission), MDHP (Minister's Home Detention Program), YAP (Youth Advocate Program), and YSC (Youth Service Commission). That's just a partial listing. Somehow, the judge and his staff knows each one, its role, and who's the best person within the agency for a particular offender. Sometimes there are turf wars, and the judge presides over these as well.

Things don't always go as planned, and Judge Jackson can't please everyone, whether child, parent, guardian, or lawyer—but he tries. As one attorney commented, "His door is always open and lots of times I go in to question him on a decision. We don't always agree and he knows I'm upset, but by the time I leave I understand how he got to the result and know that he respects my concerns."

Judge Jackson's vantage point gives him a unique perspective on the challenges confronting children growing up in Atlantic City and, for that matter, most of urban America. While discussing how disconnected conventional thinking is from the reality of the experience of children he sees in his courtroom, he said, "For most of the kids that appear in front of me, I could write their predisposition reports. *One*, the father's not there. He's either in prison or on the street doing drugs but he's not at home. *Two*, substance abuse exists in the family. Either Dad, Mom, or a sibling, but there are convicted offenders in the child's immediate family. *Three*, the child is being raised by his mother or, if she has legal problems of her own, is being raised by his grandmother or aunt or a cousin or a friend. *Four*, these kids have a high level of survival instincts. They are on the street. They learn early, *I'm pretty much on my own*. There's no guarantee where they will be sleeping that night. It could be a cousin, could be a friend, could be a neighbor. These kids live in the moment. They are surviving without judgment. They don't think, *If I do that, this could happen*. They just do whatever they think the moment requires without regard to the consequences."

He continued, "Think about this type of child. He's basically homeless. He doesn't know where he's going to sleep tonight or where his next meal is coming from, yet we want him to learn algebra. We want him to learn things in school that have no connection to his life. We want him to take standardized tests when all he's trying to do is to survive. A child in that situation doesn't see the relevance of education to his life. He's got more pressing issues to deal with."

One of those issues for some children is dodging bullets. When the judge contrasts his childhood with the situations that come before him in court, one Northside neighborhood stands out, namely Stanley S. Holmes Village. A crowning achievement of Morris Cain's career, the village is no longer a haven for children or a stepping stone for families on their way up.

"As a child, I spent a lot of summer days playing at Stanley Holmes," the judge recalled. "My friends' mothers would scold us for chasing one another through their laundry hanging on clothes lines or for running across their lawns. Today they worry about their children being shot." Judge Jackson believes the drug culture is the culprit. "Stanley Holmes has become a marketplace for the sale of drugs. Because of its location and how the buildings are arranged, it's a natural place for dealing drugs." In the 50 years since Boo Jackson played with his friends in the courtyards of the village, the lives of urban children haven't changed for the better.

"When I look back on my life, I realize that my family gave me the *leisure* of being able to pursue my education. The kids that come before me have to worry about what they're going to eat and where they're going to sleep. Every day is a fight for survival. They don't have the leisure time to think about education. When you combine that with the peer pressure to do drugs, the results are predictable.

These children don't have a childhood. Education, like the one I received, is a luxury few of them will ever know about."

Judge James L. Jackson knows that a community that fails to invest in its children by granting them the *leisure* to pursue an education is in danger of having no future. In his 13 years on the Superior Court bench, not only has he seen many repeat offenders, but children of some of the juvenile offenders he represented while with the Public Defender's Office are now charged with crimes of their own. But the biggest crime may be how our society expects these children to "learn algebra" when all that's on their mind is survival. As one respected educator has said, "Poor children simply face too many problems outside the classroom. If you don't buttress whatever happens in school with social and economic changes that give kids a better chance in life and put their families on a more stable footing, then schools alone are not going to solve the problems of poor student performance."

American society is slow to grasp that investments on the front end of social issues are cheaper than those on the back end. Day-care centers, schools, and teachers consume fewer tax dollars than prisons, police officers, and the alphabet soup of agencies that Judge Jackson works with daily. Dollars spent on education also go farther in rebuilding urban America than money spent on penal institutions.

Redenia Gilliam-Mosee and James L. Jackson are just two of the success stories involving Northside residents since legalized gambling came to the resort. As their careers demonstrate, their lives are very much about helping children to get past the "survival" stage so they can move on to being mature, responsible citizens. Despite their efforts and those of many unsung heroes, Atlantic City's black community continues to struggle. The diaspora set in motion by the American Civil Rights Movement, together with the tumult of casino gaming, have been traumatic. Nevertheless, the casino industry is hardly an enemy of the community. Significant strides in creating employment opportunities have been made since the 1976 Referendum.

No longer are black people relegated to changing sheets and denied access to management positions and corporate boardrooms. Opportunities *do* exist and doors *are* open today in situations that would make Morris Cain chortle in delight. He would probably still be sending his disciples off to Lincoln University, but he would likely be urging some of them to pursue careers in the casino industry and related businesses.

Sadly, the single biggest problem facing Atlantic City's Northside and many communities across America is that there aren't enough positive role models coming forward to lead the way. Role models can make lasting impressions. The two most prominent in resort history are Morris Cain and Nucky Johnson. Morris Cain had a ferocious belief that *all* people have the power to transform their lives through education and hard work. He lived what he believed. Nucky Johnson personified the greed, corruption, and high times that were Atlantic City in its glory days. He lived for power and to party. Today, the memories of both men are all but erased from the community's psyche. Nevertheless, their legacies linger.

Cain's legacy can be seen in the Boys and Girls Club. Johnson's legacy lives in the continuing corruption in City Hall. Were both men alive today, they would smile at the success of the local youth groups. As for local politics, Cain would be dismayed by the self-dealing of public officials and the squandering of opportunities for uplifting the community. Nucky would have a different take. He'd accept the corruption but would scorn the incompetence at managing the levers of power, making a shambles of local government. Neither would be proud of what they saw. They would conclude that Atlantic City's elected officials have failed to lead. That failure is best illustrated by the fact that all these years later, a new partnership to replace the one forged by the Commodore—only this time among City Hall, Trenton, and Wall Street—has yet to materialize. The history of this town reveals that in order for the local hotel-resort economy to excel to its full potential everyone must be working from the same playbook. Unfortunately, too few in City Hall think in such terms.

Thirty-plus years into the gambling era, much of Atlantic City looks as grim and beaten down as it did before the casinos. The crumbling continues unabated. Although there has been new and exciting noncasino development, it's been far more limited than even the least optimistic supporters of gambling anticipated. For many residents and neighborhoods, it's as if gambling never happened. The fundamentals of government have been neglected by smaller-than-life politicians with larger-than-life ambitions. Distressingly, their ambitions aren't for their city but for themselves. With few exceptions, the success stories of the casino gaming era have come in *spite* of the city's elected officials, not because of them.

What could have been a dominant position in the gambling world has been frittered away. Rather than dedicating themselves during the past 30 years to rebuilding the city into a clean, safe, first-rate resort, those in charge of City Hall have been building political fiefdoms. An audit of the New Jersey Comptroller's Office released in early 2010 revealed widespread mismanagement and misuse of millions of tax dollars. Sadly, no one was surprised at the news.

Say what one may of the Kuehnle/Johnson/Farley machine, its leaders made government *work*. Essential municipal services were delivered in a competent manner. The three "bosses" understood that for the resort's residents to prosper, City Hall had to be responsive not only to the needs of their supporters but to the entire community, including the interests of the hotel-resort industry. They didn't permit an adversarial relationship to exist between politicos and businesspeople. They understood that what was good for industry was generally good for the entire town.

History and its consequences abide. There are few landscapes in our nation in which black people have immortalized themselves as they have on Absecon Island. The people of the Northside were the key ingredient in the formula for success the first time around. Their story is entangled with the resort's history as inseparably as the tides.

Nearly as critical as the presence of African Americans in building the original resort was the unique role of local government and the political ward system. An aspect of Nucky Johnson's legacy more troublesome than corruption is the political chaos that ensued following the collapse of the Republican organization upon the defeat of Senator Frank Farley in 1971.

Because Atlantic City never developed the customs and practices of most American cities for the exercise and transfer of power, machine politics has been replaced by one wannabe boss after another, some ending their careers in prison. And, so, resort politicians make their schemes, bend the rules to benefit their cronies, and bang heads in pursuit of a throne from a bygone era. This never-ending brawl for power has bred a toxic political environment.

Absent dramatic changes in the political culture of City Hall, it's hard to envision the transformation of Atlantic City into a world class resort or to hope for the revival of a vibrant African-American community resembling the one that previously existed. Nor is it possible to envision the long-term success of casino gaming if government remains in disarray. It's folly for the CEOs of the publicly traded companies that own Atlantic City's casinos to think that their business interests are somehow immune from what's happening in local government. The people who have come to Atlantic City following the gambling referendum can make history, but they cannot escape it. Atlantic City remains an experiment in social planning. Today, as was true in 1854, the sole reason for the town's existence is to provide leisure-time activities for visitors. Today as then, repeat visitors are vital to survival, but that is becoming more difficult each year. Gone are the heady days of the 1990s when the industry was flush with cash, employing nearly 50,000 people at its peak in 1997; today's number stands at little more than 35,000. While other key indicators are down as well, the employment figures alone prompt the question: Is the experiment in jeopardy? More pointedly, will decline—yet again—be Atlantic City's future?

In significant part, Atlantic City's casino industry is a victim of its own success. Since 1976, the municipal finances of many regions in the Northeast have deteriorated to where the resort was 35 years ago. State governments (and Native American tribes) in Connecticut, New York, Delaware, and Pennsylvania have become desperate for new revenue sources. They eyed the hundreds of millions of dollars in tax revenues flowing into Trenton's coffers from Atlantic City's casinos and decided it could work for them. As the 20th century ended, no one could have imagined the level of competition Atlantic City now faces from gaming operations in nearby states. Ten short years later, with more than 25 new casinos throughout the greater Northeast region, market saturation may well be upon us. With profits declining precipitously, casino executives fret over a "race to the bottom" in competing for patrons. It adds up to a major challenge.

The wisdom of the Book of Proverbs is helpful to understanding Atlantic City's predicament: *Where there is no vision, the people perish.* Whether it is reinvigorating the Boardwalk, pursuing a more aggressive marketing strategy, staging more concerts, deregulating the casino industry, or accelerating improvements to the city's infrastructure, everything pales in comparison to the need for honest, competent municipal government. Only enlightened leadership and a professionally run local government—free of corruption and cronyism—can create the environment needed to breath new life into Morris Cain's vision for uplifting Atlantic City.

Appendix

Northside Leaders

This appendix could be titled "Ordinary People Doing Extraordinary Things." When looking back at the first half of the 20th century, an era ostensibly pre-American Civil Rights Movement, what is most striking is the number of ordinary people in Atlantic City who refused to be intimidated by discrimination. Bigotry was a nasty adversary, and it didn't give way without a fierce fight. The Northside had people of its own comparable to Fannie Lou Hamer, Rosa Parks, Robert Moses, Cecil Moore, and so forth. These community leaders stood up for themselves and others, battling racial prejudice whenever the situation required.

It's not an overstatement to say that many of today's leaders in the African-American community received their start standing on the shoulders of the unsung heroes who went before them, much the same way that Jackie Robinson owed a debt of gratitude to Pop Lloyd.

The people listed here were, and are, all leaders in their own time. It's not possible to name everyone from the Northside whose careers made a difference in shaping the future, but there are many noteworthy lives. The names discussed here have been, in large part, compiled from review logs, transcripts, and tapes of interviews created 25 to 50 years ago and included in the archival materials in the Heston Room of the Atlantic City Free Public Library (ACFPL). Additionally, I sifted through news reports, magazine articles, special event bulletins, and records of the Atlantic County Women's Hall of Fame, as well as interviews I conducted. Dates of birth for many of those profiled were not available.

The individuals profiled here all share a common trait: They are accomplished individuals who command respect. Most have a certain intangible that can best be described as *confidence*. In my talks with Horace Bryant, he often chuckled about how some white people were unnerved by being in the presence of an intelligent, self-confident black person. He believed that during his career many whites viewed him as an "uppity nigger." It's a safe bet that at one time or another most of the "Northside Leaders" have unnerved some white people much the way Bryant did.

It wasn't possible to weave every notable person into the narrative of my history on the Northside. My research comprised many great lives and important stories. As with *Boardwalk Empire,* my goal was to make sense of Atlantic City's unique experience. In *The Northside*, my goal is to demonstrate that *but for* the black experience, the town we know today would never have come to be.

Regrettably, the trajectory of the story line of *The Northside* doesn't accommodate inclusion of every story or worthy person. Acknowledging that there are many additional persons who warrant recognition, what follows is a partial listing. I compiled this list with *much* trepidation, because I know there are many worthy names that aren't included. (The listing is alphabetical for convenience only.)

Hubert U. Barbour

Hubert U. Barbour was born in Catawba, South Carolina, circa World War I. A graduate of Johnson C. Smith University, he moved to Atlantic City and joined the Atlantic City Police Department in 1940. He enlisted in the U.S. Army during World War II and served in the Pacific Theater of Operations as a signal company First Sergeant setting up communications facilities in support of airfields. He returned to police duty in 1946 and was promoted to sergeant in 1948. Barbour was promoted to police captain in 1959, becoming, at the time, the highest-ranking African-American police official in Atlantic City. During the 1964 Democratic National Convention, he commanded a protective detail for government VIPs. His diligence and attention to duty made him a role model as a police officer.

Robert Bell

Robert "Bob" Bell was a favorite in the Northside entertainment world. "Neighbor," as he was known to many, was born in Mississippi circa World War I and began his career playing the guitar on riverboats traveling between St. Louis and New Orleans. He organized the Three Peppers Trio and appeared in the movie, *The*

Lady Takes a Chance, starring John Wayne. In 1953, while Bell was appearing at the Bamboo Club, he and his wife Thelma (née Campbell, from Atlantic City) decided to make the Northside their permanent home. His days on the Chitlin' Circuit behind him, Bell was the developer, owner, and operator of the Wonder Gardens, a nightclub and showroom that featured outstanding talent of the day, adding sparkle to the Northside. "Neighbor's" charitable activities and instances of giving back to his church and community were many.

Yvonne Bonitto-Doggett

Dr. Frank B. Doggett Jr.'s partner in life is an extraordinary lady in every sense of the word. A graduate of historically black college and university (HBCU) Lincoln University, from which she holds a master's degree, Yvonne Bonitto-Doggett is a member of the Alpha Lambda Graduate Chapter of Phi Gamma Mu International Honor Society in Social Science. Bonitto-Doggett moved to Atlantic City in 1964 following her marriage to Dr. Doggett. She has been active in the community ever since. In 1978, she joined the opening team of Bally's Park Place Casino Hotel. From 1984 to 1992, she was director of economic development for Atlantic County and has also served as a member of the board of directors and as deputy director of the Casino Reinvestment Development Authority and with the Atlantic City Planning Board. In all her public roles—sometimes at meetings that could become quite contentious—Bonitto-Doggett has always injected a tone of civility, which helped level heads to prevail. She is active in the Hughes Center for Public Policy at the Richard Stockton College of New Jersey and remains a respected voice and important force in the community.

Dennis Braithwaite

Judge Dennis Braithwaite (AJSC) is a longtime Atlantic City resident. The Braithwaite family has been here for generations. Judge Braithwaite received his BS degree (cum laude) from LaSalle University and his law degree from University of Pennsylvania Law School (1973). He also attained a Master of Law from the University of Virginia School of Law (2001). Prior to his appointment to the Superior Court Bench, the judge had an active law practice providing counsel to the Institute for Human Development (IHD, formerly NARCO) and the Atlantic City Planning Board. He also served as the first solicitor to the City Council of Atlantic City. A savvy attorney and wise counselor, one of the lawyers he mentored early in his career was the Honorable James L. Jackson, who is profiled in Chapter 12.

From August 1984 until his retirement in 2005, Judge Braithwaite served in the New Jersey Superior Court and was the first African-American Presiding Judge of the Atlantic County Superior Court, serving in the Criminal Division. During the last 11 years of his tenure, he was a distinguished member of the Appellate Division, New Jersey's intermediate appellate court. During his tenure as judge, he authored approximately 75 published opinions and was a member of the panel on numerous others. Judge Braithwaite continues to share his extensive knowledge of the law by serving as a professor at Rutgers Law School, where he teaches torts and criminal procedure investigations.

John Herbert Brooks

An Atlantic City native, John Herbert Brooks came of age in the early years of the American Civil Rights Movement and, regrettably, spent his teens and early twenties in a life-and-death struggle with drug addiction. After conquering his own addiction, he went on to found what is known today as the Institute for Human Development (IHD), formerly known as NARCO, a substance abuse program that set the bar for treatment programs across the nation. Brooks served as the institute's executive director from 1969 to 1993. As a frontline soldier in the war against substance abuse, he turned many lives around because he cared. Brooks was a dynamic communicator and his passion for helping others was palpable. Under his leadership, the IHD became one of most respected drug and alcohol treatment facilities in the state of New Jersey.

Anna L. Butler

Anna L. Butler taught in the resort school system for 42 years and touched the lives of thousands of children. A graduate of Trenton State College (now The College of New Jersey), with advanced degrees from Temple University and Maryland University, her primary focus was helping black children learn how to express themselves. Butler staged an annual poetry contest for 30-plus years (circa 1945–1980), and everyone was a winner. She also knew how to express herself and was the author of two successful books of poetry, *Love Letters Unsent* and *Touchstones*. She was listed in *Who's Who in America* for many years.

Rosalind Cash

Rosalind "Roz" Cash was restless to star on stage and screen. She left town shortly after graduating from high school in 1956 and studied voice, dance, and acting in New York City. She was a founding member of the "Negro Ensemble" in 1967. Her stage debut on Broadway was in the *Wayward Stork*. Other Broadway productions included *Ceremonies in Dark Old Men, Boesman and Lena, Fiorella!*, and *King Lear.* Her appearances in live productions in New York, London, and Rome are too numerous to recite. After the stage, it was on to Hollywood. Her movie credits include *Omega Man, Klute, Centurion, Uptown Friday Night, I Am a Legend,* and *Circle of Pain.* Her television credits are numerous and include her most memorable performance in *Go Tell It on the Mountain*, for which she received an Emmy nomination.

Cash refused to play the stereotypical roles that were usually offered to female African Americans: "I am not good at playing stereotypes." She said, "I don't ingratiate myself to the powers that be as some nice, Negro, colored abiding person. You cannot depend on me to be that Negro that you have come to know and love, that you are used to." In 1987, she was awarded the Black American Cinema Society's Phoenix Award for her film achievement. In 1992, she was inducted into the Black Filmmakers Hall of Fame. She is a member of the Atlantic County Women's Hall of Fame.

Alice Cuff

Family, church, school, and community: Born circa World War I, Alice Cuff excelled in the things that matter, enriching the lives of everyone she encountered. Cuff taught the fifth grade at Indiana Avenue School for 30-plus years, and if that was all she did, she would have warranted recognition in anyone's hall of fame of the Northside. Hundreds of students gained the fundamentals of geography, history, math, and social science in a classroom where they came to know all things were possible through education. It's said that she maintained perfect classroom decorum without ever having to raise her voice. She had a frown for poor behavior that no student wanted to see and a smile for commendable conduct that her students craved. But there was more to Cuff than school. She was active in Jethro Church, and after retiring from teaching, she served as a member of the Atlantic City Planning Board. I became friends with her then. Cuff was *always* prepared to review *every* application. She *never* acted on an application with anything but total objectivity and professionalism. It was a privilege and an honor to have known Alice Cuff.

Clarence C. Davenport Sr.

Clarence C. Davenport Sr., born circa World War I in Newark, New Jersey, was a longtime Atlantic City resident who served in the U.S. Marine Corps in the South Pacific during World War II before settling here. He worked for Penn Reading Seashore Line and later for the U.S. Postal Service until retirement. He played softball with the Bill Marks Sportsmen Club and co-founded the Trailblazers Sportsmen Club, which offered youth positive recreational activities fostering civic responsibility. Often sought as a neighborhood counselor and advocate for senior citizens, he also advised and inspired young people. Davenport served as president of the Bungalow Park Civic Association and was a member of the Atlantic City Zoning Board. He attended New Hope Baptist Church, sang with the male chorus, and was an avid supporter of its youth group. In 1998, the Davenport Community Center was named after him by the city of Atlantic City in recognition of his dedicated community service.

Elwood Davis

You can't find anyone to speak ill of Elwood Davis. Coming of age in Atlantic City during the Great Depression, he learned from hard times. Davis is the consummate gentleman who has devoted his life to helping others. An Atlantic City native, the local banker and accountant was a graduate of the New Jersey College of Commerce and the American Institute of Banking. He served as assistant vice president and personnel director at Atlantic National Bank and as deputy commissioner of the Department of Revenue and Finance for the city. His community activities are many, including serving as chairman of the Atlantic City Housing Authority and the Atlantic City Zoning Board of Adjustment; member of the executive committee of the National Association for the Advancement of Colored People (NAACP), Prince Hall Masons, and the Venice Park Civic Association; director and incorporator of Atlantic Human Resources; director of the Atlantic County United Way; and member of the New Jersey Department of Community Affairs, Local Finance Board. As recounted in Chapter 10, Davis played an active role in the Summer of Freedom during the 1964 Democratic National Convention. In his religious life, Davis has served as a member and trustee of the Mt. Pleasant United Methodist Church.

Theodore Dobson Jr.

Theodore "Ted" Dobson Jr. loved his hometown and the people in it. A graduate of Atlantic City High School (ACHS) class of 1953, he was part of a special group of graduates who celebrate Atlantic City 365 days a year. Dobson graduated from Glassboro State College in 1957 and was employed in the Pleasantville school system as a classroom teacher and principal for 40-plus years. He was respected by everyone and touched the lives of thousands of children.

Were Dobson with us today, his adoring wife, Alma, believes he would tell us, "I am a product of the loving Westside Village in which everyone played a part of defining the kind of man I should become." As Alma said to me, "Ted discovered a love of reading and learning about his people in that segregated school [Indiana Avenue School] where the teachers demanded the best of their students." His love of sports led him to found the Greater Atlantic City Youth Association, which sponsored the Dolphins football team. Dobson was a member of the Battle of the Bay Basketball Tournament Committee, former president of Kiwanis, and former president of Omega Psi Phi Fraternity, Upsilon Alpha Chapter.

Dobson's love for his hometown motivated him to become a historian. He gathered photos, news articles, and memorabilia and was a go-to person for answers to many questions about both the Northside and Atlantic City. His love for his city was acknowledged by City Council when it renamed the street he lived on Theodore Dobson Lane.

Frank B. Doggett Jr.

Dr. Frank B. Doggett Jr. was well educated (a BA from Lincoln University, 1942, and an MD from Howard University, 1946), caring and attentive to his patients needs, but tough and persistent when he needed to be. A captain in the Air Force and veteran of the Korean War, he demanded staff privileges at the Atlantic City hospital in a time when other South Jersey hospitals had no black physicians. Who was going to tell a highly qualified local veteran no? He helped lead the way, and black people began receiving first-rate hospital care. (Doggett was not the first African-American physician employed at the hospital—that distinction belonged to Dr. Arthur Lee, whose career is discussed later.) Dr. Doggett is also remembered as the longtime "ring doctor" for the New Jersey Boxing Commission.

Art Dorrington

Art Dorrington learned to ice skate not long after he learned to walk. Born in Truro, Nova Scotia, during the Great Depression, he was destined to be a hockey player. He began playing ice hockey at age six and, by his late teens, was good enough to be noticed by the New York Rangers. In 1950, they offered him a contract to play for the New York Rovers, an Eastern League team affiliated with the National Hockey League. The Rovers were on an extended road trip, and Dorrington got impatient waiting in a New York hotel room. The Rangers had him go to Atlantic City to play with the local professional team, the Sea Gulls. No black man had ever played professional hockey in the U.S. before. The Northside embraced Dorrington, and eventually he made it his home.

In 1951, Dorrington didn't have a week off. Besides hockey, he also played baseball for the Watertown farm club of the Boston Braves' organization. By the next year, he concentrated his efforts in hockey. Dorrington played for six different teams in the Eastern League, but unfortunately his career came to an abrupt end in 1958 when he suffered a broken leg. He returned to Atlantic City where he met his wife, Dorothie, and made the resort his home. Today, he pursues his love of hockey through a foundation, working with young people and teaching them the game he loves.

Dorothie Dorrington

Dorothie Dorrington was teaching in the classroom while her husband, Art, was teaching on the ice. Born in South Carolina (not long after Art), her family moved here during the Great Depression. Overcoming a learning disability, she earned her BS, MS, and doctorate degrees in education from Glassboro State College (now Rowan University). During her 50-year career, Dorothie served in various capacities from classroom teacher and administrator to consultant and author. She wrote the widely respected *Handbook for Classroom Teachers of Reading* and served nine years on the Atlantic City Board of Education, five as president. She was a community leader and activist, touching the lives of thousands of students and scores of teachers.

Alice Earle-Cash

Alice Earle-Cash, an Atlantic City native, entered ACHS in 1947 but left due to illness. She returned three years later to graduate with the class of 1954, then from Douglass College in 1958. She was recognized by the National Sorority of Phi Delta Kappa Inc., Delta Lambda Chapter for service in education and was named Teacher of the Year by the Atlantic City Education Association in 1991. Earle-Cash co-founded the Inner City Tutorial Program that provided underprivileged students free help to prepare for their SATs. She is best remembered by her students during her 39-year career for her proper vocabulary, strict classroom decorum, and dignified demeanor. She was active in the community until her retirement in 2002.

Reggie Edgehill

Reggie Edgehill was a force on the Northside for more than 50 years (1920s through the 1970s). He was one of the leading entrepreneurs of Atlantic City's entertainment district. He was an owner, operator, and investor, and an experienced helping hand in dozens of Northside businesses, most dealing in entertainment, food, and beverages. Throughout his long and storied career, he employed hundreds of people and was a vital force in the resort's economy. One can't help but wonder what role Edgehill would have played in the new Atlantic

City had he been born 30 years later and able to take advantage of the opportunities brought by casino gaming.

Vera King Farris

Dr. Vera King Farris was best known as Stockton College's longest-serving president, leading the college through its hopeful youth, turbulent adolescence, and well into its accomplished early stages. As a mature institution, Dr. Farris "put Stockton on the map" during her years as president of the college. "Bunny," as she was known by close friends and family, graduated third in her class in ACHS in 1954. The first of her family to attend college, she attained a BA in Biology from Tuskegee University, graduating *magna cum laude*. She went on to earn her master's degree in zoology from the University of Massachusetts and a PhD in zoology and parasitology from the same university. By 1965, Bunny had the title "Dr." in front of her name.

Her career path took her into graduate research and teaching at the university level, attaining the rank of full professor at the University of Massachusetts, University of Michigan, and the State University of New York. When she was appointed as the third president of Stockton College in 1983, she was the first female African-American college president of a state college in New Jersey. Her accomplishments as leader of Stockton College, until her retirement in 2003, are too numerous to recite. Suffice it to say, she led the school on a period of growth that now makes it one of the leading public institutions in New Jersey. While her life's journey took her across the country and around the world, her roots remained in the Northside until the time of her demise. She gave back to the community by assisting local residents to pursue their careers in higher education.

Jane M. Flipping

Following graduation from Glassboro State College (now Rowan University) in 1950, Jane M. Flipping pursued graduate studies in early childhood education at Rutgers University. Upon completion of her education, teaching positions were hard to come by in the minority community and Flipping, along with several other classmates, came to Atlantic City and opened the Mary Jane Humpty Dumpty Nursery School at 130 Atlantic Avenue. It was the first integrated nursery school in Atlantic County. In addition to teaching and operating her own nursery school, Flipping served as Head Start director for Atlantic Human Resources, director of the Adriatic Day Care Center, and executive assistant to the president for Community Affairs at the Claridge Casino Hotel. Flipping's goal has always been to be an exemplary role model for women, especially minority women and children, so that they may become leaders of the future. She succeeded quite well.

Albert E. Forsythe

Dr. Albert E. Forsythe was born in Nassau, Bahamas, in 1897. He received his early education there and came to the U.S. in 1911, studying first at the Tuskegee Institute and later the University of Toledo, where he received his bachelor of science. In 1930, he graduated from McGill University Medical School in Canada.

Dr. Forsythe opened his medical practice on the Northside in 1932 and became friends with C. Alfred "Chief" Anderson, who was the first black American to receive a commercial pilot's license. It wasn't long before Dr. Forsythe was a licensed pilot, too. In July 1933, Dr. Forsythe and Anderson completed a flight from Atlantic City to Los Angeles and back. Their airplane, *The Pride of Atlantic City*, had no parachutes, landing lights, radio, or "blind" flying instruments, and much of their navigation was accomplished using a road map. It was the first transcontinental flight by black aviators.

Forsythe and Anderson also teamed up in 1934 for a flight to 10 countries in the Caribbean in an airplane they named *Booker T. Washington*. Anderson went on to a great career as a flying instructor, especially to the Tuskegee Airmen. Dr. Forsythe practiced medicine on the Northside, helping thousands of people during a career spanning nearly 50 years.

Edythe Greene

Edythe Greene, wife of Ralph, was a Northside schoolteacher who dedicated her life to her family and students. Greene was a native of Evanston, Illinois, and met Ralph in the 1940s while she was a college student and he was convalescing from an injury in the home of a relative who knew her. The two met, the chemistry was excellent, and they married not long afterward. She graduated from Chicago

Teachers College (now Illinois State University) in 1945, and in 1948, the Greenes move to Ralph's hometown, Atlantic City.

During her time as a teacher in the local school system, Greene touched the lives of hundreds of fifth graders. Her career included 22 years at the Indiana Avenue School, one year at the West Side Complex, and 12 years at the Uptown Complex where she was a supervisor of the elementary schoolteachers, "a teacher of teachers," for which she was so ably qualified. Greene remains active in St. Augustine's Episcopal Church, is an award-winning watercolor artist, and a volunteer at the ACFPL.

Ralph "Tiger" Greene

Ralph "Tiger" Greene, husband of Edythe, was a dynamic leader in the areas of education, business, and social uplift for the Northside community. Ralph was a 1936 graduate of ACHS and earned his bachelor of science degree from George Williams College in Chicago after completing service in the military. Ralph was active in numerous civic and community groups including the Gentlemen of Sports, Junior Chamber of Commerce, the AC Old Tymers, the Hap Farley All Stars, the Farley Standpatters, and the John Henry "Pop" Lloyd Committee. He also helped organize and coach baseball leagues, tennis leagues, and Biddy Basketball Teams during the 1950s. He was also a dedicated member of St. Augustine's Episcopal Church, where he served on the Vestry and was the superintendent of Sunday School.

Edna Patricia Hall

Edna Patricia Hall, an Atlantic City native, was an activist in the truest sense from the time of her youth. Coming of age during the American Civil Rights Movement, she was a founding member and former vice president of the First Ward Civic Association, an original member and vice president of the Inlet Public Private Association, and a staunch supporter of the NAACP and 101 Women Plus. She started the first Tenants Association for the Shore Park Apartment Complex, was treasurer of the Uptown Action Council, and was a member of the Uptown Coalition for Neighborhood Development. As a member of the board of directors of the City of Atlantic City Housing Corporation, she participated in the development of the Brigantine Homes Apartment

Complex. Hall fought tirelessly for housing in the Northeast Inlet as well as the restoration of the Absecon Lighthouse. Her advocacy related to both issues helped to spark a resurgence of redevelopment and building of new homes, and the preservation of a valuable historic landmark.

Edgar Harris

Education and the civil rights of African Americans are what Edgar Harris lived for. As a young graduate of HBCU Cheney University, Harris came to Atlantic City at the dawn of the American Civil Rights Movement and was hired to teach mathematics at the Indiana Avenue School. An excellent class instructor, Harris motivated his students to excel in all fields of math, and more importantly, in life. It wasn't long after he came to the Northside that he came within the orbit of Horace Bryant and Maceo Turner. He was an early member of the NAACP (serving a term as president) and took part in the activities surrounding the Democratic National Convention in 1964. He is remembered by residents of the Northside as a tireless advocate for equal rights.

W. Oscar Harris

Dr. W. Oscar Harris was one of the founding physicians of the Atlantic City Medical Association and years later the Ethical Pharmacy. Both organizations were important to the health of Northside residents. In addition, he was police and fire surgeon and a physician to the Atlantic City schools. Dr. Harris was born on December 3, 1908, in Pittsburgh, to Robert M. Harris and Genevieve Castor Harris. He attended Atlantic City public schools and then Dartmouth College in Hanover, New Hampshire, where he graduated Phi Beta Kappa in 1930. An interesting footnote to Harris's days at Dartmouth was one of the means by which he earned money for his education. As we saw in Chapter 6, the "numbers game" was a large enterprise not only in Atlantic City but throughout all of America. As confirmed by his grandson, Joseph Jacobs, Esq., to help pay his college expenses, young Harris "wrote numbers" for his classmates, making use of the services of a "banker" on the Northside.

Harris was one of the 25 medical school students accepted at Dartmouth, which had a two-year program. Upon completing his courses at Dartmouth, he continued his medical studies at Western Reserve (now known as Case Western Reserve University) in Cleveland, Ohio. While living in Cleveland, he met and married Elveta Lee. They relocated to Atlantic City where he established his medical practice. They had five children, Joseph, Ethelyn, William Oscar Jr., Robert Mark, and Joy Ann.

In April 1943, Dr. Harris was the first local black physician to be called on by the U.S. Army after volunteering for service. He made four major beach landings including Normandy, North Africa, and two in Italy as a member of the field hospital unit performing surgery under fire. Harris passed away on March 15, 1971, at 62 years of age after a long illness. He left behind a legacy of service to his community.

Pattie Harris-Young

Pattie Harris-Young got her start in entertainment in her early twenties during the 1960s, dancing for Larry Steele's *Smart Affairs*. From there, it was nightclubs throughout the Northeast, cruise ships, Broadway, and eventually Hollywood. Her movie credits include *Cotton Comes to Harlem, Stanley's Sweetheart, Bananas, The Hospital, Amazing Grace,* and *Gordon's War*. Her television credits include *The Ed Sullivan Show, As the World Turns, Soul, Leon Bibbs,* and *Someone New*. Upon retiring from stage and screen, Harris-Young returned to Atlantic City and has taught the performing arts to hundreds of young people. She has written, directed, choreographed, and produced dozens of musical presentations throughout the country. She is an extraordinarily talented person who uses her status to uplift others. Harris-Young originated Project Price, a mentoring program for disadvantaged teenage girls. The program utilizes the discipline of dance to help instill pride and self-worth in teenagers.

W. John Henry Hester

The Reverend W. John Henry Hester was a leader in two communities. While residing on North Ohio Avenue, Reverend Hester served as longtime pastor of Calvary Baptist Church in Pleasantville. A child of the Great Depression, he didn't cross political lines as many did in response to F.D.R.'s New Deal programs. A loyal member of the local Republican organization—he was a "Farley Standpatter"—

Reverend Hester was active in both city and county politics and was elected to the County Board of Freeholders, the first African American to serve in that position. People who knew him recall that Reverend Hester had a voice that could conjure up images of the Almighty whenever he prayed or spoke at a solemn occasion. He is remembered by all who knew him as a fair and generous gentleman.

Juanita High

It's hard to imagine anyone more committed to social uplift through education than Dr. Juanita High. Born and raised in Atlantic City, she graduated from ACHS with honors—a year early, at age 16—in 1947. Her degrees include a BA from Montclair State University, an MA from University of Pennsylvania, and a doctorate from Rutgers University. More telling are her accomplishments. After teaching in the Atlantic City school system for 15 years, she began several new careers, all related to education but tackling issues that went far beyond the classroom.

In the late 1960s, Dr. High was the educational director of Atlantic Human Resources, a private, nonprofit community action agency, where she had the responsibility of reviewing "Title One" funding to schools throughout Atlantic County. Before Dr. High, many of those funds never reached their intended benefactors, namely, minority students. After her, things changed. She then moved on to serve as executive director of the Educational Opportunity Fund (EOF) in the New Jersey Department of Higher Education. At the beginning of her tenure, approximately 1,600 students were benefiting from EOF funds. Upon conclusion of her term, four years later in 1974, nearly 14,000 low-income students were receiving assistance in preparing for college and being uplifted through education. Dr. High then spent eight years as assistant to the president of Millersville State College in Pennsylvania, where she headed the school's affirmative action and equal opportunity efforts.

From Millersville, Dr. High went on to Stockton College where she served for nearly 20 years as executive assistant to the president. She is "retired" but remains active as a member of the board of directors of the Richard Stockton College Foundation and with St. James AME. She is one of the most accomplished educators of her generation. She is known and respected throughout the state of New Jersey.

Ralph Hunter

Ralph Hunter wasn't born on the Northside and spent many years elsewhere, but no one loves and appreciates the role of African Americans in Atlantic City's history more than he does. Despite being born in Philadelphia, Hunter got "sand in his shoes" while working here during the summers. He sank his roots in the Northside in 1954 when, at age 17, he bought a home in Bungalow Park and has maintained a residence ever since. He had a successful career in retail sales, owning and operating several unique stores: Ginza at the Moorestown Mall, A Shop Called East at the Cherry Hill Mall, and the Lucky Elephant at Resorts International Hotel and Casino. Hunter has lived in Atlantic City full time since his "retirement" in 1994 and is working harder now than ever.

As the founder and curator of the African American Heritage Museum of South Jersey, Hunter has assembled an extraordinary collection of important artifacts, documents, and photographs. He works tirelessly at gathering, organizing, cataloging, displaying, and circulating pieces of history related to the African-American experience in Atlantic City and South Jersey. [I spent several months "mining" the museum's collection of materials on Claiborn Morris Cain, assembled by Hunter and Dennis Burroughs. (Ditto, the museum's materials on Sara Spencer Washington.) I am deeply grateful to both gentlemen for their painstaking work in organizing the materials from the Cain estate.]

Each February (African American History Month), Hunter takes portions of his museum on the road. February is a nonstop, full-tilt boogie, seven-days-per-week marathon of speaking engagements and exhibitions providing intellectual feasts for hundreds of people. Where he gets his energy, I do not know. People like Ralph Hunter make my job as a historian possible.

Gene Hudgins

A 1952 graduate of ACHS, Gene Hudgins is believed by many to be the greatest basketball player to come out of Atlantic City. On the court, his nickname was Hooks, for his extraordinary hook shot, nearly impossible to defend. For many years, throughout the Northeast Region, his name was synonymous with Atlantic City basketball. After graduating from ACHS, Hudgins went on to star at

HCBU Morgan State University in Virginia. He also played professionally for the internationally famous Harlem Globetrotters and several minor league teams in the farm system of the National Basketball Association.

Unfortunately for Hudgins, he came upon the scene in an era when pro basketball was first becoming popular, and many of the owners were afraid of having too many black faces on the basketball court. There was an unspoken quota, which limited the number of black ball players, and Hudgins never made it into the NBA, where many believe he would have been a standout. Regardless, he was a legend on the local basketball scene and for years was involved not only in organizing leagues, teaching the game, and coaching high school athletes, but he was a goodwill ambassador for the community. One of his proudest efforts was his creation of "The Yard" at Pennsylvania and Artic Avenues, which hosted both organized/league and pick-up games between some of the most talented basketball players in America. And if that weren't enough, Hudgins was a poet.

A final note of major importance was his role in reforming a local union. In 1991, following a federal probe of the Hotel Employee Union, Local 54, Hudgins was appointed by the Federal Court Monitor to restore integrity to the union. His job was to guide the transition of the union back to membership control. He spent several years forming workers' rights committees, implementing various training programs, and upgrading health insurance for members. "Hooks" was a star not only on the basketball court but in the community.

Mamie G. Jackson

Mamie G. Jackson dedicated her life to education and taught in the Atlantic City Public School System for 40 years. Coming of age in the early years of the Civil Rights Movement, education became her life. She is a graduate of Monmouth Junior College and Newark State Teachers College, and she has pursued graduate studies at the University of Pennsylvania, Widener University, and Rowan University. During her years as an elementary schoolteacher, she was a reading specialist, basic skills instructor, and administrator of the Early Childhood Education Program. She is the recipient of many honors, including "New Jersey Mother of the Year" in 1998 and "Educator in Leadership" in 2004. She has been an active member of numerous organizations working toward the improvement of life for others including Phi Delta Kappa, the local chapter of Links, Atlantic County Senior Citizens Advisory Board, and Atlantic County Retired Educators Association, and is a longtime active member (50-plus years) of Shiloh Baptist Church.

Joseph Herbert Jacobs

Joseph Herbert Jacobs was born on the Northside on September 19, 1908. He graduated from ACHS and then Temple University with a degree in music. His expertise was the violin. Upon graduating from Temple, he taught music in the local public schools. Jacobs became the supervisor (most who knew him might say, *impresario*) of music in the African-American schools and touched the lives of thousands of students. (Parenthetically, it's worth noting that his brother, Clarence, was a professional musician who played in the original Broadway play *Porgy and Bess*. Additionally, his younger sister, Gertrude, was a podiatrist. She wanted to practice podiatry in Atlantic City, but local landlords refused to rent her office space on Atlantic or Pacific Avenues. She refused to conform to the town's segregation and took her practice to East Orange where she prospered.)

Jacobs was a founding member of the Mu Lit So Society (a study group for teachers) that worked on coordinating curriculum and encouraged students to study different countries and cultures. He also taught privately to children who showed promise and took their music seriously. During his long and storied career, he led bands and orchestras that played on Garden Pier and played the violin with the Jewish Community Center Orchestra. A professional musician as well as an educator, Jacobs was one of the founding members and president of the Musicians Protective Union, Local 708.

An example of his passion for teaching music can be found in a Public School Bulletin of more than 60 years ago, where speaking of the benefits of the All-City Elementary School Band, he wrote, "It is here that the germ of good citizenship comes to life ... This [rehearsal] demands cooperation, self-control, responsibility, and efficiency. ... All religious and racial stocks speak the universal language of music. It is in living and working together that appreciation for one another develops." Through his love for music, Jacobs broke down barriers and touched the lives of thousands of people.

John R. Jasper Jr.

John R. Jasper Jr., an Atlantic City native, made history when he became the resort's first African-American fire department chief. Born during the Great Depression, he was among a handful of rookie firefighters who integrated the fire department in 1956 and later became known as one of "The Big Three" (the other two were Pierre Hollingsworth and Marvin Beatty), because he was one of three African Americans first promoted to the rank of captain. Prior to that time, African-American firefighters were only assigned to the fire station at Indiana and Grant Avenues. Jasper was assigned to the firehouse at Maryland and Arctic Avenues, acknowledging his character and commitment to duty. Often ranked number one on civil service tests, he achieved the ranks of battalion, deputy, and then fire chief by 1984. Jasper taught fire science classes and was active in the community as a master mason. He retired in 1987 after 31 years of public service, and Fire Station No. 1, at Maryland and Atlantic Avenues, is dedicated in his honor.

Earl E. Johnson

Earl E. Johnson, an Atlantic City native, served the Atlantic City School District for 40 years, retiring as an executive assistant superintendent. A World War II veteran and West Virginia State College graduate, Johnson rose through the educational ranks from classroom teacher to principal of various schools. He earned a master's degree in administration and supervision from Glassboro State College (now Rowan University) in 1964. While he served as the district's Director of Title III Planning, his project WILL (Workshop in Living and Learning) was selected as one of the most innovative in the U.S. He was later elected member of the board of education and served as chairman of the zoning board. He was active in many community groups and organizations including the Mayor's Advisory Council, New Jersey Education Association, U.S. Selective Service Board, the NAACP, the Miss America Board of Directors, and Omega Psi Phi Fraternity Inc.

Levenia Johnson-Corsey

In 1933, Levenia Johnson-Corsey became one of the first female evangelists in New Jersey. An evangelist is a preacher of the gospel, and for most women of her era, the highest *preacher* title was *evangelist*. Johnson-Corsey was born in Maryland shortly after the dawn of the 20th century. While still in her teens, she moved to Atlantic City in the 1920s with her mother, Emma Johnson, who was a licensed midwife. Johnson-Corsey was considered an "occasional or itinerant" preacher and traveled to many cities in the U.S. "ministering to people and sharing the gospel." She was a member of the Alan AME Church and St. James AME Church, as well as the Order of the Eastern Star. An entrepreneur and liberated woman before the term was coined, she owned and operated several businesses including a boardinghouse, custom tailor, and dress shop, and taught piano lessons.

James and Dorothy King

James and Dorothy King were a dynamic team. Charter members of the local branch of the NAACP, they were contemporaries of Margaret Lee Caution and coordinated their efforts in advocating on behalf of young black people stymied by racial barriers. They both grew up during the Great Depression and knew what it was like for black people to have to scratch for work. The Kings fought discrimination by Bell Telephone Company and the Atlantic City School District. They pled the case of four black soldiers who had qualified for officers' candidate school and saw to it that they were commissioned as officers before heading overseas in the U.S. Army. The Kings challenged discrimination whenever they saw it. They were civil rights activists before anyone was even using the term.

Arthur A. Lee

Dr. Arthur A. Lee was the first African-American doctor to work in the Atlantic City Hospital. A fair-skinned attractive couple, Arthur and his wife, Elvita, reveal the "one-drop rule" was conceived in fatuous and bigoted thinking. As poet, Langston Hughes wrote, "You see, unfortunately, I am not black. There are lots of different kinds of blood in our family. But here in the United States, the word 'Negro' is used to mean anyone who has any Negro blood at all in his veins. In Africa, the word is more pure. It means all Negro, therefore black. I am brown."

While still a student at ACHS, Lee was drafted into the U.S. Army to serve during World War II. At the end of the war, he went back to complete high school and was then accepted to Dartmouth College. After earning his BS degree, he went onto Meharry Medical School in Nashville. He decided to return to his hometown to do his internship (the first African American in Atlantic City to do so) and then established his own medical practice on the Northside. Years later, he was hired to work in the emergency room and delivered the first African-American child in the hospital. Because of Lee, the residents of the Northside were no longer relegated to a clinic in the back of City Hall, and blacks could count on a friendly, caring physician to look after them when they were hospitalized.

Ada H. McClinton

Ada H. McClinton was an extraordinary lady who has two things in common with Dr. Charles Wilson: They both attended Hampton Institute in Virginia, and it's impossible to find anyone with a bad word for either. A lifelong resident of the Northside, McClinton has made many a journey during her career of helping others. During World War II, she left Hampton Institute to work with the War Production Board in Washington. From there, she enlisted in the U.S. Army Air Corps. serving at Maxton Air Force Base in North Carolina. Upon her discharge from the military, she returned home and worked with the Bureau of Children's Services of the State of New Jersey. Several years later, she went to work with Atlantic Human Resources and was part of a team with Dr. Juanita High, her primary responsibility being to oversee training and developing of youth programs. She worked briefly in the private sector with private agency social programs before spending 10 years with the U.S. Department of Health, Education and Welfare (HEW).

McClinton's 10 years with HEW in the Virgin Islands (1975–1985) were spent directing staff and administering social programs for all three islands. Tragedy brought her back to Atlantic City. Her son, Oscar, who at the time was a vice president of Anchor Savings, met an early demise, and she longed to return to her roots. (The Oscar E. McClinton Waterfront Park at Main Avenue is named in his honor.) McClinton has served on the board of directors of the Atlantic City Housing Authority, the PTA, the Girl Scouts, and the YWCA. She has also worked as office manager of Attorney Joseph Jacobs, son of Judge Herbert Jacobs. Most recently, McClinton spent 10 years as director of the day-care center at Asbury Methodist

Church. Routinely, early complaints from parents about "homework" for preschoolers eventually turned into praise and thanks for the strides the children made under her excellent tutelage. In addition to her work with the NAACP, particularly during the summer of 1964 when she coordinated housing for delegates and demonstrators, McClinton was recipient of the Four Chaplains Award. The award is given to leaders of community groups who have served with distinction. She remains active in the Union Baptist Temple Church, where she serves as a trustee.

Charles A. Mills

Charles "Charlie" A. Mills, an Atlantic City native, was its first African-American architect. He studied electric engineering at the Pratt Institute before serving with the U.S. Army's 822nd Army Corps of Engineers in Korea and Okinawa. He attended classes at Maryland, Michigan, and Tokyo universities before being honorably discharged and continued his professional development at Drexel and Temple universities. Mills served as director of housing for Atlantic Human Resources, as a consultant to the National Conference of Black Mayors, and as executive director to both HOME, Inc. and the Atlantic Housing Development Corporation. He served on the Atlantic County Planning Board, Historic Gardner's Basin, Sid Trusty Memorabilia Center, and Westside Little League. He also helped found the Greater Atlantic City Youth Organization-AC Dolphins Football. Mills staunchly supported the NAACP, PleasantTech Academy Charter School, and St. Augustine's Episcopal Church.

Stanley Molock

Dr. Stanley Molock was a dentist, but before he earned his degrees from the Pennsylvania State University and Howard University he was forced to show the U.S. Army he had a bite of his own. Initially, after passing the exam for Officers Candidate School (OCS), he ran into stalling tactics and misplaced papers. He would have none of it. Molock knew his rights and held his ground. He refused to be bullied by bigoted army officers and pushed for acceptance to OCS. Upon graduation from OCS, he went on to serve with distinction during World War II. After the war, he took advantage of the G.I. Bill and completed dental school. He established his dental practice in 1954 and served the needs of Northside residents for many years.

Clifford J. Newsome

Clifford J. "CJ" Newsome was longtime owner of Newsome's Guest House and rose to prominence during the 1940s and '50s. He was one of the founders of the Atlantic City Board of Trade (ACBT), which was the Northside's chamber of commerce. Regrettably, the ACBT lost its clout as an unintended consequence of the Civil Rights Movement and the deterioration of the Northside's economy. In his prime, Newsome was a leader of St. James AME Church. Like Morris Cain, he was involved in numerous civic and fraternal organizations, and networked with his counterparts in those organizations throughout the Northeast region. As a result, many African-American organizations held their conventions in Atlantic City. He served as District Deputy Grand Exalted Ruler of the Elks for 19 years. In 1941, more than 100,000 came out on the Northside to see the parade of the Elks Convention. A master mason and shriner, he wooed many conventions to the Northside, far from the Boardwalk hotels where they were banned. Newsome was an important contributor to the vitality of the Northside economy.

Rosalind Norell-Nance

Rosalind Norell-Nance has a lifelong passion for education. She came of age during the Civil Rights Movement and is a graduate of HBCU Hampton University. Norell-Nance is a member of the National Sorority of Phi Delta Kappa and founded the sorority's historically black college Fair and Financial Aid Seminar. After completing additional courses at Glassboro State (now Rowan University), she began her career in education as a teacher in the Pleasantville and then Atlantic City school systems. Prior to becoming director of Atlanticare Behavioral Health Family Centers, she served as a member of city council. Often she was a lone voice of reason and became the first female council president. During her tenure on city council, Norell-Nance helped initiate the second wave of casino development and played a vital role in acquiring one of the largest Hope VI grants in the country. The grant has helped revitalize portions of Atlantic City's Second Ward with 300 new homes, the James L. Usry

Child Care Center, and numerous public improvements. She is a member of the Atlantic County Women's Hall of Fame and remains a vital force in the community.

Margaret and Alonzo Ridley

Margaret and Alonzo Ridley were a dynamic pair of entrepreneurs and community leaders. Originally from Baltimore, they came to town—by way of Philadelphia—prior to the turn of the 20th century. They had keen business instincts and a driving ambition to succeed. Not long after their arrival, blazing a trail that others would follow, "Maggie" and Alonzo began taking in boarders. While others were doing the same, the Ridleys were determined they were going to have more than a boardinghouse. Working diligently and saving their earnings, within a short time they accumulated enough capital to open their own hotel. The Hotel Ridley opened its doors in 1900 and was a mainstay on the Northside for more than 50 years, hosting tens of thousands of guests in summer months and renting rooms to out-of-town schoolteachers in the off-season. The annual meeting of the Northside Board of Trade was *always* held at the Hotel Ridley. Maggie was an extraordinary chef and baker, and her "Ridley Rolls" were a favorite on the Northside for several decades. It's said that the restaurant at the Hotel Ridley was Morris Cain's favorite place to dine.

Elwood Samuel Roberts II

Elwood Samuel Roberts II, known to many as Coach Elwood, was an Atlantic City native and lifelong resident. Born during the Great Depression, he attended Glassboro State College (now Rowan University) and served three years in the U.S. Navy. As a young adult he worked at Club Harlem. Roberts was a devoted football and basketball coach who worked for the Atlantic City Board of Education. He coached the Atlantic City Dolphins for many years as well as the Atlantic City High School Basketball Team and was known for his ability to teach discipline, teamwork, character building, and perseverance in the face of obstacles. He was an active member of the Police Athletic League (PAL) and numerous children's organizations. Roberts, both mentor and friend to two generations of youth, was respected for his humility, creativity, and productivity in working with children. He was a member of the Asbury United Methodist Church where he sang in the male chorus and served as a Sunday school teacher.

Wilbert Royal

Wilbert "Huff" Royal, born in Clinton, North Carolina, made Atlantic City his home after receiving his master's degree at North Carolina A&T University. Affectionately known as Huff, he spent his college summers during the 1960s in Atlantic City working as a bellhop at the Lombardy Motel and singing at Eddy's Bar. He was a manager of the famed Club Harlem and also worked as a teacher, social worker, and neighborhood facilities coordinator for the Atlantic City Board of Education. Royal was a member of Omega Psi Phi Fraternity, Inc., NAACP, and Union Baptist Temple, where he taught Sunday school.

Royal received many community service awards for his involvement in civic and professional organizations. He was the New Jersey Black Achievement & Awards Foundation's "Personality of the Decade" in 1988. His greatest legacy can be found in the 20-plus years he spent coaching the Atlantic City Dolphins football team. As my brother Ed Johnson (a football referee who officiated many of Huff's games) can attest, Coach Royal was more than a coach. He worked tirelessly in guiding hundreds of young men from troubled homes through the difficulties of adolescence. As Royal once said to me, "It's about more than the Xs & Os. I need to help these kids to get their heads screwed on so they can grow up to be men and mature members of society." Scores of his players have grown to be role models themselves. As with, Dr. Charles Wilson, it's not possible to find anyone to speak a negative word about Huff Royal.

Margaret Taliaferro

Margaret Taliaferro had a flair for fashion and found success and acclaim both locally and throughout the nation for her talents as a designer. A child of the Great Depression, she worked hard to establish herself in business. Beginning in 1951 and for the next 25-plus years, she was head wardrobe mistress for the Miss America Pageant. She also designed many award-winning pageant parade floats for the Dennis Hotel. But those efforts consumed only a fraction of time.

Taliaferro designed dresses from the House of Taliaferro, which were sold in exclusive high-fashion salons, and designed dresses for Hollywood stars, many of which appeared in movies during the 1950s and '60s.

Sid Trusty

Sid Trusty was one of the finest gentlemen I've ever met and was a true renaissance man. He was a musician, hotel worker, limousine driver, restaurant worker, and lover of history. He was a self-taught folk historian. He knew his subject well and was generous in sharing his knowledge. I've probably quoted him in my work more than anyone else, because he was such a wise person who understood the unique role played by blacks in Atlantic City's history. As the quote at the beginning of Chapter 11 exemplifies, his understanding of American history was profound.

Trusty and I met a short time after *Boardwalk Empire* was published. We were waiting to be interviewed for a TV show on Atlantic City history, and it was the first of several brainstorming sessions that led to my writing *The Northside*. It was Trusty's encouragement (I could say prodding) that gave me the impetus and, more importantly, the confidence to write this book. It was a privilege and honor to have known him as a friend.

Maceo Turner

Maceo Turner was born in Greenville, South Carolina, and found his way to Atlantic City following his service during World War II. While in the U.S. Army, he rose from the rank of private to captain. He commanded the Chemical Smoke Unit for General George Patton's Third Army and, "laying a smoke screen while exhausted and under heavy enemy fire," Turner earned a Silver Star for gallantry. After the war, he attended Howard University (working his way through school as part of the capitol police force) where he received his law degree. Shortly after graduation from law school, Turner opened his law practice in Atlantic City. Several years later, he took into his practice another Northside attorney, Herbert Jacobs (discussed in Chapter 9), who became the first African-American attorney to be appointed to the Atlantic County Court by Governor Richard Hughes.

Turner was an activist and an agitator for equal rights his entire career. A founding member of the local NAACP, Turner and Horace Bryant organized and led civil rights marches both in the resort and Trenton before there was a "movement." Serving on the boards of many legal, civic, religious, and fraternal and community organizations, he was a force unto himself. As recalled by Ada McClinton, "Maceo could be arrogant at times, but he was brilliant and fearless. He wouldn't back down from racists. They always knew where they stood with him."

It was Turner who reached out to Cecil Moore of the Philadelphia NAACP in organizing the events for the Democratic National Convention in 1964 and helped bring the nation's attention to Atlantic City during the Summer of Freedom. As Judge James L. Jackson recalls, "When I was a kid, Maceo Turner was a very visible lawyer in the community. He was an important role model in my life. He showed me that I could do it too." Maceo Turner earned the respect of the entire community. His early demise was a severe loss to the Northside.

Soundra E. Usry-Hollingsworth

Born circa World War II, educated at Shaw University in Raleigh, North Carolina, Soundra E. Usry-Hollingsworth's background was in broadcast journalism. She hosted award-winning talk show programs and was the creator of *Soundra's Surprise Gospel Hour*, which aired on WMGM TV 40. A talented entertainer, Usry-Hollingsworth performed worldwide in the venue of song and dance. She was both a performer and MC at the world famous Apollo Theater in New York City and at Club Harlem. She also acted in television shows including *Search for Tomorrow, As the World Turns,* and *One Life to Live.*

For many years, Usry-Hollingsworth hosted the March of Dimes Telethon, raising funds for local people in need. She was the founder of the Insulin Support Fund, a nonprofit organization to fight diabetes, and organized an annual diabetic telethon to provide those without insurance with the means to control diabetes by obtaining insulin and other diabetic supplies at no cost. Precious wife of Pierre Hollingsworth and beloved niece of Jim Usry, Usry-Hollingsworth touched the lives of thousands of people. Her gentle ways are sorely missed.

Daisy B. Ware

Daisy B. Ware was a longtime officer of the Atlantic County Sheriff's Department. Born during the Great Depression, she understood hard times. A member of the Union Baptist Church, she was the first female chairperson of the church's trustee board and is credited with being the first female to serve meals to in-need residents of Atlantic County. She was active in numerous community organizations, everything from the Northside Business Professional Women's Association and Stanley S. Holmes Village Senior Citizens Club to Atlantic Human Resources and the Policemen's Benevolent Association. She impacted the lives of hundreds of people and is a member of the Atlantic County Women's Hall of Fame.

Jean Webster

More than 25 years ago, casino chef Jean Webster saw a man searching for food in a garbage can on an Atlantic City street. With $5 in her pocket, she bought him a meal at a fast-food restaurant and invited him to eat at her home the next day. Soon, others followed him back to her house, and she fed all of them. Webster's kitchen grew and moved to the First Presbyterian Church at Pacific and Pennsylvania Avenues and continued to serve as many as 500 meals to the needy each day. The church's chapel doubles as a friendly dining room where 150 people at a time are served hot, generous, "sit-down meals" in a family setting (three to four settings daily). Webster personally supervises and trains her volunteers, who are always needed, to prepare and serve meals. Inspirational sing-a-longs and messages precede each meal. Sister Jean treats her "guests" with the greatest dignity, knowing that self-respect is vital to self-improvement.

Often referred to by the others as the Mother Teresa of Atlantic City, Sister Jean was the recipient of the Russ Berrie Award that recognizes those who make a difference by helping others. In 1998, she was inducted into the Atlantic County Women's Hall of Fame and has received the Humanitarian Award from Stockton College and the Thomas Jefferson Award from the American Institute of Public Services in Washington, D.C.

Author's Postscript: I am indebted to Joseph Jacobs, Esq., for his help in gathering material on both his grandfathers, Dr. Herbert Jacobs and Dr. W. Oscar Harris, plus several other Northside leaders. He also provided some striking photos for which I'm deeply grateful. Joe loves Atlantic City and is extremely proud of his heritage. Lynn Caterson, Esq., was also a contributor on several biographical sketches of women inducted into the Atlantic County Women's Hall of Fame. She had histories of several ladies that I could find nowhere else, and I am grateful for her help.

Source Notes

As with *Boardwalk Empire*, I have avoided footnotes interspersed throughout the text. They are a distraction from the story I'm trying to tell. To provide the reader with my sources and thoughts on the same, I have utilized the practice of referencing particular passages by page number, here at the end, rather than by breaks in the narrative. Hopefully, it will be easier on the reader's eye. These Source Notes list the interviews, newspapers, magazines, books, public records, studies, journal articles, and learned treatises that were the most influential in shaping my perspective on the Northside's history.

My odyssey in absorbing the information required in authoring *Boardwalk Empire* and now *The Northside* began—and remains—with the Atlantic City Free Public Library (ACFPL). It could be no other way. Libraries are our past. Libraries are our future. If you want to learn about Atlantic City's past, go to the Heston Room (named in honor of Alfred M. Heston, the ACFPL's founder). If you're interested in local history, it contains treasures to excite your imagination and fuel to ignite a fire as it did for me.

If you want to see Atlantic City's future, go to the first-floor reading room, in particular, the many computer stations at which countless residents register to go online each day. It's an amazing sight/site to behold. ACFPL director, Maureen Frank, and friends of mine in the Atlantic City School District assure me that the number of foreign languages spoken by newcomers lured by employment in the casino industry equals 35-plus. Did you know the resort was such a cosmopolitan town? The portal through which many of those people begin their assimilation into American society is the ACFPL. Go to the ACFPL and see tomorrow's Atlantic City in the making.

My love for libraries is palpable. I hope my appreciation for the people who work there is as well. Maureen Frank, Heather Halpin Perez, Pat Rothenberg, Julie Senack, and others (before them, Jane

Spitler and Marie Boyd) have all made my work easier. Books such as this aren't written alone. Whether responding to notes, telephone calls, or email, the staff at ACFPL never fails to lend a hand in my research. I am extremely grateful for all their help. In the notes, I reference the Heston Room Collection. Wherever possible, I cite specific files. Often, more than one file contained information, which, when read together, had the effect of creating variations on a central theme, not readily untangled. In those instances where I simply cite the collection, anyone who visits the Heston Room and asks for information on a particular subject may receive more than one file and then will gain an understanding why it is perplexing to try to cite one specific source on a given issue.

I caution the reader that in my research for this book, as was true in writing *Boardwalk Empire*, I had to navigate the fine line between fact and myth. On several occasions, "reliable" sources proved otherwise. Sifting the truth from fantasy was often trying. Conflicts over the accuracy/chronology/primacy of particular events, individuals, and institutions were rampant.

Finally, I believe that history is not "what happened." Rather, it's the best story that can be told with the available facts. I have peace of mind that I've told a coherent, authentic story of the historic Northside.

Prologue

i   "Discovering" Claiborn Morris Cain may be the most rewarding aspect of my research for this book. There are two African-American scholars and fine gentlemen whom I count as friends and to whom I give thanks for having introduced me to the career of Morris Cain. They are Ralph Hunter, director of the African American Heritage Museum of South Jersey, and Dennis Burroughs.

Hunter has gathered, preserved, and saved from obscurity a wealth of information essential to understanding the history of the Northside. His collection of artifacts, documents, manuscripts, and artwork at the museum in Newtonville is a treasure. Burroughs was inspired by Hunter's collection on Cain and set about the task of organizing and cataloging the many materials on Cain's life. I spent several months immersed in their materials. My discussion of Morris Cain's life would not have been possible without Hunter and Burroughs's efforts.

Cain's sense of urgency regarding the pursuit of his education resonates to my core. As a youth, my mother impressed upon me that *nothing* I would do was more important than my education *and* that my education must never cease. She preached that everyone's condition could be uplifted and all challenges conquered through education. To this day, I believe in the power of education as the principal means by which our society must transcend our most severe social problems.

I identify with the sacrifices Cain and his family made and the obstacles overcome to attain his education and achieve his life goals. Nothing came easy. Failure wasn't an option. Disappointing family members was unacceptable. The dint of hard work would prevail. Claiborn Morris Cain's life is an inspiration. He is now in my pantheon of heroes.

Chapter 1: Indispensable

1   The tale of the spring housecleaning is inspired by stories told to my parents and me by "Mr. and Mrs. Scott," who were patrons of my family's hardware store when I was a boy. My mother, Jennie Benson Johnson, was born and raised in the rural African-American community of Newtonville, a village in Buena Vista Township. She attended the Newtonville AME Church, and her roots remain there. The church was long ago destroyed by fire, but both her parents are buried in the cemetery. My mother gained a respect for her neighbors, which she passed onto her children. She often said to me, "Let's look at the word *prejudice*. It means *pre*-judge. There is nothing more ignorant than to *pre*-judge a person."

My parents' business was the first in Hammonton to extend credit to black patrons. Two of those patrons were an elderly couple from Newtonville, Mr. and Mrs. Scott. He was from Virginia, and she was (I believe) from North Carolina. They met in Atlantic City shortly after World War I. The Scotts spent their younger married days in Atlantic City and, sometime after World War II, sold their boardinghouse and moved to Newtonville. It was his desire to leave Atlantic City. Mr. Scott was her "farm boy," and Mrs. Scott was his "city girl."

My impression was that she missed living on the Northside until the day she died.

3   **Jonathan Pitney was an unlikely real estate developer …** All of the information on Pitney and much of the source materials for Atlantic City's "early days" was gleaned from portions of my earlier work, *Boardwalk Empire: The Birth, High Times, and Corruption of Atlantic City* (Medford, NJ: Plexus Publishing, Inc., 2001). In particular, I utilized the research and notes prepared in connection with Chapters 1, 2, and 3 of *Boardwalk Empire*.

4   **"Richards" was a name known and respected throughout New Jersey.** See Sarah W. R. Ewing and Robert McMullin, as cited in *Boardwalk Empire*, and Arthur D. Pierce's work, *Family Empire in Jersey Iron: The Richards' Enterprises in the Pine Barrens* (New Brunswick, NJ: Rutgers University Press, 1964), on the Richards family, which was a powerhouse in South Jersey for several generations. The chapter, "Railroad to Nowhere" (pp. 225–240), in Pierce's book is an excellent recount of Samuel Richards's efforts in making Jonathan Pitney's dream a reality.

5   **"Billy" Bright …** Mr. Bright is mentioned in several early volumes, the most reliable being work of Alfred Heston, *South Jersey, A History: 1664–1924* (5 vols., New York: Lewis Historical Publishing Co., Inc., 1924).

6   **According to historian Richlyn Goddard …** Dr. Richlyn F. Goddard is a prodigious researcher. Her doctoral dissertation earned at Howard University is titled "Three Months to Hurry and Nine Months to Worry: Resort Life for African Americans in Atlantic City, NJ (1850–1940)," a Dissertation Submitted to the Faculty of the Graduate School of Howard University (Washington, DC: Howard University, 2001). Dr. Goddard's dissertation contains many valuable facts and keen observations on the African-American experience in Atlantic City. Her U.S. Census analysis makes a strong argument that slave labor was utilized in the early days of Atlantic City.

11   **Speaking for many in the resort …** The early historical writings and news articles of the late 19th and early 20th centuries reveal what is at best a begrudging acceptance of

the presence of black people in the resort. Their presence as servants was fine, but visiting blacks who came as vacationers unnerved the white community. One newspaper in particular, the *Atlantic City Daily Union*, often portrayed black people in a sarcastic and demeaning manner.

11   **"They are patronizing ..."** *Atlantic City Daily Union*, September 3, 1898.

11   **"Yesterday was a great day for the colored population ..."** *Atlantic City Daily Press*, September 12, 1900.

12   **"Immediately the name of Atlantic City became familiar ..."** Harold F. Wilson, *The Jersey Shore* (New York: Lewis Historical Publishing Co., 1953), p. 473, as cited by Martin W. Paulsson, *The Social Anxieties of Progressive Reform: Atlantic City, 1854–1920* (New York: New York University Press, 1994), p. 24. During the initial phase of my research for *Boardwalk Empire*, Paulsson and I spent a day together traveling to Newark to examine the archives of the defunct *Newark News*, which had a fascination with both Louis Kuehnle and Nucky Johnson. Paulsson is a first-rate historian and a gentleman.

13   **The residents of Tent City ...** See *Boardwalk Empire*. I first learned of "Tent City" when interviewing Mary Ill. Her father was an itinerant laborer from Pittsburgh and a seasonal resident of Tent City. He met Mary's mother, circa 1890, while working on a construction site in Atlantic City and a resident of Tent City.

14   **... the resort became a major metropolis ...** My review of the New Jersey census figures confirms that during the early days of the 20th century, "in-season," Atlantic City was the largest urban center in the state.

15   **... the street grid designed by Osborne ...** See *Boardwalk Empire*.

16   **Atlantic City understood its role well.** See *Boardwalk Empire* and Paulsson, *Social Anxieties*.

16   **"There is no one that can visit ..."** *Philadelphia Press*, June 12, 1904 (Resort Section), p. 1.

17   **Amusement rides were ...** An excellent discussion of early entertainment and amusement rides in the resort can be found in the work of Charles E. Funnell, *By the Beautiful Sea: The Rise and High Times of That Great American Resort, Atlantic City* (New York: Alfred A. Knopf, Inc., 1975), pp. 60–65. Despite its limited focus, Funnell's book is an excellent work. I recommend it to anyone interested in early Atlantic City. Notwithstanding the fact that it was originally a doctoral dissertation, it is more accessible to the reader (and more accurate) than some of the earlier histories.

18   **"The Boardwalk was a stage ..."** Funnell, *By the Beautiful Sea*, p. 37.

18   **Historian Charles E. Funnell has estimated ...** An analysis of boardinghouses versus hotels is found in the work of Funnell, *By the Beautiful Sea,* pp. 34–35.

19   **"If the people who came to town ..."** This quote first appeared in *Boardwalk Empire* and comes from an interview with Murray Fredericks, Esq. A longtime associate in the practice of law (they were not "partners") and advisor to Hap Farley, Murray knew where "the bones are buried." He also understood what made the town tick as demonstrated by his apt explanation of the resort's penchant for bending the law to keep visitors happy. It was a privilege to know Murray. I'm honored that he was so candid with me.

19   **"A locally notorious house of ill repute ..."** Prostitution was a favorite subject of the Philadelphia newspapers. They were forever scolding Atlantic City for its brothels, at which most of the patrons were visitors from the City of Brotherly Love. Occasionally, resort papers chimed in to keep up appearances. This article appeared in the *Atlantic City Daily Press* on April 10, 1902.

20   **"Persistent rumors are heard to ..."** "The Gambling Dens Are Now Wide Open," *Atlantic City Daily Press,* April 10, 1902.

21   **"Negros are servants; servants are Negros."** W. E. B. Du Bois, *Darkwater* (New York: Schocken Books, 1919; reprinted, 1969), p. 115.

Chapter 2: Working, Not Being Worked

The vignette at the beginning of this chapter is extrapolated from old news articles in the *Philadelphia Bulletin* and stories told to me by old-timers such as Mary Ill and Sid Trusty.

24   **... three distinct groups ...** Goddard, "Three Months of Hurry," p. 8.

25   **"Schools, restaurants, trains ..."** Juan Williams, *Eyes on the Prize: America's Civil Rights Years, 1954–1965* (New York: Penguin Books, 1987), pp. 12–13. See also Darlene Clark Hine, William C. Hine, and Stanley Harrold, *The African-American Odyssey* (Upper Saddle River, NJ: Prentice Hall, 2003), p. 318.

26   **These events would freeze race relations ...** My list of the events/forces/attitudes are my own based on my readings over the years. I've spent years pondering the question: What went wrong after the Civil War? The war was over slavery, and the South lost. Why did all those people die if the end result for millions of blacks wasn't much better than slavery? My list attempts to explain why things turned out as they did.

26   **"The name Jim Crow was first heard ..."** Williams, *Eyes on the Prize,* pp. 12–13.

27   **"believed that for the good of all ..."** Hine, Hine, and Harrold, *The African-American Odyssey,* pp. 316–320.

27   **African-American historian E. F. Frazier ...** E. F. Frazier, *The Negro in the United States* (New York: Macmillan, 1957), p. 165.

28   **Reports published by the New Jersey Department of Labor ...** The information contained here and on the next several pages regarding the work opportunities available to African Americans in Atlantic City, the role played by organized labor, and the fears of whites that black workers would displace them relies in large part upon the doctoral dissertation of Herbert James Foster, "The Urban Experience of Blacks in Atlantic City, New Jersey, 1850–1915," Written in Partial Fulfillment of the Requirements for Doctor of Philosophy, Graduate Program in History, Rutgers University (New Brunswick, NJ: Rutgers

University, 1981), pp. 51–56. The scope and depth of Dr. Foster's research supporting his findings is impressive.

28 **"racial prejudice was based upon ..."** Foster, "The Urban Experience," pp. 51–56.

28 **Among the reasons stated in reply to the state's questionnaire ...** Ibid.

29 **... the AF of L acknowledged ...** Ibid.

29 **"I was a contractor ..."** Ibid.

30 **Common "Help Wanted" ads of the day read ...** I reviewed numerous ads for employment published in the *Atlantic City Daily Press.* The quotes here are from editions from March through May 1902.

32 **Implications flowed from the existence of these strata.** The discussion of "strata" was first explained by Dr. Foster's work and confirmed by longtime residents such as Sid Trusty, Pierre Hollingsworth, Mary Ill, and Dick Jackson.

34 **... the first such incident.** See *Boardwalk Empire;* Foster, "The Urban Experience"; and Paulsson, *The Social Anxieties.*

34 **... there was a similar confrontation ...** Ibid.

35 **... the scene of a third strike, in 1906 ...** Ibid.

35 **"I have been tipped more money ..."** Paulsson, *The Social Anxieties.*

37 **"The patrons were in an ugly mood. ..."** William M. Ashby, *Tales Without Hate* (Newark, NJ: Newark Landmarks and Preservation Committee, 1980).

37 **"We could in a way always get back at them. ..."** Ashby, *Tales Without Hate.*

38 **"What are we going to do with our colored people? ..."** "Down by the Sea Shore: Atlantic City," *Philadelphia Inquirer,* July 23, 1900, p. 1.

38 **"He found no serious 'problem' agitating the public. ..."** *Atlantic City Daily Union,* August 1, 1893, p. 4.

40   **Between 1880 and 1915, the pattern of residence ...** Foster, "The Urban Experience," p. 144.

43   **In 1904, a "local reform group" ...** Paulsson, *The Social Anxieties*, p. 38.

43   **Boardwalk merchants also practiced discrimination.** Ibid., pp. 36–39.

43   **"We therefore request ..."** Ibid., p. 38.

44   **"The colored man is dependent on the white man ..."** *Atlantic City Gazette*, June 29, 1906, p. 4.

Chapter 3: The Off-Season

The introductory quote is from sociologist Margaret Brett's 1912 study of the living conditions of Negroes in Atlantic City. From her writings, it appears she spent considerable time among the people of the Northside. The quote is from her work titled, "Atlantic City: A Study in Black and White," p. 724. I have yet to locate a "complete" copy of Brett's study.

45   **The winter of 1905 was brutal.** *Atlantic City Gazette Review*, January 29, 1905, p. 1.

46   **Not only must he be a leader in his neighborhood ...** The Republican organization could never have become as dominant as it was without the loyal support of Northside voters. Nevertheless, for a black man to secure a highly coveted position of year-round employment in City Hall was a big deal. This fact was confirmed by longtime residents such as Bill Ross, Mary Ill, Sid Trusty, Pierre Hollingsworth, and Dick Jackson.

46   **"Irregularity of employment ..."** Margaret Brett, "Atlantic City: A Study in Black and White," Survey, vol. 28 (September 7, 1912), p. 723.

46   **"'In-season' relatives and acquaintances ..."** Ibid.

47   **"privilege of the kitchen"** Foster, "The Urban Experience," pp. 175–176.

48   **Squalid housing and the lack of any type of community health services took its toll ...** Ibid., pp. 200–202.

49 **"Labor Day sounds the death knell ..."** Milton Palmer, "Earning a Living in Atlantic City." WPA Papers. Federal Writers' Project, New Jersey Ethnic Survey, New Jersey State Library, Archives and History Bureau, Manuscript Collection, Box WK-2.

50 **The founder of the local Republican organization ...** See *Boardwalk Empire*.

51 **"Its sixty-foot bar ..."** Paulsson, *The Social Anxieties*, p. 45.

51 **"In 1890, Kuehnle waged a legal fight with the Pennsylvania Railroad ..."** Ibid., pp. 45–46.

51 **"Kuehnle challenged him to a footrace ..."** Ibid., p. 47.

52 **The Atlantic City municipal election of 1892 ...** Ibid., pp. 52–55.

53 **"Last summer a party of colored gentlemen ..."** *Philadelphia Bulletin*, March 7, 1892, p. 4.

53 **"The number of colored men ..."** *Atlantic City Daily Union*, February 17, 1892, p. 1.

54 **"The colored people are taking more ..."** *Philadelphia Bulletin*, March 7, 1892, p. 4.

55 **"Mr. Stroud has always been ..."** Ibid.

55 **"who was tainted locally ..."** Paulsson, *The Social Anxieties*, p. 48.

55 **"who might have coalesced into ..."** Ibid.

56 **Enduring institutions evolve organically.** The hypothesis expressed here is my own, based on philosophical and historical readings over the years. Of particular influence are the writings of 18th-century French political philosopher, Charles Montesquieu, and my political philosophy professor at St. John's University, Dr. Richard Clark.

57 **"Boss rule in most communities is regarded as an affliction ..."** *Atlantic City Daily Press*, December 14, 1903, p. 4. This is an *amazing* quote, especially when you consider that Walter Edge is likely the most distinguished self-made man in Atlantic City's history. He was first elected governor in

1916. He went on to serve as U.S. senator and ambassador to France. He was elected governor a second time in 1943. The candor of this editorial is startling for then or any time in American history.

57   **... the Commodore understood the need for making investments ...** See *Boardwalk Empire.*

58   **Kuehnle was corrupt, but he had a vision ...** See *Boardwalk Empire.*

59   **"The Commodore would personally hand out turkeys ..."** Interviews with Mary Ill and Dick Jackson.

59   **They each had a list of deceased and fictitious voters ...** "The Rise and Fall of Kuehnle," *Literary Digest*, December 27, 1913, pp. 1285–1293.

60   **"Such fraudulent registration ..."** New Jersey State Senate, Protest, Testimony taken before the Committee in the Matter of the Contest for State Senator of Atlantic County between Wm. Riddle and S. Hoffman (Trenton, NJ: MacCrellish and Quigley, State Printers, 1893), p. 2.

61   **Allied with the Quakers were a handful of "progressives"** ... Martin W. Paulsson, *Politics and Progressivism in Atlantic City: A Brief Hour of Reform* (Ann Arbor, MI: University Microfilms, 1992), pp. 20–21, 25–26.

63   **"You are getting that man to vote ..."** "The Rise and Fall of Kuehnle," *Literary Digest.*

63   **"So after that, men came out ..."** Ibid.

63   **"Why, my instructions to the workers ..."** Ibid.

65   **"With Nucky, it was all business ..."** Interview with Dick Jackson.

65   **After the Commodore's return ...** See *Boardwalk Empire.*

66   **Throughout the nearly 30 years that Nucky was boss ...** See *Boardwalk Empire.*

66   **"... running for election was beneath a real boss."** See *Boardwalk Empire.*

66   **"If your kid needed a winter coat ..."** Interview with Dick Jackson.

Chapter 4: The Disinherited

The single most important institution in the African-American community is the black church born in the slavery experience. It is the mighty thread that prevents a frayed cloth from shredding to tatters.

70   **"has been something less and something more …"** Gayraud S. Wilmore, *Black Religion and Black Radicalism: An Interpretation of the Religious History of Afro-American People* (Maryknoll, NY: Orbis Books, 1983), p. 1.

71   **Most Africans understood slavery.** James Oliver Horton and Lois E. Horton, *Slavery and the Making of America* (New York: Oxford University Press, 2005), p. 20.

71   **"I assert most unhesitatingly …"** Frederick Douglass, *Narrative of the Life of Frederick Douglass* (New York: Dover Publications, 1995), p. 71. Thanks, in part, to the endorsement of his writings by abolitionists William Lloyd Garrison and Wendell Phillips, Douglass's *Narrative* reached a wide audience. Douglass spoke as eloquently as he wrote. It's said he mesmerized his audiences.

73   **Christ's view of life and his teachings …** Howard Thurman, *Jesus and the Disinherited* (Richmond, IN: Abingdon Press, 1949), pp. 15–20. I found Dr. Thurman's work revelatory. Dr. Thurman's thesis is essentially that you can't take Jesus out of context. He was a poor Jew whose people were struggling for survival. Both Jesus and the Negro in slavery lived in a climate of "deep insecurity." His discussion of "fear" at page 37 is profound. I read this book several times and portions of it countless times. In my opinion, he provides keen insights to the African-American religious experience.

73   **"This is the position of the disinherited in every age."** Ibid., p. 23.

74   **"Jesus' teachings are in large part instructions …"** Ibid., p. 29.

74   **"The basic fact is that Christianity …"** Ibid.

75   **The early spiritual leaders, or "African Priests" …** Wilmore, *Black Religion,* pp. 17–18.

75   **"... where the gods of their fathers walked and talked ..."** Ibid.

76   **"The Negro Church is the only social institution ..."** W. E. B. Du Bois, *Some Efforts of American Negroes for Their Own Betterment* (New York: Schocken Books, 1898), p. 4.

76   **"Born in slavery ..."** Wilmore, *Black Religion,* p. 27. Quoting Joseph R. Washington Jr., *Black Religion* (Austin, TX: Beacon Press, 1964), p. 33.

77   **"a veneer of Christianity."** Wilmore, *Black Religion,* p. 5, quoting W. E. B. Du Bois from *The Negro Church* (Atlanta, GA: Atlanta University Press, 1903), p. 5.

77   **The "invisible institution".**.. George F. Bragg, *History of the Afro-American Group of the Episcopal Church* (New York: Schocken Books, 1922).

77   **"bitterly hostile people hating with a deepening despair."** Carl Sandburg, *Abraham Lincoln: The Prairie Years,* vol. 2 (New York: Harcourt, Brace & World, Inc., 1939), p. 619. In my opinion, Sandburg's *Lincoln* may be the most beautifully written and exhaustively researched biography (some might say *elegy*) by an American historian. I first picked it up during final exams of my junior year at St. John's. Once I began reading, I had to struggle to put it down and return to my study for exams.

78   **"The black church has no challenger ..."** C. Eric Lincoln and Lawrence H. Mamiya, *The Black Church in the African American Experience* (Durham, NC: Duke University Press, 1990), p. 8.

78   **"A colored camp meeting is in progress on Illinois Avenue ..."** Foster, "The Urban Experience," p. 188.

79   **"The persons having charge of the colored ..."** "Current Projects," *Atlantic City Daily Review,* August 23, 1873, p. 3.

79   **The first traditional black church in Atlantic City ...** St. James is a bulwark of the Northside. Over the years, church members have prepared and updated the history of their church. Those histories are on file in the Heston Room.

81   **The original Methodist Church began ...** Lincoln and Mamiya, *The Black Church*, pp. 47–49.

81   **"pulled from their knees ..."** Ibid., p. 51.

81   **"All went out of the church ..."** Ibid.

82   **"had a clear perception of what education would mean ...** Ibid., p. 52.

83   **"We assure you, dear brothers ..."** Ibid., p. 53.

84   **"an encroachment on their [New York Methodists'] territorial prerogatives" [by Philadelphia Methodists]."** Ibid., p. 57.

85   **"led the small flock until his death in 1917."** Heston Room Collection, "History of the Negro Church in Atlantic City," Federal Writers' Project, p. 6.

88   **the Holiness Movement and Pentecostalism.** The Holiness Movement and Pentecostalism emerged as a response to (some might say as a reform movement) the traditional Methodist Church. See generally Lincoln and Mamiya, *The Black Church*, and Wilmore, *Black Religion*.

88   **"Just as Methodism was originally ..."** Lincoln and Mamiya, *The Black Church*, p. 78.

Chapter 5: Cornerstones

93   **Cain's career personifies ...** The entirety of the facts used to profile the life of Morris Cain are derived from the materials provided to me by Messrs. Hunter and Burroughs. I owe them a large debt of gratitude. I reference their work herein as the "Hunter Collection."

95   **Pursuing a formal education ...** Cain's generation were true believers in the absolute necessity of creating "social capital" through education and then using it to improve the lives of those around them. Cain is not unlike Professor Melvin Tolson of Wiley College whose career was dramatized in the 2007 Hollywood production, *The Great Debaters*. Incidentally, like Cain, Professor Tolson was a graduate of Lincoln University.

95   **"the first institution found anywhere ..."** *The Full Fruits of Freedom*, published by Lincoln University, 1934.

98   **"I saw Morris Cain work and apply himself so conscientiously ..."** Letter written by Christine M. Howell, dated May 19, 1938, from the Hunter Collection.

98   **The YMCA movement began in America prior to the Civil War.** Like so many otherwise excellent institutions of the era, the "Y" didn't have the confidence to conduct racially integrated operations. Bigots are some of the worst bullies, and the YMCA's failure to stand up for its expressed Christian values tarnished its image in history.

100   **"One of the most talked about weddings of the season ..."** *Atlantic City Daily Press*, February 23, 1924, p. 6.

106   **"You had to abide by the rules ..."** Interview with Dick Jackson.

106   **Repeal of Prohibition in 1933 made things worse.** What's difficult for many to appreciate, even some old-timers, is that Atlantic City's popularity with vacationers reached its apex during Prohibition. Upon its repeal on December 5, 1933, there was a steady decline in visitor enthusiasm.

106   **"Come the Great Depression ..."** Interview with Sid Trusty. Sid was a true renaissance man: musician, businessman, historian, and storyteller *par excellence*. Sid and I appeared together at several historical symposiums and on a television talk show on Atlantic City precasino gaming. We had much fun quizzing one another and trying to make sense of race relations in America.

        Sid was one of the people who encouraged me to write this book. He told me he had read Chapter 3, "A Plantation by the Sea," of *Boardwalk Empire* many times and believed strongly that a book on the history of the Northside needed to be written. I hope I've met his expectations.

107   **"provide public housing to counteract the ill effects ..."** *Atlantic City and Public Housing,* compiled and written by the Writers' Project, Work Projects Administration of New Jersey, December 1, 1941, p. 13.

107   **"were economically and socially homogeneous ..."** Ibid., pp. 13–14.

107   **"Of the 2,843 structures in Tract No. 6, 1,059 needed major repairs ..."** Ibid.

108   **"16 two- and three-story fireproof buildings containing 277 apartments ..."** *Atlantic City and Public Housing*, compiled and written by the Writers' Project, Work Projects Administration of New Jersey, December 1, 1941, p. 25.

109   **"On May 4, 1939, President Roosevelt approved ..."** Ibid. p. 8.

109   **"The name of Cain was ..."** *Philadelphia Tribune*, May 26, 1938.

110   **"The light is placed as a symbol ..."** Ibid.

110   **"... honest in business, outstanding in character ..."** Ibid.

110   **"So, helping young men in their battle with life ..."** Ira Yemmens's entire poem is worth the read.

111   **Born two months apart, Morris Cain and Nucky Johnson were contemporaries.** It's a challenge to compare the lives of two such different leaders, each of whom left their imprint on the town. I hope I have done justice to each gentleman. I'm confident the reader knows who I admire the most of the two. Interestingly, Cain shared a trait with Nucky's successor, Hap Farley. Both Cain and Farley had a knack for—some might say *need* for—maintaining friendships. They each seemed to remain close with every friend they made throughout their lives. New acquaintances found themselves part of a network and discovered they had someone who remembered their birthday, sent a note when they were ill, or reached out to them unexpectedly to say hello. Cain and Farley knew how to cultivate a friendship.

113   **By 1930, the Northside had in residence ...** This list was compiled by combing through various documents in the Heston Room Collection.

113   **"When my father first started, he had a horse and buggy ..."** Interview of Dr. Morris's daughter, Amaza Lockett, conducted by Cynthia Ringe, May 23, 1978. Mrs. Lockett taught in the Atlantic City school system for 40-plus years. She was known and loved by thousands of students.

114   **"The one thing I remember about him is ..."** Interview with Amaza Lockett.

114   **"I knew Miss Fletcher and Miss Gamble as a boy ..."** Interview with Sid Trusty.

114   **The mission of the Old Folks Home ...** This thumbnail sketch was derived from various documents in the Heston Room Collection.

115   **The home's original policy ...** Ibid.

Chapter 6: Building Blocks

117   **Attired in a silk brocade dress ...** The story of Madame Washington's encounter with the salesgirl at Wanamaker's has been told before by others, the best probably conveyed by Jim Waltzer in the February 1998 edition of the defunct *Atlantic City Magazine*. I ran my version past Madame Washington's grandson, Royston Scott (son of Madame Washington's adopted cousin, Sara Joan Hayes), and he told me I had recounted the tale accurately.

120   **Apex's Atlantic City plant ...** This sketch was derived from various documents in the Hunter Collection.

121   **Apex Rest was a 15-room hotel-resort center ...** Ibid.

124   **A partial listing from the 1940 Board of Trades annual publication ...** This list was compiled by combing through various documents in the Heston Room Collection.

125   **Gambling was a luxury few people on the Northside could afford.** This sketch and much that follows was based in large part on discussions with Joseph Bair, son of Walter Greenidge. For me, Bair illustrates the loss the Northside suffered as result of the "diaspora," which occurred during the 1960s and 1970s.

126   **The numbers game consisted of ...** Ibid.

126   **The profits of the "policy bankers" were large ...** Ibid.

127   **Nucky knew easy money when he saw it.** Ibid.

127   **"With Nucky, the payments weren't voluntary ..."** Interview with Dick Jackson.

128 **... the enormous volume of play is revealed ...** Some of this information first appeared in *Boardwalk Empire* and relies on the FBI report on Nucky's conviction titled, "The Case of Enoch L. Johnson, a Complete Report of the Atlantic City Investigation," prepared by William E. Frank, Special Agent, Intelligence Unit, Treasury Department, and Joseph W. Burns, Special Assistant to the U.S. Attorney for the District of New Jersey. Despite the title and the fact that it was written by FBI agents, the report is an entertaining read.

128 **"If you went to the corner store ..."** Interview with Dick Jackson.

129 **The Elks, or the Independent Benevolent ...** My discussion of the Elks national convention relies in substantial part on the research of Dr. Richlyn F. Goddard in her doctoral dissertation, "Three Months to Hurry and Nine Months to Worry: Resort Life for African Americans in Atlantic City, NJ (1850–1940)" (pp. 151–152), which is a must read for any serious student of Northside history. Ponder again the annual Elk parade on the Boardwalk: 15,000 marchers and 150,000 spectators.

131 **"The men at Engine Company #9 were amazing!"** Interview with Dick Jackson.

133 **"The issue was debated and ..."** Foster, "The Urban Experience," pp. 218–224.

134 **"interfering with the harmonious affiliation ..."** Ibid.

134 **"This young man is right. ..."** Ibid.

135 **"It is doubtful that in deciding on this course of action ..."** Ibid.

136 **"The employment of colored teachers ..."** Annual Report of the NJ Board of Education, 1903, p. 93.

136 **"Our teachers made us believe in ourselves. ..."** Interview with Amaza Lockett conducted by Cynthia Ringe, May 23, 1978. This extraordinary lady is a legend on the Northside. During her 40-plus years in the classroom, she molded the lives of thousands of young people. Compare her expression of how important her teachers were in her life to that

expressed by Judge James Jackson in Chapter 12: "By the time I got out of Indiana Avenue School, I knew who I was. I knew I was someone capable of doing whatever I wanted with my life." For three generations, the Northside's schools turned out self-confident students. Something has been lost.

137 **"By the time I got out of Indiana Avenue School ..."** Interview with the Honorable James L. Jackson by the author.

137 **"I can remember one teacher ..."** Interview with Amaza Lockett.

138 **One historian has determined that, by 1920, ...** Hine, Hine, and Harrold, *The African-American Odyssey*, p. 355.

Chapter 7: "Pop"

John Henry Lloyd is the only person who receives his own chapter in my history of the Northside. As a member of the Baseball Hall of Fame, he warrants that distinction. Thanks to the efforts of Michael Everett and the John Henry "Pop" Lloyd Committee (the "Committee"), there is a wealth of information on "Pop." The Committee had the wisdom to deposit its archival materials with the Richard Stockton College Library. There is also a wealth of information on file with the Heston Room. There are numerous brochures, pamphlets, interviews, biographical sketches, and essays on Pop prepared and/or compiled by members of the committee. There's a great deal of information available on Pop, and it's all interesting.

I relied on both the Stockton and Heston collections and reference them generally as the "Pop Lloyd Archives." Additionally, Michael Everett of the committee was generous with his time and reviewed a late draft of this chapter, assuring me I was telling Pop's story accurately.

140 **"The quintessential shortstop ..."** This sketch and much that follows was written via combing through various documents in the "Pop Lloyd Archives." It's difficult to cite any one document because they duplicate one another, and for some issues addressed, it's unknown to me who could claim original authorship. If that isn't clear to the reader, a review of the Pop Lloyd Archives will demonstrate my dilemma.

140 **"the Jekyll and Hyde of baseball ..."** Ibid.

141 **"Pioneer baseball historian Sol White tells us ..."** Quoted from a pamphlet in the Pop Lloyd Archives titled "Everybody Called Him Pop" by Max Manning, Lawrence Hogan, and James DiClerico (undated).

142 **Prior to the 1890 season ...** See my note at page 26 and the discussion of six "events/forces/attitudes ..." contained in Chapter 2. It's the best explanation I can provide.

143 **For years, it was common for black teams to "barnstorm" ...** Lawrence D. Hogan, *Shades of Glory: The Negro Leagues and the Story of African-American Baseball* (Washington, DC: National Geographic, 2006), p. ix, from the Foreword by Jules Tygiel.

144 **One season in Havana ...** Pop Lloyd Archives.

146 **Soon, Negro Baseball was staging a "world series" of its own ...** *Press of Atlantic City*, October 23, 1996, p. D5.

146 **"to keep the colored element off the Boardwalk ..."** Ibid.

147 **"You see, in the first place ..."** Pop Lloyd Archives.

147 **Local lore has it ...** Ibid.

149 **"Never in the history of the game ..."** Lawrence D. Hogan, "Joe D., the Babe and Pop," *New York Times*, July 5, 1998.

149 **"When the Yankees were on the road ..."** Ibid.

149 **"In 1931, now 47, Pop finished his career ..."** Pop Lloyd Archives.

150 **"John Henry Lloyd contributed quite a bit to my knowledge ..."** Ibid.

150 **"Pop Lloyd was the greatest player ..."** Interview with Bill Yancey contained in Pop Lloyd Archives.

151 **Farley was a ballplayer himself and he admired Lloyd greatly ...** Pop Lloyd Archives.

151 **"I gave my best when I was playing ball, ..."** Ibid.

152 **"I do not consider that I was born ..."** Ibid.

152 **"The big league doors suddenly opened ..."** Hogan, *Shades of Glory,* p. ix.

153 **"In the enlightened age of integration ..."** Ibid.

154 **"I hope that someday ..."** Pop Lloyd Archives.

154 **"I was just as good as the white boys ..."** Hogan, *Shades of Glory,* p. xviii.

155 **"Pop was an exemplary player ..."** Pop Lloyd Archives.

156 **The John Henry "Pop" Lloyd Committee preserves his memory ...** Michael Everett and the committee have done a yeoman's job of preserving wonderful materials on Pop and in perpetuating his legacy. The greater Atlantic City community—not just the Northside—owes the committee a debt of gratitude for their efforts.

Chapter 8: "K-y at the Curb"

I use the term "K-y at the Curb," although I'm told some refer to it as "K-y *and* the Curb." My wording quotes Sid Trusty and others. The story of the Northside's entertainment district is a rich one. Before beginning my research and interviews, I didn't have a feel for just how valuable the Kentucky Avenue nightclubs were to Atlantic City's economy. Tens of thousands of visitors came to town each summer because of the nightlife on Kentucky Avenue. Following the repeal of Prohibition, K-y was still a major part of the town's draw. There is so much valuable information floating around out there. It was difficult containing the available material to a single chapter. I believe the complete story of "K-y at the Curb" warrants a book unto itself. Hopefully, someone will step forward and do the necessary work to make that occur.

157 **"The blues is truth music ..."** Interview with Chris Columbo, conducted by Cynthia Ringe, May 4, 1978.

158 **"The breakfast shows were the biggest things at Club Harlem ..."** Patti Harris, a dancer at Club Harlem in 1950s and a featured performer in 1960s, quoted in "Echoes of the Night," *Atlantic City Magazine,* September 1998.

158 **"That place had a groove ..."** Sid Trusty, quoted in "Echoes of the Night," *Atlantic City Magazine*, September 1998.

158 **"People were unified ..."** Sid Trusty, quoted in the *Press of Atlantic City,* July 17, 1994, p. B1.

158 **"And one of the great things about the shows at Club Harlem ..."** Interview with Joanna LaSane, conducted by Carnegie Library Center Oral History Project, December 2004.

159 **"a wonderful job and a real education ..."** Discussion with James Usry. In the 1980s, I did legal work for a citizen's group headed by Jim Usry and Jim Masland. We successfully fought the construction of a behemoth parking garage proposed for Missouri and Fairmount Avenues. It was a privilege to work with these two fine gentlemen.

159 **"It was better than any showroom you had in the casinos ..."** Interview with Chris Columbo, conducted by Cynthia Ringe.

161 **"glorify the beauty, the soul and the talent of the black woman."** Sonny Schwartz, "Spotlight on Larry Steele," *Press of Atlantic City,* August 24, 1975.

161 **"There'd be a 15-piece band ..."** Interview with Chris Columbo, conducted by Cynthia Ringe.

162 **"I only had one man that I ever got angry with ..."** Ibid. This is such a great story; unfortunately, Chris Columbo was long dead before I started work on this book. I'm grateful the ACFPL has preserved Ms. Ringe's interviews.

163 **"You don't need gimmicks ..."** Interview with Mamie Staples of the Staple Sisters on National Public Radio, June 15, 2007.

166 **"The blues is where we came from ..."** W. C. Handy, widely respected blues musician, quoted in *African American Quotations*, compiled by Richard Newman (New York: Checkmark Books, 2000).

166 **"a pool room downstairs ..."** Interview with Chris Columbo, conducted by Cynthia Ringe, and confirmed in my interviews with Sid Trusty.

167   **When Williams was asked ...** "Atlantic City Life," *Press of Atlantic City,* June 30, 1994, p. 14.

168   **"Ben was in his office every morning between ..."** Interview with Steven Alten by the author. The "Alten guys" were extremely helpful in filling in several important gaps in my history of Club Harlem. Richard Alten, my longtime friend and distinguished member of the Atlantic County Bar, introduced me to his cousins, Allen and Steven, the sons of Ben Alten, club owner and manger for many years. The three of them had worked at the club with Ben and shared with me a wealth of information I would learn nowhere else. I am grateful to all three of them. I hope I did their stories justice.

169   **"had to go to the back door ..."** Interview with Chris Columbo, conducted by Cynthia Ringe.

169   **"I was a young man when I saw Eubie ..."** Interview with Sid Trusty. He had great admiration for Eubie Blake.

171   **"The black folk said [to the Jews] ..."** Cornel West, chair of African American Studies at Princeton University, speaking at a Stanford University symposium, "African American and American Jews: Bridges, Boundaries, Identity," February 12, 1993.

172   **"The Paradise Club was the first nightclub ..."** Interview with Chris Columbo, conducted by Cynthia Ringe.

172   **"The manager of the Paradise would send telegrams ..."** "This Side of Paradise," *Press of Atlantic City,* June 12, 1977.

173   **"During one breakfast show ..."** Ibid.

173   **"In black entertainment the last show of the season ..."** Interview with Chris Columbo, conducted by Cynthia Ringe.

173   **"Club Harlem was preceded by another club ..."** Interview with Joanna LaSane.

174   **"They went on tour to see, feel, smell ..."** Bryant Simon, *Boardwalk of Dreams: Atlantic City and the Fate of Urban America* (New York: Oxford University Press, 2004), p. 51.

175   **"There was a time when you couldn't see the ground ..."** Sid Trusty, quoted in the *Press of Atlantic City,* July 17, 1994, p. B1.

175   **"They say you could always tell ..."** Interview with Chris Columbo, *Press of Atlantic City,* August 23, 1995.

175   **"He brought the organ out of ..."** Ibid.

176   **"Our big extended engagement for that summer ..."** Count Basie and Albert Murray, *Good Morning Blues: The Autobiography of Count Basie* (New York: DaCapo Press, 2002), p. 275.

177   **"When I look at Count Basie, I think ..."** Interview with Chris Columbo, conducted by Cynthia Ringe.

177   **"As long as our workday at Atlantic City was ..."** Basie and Murray, *Good Morning Blues*, p. 276.

178   **"We used to go bathing at Indiana Avenue ..."** Interview with Chris Columbo, conducted by Cynthia Ringe.

178   **Two blackface characters nearly always depicted ...** Donald Bogle, *Toms, Coons, Mulattoes, Mammies, & Bucks: An Interpretive History of Blacks in American Films* (New York: Continuum, 1973/1994), p. 8.

179   **"Before its death ..."** Ibid.

179   **"Blacks knew how to fry chicken. ..."** Interview with Chris Columbo, conducted by Cynthia Ringe.

179   **"That beach was beautiful. ..."** "Echoes of the Night," *Atlantic City Magazine*, September 1998.

180   **"Every day he served champagne in silver goblets ..."** Interview with Russell Levan, conducted by Cynthia Ringe, June 1978. I became acquainted with Mr. Levan through Dick Jackson when I was researching *Boardwalk Empire.* Curiously, he never mentioned his summers as a beach chair concessionaire. Nevertheless, the words spoken in his interview with Ms. Ringe sound just like him.

180   **"He was a big gambler ..."** Ibid.

180   **"There was many a day ..."** Ibid.

180   **"They would put on all kinds of skits ..."** Ibid.

Chapter 9: Breaking Down Barriers

I must confess. The "dumb ass" in the opening exchange between Horace and Lillian is *yours truly*. It wasn't the only instance I came up short in Horace Bryant's eyes, but he was ever the helpful (if not always patient) counselor. Horace was such a shrewd political tactician that every time I was in his presence, I felt like I should be taking notes. In the early 1980s, when I was contemplating a run for political office, I visited Horace several times at the Linwood Convalescent Center. Those sessions were a real education. Now, I wished I had taped those conversations. It's a shame that a video-taped interview of Horace, akin to the one done of Hap Farley at Stockton College, wasn't made. It would have been a gem. We are all the poorer for it.

184   **Horace Sr. and Sarah were significant players ...** The information about Horace Sr. and Sarah throughout the beginning of this chapter was obtained via interviews with Horace's daughter, former Atlantic County Freeholder, Lillian Bryant, and his nephew, former State Senator Wayne Bryant.

185   **The "railroad" was a vast network ...** Giles R. Wright, Director, Afro-American History Program, New Jersey Historical Commission, has prepared an excellent study on the Underground Railroad titled, *"Steal Away, Steal Away...": New Jersey's Underground Railroad Heritage.*

186   **It wasn't possible for Horace Bryant Jr. to grow up ...** The biographical sketch of Horace J. Bryant Jr. and any related quotes throughout the rest of this chapter rely on interviews with Lillian Bryant (his daughter), Wayne Bryant, and Pierre Hollingsworth, together with the extensive files on Bryant's career maintained in the Heston Room Collection.

195   The individual profiles and any related quotes featured throughout the rest of the chapter rely on the Heston Room Collection and personal interviews.

Chapter 10: The Summer of Freedom

208   **"I understand very well ..."** This story was told to me many times by Harold Lillienfeld, a political science professor at

St. John's University. He was an early 1960s "Freedom Bus" rider and had many "war stories" from the summer of 1964.

208   **"a highly rational emotion ..."** Joshua Zeitz, "Democratic Debacle," *American Heritage Magazine*, vol. 55, Issue 3, June/July 2004.

209   **"The work was dangerous, lonely and hard."** Ibid.

209   **"He was beaten by local police ..."** Ibid.

209   **"The MFDP followed Mississippi election law ..."** Ibid.

210   **"Maybe they went to Cuba."** Ibid.

210   **"If you go back home ..."** Ibid.

211   **"You're either the party of Lincoln or you ain't."** Robert A. Caro, *The Years of Lyndon Johnson: Master of the Senate* (New York: Alfred A. Knopf, Inc., 2002), p. 937.

211   **"Lyndon Johnson cared ..."** Caro, *The Years of Lyndon Johnson*, p. xxi.

212   **"The NAACP stands for ..."** Zeitz, "Democratic Debacle."

212   **"on a platform of segregation and race ..."** Theodore H. White, *The Making of the President, 1964* (New York: Antheneum Publishers, 1965), p. 129.

212   **"a hymn-singing group ..."** Ibid.

212   **"It was orderly, yet exciting ..."** The story of the Northside's role in the proceedings surrounding the Democratic National Convention is based on interviews with Ada McClinton, Elwood Davis, and Pierre Hollingsworth.

214   **Hamer began her career as a civil rights activist ...** The Heston Room Collection, and Zeitz, "Democratic Debacle."

217   **"For most of the post–Civil War era ..."** Rick Perlstein, "The Southern Strategist," *New York Times*, Sunday Magazine, December 30, 2007.

217   **"while appearing publicly to endorse them. ..."** Ibid.

217   **The two-party system hasn't been the same ...** What once was the bellwether of the "Solid South," South Carolina—the state that to this day flies the Confederate Flag (a flag of treason) and that continues to honor the likes of "Pitchfork"

Ben Tillman—is now the most important state in the Republican presidential primaries.

218   **"By mid-morning switchboards would collapse ..."** White, *The Making of the President*, p. 290. As noted by White, more than 5,000 newspersons descended on Atlantic City in August 1964 for the Democratic National Convention. Instead of a *marker on the road back,* the convention was a public relations disaster. The reports published and broadcast throughout the nation destroyed what was left of Atlantic City's aura and revealed it for the beat town it was.

219   **"Never had a town ..."** White, *The Making of the President*, p. 291.

219   **"Today aside from the conventioneers, ..."** *TIME*, August 31, 1964.

220   **"It was somethin' to see ..."** Interview with Pierre Hollingsworth.

220   **"Farley could never cultivate the blacks the way Johnson had. ..."** Interview with Dick Jackson.

222   **"The real Democrats were rising. ..."** Ibid.

224   **"Karlos LaSane was a novice ..."** Anonymous source.

Chapter 11: Unintended Consequences

Sid's quote at the beginning of this chapter came during a conversation in which I was probing him in an effort to untangle his views on the unintended consequences of the American Civil Rights Movement. Sid's pithy comment speaks volumes. He was a wise and gracious gentleman. It was a privilege and an honor to call him a friend.

227   **"It was bedlam—sheer hysteria."** Interview with Hank Tyner.

228   **"Unable to spot the assailants ..."** *Press of Atlantic City,* April 3, 1972. The reporter who covered this story for the *Press* was Alex Stern. Sten was tough, smart, thorough, and accurate.

228   **"I survived Vietnam ..."** Ibid.

228 **"Warring gangs from Philadelphia ..."** Jim Waltzer and Tom Wilk, "Club Harlem," *Tales of South Jersey* (New Brunswick, NJ: Rutgers University Press, 2001).

230 **"Prohibition didn't happen in Atlantic City."** Interview with Dick Jackson.

233 **"This town was goin' down the drain ..."** Interview with Sid Trusty.

235 **"How could you get anyone to stay ..."** Interview with Dick Jackson.

237 **"Family resort, my ass. ..."** Interview with Sid Trusty.

237 **As early as 1958 ...** See *Boardwalk Empire*.

239 **Remove Perskie's relationship with Byrne ...** I had the good fortune of observing Assemblyman Steven Perskie (later state senator and now Superior Court Judge) up close in some of his interactions with Governor Brendan Byrne. There was a true big brother/little brother, mentor/protégé relationship. Without that chemistry between these two gentlemen, there wasn't a chance Atlantic City would have been able to secure legislative approval for a second referendum.

241 **"Probably one of the few people on the Northside ..."** Interview with Sid Trusty.

242 **"In Europe, we habitually regard ..."** Alexis de Tocqueville, translated by George Lawrence, *Democracy in America,* vol. I, Part II (New York: Anchor Books, 1969), p. 284.

244 **"The migrant is the maverick ..."** Peter C. Whybrow, *American Mania: When More Is Not Enough,* (New York: W.W. Norton & Company, 2005), p. 53.

Chapter 12: Embracing the Future

Writing the profiles of Redenia Gilliam-Mosee and the Honorable James L. Jackson were particularly challenging. I've known both these distinguished persons for 25-plus years and consider it a privilege and honor to have their friendship. The difficulty was to remain objective and to put their careers into proper context, meaningful to today's events. I hope I've succeeded.

The bulk of the quotes throughout this chapter are based on interviews with Ms. Gilliam-Mosee and Judge Jackson as well as my personal knowledge from having followed their careers. There are several exceptions, namely, anonymous quotes from attorneys who appear regularly in Judge Jackson's courtroom. At their request, I have not used their names but I am grateful for their cooperation.

266   **Poor children simply face ...** Paul Tough quoting educator Diane Ravitch in "A Teachable Moment," *New York Times Magazine*, August 17, 2008.

Selected Bibliography

Ashby, William M. *Tales Without Hate*. Newark, NJ: Newark, Landsmark and Preservation Committee, 1980.

Basie, Count and Albert Murray, *Good Morning Blues: The Autobiography of Count Basie*. New York: DaCapo Press, 2002.

Beard, Charles A. *An Economic Interpretation of the Constitution of the United States*. New York: The Free Press, 1913.

Bogle, Donald. *Toms, Coons, Mulattoes, Mammies, & Bucks: An Interpretive History of Blacks in American Films*. New York: Continuum, 1973/1994.

Bragg, George F. *History of the Afro-American Group of the Episcopal Church*. New York: Schocken Books, 1922.

Carnesworth [pseudo.] *Atlantic City: Its Early and Modern History*. Philadelphia: William C. Harris & Co., 1868.

Caro, Robert A. *The Years of Lyndon Johnson: Master of the Senate*. New York: Alfred A. Knopf, Inc., 2002.

Cone, James H. and Gayraud S. Wilmore. *Black Theology: A Documentary History, Volume One: 1966–1979*. Maryknoll, NY: Orbis Books, 1993.

Cook, W. George and William J. Coxey. *Atlantic City Railroad: The Royal Route to the Sea*. Ambler, PA: Crusader Press, 1980.

Cunningham, Hugh. *Leisure in the Industrial Revolution*. New York: St. Martin's Press, 1980.

de Tocqueville, Alexis. translated by George Lawrence. *Democracy in America*. New York. Anchor Books, 1969.

Donald, David Herbert. *Lincoln*. New York: Simon & Schuster, 1995.

Douglass, Frederick. *Narrative of the Life of Frederick Douglass, an American Slave: Written by Himself*. New York: Dover Publications, 1995.

Du Bois, W. E. B. *Darkwater*. New York: Schocken Books, 1919; reprinted, 1969.

Du Bois, W. E. B. *Some Efforts of American Negroes for Their Own Betterment*. New York: Schocken Books, 1898.

Dulles, Foster Rhea. *A History of Recreation: America Learns to Play*. New York: Appleton Century Crofts, 1965.

Edge, Walter Evans. *A Jerseyman's Journal*. Princeton, NJ: Princeton University Press, 1948.

Ellis, Joseph J. *Founding Brothers: The Revolutionary Generation*. New York: Alfred A. Knopf, 2001.

English, A. L. *History of Atlantic City, New Jersey*. Philadelphia: Dickson and Gilling Publishers, 1884.

Ewing, Sarah W. R. and Robert McMullin. *Along Absecon Creek: A History of Early Absecon, New Jersey*. Bridgeton, NJ: C.O.W.A.N. Printing, 1965.

Finkelman, Paul. *Slavery and the Founders: Race and Liberty in the Age of Jefferson*. Armonk, New York: M.E. Sharpe, Inc., 1996.

Foster, Herbert James. *The Urban Experience of Blacks in Atlantic City, New Jersey, 1850–1915*. (Written in Partial Fulfillment of the Requirements for Doctor of Philosophy, Graduate Program in History, Rutgers University, 1981.) A Dissertation Submitted to the Faculty of the Graduate Program in History.

Frazier, E. F. *The Negro in the United States*. New York: Macmillan, 1957.

Funnell, Charles E. *By the Beautiful Sea: The Rise and High Times of That Great American Resort, Atlantic City*. New York: Alfred A. Knopf, Inc., 1975.

Goddard, Richlyn F. *Three Months to Hurry and Nine Months to Worry: Resort Life for African-Americans in Atlantic City, NJ (1850–1940)*. A Dissertation Submitted to the Faculty of the Graduate School of Howard University, Washington, D.C., 2001.

Hall, John F. *The Daily Union History of Atlantic City and County, New Jersey*. Atlantic City, NJ: Daily Union Printing Company, 1899.

Heston, Alfred M. *Hand Book of Atlantic City Illustrated*. Philadelphia: Franklin Printing House, 1887.

Heston, Alfred M. *South Jersey: A History: 1664–1924* (5 vols.). New York: Lewis Historical Publishing Co., Inc, 1924.

Hine, Darlene Clark, William C. Hine, and Stanley Harrold. *The African-American Odyssey*. Upper Saddle River, NJ: Prentice Hall, 2003.

Hogan, Lawrence D. *Shades of Glory: The Negro Leagues and the Story of African-American Baseball.* Washington, DC: National Geographic, 2006.

Hollifield, Ambrose Nelson. *Shall We Legalize Sabbath Desecration, and Races, and Gambling on Race Courses?* Newark, NJ: Advertiser Printing House, 1891.

Horton, James Oliver and Lois E. Horton. *Slavery and the Making of America.* New York: Oxford University Press, 2005.

Johnson, Nelson. *Boardwalk Empire: The Birth, High Times, and Corruption of Atlantic City.* Medford, NJ: Plexus Publishing, Inc., 2001.

Kerney, James. *The Political Education of Woodrow Wilson.* New York: The Century Co., 1926.

Laband, David N. and Deborah Hendry Heinbuch. *Blue Laws: The History, Economics, and Politics of Sunday-Closing Laws.* Lexington, MA: D.C. Heath and Company, 1987.

Lincoln, C. Eric and Lawrence H. Mamiya. *The Black Church in the African American Experience.* Durham, NC, and London: Duke University Press, 1990.

Link, Arthur S. *Woodrow Wilson and the Progressive Era, 1910–1917.* New York: Harper and Row, 1954.

MacLeod, Duncan J. *Slavery, Race and the American Revolution.* New York: Cambridge University Press, 1974.

McDougall, Walter A. *Freedom Just Around the Corner: A New American History, 1585–1828.* New York: HarperCollins Publishers, Inc., 2004.

McMahon, William. *South Jersey Towns: History and Legend.* New Brunswick, NJ: Rutgers University Press, 1973.

McManus, Edward J. *Black Bondage in the North.* Syracuse, NY: Syracuse University Press, 1973.

Muelder, Walter G. *Methodism and Society in the Twentieth Century,* vol. II. New York: The Abingdon Press, 1961.

Nevins, Allan. *The Emergence of Lincoln: Douglas, Buchanan, and Party Chaos, 1857–1859.* New York: Charles Scribner's Sons, 1950.

Newman, Richard. *African American Quotations.* New York: Checkmark Books, 2000.

Paulsson, Martin W. *Politics and Progressivism in Atlantic City: A Brief Hour of Reform.* Ann Arbor, MI: University Microfilms, 1992.

Paulsson, Martin W. *The Social Anxieties of Progressive Reform: Atlantic City, 1854–1920.* New York: New York University Press, 1994.

Phillips, Kevin. *The Cousins' Wars, Religion, Politics, Civil Warfare, and the Triumph of Anglo-America.* New York: Mark Stein Studios, 1999.

Pierce, Arthur D. *Family Empire in Jersey Iron: The Richards' Enterprises in the Pine Barrens.* New Brunswick, NJ: Rutgers University Press, 1964.

Sandburg, Carl. *Abraham Lincoln, The Prairie Years,* vol. 2. New York: Harcourt, Brace & World, Inc., 1939.

Sandburg, Carl. *Abraham Lincoln, The War Years,* vol. 3. New York: Harcourt, Brace & World, Inc., 1939.

Simon, Bryant. *Boardwalk of Dreams: Atlantic City and the Fate of Urban America.* New York: Oxford University Press, 2004.

Sinclair, Andrew. *Era of Excess: A Social History of the Prohibition Movement.* New York: Harper and Row, 1962.

Sitkoff, Harvard. *The Struggle for Black Equality, 1954–1980.* New York: Hill and Wang, 1981.

Sternleib, George and James W. Hughes. *The Atlantic City Gamble: A Twentieth Century Fund Report.* Cambridge, MA: Harvard University Press, 1983.

Thurman, Howard. *Jesus and the Disinherited.* Richmond, IN: Abingdon Press, 1949.

Waltzer, Jim and Tom Wilk. *Tales of South Jersey.* New Brunswick, NJ: Rutgers University Press, 2001.

White, Ronald C. Jr. *The Eloquent President: A Portrait of Lincoln Through His Words.* New York: Random House, 2005.

White, Theodore H. *The Making of the President, 1964.* New York: Antheneum Publishers, 1965.

Whybrow, Peter C. *American Mania: When More Is Not Enough.* New York: W.W. Norton & Company, 2005.

Williams, Juan. *Eyes on the Prize: America's Civil Rights Years 1954–1965.* New York: Viking Penguin Books, 1987.

Willis, Laura L., L. Dow Balliett, and M. R. M. Fish. *Early History of Atlantic County, New Jersey.* Somers Point, NJ: Atlantic County Historical Society, 1915.

Wilmore, Gayraud S. *Black Religion and Black Radicalism: An Interpretation of the Religious History of Afro-American People.* Maryknoll, New York: Orbis Books, 1983.

Wilson, Harold F. *The Jersey Shore.* New York: Lewis Historical Publishing Co., 1953.

About the Author

Nelson Johnson, whose family's presence in Atlantic County predates the founding of Atlantic City, is a lifelong resident of Hammonton, New Jersey. He practiced law for 30 years and was active in Atlantic City and Atlantic County politics through much of that period.

Johnson's previous book, *Boardwalk Empire: The Birth, High Times, and Corruption of Atlantic City*, inspired the critically acclaimed HBO series from Martin Scorsese and Terence Winter.

Index